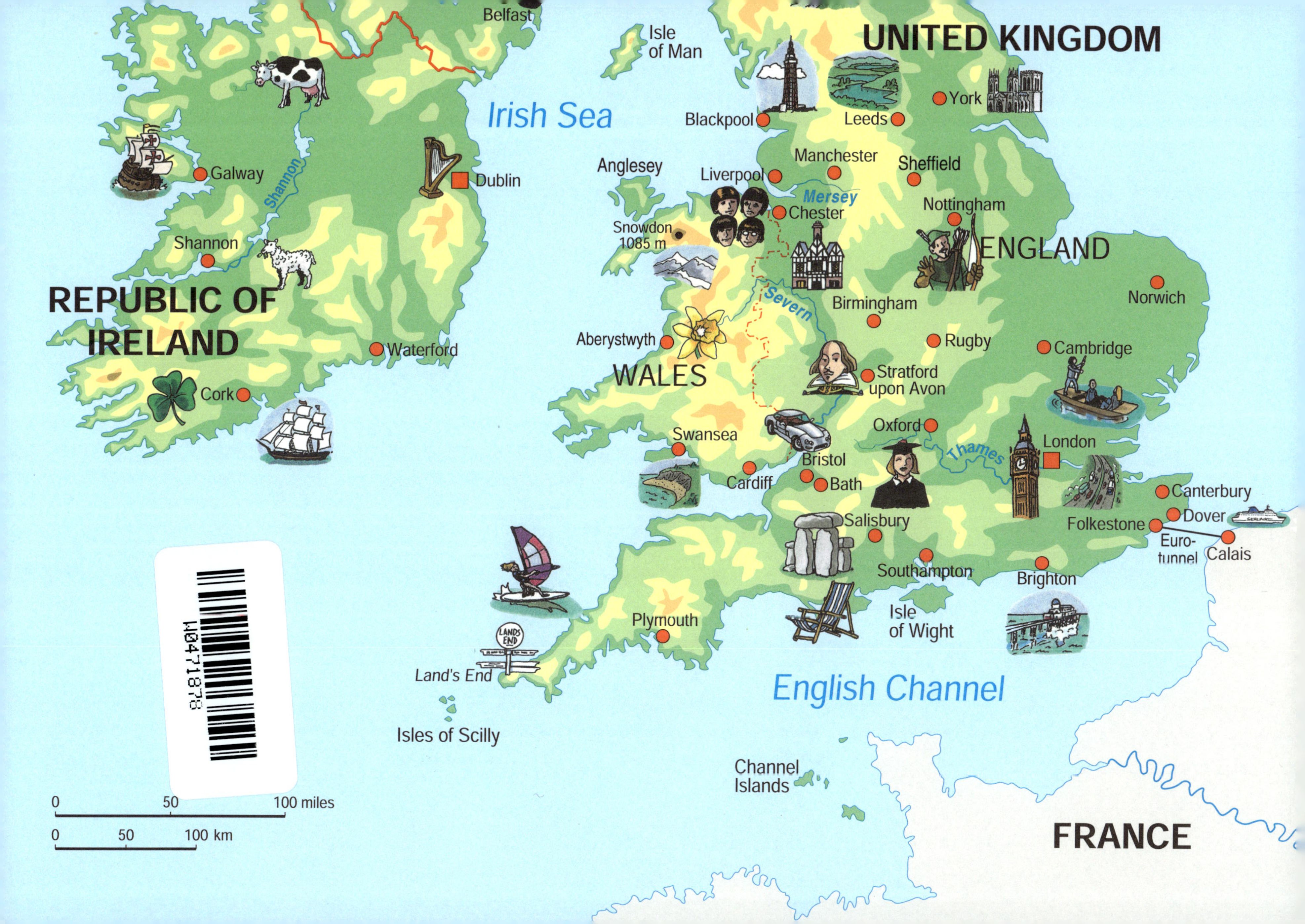
UNITED KINGDOM
REPUBLIC OF IRELAND
ENGLAND
WALES
FRANCE
Irish Sea
English Channel
Belfast
Isle of Man
Blackpool
Leeds
York
Galway
Shannon
Dublin
Anglesey
Liverpool
Manchester
Sheffield
Mersey
Chester
Nottingham
Snowdon 1085 m
Shannon
Severn
Birmingham
Norwich
Aberystwyth
Waterford
Rugby
Cambridge
Stratford upon Avon
Cork
Oxford
Swansea
London
Thames
Bristol
Cardiff
Bath
Canterbury
Dover
Salisbury
Folkestone
Euro-tunnel
Calais
Southampton
Brighton
Isle of Wight
Plymouth
LANDS END
Land's End
Isles of Scilly
Channel Islands
0
50
100 miles
0
50
100 km

Notting Hill Gate 3B

Für Klasse 7 an Gesamtschulen
und anderen integrierenden Schulformen
(zum Beispiel Gemeinschaftsschulen)

Diesterweg

Notting Hill Gate 3B

Für Klasse 7 an Gesamtschulen und anderen integrierenden Schulformen (zum Beispiel Gemeinschaftsschulen) Differenzierende Ausgabe Basic course

Herausgegeben von: Dr. phil. h.c. Christoph Edelhoff, StD a.D., Vorsitzender THE ENGLISH ACADEMY
Erarbeitet von: Michael Biermann (Hamburg), Otfried Börner (Hamburg), Hannelore Debus (Mörfelden), Pamela Hanus (Hamburg), Phil Mothershaw-Rogalla (Siegen), Ingrid Preedy (Dortmund), Kathleen Unterspann (Halstenbek), Jürgen Wrobel (Oberursel) **sowie** Ruth Barker (Plauen), Simone Collenberg (Hennef), Ingrid Gebhard (Wetzlar), Pat Jüngst (Kassel) und Tanja Ripke (Hamburg)
Fachliche Beratung: Natalie Beer (Duisburg), Lieselotte Bohnsack (Essen), Melanie Dahm (Wiesbaden), Arno Esser (Ebsdorfergrund), Rolf-Olaf Geisler (Gelsenkirchen), Elvira van Haasteren (Mainz-Kostheim), Susanne Hooß-Biehl (Buseck), Stephanie Mayer (Bochum), Angelika Pohlmann (Hanau), Cornelia Scherer (Bielefeld), Dr. Annegret Staufer (Dortmund), Noah Tauche (Kassel), Michael Tetzlaff (Mörfelden-Walldorf)

Dieses Werk folgt der reformierten Rechtschreibung und Zeichensetzung 2006. Ausnahmen bilden Texte, bei denen künstlerische, philosophische oder lizenzrechtliche Gründe einer Änderung entgegenstehen.

Zusatzmaterialien zum vorliegenden Schülerbuch

Schülermaterialien

- Workbook 978-3-425-11613-6
- Multimedia-Sprachtrainer 978-3-425-11653-2
- Audio-CDs für Schüler 978-3-425-11663-1
- Workbook mit Audio-CDs 978-3-425-11623-5
- Workbook mit Multimedia-Sprachtrainer 978-3-425-11633-4
- Workbook, Multimedia-Sprachtrainer und Audio-CDs 978-3-425-11643-3

Lehrermaterialien

- Teacher's Manual mit Unterrichtskommentaren und Lösungen 978-3-425-11673-0
- Vorschläge für Lernerfolgskontrollen mit CD-ROM 978-3-425-11683-9
- Copymasters mit Unterrichtskommentaren 978-3-425-11693-8
- Audio-CDs für Lehrer 978-3-425-11713-3
- Lehrersoftware 978-3-425-11703-4
- Folien mit Unterrichtskommentaren 978-3-425-11723-2

Druck A³ / Jahr 2010
Alle Drucke der Serie A sind im Unterricht parallel verwendbar.

Redaktion: Barbara Drauschke, Jutta Eckardt-Scheurig, Dr. Katja Nandorf und Verena Nungesser sowie Thomas Newman
Vokabelanhang: Doris Bos, Hanau
Herstellung: Harald Thumser, Frankfurt
Karten: Joachim Zwick, Gießen
Illustrationen: Ulf Marckwort, Kassel
Umschlaggestaltung: Blum Design & Kommunikation, Hamburg
Layoutkonzeption: Claudia Ehrlich, Jesse Konzept & Text GmbH, Hannover
Satz und Gestaltung: tiff.any GmbH, Berlin
Druck und Bindung: westermann druck GmbH, Braunschweig

ISBN 978-3-425-**11603**-7

Butterfly
Mrs Collins
Mr Patel
Mrs Johnson
Mr Ross
Mr Batson
Mr Williams
Mrs Williams
Mr Johnson
Josephine Batson
Mrs Batson
Mrs Patel
Mrs Ross
Sheree Patel
Jack Johnson
Rosemary Hastings
Sharon Batson
Susan Johnson
David Williams
Gillian Collins
Cheryl o'Neill
Charlie Batson
Rajiv Patel
Rita Johnson
Vanessa Ross
Kenny

Last year in Notting Hill Gate

Gillian Collins
- is from Notting Hill
- lives with her mother
- birthday: 15 January
- her best friends are Susan, Rajiv and her cousin David
- has got a cat, Butterfly
- plays football
- collects CDs, cassettes and old records
- likes all kinds of music: rock and pop, reggae and rap

Susan Johnson
- lives in Notting Hill
- goes to Holland Park School
- is now thirteen years old
- her best friends are Gillian, Rajiv and Vanessa
- loves animals
- likes pop music
- her favourite sport is in-line skating

Rajiv Patel
- lives in Notting Hill
- his best friends are Gillian, Susan and David
- his family is from India
- his parents have got a shop
- loves his computer
- plays the guitar
- his favourite hobby is football

Vanessa Ross
- is from Hendon, but she is now living in Notting Hill
- has no brothers and sisters
- her friends are Gillian, Charlie, David and Susan
- is in a girls' football team
- likes music and dancing
- has got a lot of CDs

Charlie Batson
- is from Hendon and goes to Hendon School
- his best friends are David and Vanessa
- his family is from Barbados
- has got a goldfish
- his favourite hobby is football
- is a great football fan
- loves riding his bike
- loves stories
- is the president of the *Hendon Goldfish Club*

David Williams
- lives in Hendon
- is Gillian's cousin
- has no brothers and sisters
- birthday: 15 April
- his friends are Vanessa, Rajiv and Charlie
- his parents have got a small supermarket, he sometimes helps them after school
- history is his favourite subject

New in Notting Hill Gate

Rosemary Hastings
- is fourteen years old
- lives in Notting Hill
- has no brothers and sisters
- her best friends are Rajiv and Gillian
- her father is an international banker
- she likes travelling and exotic food

Inhalt

Textsorten	Land & Leute	Sprachliche Mittel / LiF
Steckbrief		
Speisekarten, Hörtext, Dialog, Gedicht, Erzähltext		1. much / many / a lot of 2. Das Perfekt (R) 3. Die einfache Vergangenheit oder Perfekt?
Dialog, Hörtext, Cartoons, Kochrezept	Indien S.18	4. Bestätigungsfragen
Sachtext		
Fitnesstest, Erzähltext, Gedicht	Schulsport S.29	5. Die ing-Form als Nomen 6. Vergleichsformen des Adjektivs (R)
Telefongespräch, Dialog, Erzähltext		7. be able to
Bericht		
Veranstaltungsprogramm, Hörtext, Bildcollage, Erzähltext, Liedtext Zeitungsartikel	Notting Hill Carnival S.42	8. Relativsätze 9. Die Verlaufsform der Gegenwart (R) 10. Die Verlaufsform der Vergangenheit
Liedtext		
Comic, Liedtext, Gedicht, Hörtext, Wortcollage, Problem page im Jugendmagazin, Personenbeschreibungen, Liedtext		11. Die einfache Vergangenheit (R) 12. Die Stellung der Satzglieder 13. Der Infinitiv mit to
Gedicht		

Inhalt

Textsorten	Land & Leute	Sprachliche Mittel / LiF
Dialog, Museumsführer, Hörtext, Schülerzeitung, Informationsbroschüre	Museen zum Anfassen S. 70	14. have to 15. Das Passiv
Erzähltext		
Dialog, Kettensätze, Liedtext, Zeitschriftenartikel, Stadtplan, Zeitungsartikel enzyklopädischer Text	Red Nose Day S. 85	16. Bedingungssätze 1 17. something / anything 18. some / (not) any (R)
Sachtext		
Starportrait, Liedtext, Comicstrip Veranstaltungsprogramm		19. Berichtete Rede 1
Geschichte, Liedtext		
Werbebroschüren, Liedtext, Webseite, Hörtext, Comicstrip	Englisch – eine Weltsprache S.111	
Liedtext		

Inhalt

CD	Der Hörtext ist auf der Schüler-CD.
workbook A1	Hierzu gibt es Übungen im Workbook.
LiF 1	Hierzu gibt es eine Erklärung im LiF-Teil.
wordbank sport	In den *wordbanks* findest du die wichtigsten Wörter und Ausdrücke zu einem Thema.
how to … talk	Auf den *How to*-Seiten findest du Lernhilfen.
project	Projekte sind umfangreiche Aufgaben für Gruppen.
portfolio dossier	Du kannst deine Arbeit im Portfolio-Dossier (Mappe) aufbewahren.
portfolio I can listen	Zu dieser Aufgabe gibt es in den Portfolio-Bögen im Workbook einen Eintrag.
model	Ein *model text* ist eine Vorlage für deinen eigenen Text.
Tipp $ = amerikanischer Dollar	Hier bekommst du kleine Tipps und Hilfen.
film	Verweise auf Filme
★	leichte Aufgabe
☀	schwere Aufgabe
Choose	Suche dir eine Aufgabe aus.
○ ○ ○	Diese Aufgaben gehören nicht zum Basisweg und bieten Vertiefungsmöglichkeiten.

Eating out 1

In diesem *Theme* ...

- unterhältst du dich über Restaurants und Essen.
- lernst du, wie man in einem Restaurant Essen bestellen kann.
- übst du, Texten Informationen zu entnehmen.
- erfährst du etwas über Indien und indisches Essen.
- beschäftigst du dich mit Essgewohnheiten in anderen Ländern.

A1 ● Your ABC of food and drink

a) Think about food and drink and write down your ABC. What is your **favourite food?**

b) Work in small groups and compare your alphabets. Add more words to your list.

A2 ● Are you hungry?

wordbank
food and drink

a) What is your **favourite place to eat at?**

b) Look at the menus and the pictures of the restaurants on these two pages. Choose one restaurant and say why you would like to go there.

portfolio
I can read, I can work with words

I'd like to go to	Burger Queen the Windsor Castle Pizza World	because it is not so expensive. because the food is … because my favourite food is … because I love … because …

BURGER QUEEN

Queen Hamburger	£2.95
Queen Cheeseburger	£3.50
Queen Burger & Beans	£3.95
Queen Special *(Burger, Chips & Salad)*	£4.95
Queen Sausage	£2.95
Queen Muffin	£1.50
Soft Drinks	£1.10

Windsor Castle

Starters	
Soup of the day	£3.75
Tomato soup	£2.95
Garden salad	£3.95
Windsor Castle salad	£4.95
Fresh melon salad	£3.50
Garlic bread	£2.25
Main Courses	
Chicken curry	£12.00
Roast lamb and mint sauce	£14.95
Fish pie	£12.75
Vegetarian lasagna	£9.50
Desserts	
Apple crumble	£4.50
Fruit salad	£4.60
Chocolate cake	£4.50
Ice cream	£4.60
Drinks	
Soft drinks	£1.90
Tea or coffee	£1.95

Pizza World

Pizzas	regular	large
Ciao Bambino *(Tomatoes, cheese)*	£5.95	£7.75
Via Veneto *(Ham, olives)*	£7.95	£10.35
Pizza Mexicana *(Beans, chillies, onions)*	£8.95	£11.65
Pizza Capri *(Salami, mushrooms)*	£9.45	£12.25
Pizza Verde *(Broccoli, mushrooms)*	£9.45	£12.25

Fresh Salads	
Italian Salad	£6.45
Tomato Salad	£5.45
Chicken Salad	£7.45

Drinks	
Soft drinks	£1.50
Tea	£1.45
Coffee	£1.75

A3 ● In a restaurant

Listen to the four dialogues on CD. Which restaurants are the people in?

CD 1/1

The people in the first dialogue are in …

1

Waiter: Good evening. Are you ready to order?
Pete: Yes, I think so. How about you, Ann?
Ann: I'd like …

2

Dave: What are you having?
Joe: I don't know. I'm not very hungry. I think I'll only have …

3

John: What's your food like? Is it good?
Mary: Oh, it's great …

4

Jennifer: Excuse me, could we have the bill, please?
Waitress: Of course. So that was …

portfolio I can listen

workbook A1, A2

A4 ● Going out

You have got £15 and want to go to one of the restaurants. What do you want to eat and drink? Write it down and tell your partner.

portfolio I can talk

A5 ○ Choose

1. Look at the menus in A2. Choose meals for your friends and family.
2. Write your dream menu. Compare it with your partner's dream menu.
3. Design and draw a menu for your pet.

portfolio I can write, dossier

A6 ● Eating out?

CD 1/2 1/1

a) Listen and read along. What are Mrs Collins, Gillian and Vanessa discussing?

It is the last day of the holidays. Mrs Collins wants to take Gillian and Vanessa out for a meal. But they can't decide where to go, because there are so many restaurants in Notting Hill. Gillian wants to go to Burger Queen because her favourite meal is hamburger and chips. Mrs Collins wants to go to the Windsor Castle, a nice restaurant, because they have a lot of different salads. Vanessa loves pizza and she hopes that they will go to an Italian restaurant. But she doesn't know how much money Mrs Collins wants to spend.

Mrs Collins: You eat too many hamburgers and too much ketchup, Gillian. And I don't want to go to Burger Queen and sit inside. There are always so many people there. We can sit outside at the Windsor – and the salads are really good …
Gillian: I don't want to sit outside! Anyway, I've had a lot of salad this week. I'm turning green!
Mrs Collins: Don't be silly, Gillian! What about you, Vanessa? Where would you like to go?
Vanessa: We could try that new pizza place – Pizza World. Have you been there?
Mrs Collins: No, we haven't been there so far. But it sounds good.
Gillian: Pizza is better than salad. But I don't like cheese. And many pizzas have a lot of cheese on them.
Vanessa: Well, some pizzas don't have much cheese on them. But, wait a minute. I've got an idea. A lot of restaurants do takeaway food. Why don't we ring up and ask? Then we can all eat what we want.
Gillian: You're brilliant, Vanessa. And we can watch a DVD at the same time.
Mrs Collins: Oh, Gillian!

b) What different restaurants are Mrs Collins, Gillian and Vanessa talking about?

workbook A3, A4

c) Who wants to eat what? And where?

Act out the scene in groups of three.

Mrs Collins Gillian Vanessa	wants to doesn't want to	eat … go to …

A7 ● Language detective

portfolio I can work with grammar

a) Read A6 again. Find the words that go with "much" and "many". Make a list.

much	many
money	restaurants
…	…

LiF 1

b) When do you use "much", when do you use "many"?

workbook A5, A6

c) Make a list for "a lot of".

When can you use "a lot of"?

A8 Are you ready to order?

a) Listen to the funny dialogue between the waiter and the lady.

Are you ready to order?
Oh, yes, please.
A bowl of soup and a plate of cheese.
Or possibly that chicken with a chocolate sauce.
And have you got wine?
Of course!

Anything else?
Yes, I'll have some fish.
Or maybe just some cornflakes put into a dish.
The meat looks nice but I've changed my mind,
I think I'll eat some other time!

Er … sorry about that!
Not at all, Madam, come again soon!
I could just try some dessert!

b) Read the dialogue. Who says what?

Act out the dialogue.

A9 At the restaurant

a) Collect restaurant phrases. Look at A3 and A8 for ideas.

b) Sort your phrases into two lists: one for waiters or waitresses and one for guests.

Form groups of three or four. Write a scene in a restaurant. One of you is the waiter or the waitress, the others are the guests and order their meals. Use one of the menus on pages 12/13 or your dream menu.

A10 Eating in foreign restaurants

a) Read about Rosemary.

At the supermarket Rajiv met Rosemary, a girl from school. Her father travels a lot for his job. Sometimes he takes Rosemary with him. She likes going to foreign restaurants but she doesn't always understand the menu. She has tried a lot of interesting food. And sometimes she is surprised when she finds out what she has eaten …

b) Now listen to Rosemary. What surprised her?

c) Have you ever eaten snake? What was it like? Work with a partner. Ask questions and answer them.

Have you ever	eaten been to drunk …	snake? green tea? an Italian restaurant? …

Yes, I have.
No, I haven't.
It tasted awful.
What was it like?
It was good.
…

CD 1/3

wordbank: food and drink

portfolio: I can talk, I can learn English, I can work with words

portfolio: dossier

workbook: A7–A9

CD 1/5 1/4

CD 1/6 1/5

portfolio: I can talk, I can work with grammar

LiF 2R, 3

workbook: A10–A12

B1 ● Rajiv's curry party

a) Look at the picture. What do you think the dialogue is about?

CD 1/7 1/6

b) Listen to the CD and read along. What are the friends doing?

Rajiv is a great cook. It's Saturday and he has invited some friends for an Indian meal: Gillian, Charlie, Vanessa and Rosemary. They are making a curry and banana raita.

Gillian: Mmm. Smells good, doesn't it?
Rajiv: I always cook it like my grandmother did. When she came here from India, she brought lots of spices with her.
Charlie: I thought you could buy everything at the supermarket.
Rajiv: Well, now you can. But when she came here, people had no idea about Indian food. Now there are a lot of Indian supermarkets and I can buy everything I need.
Vanessa: How many onions do you want? Ow, I can't see very much and … ouch! – Now I've cut my finger.
Rosemary: Poor you! Here. Hold your finger under cold water. Have you got any more spices, Rajiv?
Rajiv: Sure. Here's my extra-hot chilli paste.
Rosemary: Mmm, it's delicious now, isn't it? Try it!
Gillian: Phew, it's sooo hot!
Charlie: Yeah, you're right … Rajiv, what have you done?
Rajiv: Come on, it's not that bad.
Vanessa: I can't eat it. Let's …

c) Read the dialogue again.

how to … read

portfolio I can read

1. What did Rajiv's grandmother bring from India?
2. What does Rajiv need for his curry?
3. What happens to Vanessa?
4. Who thinks the curry is too hot?

Read the dialogue again and take notes: who, where, when, what?

workbook B1

B2 ○ Guess what

a) Look at B1 again. What do you think Vanessa is going to say?

CD 1/8

b) Listen to the CD and find out.

c) Do you think this is a good idea?

workbook B2

B3 ● Clever, aren't they?

a) What is happening in these pictures? Describe the situations.

In picture number one there are …

b) Now look at the speech bubbles that go with the pictures and translate them into German. Which is your favourite translation for the question tags?

… nu? … ne? … nicht? … gell? … wa? … oder? … woll?

B4 ● Question tags

a) Write the sentences in your exercise book and add these question tags.

1. Rajiv is a good cook,
2. Gillian is helping Rajiv,
3. Rosemary likes chilli paste,
4. Indians eat curry every day,
5. Curry can be very hot,
6. Rajiv has got extra-hot chilli paste,
7. You can buy lots of spices in Indian supermarkets,

Rajiv is a good cook, isn't he?

b) Listen to the CD and check your sentences.

c) Listen again and repeat what you hear.

Find a rule for the question tags.

LiF 4
portfolio I can learn English
CD 1/7
workbook B3
portfolio I can work with grammar

LAND & LEUTE 1

Indien

Rajivs Familie kommt aus Indien. Indien ist fast zehnmal so groß wie Deutschland und hat mehr als dreizehnmal so viele Einwohner, nämlich 1,12 Milliarden. Es werden 300 verschiedene Sprachen und Dialekte gesprochen, aber mit Englisch kommt man fast überall zurecht.
Rajiv spricht Englisch. Er versteht aber auch Urdu, eine der 15 wichtigsten Sprachen in Indien. Sein Leben in Notting Hill unterscheidet sich kaum von dem seiner britischen Freundinnen und Freunde.

Im Gegensatz dazu ist das Leben in Indien sehr stark vom Hinduismus geprägt. Dieser Religion gehören rund 80 % der Bevölkerung an. Auf das tägliche Leben hat die Einteilung in voneinander getrennte gesellschaftliche Gruppen – so genannte Kasten (*castes*) – noch immer Einfluss. Am höchsten sind die Brahmanen (*Brahmins*) angesehen. An unterster Stelle stehen die so genannten Unberührbaren (*untouchables* oder *Dalits*).

Die Mehrzahl der Familien lebt unter einfachsten Bedingungen und Arbeit gehört zum Alltag vieler Kinder. Sie müssen mithelfen, den Lebensunterhalt ihrer Familien zu verdienen. Obwohl es eine Schulpflicht gibt, lernt jedes fünfte Kind weder Lesen noch Schreiben. Zugleich entwickelt sich die Wirtschaft rasant. Textilien, Schmuck und Computersoftware gehören zu den wichtigsten Exportartikeln Indiens.

Versuche weitere interessante Informationen über Indien zu finden, zum Beispiel:

- **die Wirtschaft**
- **die Filmindustrie (Bollywood)**
- **das Kastensystem**
- **Kinderarbeit.**

B5 Banana raita

a) Traditional Indian food is not always hot and spicy. Read this recipe for a mild Indian dish. It is easy to make at home.

Banana raita

for 4 people

What you need:
2 bananas
450 g yoghurt
1 teaspoon honey
½ teaspoon cinnamon
½ teaspoon cardamom
1 teaspoon fresh lemon juice

What you do:
Mash one of the bananas with a fork and mix it with some of the yoghurt. Add the honey, the spices and the lemon juice. Cut the other banana into little pieces and then mix everything.

Tipp
man sagt:
450 grams of yoghurt, one teaspoon of honey und *half a teaspoon of cinnamon*

b) What is Rajiv doing? Listen to the CD.

CD 1/10

c) Tell your partner in German how to make banana raita.

portfolio
I can listen

Find another recipe on the Internet. Go to www.mamtaskitchen.com for example. Present your recipe to your class.

workbook B4, B5

B6 Choose

Find as many words about food as you can. You can also use your dictionary to find more words. Then choose one of these tasks:

wordbank
food and drink

1. Make two lists: one list for food and one list for other words to do with food.

food	other words
fish	eat
hamburger	knife

2. Make a word web of all the words to do with food.

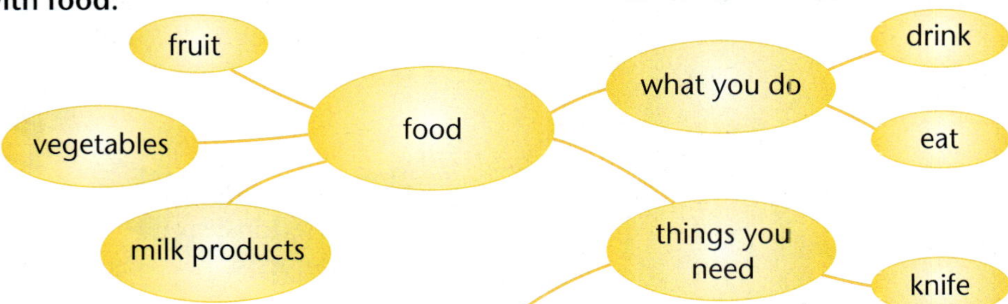

portfolio
I can learn English

3. Make a word snake or a hidden word puzzle for a classmate. Do your classmate's puzzle.

workbook B6–B8

Oriental Food
Oriental Food
Kebab
MIXED VEG CURRY
SPINACH & POTATO
DHAL CURRY
CHICK PEAS
KEBAB

INDIAN
FOOD

P1 Say it in English

Match the sentences.

1. Wie bestellst du einen Hamburger?
2. Was sagt man, wenn man die Rechnung haben möchte?
3. Wie kann man jemanden bedauern?
4. Wie kannst du sagen, dass etwas gut riecht?
5. Wie kannst du sagen, dass du das Essen lecker findest?
6. Wie kannst du sagen, dass du zu Pizza World gehen möchtest?
7. Wie fragt man jemanden, was er sich bestellen möchte?
8. Wie sagst du, dass du keinen Käse magst?

a. I'd like to go to Pizza World.
b. Poor you!
c. I'd like a hamburger, please.
d. I don't like cheese.
e. Could we have the bill, please?
f. What are you having?
g. It's delicious, isn't it?
h. Smells good, doesn't it?

P2 Pairs

Find the words.

muffins – eat
tea – ???

school – teacher
restaurant – ???

melon – fruit
broccoli – ???

chicken curry – main course
ice cream – ???

roast lamb – knife and fork
soup – ???

hot – cold
mild – ???

spoon · waiter · dessert · drink · hot · vegetable

P3 Sound check

CD 1/10

a) Listen to the words and repeat them.

b) Make lists in your exercise book and put the words in the right list.

fish · Gillian · much · vegetables · cheap · dictionary · question · English · fresh · ketchup · enjoy · juice · chocolate · cheeseburger · geography · short · she · German

[ʃ]	[dʒ]	[tʃ]
fish	Gillian	much

CD 1/11

c) Listen to the CD and check your lists.

P4 In the kitchen

LiF 1

Put in "much" or "many".

1. There aren't **???** spices on the shelf.
2. There isn't **???** ice cream in the fridge.
3. There aren't **???** books on the table.
4. There aren't **???** cups in the cupboard.
5. There isn't **???** cheese in the fridge.
6. There aren't **???** lemons on the table.
7. There isn't **???** fruit juice on the shelf.

P5 Have you tried chicken curry?

chicken curry

tomato soup

spaghetti

baked potato

LiF 2R, 3

portfolio
I can work with grammar

Which of these dishes have you tried? Did you like it? What else have you tried? Write sentences about at least five dishes.

I have tried … I have had …	and I liked it. but I didn't like it.

It was	delicious. wonderful. great. good. not so good. terrible. awful. …

I have tried chicken curry and I liked it. It was delicious.

P6 You like milk, don't you?

LiF 4

portfolio
I can work with grammar

a) Ask questions. Use the question tags.

1. Your grandma can make a curry, …?
2. You like hot food, …?
3. Your mother is a perfect cook, …?
4. Vanessa hates cutting onions, …?
5. You have a favourite meal, …?
6. You can make a fruit salad, …?
7. Your dad always drinks coffee, …?
8. Your friends like tea, …?
9. You have got a sandwich in your schoolbag, …?
10. We are good cooks, …?

aren't we | isn't she | haven't you | haven't you | doesn't she | can't you | don't they | can't she | don't you | doesn't he

b) Listen to the CD and check your questions.

CD 1/12

P7 Food words

Make a list of food words that are similar to German food words.

English	German
tomato	*Tomate*
butter	*Butter*

wordbank
food and drink

Eating habits

People in different countries have different traditions and eating habits.

Britain
In Britain some people don't use their fork like a spoon. They press the peas onto the back of a fork with a knife. They also do this to eat small pieces of meat and potatoes.

China
In China, people eat food with chopsticks. You hold them between your fingers as you can see here. The food is served in bowls.

India
People don't usually use knives or forks. With pieces of chapati they pick up their food. Then with three fingers and the thumb of the right hand, they make a little ball of food and eat it.

Iran
Family meals in Iran are very important. Traditionally the family sits on the floor around a large cloth. All the different food is in a great number of dishes.

Germany
What do you think people from other countries find interesting about German eating habits?

Be a sport

2

In diesem *Theme* ...

- lernst du zu sagen, ob dir etwas leicht oder schwer fällt.
- beschäftigst du dich mit verschiedenen Sportarten.
- übst du, mit Hilfe von Notizen über etwas zu sprechen.
- lernst du, gesundheitliche Probleme zu beschreiben.
- lernst du zu sagen, wozu jemand nicht in der Lage ist.

A1 ● Are you fit?

a) Do you lead a healthy life? Copy the questions and answer them.

1. Do you walk to school?

a) Yes, always.
b) No, never.
c) Sometimes.
d) Only if the weather is nice!

2. What do you do in your free time?

a) I play computer games.
b) I do sport.
c) I watch TV.
d) I hang out with friends.

3. Do you do sport regularly?

a) Yes, I love sport.
b) No, I don't.
c) Every now and then.
d) I watch it on TV.

4. How much fast food do you eat?

a) Not much.
b) I never eat fast food.
c) I go to a fast food restaurant every day after school.
d) I eat too much fast food.

b) Talk to your partner. What do you do to stay healthy?

portfolio
I can talk

I never …

I do …

… but not very often.

I go …

I sometimes …

… once a week.

I often …

…

… at least twice a week.

A2 ● Test your fitness

a) Read the fitness test on the next page. How well do you think you will do? Write down your guesses on a piece of paper first.

b) Now do the test with a partner. Write down your answers.

Fitness Test

① *Jump up and down for one minute. Are you out of breath?*

a) Yes, I am.
b) No, not at all.
c) Yes, a bit.

② *Step on and off a chair ten times quickly. Was that difficult?*

a) Yes, it was.
b) No, it was easy.

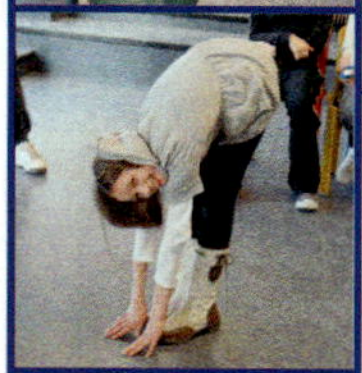

③ *Touch the floor like this ten times. Can you do it?*

a) Yes, of course I can.
b) I can, but it wasn't easy.
c) No, I can't. That's really hard.

④ *Do press-ups. How many can you do?*

a) 0–5
b) 6–10
c) 11–15
d) More than 15

⑤ *Hop on your right foot for thirty seconds. Then do the same on your left foot. Can you do it?*

a) Yes, I can.
b) No, I can't, it's too difficult.
c) Thirty seconds on one foot is a long time, but I did it.

⑥ *Walk up and down 15 stairs quickly. Are you out of breath?*

a) Yes, I am.
b) Just a little.
c) No, of course not! That's not difficult.

portfolio
I can read

c) Now report to your class.

Jumping Stepping Touching Doing Hopping Walking	press-ups up and down for one minute on and off a chair ten times up and down 15 stairs quickly the floor on my right and left foot	was	easy. very easy. difficult. hard, really hard. too hard. no problem. …

Jumping up and down for one minute was very easy.

LiF 5

portfolio
I can talk

workbook A1, A2

CD 1/12 1/13

portfolio I can listen

how to ... read

A3 My sport

a) Listen to Jennifer. What sport is she talking about? Why does she like it?

b) Read the texts and take notes.

Karate

I started karate six years ago. It is a great sport because you learn to defend yourself! I enjoy it very much. I am much better at school sports now because I am fitter. And I have no more problems with boys ...

Becky, 13, Cardiff, Wales, UK

Me and my first mini-triathlon

Yesterday I had my first mini-triathlon. A triathlon has three parts: swimming, running and cycling. I enjoyed the cycling less than the rest because my bike broke down in the middle of the race. I still did really well because I was the fastest swimmer. I can't wait until my next triathlon! Next time I want to do even better!

Caitlin, 11, Perth, Australia

portfolio I can read

model

I like hockey

I really like playing hockey. It is my favourite sport because it is exciting and fast! I think that it is better than ice hockey, because we don't need special clothing or helmets. It is less dangerous, but just as exciting! I enjoy playing outside. It is nicer than being inside a sports hall.

Amar, 15, Delhi, India

portfolio I can learn English

name?	age?	country?	what sport?	why do they like it?	other information?
Becky	13	UK	karate	...	...

portfolio I can talk

c) Use your notes and talk to a partner.

1. What sports do they do?
2. Why do they like their sports?
3. What other information do they give?

workbook A3

portfolio I can talk, I can write

wordbank sport

workbook A4

A4 Choose

1. Interview your partner. What sport does he or she do? Take notes.
2. Write about **your** sport. Look at the texts in A3 for help.
3. Make a poster about your favourite sport.

I play ...

I practise twice a week.

What sport do you ...

You only need ...

I started ... years ago.

Land & Leute 2

Schulsport

Sport ist eines der wichtigsten Schulfächer in Großbritannien. An vielen Schulen gibt es tolle Sportanlagen und Turnhallen auf dem Schulgelände. Die Schüler sollen die Chance haben, möglichst viele Sportarten kennenzulernen. Neben den besser bekannten Mannschaftssportarten wie Fußball, Hockey, Kricket oder Basketball bieten viele Schulen auch Individualsportarten wie Golf, Tennis oder Geländelauf an. Schulmannschaften treten in Trikots mit den Farben ihrer Schule an. Die Schüler tragen also nicht nur eine Schuluniform, sondern auch die entsprechende Sportkleidung. Wenn sie gegen Teams aus anderen Schulen spielen, kann jeder sehen, zu welcher Schule sie gehören. Wenn die Schülerinnen und Schüler die Schulfarben tragen, haben sie ein Gefühl der Zusammengehörigkeit.

Sporttag

Im *summer term* gibt es an den meisten Schulen einen besonderen Sporttag (*sports day*), an dem alle teilnehmen. Der Nachmittag beginnt mit verschiedenen Sportangeboten auf den Sportplätzen und endet mit den eher traditionellen Wettläufen. Das Besondere daran ist, dass jeder Schüler, der an den Aktivitäten des Sporttages teilnimmt, Punkte für sein „Haus" (*school house*) gewinnen kann. An jeder Schule gibt es nämlich vier oder fünf verschiedene Häuser, und jeder Schüler gehört zu einem dieser Häuser. Viele Schulen veranstalten auch Wettbewerbe zwischen den Häusern.
Während des ganzen Schuljahres können Schülerinnen und Schüler Punkte für ihr „Haus" sammeln. Am Ende gewinnt das Haus mit den meisten Punkten einen Pokal.

„Der Sporttag ist viel aufregender, wenn du die anderen Mitglieder deines Hauses unterstützen kannst", sagt Debbie Barclay, Schülerin an der Emerson Park School. Sie ist außerdem *House Captain*, also Sprecherin für ihr Haus: „Du hast das Gefühl, dass du wirklich dazu gehörst."

Was gefällt dir am britischen Sporttag? Wie sehen Sporttage an deiner Schule aus?

A5 Sports poems

CD 1/13 1/14 1/14 1/15

a) Listen to the poems and read along.

Swimming

I love swimming!
It's really fun!
Some people go to lessons
at half past one!

I like breaststroke,
I think that is the best.
Some people don't like that stroke,
they like the rest.

I don't like front crawl,
I think that's the worst.
When I do front crawl
I really want to burst!

When it's time to get out
I sometimes start to cry;
I never want to leave
or even say bye-bye!!!!

Dayna, 12, Croydon, UK

The cricket ball's story

He's holding me tightly
with fingers and thumb
He's about to release me
Here I come!
I spin through the air
The crowd gives a gasp
As the batter steps back
lifting his bat

WHACK!

Helen, 11, Nottingham, UK

b) Which poem do you like better?

A6 Be a poet

how to ... write

portfolio: I can work with words

portfolio: dossier

workbook A5

Write a sports poem like this: one word, two words, three words, two words, one word.

a) Think of some rhyming words which have to do with sport.

ball – small – fall – sports hall

b) Write some two-line poems.

Dirk is tall
And good at basketball

A7 ● Sports favourites

a) Look up these words in your dictionary. Write down the words and their German meaning in your exercise book.

tall · fast · muscular · young · successful · fit · strong · small · clever · powerful · skilful · big

b) What do you think? Write five or more sentences.

Someone who	plays football goes swimming does aerobics plays basketball does karate …	must be can be doesn't have to be …	…

Someone who plays football must be fast.

c) With a partner talk about **your** sports hero.

I think	…	is the	tallest fittest most powerful most wonderful most successful …	basketball player. swimmer. goalkeeper. football player. football team. …

I think … is the most successful football team in Germany.

Yes, that's right. I think so, too.

I don't think so. I think … is	taller fitter more powerful more wonderful more successful …	than …

I don't think so. I think … is more successful than …

wordbank
sport

LiF
6R

portfolio
I can work with grammar

workbook
A6–A11

B1 Phoning the doctor

a) Look at these phrases. Write down the dialogue in the correct order.

wordbank
health

- Good morning. Dr Ewalski's surgery.
- You could come tomorrow at four.
- Well, yes. You could come today at five, but you'll have to wait.
- You're welcome. Goodbye.
- A cold? Do you have a temperature?
- Yes, I do. And my throat hurts.
- That's OK. Thank you.
- Good morning. My name is Miller and I have a bad cold.
- Tomorrow? But I feel really bad! Could I come today?
- Goodbye.

CD 1/15 1/21

b) Now listen to the telephone call.

portfolio
I can talk

c) Work with a partner. Act out the scene.

Work with a partner. You feel terrible and can't go to school. Phone the doctor's surgery. Say what's wrong with you and ask for an appointment.

B2 At the doctor's

a) Look at the pictures. What do you think is happening in the scenes?

I think …

Perhaps …

CD 1/16 1/22

b) Now listen to the two dialogues and read along.

In the waiting room:

Charlie: Ow! It hurts. I can't move my arm.
Rajiv: Huh! You've only got a broken finger. That's all!
Charlie: But it hurts! And it's swollen. Look!
Rajiv: The doctor will just put a bandage or something on it. We'll be playing football again soon.
Charlie: OK, but next time kick the ball, not my finger!
Receptionist: Charlie Batson? Doctor Ewalski will see you now.

In the surgery:

Dr Ewalski: Now, what's the matter with you?
Charlie: Well, I was playing football and … I fell … and … I think I've broken my finger.
Dr Ewalski: Let me see.
Charlie: Ouch!
Dr Ewalski: Ah, yes. We'll take an X-ray and then we'll see what the problem is.

c) Listen to the dialogues again. Then match the sentence halves and write down the sentences.

1. Charlie has …
2. Rajiv thinks …
3. Charlie's finger hurts …
4. The receptionist tells Charlie …
5. Dr Ewalski wants to …

a. … take an X-ray.
b. … that the doctor is ready to see him.
c. … broken a finger.
d. … that Charlie only needs a bandage.
e. … and it is swollen.

workbook
B1–B5

B3 ● What's the problem?

a) Look at the picture and listen to the CD. Who is talking?

CD 1/17

b) What is the matter with these patients?

The old lady has a stomach ache.

stomach ache · bad cold · backache · cut foot · sore leg · broken arm

wordbank health

portfolio I can listen

workbook B6

B4 ● Too bad

What are the patients not able to do? Match the pictures and the sentences.

1 

2 

3 

4 

5 

6 

a. The man with the black hair is not able to smell anything.
b. The girl with the blonde hair is not able to play football.
c. The old lady is not able to eat very much.
d. The boy is not able to ride his bike.
e. The man with the glasses is not able to go dancing.
f. The woman with the red hair is not able to clean the windows.

LiF 7

portfolio I can work with grammar

workbook B7, B8

B5 The story of Christy Brown

a) Look at the five photos on these two pages before you read the text. What do you think the story is about?

CD 1/18 1/24

b) Now listen and read along. Who was Christy Brown?

how to … read

c) Look through the story again and take notes. Where and when did Christy live? What do you know about his family?

portfolio I can read

Christy Brown was born in Dublin in 1932. His family was very large and he had 22 brothers and sisters. The family lived in a small house. Christy's father worked as a bricklayer.

Christy was a few months old when his mother noticed that he could not move properly. It was clear that Christy was disabled. When he was a little older, he was not able to feed himself or put on his clothes. He could not walk but he could control his left foot. He could not talk because he was not able to control his tongue. But he was able to hear.

His mother was a very strong woman. She decided to help him. She had a very busy life because there were younger children in the family and there were no modern machines to help her with the housework. But she always found time to help Christy to learn his alphabet and to write with his left foot.

Christy was a very intelligent child. He started to draw pictures and people bought them. His brothers made him a box on wheels, so he was able to play with them in the streets. Later, they built a little house in the garden for him where he could write his stories, read and draw. But Christy was never able to go to school.

One day, a doctor visited him. She worked in a clinic for children and young people. Christy went to this clinic and learnt how to control his body a little. His family always helped him. He wrote about them in his book *My Left Foot*, which made more money than his father earned in a year as a bricklayer. Later, he wrote more books and articles and won many prizes as a writer. Christy died in 1981. Eight years later, his life story was made into a film called *My Left Foot*.

B6 Christy's life

a) Read the story in B5 again and complete the sentences:

His mother
Christy Brown
A doctor
His father
His brothers

... had 22 brothers and sisters.
... worked as a bricklayer.
... helped him to learn the alphabet.
... started to draw pictures.
... made him a box on wheels.
... wrote stories in a little house in the garden.
... helped him to learn to control his body.
... won many prizes as a writer.

Match the two parts of the sentences and write them down. You will then have a summary of the story.

1. Christy Brown was born ...
2. He had ...
3. The family lived ...
4. Christy was ...
5. He was not able to ...
6. His mother ...
7. She helped him ...
8. He was able to ...
9. People bought ...
10. Christy went ...
11. He learned ...
12. He wrote ...
13. He won ...
14. He died ...

a. ... write and draw with his left foot.
b. ... a book about his life.
c. ... many brothers and sisters.
d. ... in a small house.
e. ... disabled.
f. ... many prizes as a writer.
g. ... in Dublin in 1932.
h. ... walk or talk.
i. ... to learn his alphabet.
j. ... to a special clinic.
k. ... in 1981.
l. ... his pictures.
m. ... found time to help him.
n. ... to control his body a little.

b) What do you think Christy learned to do by himself?

B7 My left foot

Watch the film "My left foot" (min. 11:00 to min. 14:00). In the scene, Christy's mother falls down the stairs. People think that she fell because she carried Christy. What really happened?

film

workbook B9–B12

P1 Say it in English

Match the sentences.

1. Wie fragst du, ob jemand regelmäßig Sport macht?
2. Wie sagst du, dass du zu viel Fastfood isst?
3. Wie fragst du, was jemand in seiner Freizeit macht?
4. Wie sagst du, dass du etwas schwer findest?
5. Wie sagst du, dass du zweimal pro Woche trainierst?
6. Wie sagst du, dass dein Hals weh tut?
7. Wie sagst du, dass du deinen Arm nicht bewegen kannst?

a. My throat hurts.
b. That's really hard.
c. I eat too much fast food.
d. I can't move my arm.
e. What do you do in your free time?
f. Do you do sport regularly?
g. I practise twice a week.

P2 Your favourite team game

Make a word web for your favourite team game. Think about

- where you can play it
- what things you need
- what you wear
- people who do this sport
- …

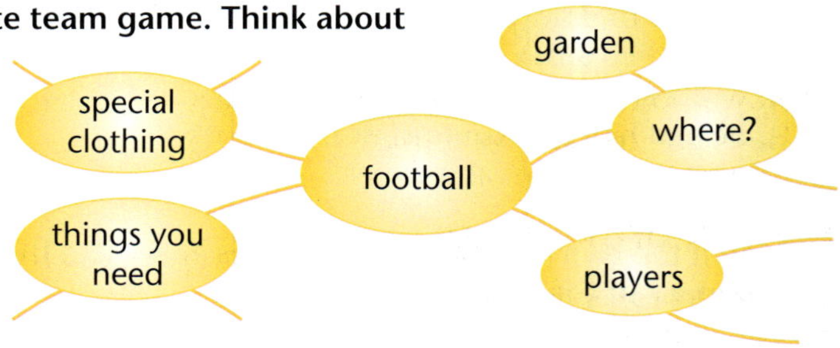

P3 Swimming is …

LiF 5

a) **What do you think about these sports? Write sentences.**

Swimming Playing football Playing hockey Running Cycling …	is can be is not	fun. boring. dangerous. interesting. difficult. …

I like cycling because it is …

b) **Now talk to your partner.**

I think swimming is …

I don't like …

P4 Fit, fitter, fittest

LiF 6R

a) **Put these adjectives in alphabetical order and add the comparative and superlative forms. Watch your spelling.**

fit · slow · safe · fast · cheap · good · exciting · successful · big · happy

CD 1/25

b) **Listen to the CD and check your words.**

c) **Think about sport. Use five of these adjectives to write comparisons with "than" or "as … as".**

The football field is bigger than the swimming pool.

P5 ○ A healthy life?

a) Work with a partner. Give short answers.

1. Do you eat a lot of crisps?
2. Have you got a bike?
3. Is chocolate your favourite food?
4. Did you spend more than two hours in front of the TV yesterday?
5. Can you swim for 15 minutes?
6. Have you ever missed a sports lesson at school?

No, I don't.
Yes, of course I have.
No, I didn't.
No, of course I haven't.
Yes, I have.
Yes, I did.
No, I can't.
No, it isn't.
Yes, I can.
Yes, it is.
No, I haven't.
Yes, I do.

b) Now find three more questions to ask your partner. He or she has to give a short answer.

P6 ○ A broken leg

Tim has a broken leg. Write about what he is able to do and what he is not able to do.

read comics
play football
play his guitar
watch DVDs
walk to school
go swimming
...

Tim is able to read comics. He ...

LiF 7

P7 ○ Christy Brown

a) There were lots of things that Christy could not do. But he had people who helped him. Write notes like this:

His mother: feed, dress, ... | His brothers: make box, ... | The doctor: ...

b) Now write sentences.

His mother fed him. She dressed him, she ...

Paralympics

SPORTS · SPORTS · SPORTS · SPORTS · SPORTS

Everyone has heard of the Olympic Games. But how many know about the Paralympics? After the first athletes have gone home from the Olympics with their gold, silver and bronze medals, the races go on. Hundreds of athletes from all over the world come together. They run, cycle, play basketball and swim just as other international athletes.

The difference is that the athletes in the Paralympics are disabled. Some are blind or in wheelchairs but they want to compete for their countries in the Olympic stadium. The Paralympics began in 1948 after the Olympic Games in Rome. The "para" means parallel, it means that the games take place parallel to the Olympics.

In 2008 there were 4,124 disabled athletes competing in Beijing, China. One of them was Oscar Pistorius who won three gold medals. He ran the 100m race in 11.17 seconds and defended his Paralympic title in the 200m race. After breaking the Paralympic record in a time of 21.67 seconds he finally became the 400m champion in a world-record time of 47.49 seconds. What was so special about that? Oscar Pistorius lost his legs at the age of 11 months. He was the first disabled athlete ever to run the 200m in under 22 seconds. Currently, he holds three world records. He smiles whenever he is introduced as "The fastest man on no legs". "I'm not disabled," he says, "I just don't have any legs."

He has started to run against athletes with no handicaps because he wants to show the world that disabled people can do just as well. He hopes to be good enough to run in the Olympic Games in London in 2012.

Have you ever heard of the Paralympics? Do you know the names of any athletes?

On the street 3

In diesem *Theme* ...

- lernst du den *Notting Hill Carnival* kennen.
- übst du, einen Text nach Informationen zu durchsuchen.
- kannst du etwas über Feste in deiner Stadt berichten.
- übst du, Personen und Dinge näher zu beschreiben.

A1 ● Here comes the carnival

portfolio
I can talk,
I can work
with words

a) Look at the photos on this page. Talk to your partner.

dancer · mask · costume · witch · parade · …

In photo number one I can see …

1 2 3

b) What is the German word that you use for "carnival"? Do you know any other German words for carnival?

wordbank
festivals

c) How do you celebrate carnival?

I My parents My friends …	dress up. watch a parade. have parties. watch a parade on TV. don't celebrate carnival. …

workbook
A1

d) What do you know about carnival in other parts of Germany?

A2 ● Notting Hill Carnival

Every year in August, there is a big carnival in Notting Hill. Thousands of people walk, dance and sing in the streets. There are thousands of tourists who take photos and make videos of the carnival. A lot of police officers are there to help people.

CD
1/19

a) Listen to the music and look at the photos on the next page. Then talk about the carnival.

how to …
use the
Internet

b) When is Notting Hill Carnival this year? Search the Internet.

1

2

3

4

Land & Leute 3

Notting Hill Carnival

Der Londoner Stadtteil Notting Hill ist bekannt für seinen *carnival*. Die berühmten Umzüge finden jedes Jahr am letzten Wochenende im August statt. Samstags gibt es unter anderem einen Wettbewerb für *steel bands*. Die Bands spielen Musik auf *steel drums*, die aus alten Ölfässern hergestellt werden. Am Sonntag folgt dann ein Umzug, bei dem vor allem Kinder und Jugendliche in farbenprächtigen Kostümen durch die Straßen von Notting Hill ziehen.
Am Montag findet dann der ganz große Umzug statt. Jedes Jahr kommen bis zu anderthalb Millionen Zuschauer, um die *main parade* zu sehen. Auf einer Strecke von fünf Kilometern ziehen verschiedene Gruppen in fantastischen Kostümen durch die Straßen, begleitet von Festwagen mit Musikanlagen und Bands. Dabei wird die karibische Kultur gefeiert und es herrscht ausgelassene Stimmung.

Eigentlich hat der *Notting Hill Carnival* einen ernsten Hintergrund. Im Jahr 1959 wurde das Fest zum ersten Mal gefeiert, um auf rassistische Übergriffe gegen Einwanderer aus der Karibik aufmerksam zu machen. Im Laufe der Zeit hat es sich von einer kleinen Feier zu einem Stadtteilfest mit einem der größten Straßenumzüge Europas entwickelt.

Finde heraus, woher das Wort *carnival* kommt und was es eigentlich bedeutet. Das Internet kann dir dabei helfen: www.askkids.com.

workbook A2

A3 ● The steel drummer

CD 1/20

a) Listen to the CD. Whose uncle plays the steel drums?

how to ... listen

b) Listen to the CD again and find out:

1. Where did Charlie start to drum?
2. What did Charlie use to drum with at the beginning?
3. Who didn't like the noise?
4. Where did Charlie's mother send him?
5. What did he hit in the garden?
6. Who rang the doorbell?

portfolio I can listen

Notting Hill Carnival programme

Date & Time	Event	Location
Saturday 29 Aug 5.30 pm – 9.30 pm	Steel Band competition	Hyde Park
6 pm – 12 midnight	Grand Carnival Costume Splash A competition for the titles of: • Best King • Best Male Individual • Best Queen • Best Female Individual	Alexandra Palace, Wood Green
Sunday 30 Aug 9 am – 9 pm	Parade & Festival 5 steel bands start official opening of Carnival Children's Day Parade	

A4 ● Rajiv in business

Look at the picture and read about Rajiv. Where is he and what is he doing?

CD 1/21 1/27

how to … read

portfolio I can read

Rajiv loves the carnival. He loves watching the crowds of people who walk from Notting Hill Gate to Portobello Road. He loves listening to the singers and bands. Then there are a lot of dancers and brightly coloured floats that pass by in the parade – and the tourists who take photos. But there are also pickpockets who try to steal purses and watches. The police put up posters which tell everybody to be careful.

"Hi, Rajiv, how are you?" asked David.
"Oh, hi, David. I'm fine! Everybody wants my samosas. I think I've sold at least 50 already! Remember last year? Nobody was hungry and I had to eat samosas for a week after carnival."
Rajiv was standing behind a stall outside his parents' shop with a sign that said: "Buy the best samosas in Notting Hill here".
"Have you got any for me? I'm really hungry and I love your samosas," said David.
"Don't worry, I've always got enough for an old friend. Hey, here come the steel bands."
"And guess who's in a steel band this year!" said David. "Who?" asked Rajiv. "Look and see if you can find him." "Oh, wow, it's Charlie. Charlie's in a steel band? Can he play?" asked Rajiv.
"Well, I'm not sure he can. What's he doing now? Oh, no …"

workbook A3

A5 ● Lots to see

What can you see at the carnival? Look at the pictures on page 41 and the programme on page 42 and read "Rajiv in business" again.

There	is are	a programme police officers steel bands tourists a Children's Day Parade pickpockets …	who which that	start the opening of the carnival. you can watch on Sunday. tells you what's on. help people. try to steal purses. …

LiF 8

portfolio I can work with grammar

workbook A4–A6

A6 Tips for the carnival

CD 1/23

portfolio I can listen

a) Listen to the interview on the radio and find out:

1. Who is Robert Taylor?
2. When does the carnival start?
3. How many important things are there to remember?
4. "It's better to be safe than …" what?

b) Listen again and find the dos and don'ts. Make a list.

Don't take the car.

workbook A7–A8

Listen again. Write down all the don'ts and say why you should not do this.

Don't take the car because …

A7 A street festival

a) Read about the street festival.

model

Every year in September, there is a street festival in our town. It is called "Burgstraßenfest". In the morning the fire brigade band plays music in the street. Children and adults set up stalls for a flea market where you can buy all kinds of things, old and new. Some people sell things to eat, for example cakes, hot dogs, hamburgers, sausages or ice cream.

In the afternoon there are drama groups, choirs, dancers and magicians in the streets. When the weather is fine, people sit and watch and eat and drink until late.

The profit from the festival always goes to a children's home in our town.

b) Copy the table into your exercise book and fill in the information.

portfolio I can learn English

WHEN is it?	WHERE is it?	WHO is there?	WHAT do people do?	WHY do they organize this festival?
…				

workbook A9, A10

c) Work in small groups and compare your tables.

A8 Choose

how to … present

portfolio I can talk, I can write, dossier

workbook A11

1. **Write about a street festival in your town.**
2. **Prepare a talk about a festival in your town. Use the questions from the table above to plan your talk. You can add more information.**
3. **Write about your favourite carnival costume.**

B1 ● A narrow escape

a) Look at the pictures. What is happening?

Photos of the incident by M. Parlemois from Chartres

portfolio
I can talk

b) Now read the newspaper article. Find out why the boy almost had an accident.

Notting Hill Evening News

PAGE 2
Monday, 31 August

NARROW ESCAPE
Six-year-old John Scott from Wembley had a narrow escape yesterday while he was watching the carnival parade. A pickpocket who was running away knocked the boy under a float.
The boy's mother saw what was happening and managed to pull her son away before the front wheel of the float ran over him. The police are now questioning a young man. Anybody with further information please phone the police: **020 8743 5520.**

portfolio
I can read

c) Look at the text and find the English phrases for these German phrases.

portfolio
I can work with words

- ist gerade noch einmal davongekommen
- stieß den Jungen unter einen Festwagen
- konnte ihren Sohn gerade noch wegziehen
- bevor das Vorderrad des Festwagens ihn überrollte

d) Finish these sentences:

1. A boy was watching …
2. A pickpocket knocked him …
3. The pickpocket was running …
4. The boy's mother saw …
5. She managed …
6. The police …

workbook
B1–B5

A friend sees the pictures and wants to know what happened. Tell him or her in German.

portfolio
I can help out in English

B2 ● What is he doing?

Look at these pictures and write down what the young man is doing.

LiF
9R

1

have a drink

2

watch the parade

3

listen to a steel band

4

watch a film

5

eat at Burger Queen

6

talk on the phone

7

steal wallets

8

drive a car

workbook
B6

1. He is having a drink.

B3 ● A police interview

Listen to the police interview and take notes. What was the young man doing yesterday afternoon?

He was He wasn't	playing watching stealing wearing	the parade. the same jacket. TV. football. wallets.

CD 1/26

LiF 10

portfolio I can listen

B4 ● What were you doing?

a) **Think about the situation in your class this morning. Write down what you were doing when the teacher came in.** *I was …*

b) **Work in small groups. Ask and answer each other.**

What were you doing when Mr … / Mrs … came in?

I was …

c) **Walk around and try to find somebody who was doing the same.**

d) **Work in groups again. Ask and answer more questions like this.**

What were you doing at six o'clock yesterday evening?

LiF 10

portfolio I can talk, I can work with grammar

workbook B7–B10

B5 ○ Not around

a) **Listen to the CD. What were the young people doing when Jack tried to phone them last Saturday? Take notes. Then write sentences in your exercise book.**

CD 1/27

portfolio I can learn English

When Jack called,	Greg Lindsay Robert Ann Emily	was	watching a football match. listening to a band. visiting a museum. watching a film. looking at snakes.

LiF 10

When Jack called, …

Greg Lindsay Robert Ann Emily	listen visit watch look at watch

b) **Listen again and find out more about Jack's friends. Take notes and collect all the information in class.**

P1 Say it in English

Match the sentences.

1. Wie sagst du, dass du einen Festumzug anschaust?
2. Wie sagst du, dass du dich verkleidest?
3. Wie fragst du, was jemand gestern Abend um sechs Uhr getan hat?
4. Wie sagst du, dass es jedes Jahr im September ein Straßenfest in eurer Stadt gibt?
5. Wie sagst du, dass der Gewinn einem Kinderheim gestiftet wird?
6. Wie fragst du, wie jemand Karneval feiert?

a. Every year in September, there is a street festival in our town.
b. How do you celebrate carnival?
c. What were you doing at six o'clock yesterday evening?
d. I dress up.
e. The profit goes to a children's home.
f. I watch a parade.

P2 The little boy who …

Write about the parade. Match the sentence halves.

LiF
8

portfolio
I can work with grammar

1. John is the little boy		are playing in the parade.
2. This is the float		pulled her son away from the float.
3. Mrs Scott is the woman		almost had an accident.
4. This is the telephone number	who	felt a hand in his pocket.
5. These are the steel bands	which	is talking to the police.
6. Bill is the young man	that	you can call to talk to the police.
7. M. Parlemois is the tourist		took the photos.
8. Mr Gordon is the man		nearly ran over the little boy.

John is the little boy who almost had an accident.

P3 Sound check

CD 1/33

a) Listen to these words on CD and repeat them.

sorry · zoo · that · police · there · yes · answer · mother · zebra · seven · them · lesson

b) Which words are spoken with [s] as in *sorry*?
Which are spoken with [z] as in *zoo*?
Which are spoken with [ð] as in *that*?
Make lists.

CD 1/34

c) Listen to the CD and check your lists.

[s]	[z]	[ð]
sorry	*zoo*	*that*

P4 Check your spelling

Copy the lists into your exercise book. Fill in the ing-forms of the verbs in the box.

Verdoppelung des letzten Buchstabens	Wegfall des -e	nur -ing wird angehängt
run → running	have → having	watch → watching
…	…	…

run · have · happen · watch · do · put · talk · take · listen · make · sit · dance · visit · drive · write · swim

P5 What a class

What were the pupils doing yesterday when Mr Dickson came in?

LiF 10

Lennie was listening to his MP3 player.

Tipp
was/were
+ verb
+ ing

P6 Last Saturday

a) When Audrey tried to call her friends last Saturday they did not answer the phone. Listen to the CD. Find out what Amir, Ryan and Hannah were doing and take notes. Then write about it like this:

CD 1/35

When Audrey called Amir last Saturday he was …

b) Listen to the children again and answer the questions.

1. When does Amir have a lesson?
2. When did he play his last games?
3. Did Amir win or lose the games?
4. What colour was Ryan's room and what colour is it now?
5. Who paid for the paint?
6. What does Hannah want to buy?
7. What does she sell at the stall?
8. What did she buy last Saturday?

All night long

CD 1/28 1/36

Well, my friends, the time has come
Raise the roof and have some fun
Throw away the work to be done
Let the music play on (play on, play on)

Everybody sing, everybody dance
Lose yourself in wild romance
We're going to party
Karamu, fiesta, forever
Come on and sing along!
We're going to party
Karamu, fiesta, forever
Come on and sing along!

All night long! (all night)
All night long! (all night)
All night long! (all night)
All night long! (all night)

People dancing all in the street
See the rhythm all in their feet
Life is good, wild and sweet
Let the music play on (play on, play on)
Feel it in your heart and feel it in your soul
Let the music take control
We're going to party
Liming, fiesta, forever
Come on and sing my song!

All night long! (all night)
All night long! (all night)
All night long! (all night)
All night long! (all night)

Yeah, once you get started you can't sit down
Come join the fun, it's a merry-go-round
Everyone's dancing their troubles away
Come join our party, see how we play!

Oh, yes, we're going to have a party!

All night long! (all night)
All night long! (all night)
All night long! (all night)
All night long! (all night)

Everyone you meet
They're jamming in the street
All night long!
Yeah, I said, everyone you meet
They're jamming in the street
All night long!

Music and lyrics: Lionel Richie

Which of the words and phrases in the song make you think of carnival?

No man is an island

4

In diesem *Theme* …

- beschäftigst du dich mit der Geschichte von Robinson Crusoe.
- sprichst du darüber, was *home* für dich bedeutet und was du magst und nicht magst.
- beschäftigst du dich mit dem Thema Familie.
- liest du über persönliche Probleme und wie man sie lösen kann.

A1 ● Robinson Crusoe

The English writer Daniel Defoe wrote the adventure story *Robinson Crusoe* in 1719.

a) Have you ever heard of Robinson Crusoe? What do you know about him?

b) Read this very short version of the adventure story.

portfolio
I can read

workbook A1–A3

LiF 11R
portfolio I can write
workbook A4–A6

A2 ● Back home

When Robinson Crusoe was back in York he told the people his story. Write down what he said.

Well, I left my parents in York on 1st September 1651.
I boarded a ship …
Then I left London on …
Later …
After some time …
One day …
…

CD 1/29 1/42
LiF 12

A3 ● Interviewing Robinson Crusoe

a) After Robinson's adventure, people had lots of questions. Listen and read.

Tipp
Eine Liste mit unregelmäßigen Verben findest du hinten im Buch.

portfolio I can talk
workbook A7

b) What do you think were Robinson Crusoe's answers?

A lot of things – the houses, the people, …
With a small stick.
Well, I pointed to things and told him the word.
Just for a holiday.
…

What would *you* ask Robinson Crusoe?

Did you …? *When did you …?* *What did you …?* *How did you …?*

A4 Island in the sun

a) Listen to the song.

This is my island in the sun
Where my people have toiled since time begun.
I may sail on many a sea,
Her shores will always be home to me.

Chorus:
O, island in the sun,
Willed to me by my father's hand.
All my days I will sing in praise
Of your forest, waters, your shining sand.

As morning breaks the heav'n on high,
I lift my heavy load to the sky.
Sun comes down with a burning glow,
Mingles my sweat with the earth below.

Chorus

I see woman on bended knee
Cutting cane for her family.
I see man at the waterside
Casting nets at the surging tide.

Chorus

I hope the day will never come
That I can't awake to the sound of drum.
Never let me miss carnival
With calypso songs philosophical.

Chorus

Music and lyrics: Harry Belafonte

CD 1/30 1/43

b) What does the singer love about the island?

c) The singer loves his island home. What do you love about your home?

wordbank
places

A5 An island poem

a) Listen to the poem and read it.

CD 1/31 1/44

Ocean breezes

Breezes
from the ocean
fanning my island's shores
lure rich and poor to swim in the
same seas.

Monica Gunning

b) Copy the poem and draw a picture that illustrates the poem.

Learn the poem by heart and present it to the class.

A6 ○ Your survival kit

a) Which of these things would you have in your survival kit for a lonely island?

a rope · a trumpet · soap · a knife · a packet of seeds · a first aid kit · a toothbrush · a strong plastic bag · a pair of scissors · books · a spade · sunglasses · a laptop · sweets · matches · a watch

b) Think of more things you would take and write them down.

c) Write down your top three.

portfolio
I can talk

d) Talk about your top three with your partner.

I think a watch is very important. What about you?

I think you are right.

Well, I'm not sure. I think I'd rather take scissors.

A7 ● Dream islands

CD 1/32

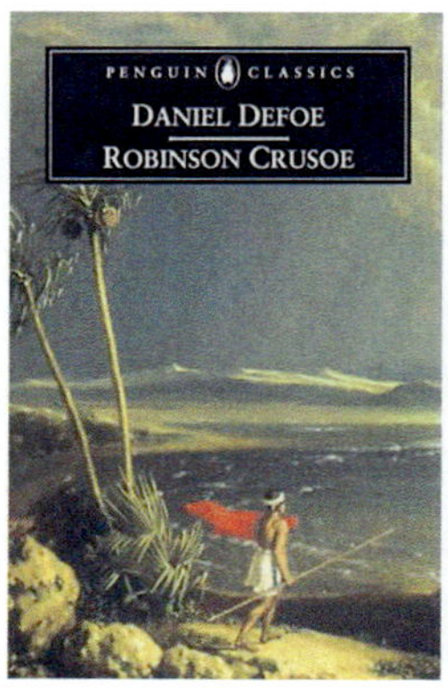

Gillian, Charlie and David have read the book *Robinson Crusoe*. They all loved it. Now they are talking about their dream islands.

portfolio
I can listen

Listen and find out:

1. Who wants to live on an island with a high mountain?
2. Who wants to live on an island with a beautiful lake?
3. Who wants to live on an island with a big waterfall?
4. Who wants to live on an island with a big forest?

Listen and find out: who wants to live where and why?

A8 ○ Choose

1. Imagine you are stranded on an island. What would you do to survive? Make notes like this:

   find food, build a hut, look for wild animals, ...

   Then write about it.

2. Imagine you are stranded on an island. Write a message in a bottle.

3. Draw and describe your dream island. Think about the plants and the animals, mountains, lakes and rivers.

4. In the film "Cast away" Chuck Noland is stranded on an island. He finds lots of packages on the beach and opens them. Watch the scene (0:59:05–1:03:01) and find out: what is in the packages? Which of these things are useful to him? What does he use the things for? Talk about the scene in class.

wordbank feelings

portfolio I can learn English

portfolio dossier

film

workbook A8–A11

A9 ● What is home?

Home is where the heart is

MY HOME IS MY CASTLE

There is no place like home

EAST, WEST – HOME IS BEST

a) Work with a partner and make a word web about home.

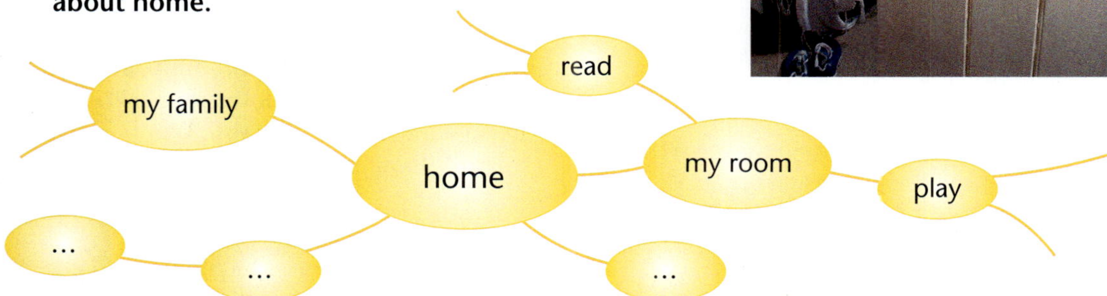

portfolio I can work with words

b) Use your word web to talk about your home. What do you like? What don't you like?

I love my room.

I like playing ...

I hate ...

I enjoy ...

Write an acrostic about home.

workbook A12

B1 ● Letters to Sarah

Sarah

Send all your problems to me. I can only answer a few letters on this page, but I'll send an answer to everyone who writes to me.

portfolio
I can read

1 Text bullying

I'm a 13-year-old boy and my big problem is text bullying. For my last birthday I got a new mobile. At school we shared all our numbers in my class and since last month I have received some terrible text messages. Someone wants to beat me up. I'm desperate. What can I do?

Desperate from London

Sarah says …

First: Remember it's not your fault. Tell your parents and your teachers. Talk about it with your friends. Maybe they have problems like that, too. Together you'll stop the bullying.

2 I'm so shy

I'm 13 and have a big problem. I'm very shy. I hate it when teachers ask me questions at school. I forget everything. I'm too shy to talk to girls. When a girl talks to me, I go red in the face. I don't know how to answer her.

Shy from London

Sarah says …

Don't worry so much! Think about the things you CAN do! When the teacher asks you a question, take a breath and don't WORRY! Stay cool and forget the other pupils in the classroom. Try to talk to girls as friends and not as girlfriends. And don't think about what the others think. YOU are important. YOU are YOU.

3 My love is a secret

I'm a 14-year-old girl and I've been going out with a boy for some weeks. The problem is he's already 18. When my parents were away we spent a lot of time together and I was so happy, but now we have to keep it a secret. We love each other and we don't want to break up, but I can't see a way out, my parents will think he is too old.
I can't concentrate on my schoolwork. I want to run away from home. What can I do? My parents will not understand.

Secret from London

Sarah says …

This is a difficult decision, but running away from home will solve nothing. You'd better cool things down with this boy and sort out your schoolwork first. If he loves you, he'll understand and wait for you. Why not talk about it with your friends?

Write to Sarah at:

Go! magazine
325 Alexandra Road
NW2 3PO London
sarah@go.co.uk

a) Read one or more of the letters and the answers. What is your reaction?

b) What are the problems? Work in groups.

In the	first letter second letter third letter	Desperate Shy Secret	has problems with …

Someone He She	wants to would love to would like to	talk to girls in class. tell her parents about her boyfriend. beat him up. answer questions in class. run away from home because … …

c) What do **you** think about Sarah's advice? Talk to your partner.

I think the	first second third	answer is	(very) (quite) (not very)	OK. helpful. silly. good.

Choose one of the letters to write your own answer or write an answer to "Dog lover" from Brighton. Look for useful phrases in Sarah's answers.

Dad says: No dog

I'm so sad. I've always wanted a dog but my father won't let me have one. He says our flat is too small. I've told him I will walk the dog and feed it. But Dad says we can't leave a dog at home all day. I'm sure I can find someone to look after it. Perhaps I could take it to school with me.

Dog lover from Brighton

how to … read
LiF 13
wordbank feelings
portfolio I can talk
workbook B1 – B6
portfolio I can write
portfolio dossier

B2 ● Meet Charlie's family

CD 1/36 1/47

portfolio
I can read

a) Read about Charlie and his family. What are the problems?

Charlie's father, Mr Batson, is an engineer. He is out of work at the moment. So he does the housework and the cooking. He is looking for a new job – but that is very difficult. Every morning he checks the newspaper and searches the Internet.

Charlie's mother works in a supermarket. She normally works the early shift, so she has to get up very early – at 6 o'clock. It's a boring job. First she has to fill up shelves. Afterwards she sits at the cash desk for hours. She would love to give up the job but they need the money for the family.

Charlie's older sister, Josephine, is 19. She is a trainee nurse at St Mary's Hospital in Paddington. She works very hard but she loves her job. She is often tired when she comes home after her 12-hour shift. She has a boyfriend who likes to drive fast cars. When she goes out with him, her mum is always worried.

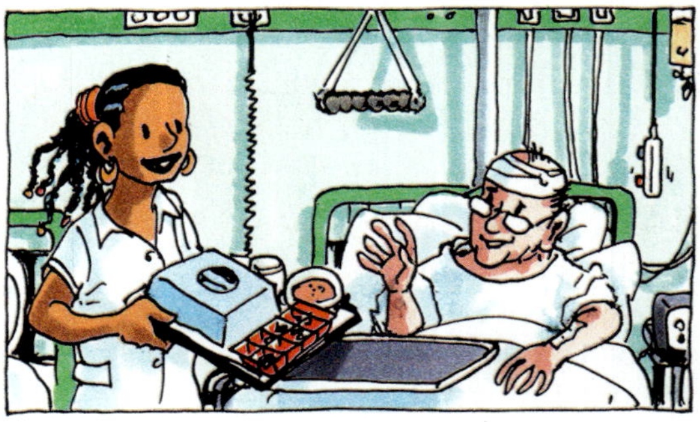

Sharon is Charlie's younger sister. She is 11 years old. She doesn't like helping in the house and never cleans her room. She'd love to go back to ballet lessons but she can't go to her lessons now because they are too expensive.

Charlie is now 13. He loves playing football after school. He still plays for his school team. He likes his work as president of the Hendon Goldfish Club better than his homework. And then there's Lisa. He thinks about her all the time. His last school report was not very good.

b) Read the text again. Who says what?

1. Finding a new job is really hard.
2. I'd love to have a more interesting job.
3. I think Lisa is a beautiful girl.
4. I hate getting up so early.
5. I don't want to help in the house.
6. I'd like to have ballet lessons again.
7. These shifts are just too long.
8. I wish mum wouldn't be so worried.

c) Write down the most important facts from the text like this. Then present one member of the family to the class.

What questions would you ask the Batsons? Write at least six questions.

Charlie: 13 – plays football – …
Mr Batson: …
Mrs Batson: …
Josephine: …
Sharon: …

portfolio
I can talk,
I can learn English

workbook
B7–B9

B3 Choose

1. Work with a partner. What is happening in the picture? Make notes. Then write a dialogue and act it out.
2. You are Sharon, Josephine or Charlie. Write a letter to Sarah. Ask for help with your problems. Use the letters in B1 for help.
3. Write a letter to Sarah about a problem you have. Use the letters in B1 for help.
4. Present members of your family to the class. Look at B2 for help.

wordbank
feelings

portfolio
I can talk

portfolio
dossier

B4 Wonderful world

a) Listen and read along. How does the singer feel?

CD
1/37 1/48

Don't know much about history
Don't know much biology
Don't know much about a science book
Don't know much about the French I took
But I do know that I love you
And I know that if you love me too
What a wonderful world this would be

Don't know much about geography
Don't know much trigonometry
Don't know much about algebra
Don't know what a slide rule is for
But I do know one and one is two
And if this one could be with you
What a wonderful world this would be

Now I don't claim to be an A student
but I'm trying to be
For maybe by being an A student, baby
I can win your love for me

Chorus

History – biology
Science book – French I took
But I do know that I love you
And I know that if you love me too
What a wonderful world this would be

Music and lyrics: Sam Cooke / Lew Adler / Herb Alpert

b) What is your idea of a wonderful world? Make a word web.

workbook
B10

P1 Say it in English

Match the sentences.

1. Wie kannst du jemanden fragen, was er am meisten vermisst hat?
2. Wie kannst du jemandem sagen, er solle sich nicht so viele Sorgen machen?
3. Wie kannst du jemanden nach seiner Meinung fragen?
4. Wie kannst du sagen, dass du nicht sicher bist?

a. Don't worry so much.
b. I'm not sure.
c. What about you?
d. What did you miss most?

P2 Why is that?

a) **Match the questions and answers.**

1. Why don't you help your mum with the housework?
2. Why don't you help your dad in the garden?
3. Why don't you talk with your sister about this problem?
4. Why don't you buy a parrot as a pet?

a. Because she never listens.
b. Because I've got a cat.
c. Because there is so much homework to do.
d. Because I already helped him yesterday.

CD 1/49

b) **Listen to the CD and check your questions and answers.**

c) **Write more "why don't you …" questions for your partner.**

d) **Answer your partner's questions.**

P3 Simple past forms

LiF 11R

portfolio I can work with grammar

a) **Find the simple past forms in Theme 4.**

talk | write | go | collect | leave | know | miss | come | be

b) **Use the simple past forms to write a story about an island.**

P4 Working with words

how to … work with a dictionary

a) **Use a dictionary to find opposites of these adjectives:**

- difficult
- early
- boring
- unfriendly
- fast
- expensive
- good
- fair
- right
- small
- happy
- terrible

b) **Combine ten adjectives with nouns.**

good news

P5 Scrambled sentences

a) Unscramble the sentences.

LiF 12

1. for – lived – He – many – years – alone – .
2. miss – did – most – you – What – ?
3. came – some cannibals – to – One day – the island – .
4. much – worry – so – Don't – .
5. give up – Charlie's mother – love to – would – the job – .

b) Listen to the CD and check your sentences.

CD 1/50

P6 Imagine

a) Imagine you want to travel to a far away country. Make notes.

- Where would you like to go?
- What would you love to see?
- What would you love to do?
- What would you like to take with you?
- What would you hate to do?

b) Talk to your partner. Take turns.

wordbank travelling

LiF 13

portfolio I can work with grammar

P7 Home poem

Write a home poem like this:

Home	(One word)
My room	(Two words)
Not enough shelves	(Three words)
Just too many things	(Four words)
Home	(One word)

model

P8 Sound check

a) Listen to the words and repeat them. Which are stressed on the first syllable? Which are stressed on the second syllable? Make two lists. Which word is different?

CD 1/51

island · biology · disabled · medicine · goodbye · magazine · interview · American · successful · normally · accident

b) Listen to the CD and check your lists.

CD 1/52

Tuff

CD 1/38 1/53

I'm tough!
Mighty tough!
T-U-Double F!
See!
Good word "tough" –
Strong! Rough!
For me,
See!

Don't need anyone,
Not me;
See!

Nobody loves me.
Love! Huh!
Who needs it!
L-U-V.
Silly word, love …
They say "I love you"
Then they leave.

Empty words –
Just deceive.

I get by.
Don't cry
Not me.
Got enough;
I'm tough.
See!

Plenty friends
On the street;
Plenty places we can meet;
Plenty food
For us to eat;
Don't need shoes on our feet;
We're tough!
T-U-Double F!
See!

Friends are mates,
There for me.
Special mates;
They care for me.
See!

Is that love? …

Could be …

We'll see …
We'll see …
We'll see.

Annette Kosseris

tough

How does the young man feel? What makes you think so?

The world of science

5

In diesem *Theme* ...

- erfährst du etwas über das *Museum of Science and Industry* in Manchester.
- beschäftigst du dich mit dem Thema Erfindungen und sprichst darüber, was sie für dich und deinen Alltag bedeuten.
- lernst du, wie man etwas im Passiv ausdrückt.
- übst du, einem Bericht Informationen zu entnehmen.

A1 ● Going up north

a) Look at the title and the pictures. What do you think David, Gillian and the woman are talking about?

CD 2/1 1/54

b) Now listen to the CD and find out where they are going.

Gillian and David are going to spend the weekend with David's uncle George in Manchester.

Gillian: I've never been to Manchester before. Have you?
David: No, but Charlie says it's really cool. He came up to see Arsenal play Manchester United last year.
Gillian: And I checked it out on the Internet. Lots of super shops and places to go.
David: Well, Uncle George is taking us to the Museum of Science and Industry first. It sounds brilliant.
Gillian: Oh yes, I went to their website. Looks really good.
David: And it'll be useful for my school project. Look, here's a flyer Uncle George sent me.
Gillian: Great! Then you needn't spend hours in the library.
Ticket inspector: Tickets, please? Any more tickets please?
Gillian: David, you've still got our tickets, haven't you?
David: Sure! Here you are!
Ticket inspector: Thank you.
Woman: Oh, you're going to the Museum of Science and Industry, are you? That's a wonderful place. And it's free!
David: Yes, my uncle told us about it.
Woman: You'll need lots of time, though. There's so much to see. My favourite is the Power Hall. You can see the old machines from the cotton mills. They're so big, and what a noise!

David's uncle meets them at the station.

Uncle George: Hi, you two! Had a good journey?
David: Yes, fine, thanks.
Uncle George: OK, shall we go to the museum now?
Gillian: Is it far?
Uncle George: No, only about 20 minutes' walk. But we can get the bus if you like. It's free!

c) Read the dialogue. Who was it?

1. Who says Manchester's a cool place?
2. Who checked out Manchester on the Internet?
3. Who is working on a school project?
4. Who has got the train tickets?
5. Who thinks the Museum of Science and Industry is a wonderful place?
6. Who talks about the free bus to the museum?

workbook A1

A2 ● Welcome to MOSI

When you are inside MOSI, the first thing you have to do is to decide where to start! There's so much to see, you can't possibly see everything in one visit.

Tipp
MOSI = Museum of Science and Industry

a) Read this small part of the museum brochure.

mOSI MUSEUM OF SCIENCE & INDUSTRY

Great things to see and do

1. Crawl underground through a spooky sewer – over 100 years old – with smells, sounds ... and worse!
2. Ride on the old locomotive *Planet*. Start from the oldest railway station in the world.
3. Lift a *Mini* car with your little finger! Can you do it?
4. Hear the noisy machines of the cotton industry, but cover your ears!
5. Watch the ghosts of Manchester's famous scientists. Hear them explain their discoveries and inventions!
6. Compare your computer at home with *Baby*, the world's first computer.
7. See the Avro Shackleton aeroplane, designed in 1954.
8. Find out what living rooms looked like in the 1930s and 1950s. Ask your grandparents!

5

b) Look at the brochure again.

portfolio
I can read

1. What can you *see* in the museum?
2. What can you *hear* there?
3. What can you *smell* there?
4. What can you *do* there?

c) Which parts of the museum would you look at?

I'd first look at ...

Then I'd go to see ...

Which parts of the museum would you look at? Say why.

I'd first have a look at ...
Then I'd go to see ...

because

I like ...
I'm interested in ...
I've never seen ... before.
It sounds interesting / fun / ...
...

portfolio
I can talk

workbook
A2

A3 ● Where are they?

CD 2/2

Look at the museum brochure in A2 again and listen to the two children in the museum. Which parts of MOSI are the children in? Take notes.

A4 ○ Inventions

In MOSI you can find out about inventions.
Which inventions are important for everyday life?
Write down what you think is …

- the most important for you.
- very important for you.
- good to have.
- not important for you.

bicycle

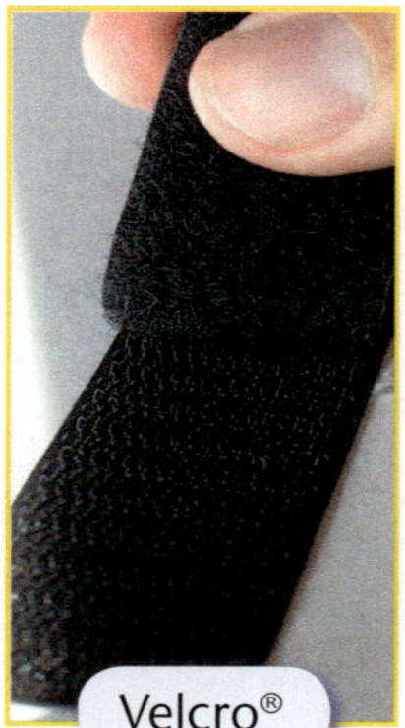
Velcro®

mobile phone

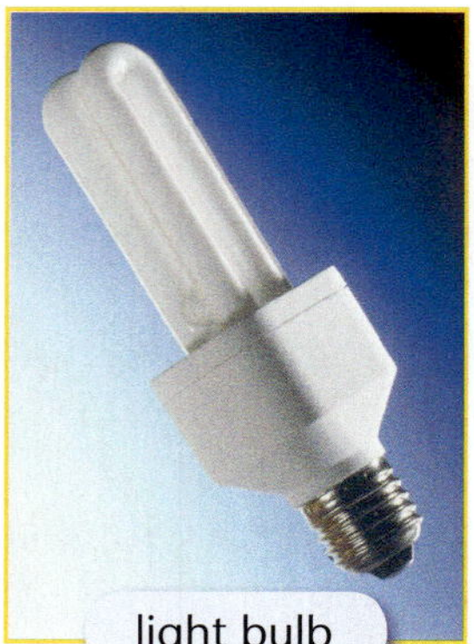
light bulb

laptop

wordbank
science

matches

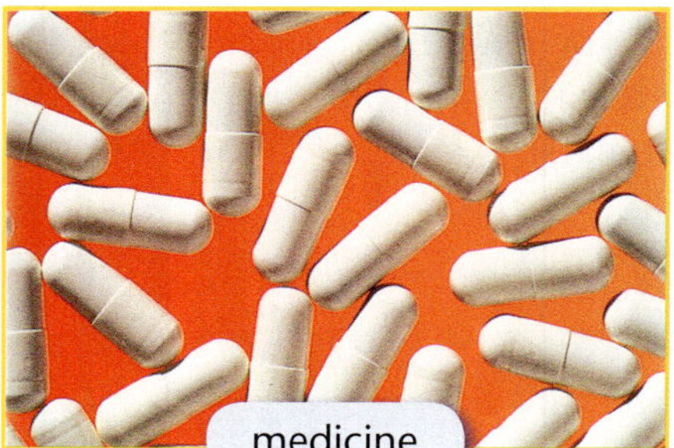
medicine

TV set

The … is … s are	the most important for me. very important for me. good to have. not important for me.

The … is very important for me.
I couldn't live without …
I don't need …

workbook
A3

Work with a partner and write down some more inventions. Decide how important they are for you.

A5 ● Life without electricity

a) Think of your home. Think of the things you do every day.
Which of the things do you need electricity for? Write them down in a list.

b) Compare your list with the lists of your classmates. Make a class list and talk about it.

I We	need	electricity for	the radio. the TV. … cooking. washing. …

I need electricity for the radio.

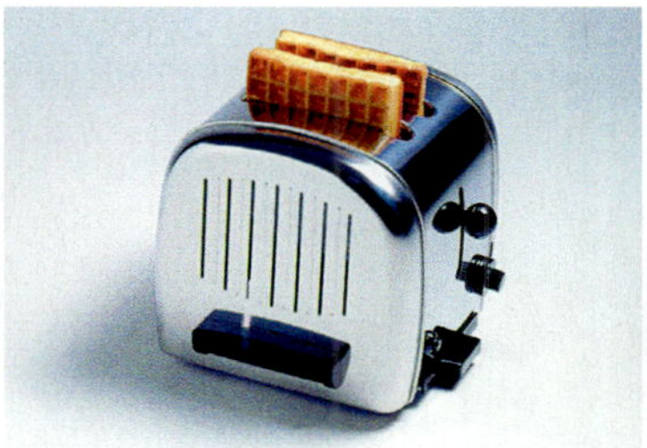

wordbank science

portfolio I can talk, I can learn English, I can work with words

c) Imagine life without electricity. Talk about it.

Without electricity	I we	can't have to	eat … watch … make … …

Without electricity we have to eat cold food.

LiF 14

portfolio I can work with grammar

d) Have you ever been without electricity? What happened?

When we had no electricity,	I we	had to … couldn't …

When we had no electricity, we had to use candles.

workbook A4–A7

A6 ○ Choose

1. Make a list of inventions you think the world could live without. Make notes and give reasons.
2. Which inventions will no longer be in use 30 years from now? Make notes and give reasons.
3. Describe an invention to your partner but don't say what it is. Your partner must guess. Take turns.
4. Which inventions don't use electricity? Make a list. Compare your list with your partner's list.

wordbank science

LAND & LEUTE 4

Museen zum Anfassen

Die Briten sind Weltmeister, wenn es um Museen geht. Wenn du in Großbritannien Ferien machst, bist du nie weit entfernt von einem Kanalmuseum oder einem Museum für Dampfeisenbahnen. Ob Teekannen oder Rasenmäher, Spielzeug oder Pferde – es gibt Museen für alles.

Viele der Museen zeigen, wie die Menschen früher gelebt haben. Man kann in ehemaligen Fabriken und Bergwerken umherspazieren, in alten Läden stöbern und auch einkaufen. Per Dampfeisenbahn kann man ganz gemütlich wie die Menschen vor der Einführung der Hochgeschwindigkeitszüge reisen. Man kann aber auch eine Fahrt mit einem Kanalboot machen, das von einem Pferd gezogen wird.

Im *Viking Centre* in York erfährst du, wie die Wikinger Britannien angegriffen und besiedelt haben. *Robin Hood* triffst du im *Sherwood Forest* und in *Liverpool* kannst du ein *Beatles*-Museum besuchen. In Manchester gibt es für Fußballfans sogar ein *Manchester United Museum*.

Doch nicht in allen Museen geht es um die Vergangenheit: Im *Centre for Alternative Technology* in *Wales* kannst du alles über Wind- und Wasserkraft herausfinden und tief unten in einem Berg kannst du ein Hightech-Elektrizitätswerk besichtigen.

Das Besondere an den meisten Museen ist, dass man die Dinge nicht nur ansehen darf, sondern vieles auch anfassen und ausprobieren kann. Wer Urlaub in Großbritannien macht, bekommt in den *Tourist Information Centres* alle Informationen über die Museen in der Umgebung.

Finde im Internet heraus, welche anderen Museen in Großbritannien dich interessieren könnten.

A7 ○ Museums in your area

how to ... help out in English

portfolio dossier

workbook A8–A10

Which museums are there in your area? Choose one. What can you see and do there? What is the best thing about it? When is it open? What does it cost? How can you get there?

a) Bring an information leaflet and report to the class in English.

b) Make an English-German leaflet for English-speaking visitors to your area. Have an exhibition in class.

B1 ● An amazing day out

a) Read David's report about his trip to MOSI. What parts of the museum does David mention?

how to … read

Hot tip in Manchester

There's more to Manchester than Man United! It's an interesting city with lots to see and do.

We had a great day at the Manchester Museum of Science and Industry last weekend. There's so much to see there – too much for one day! And it's free!

Power Hall
There are five different buildings and it was hard to know where to start. So we followed the terrific noise to the Power Hall. The big water-powered and steam-powered engines were already working. What a noise! The old cotton mills of Manchester were powered by these machines. Even noisier were the spinning and weaving machines, and you could really get an idea of what it was like for the hundreds of men, women and children who had to work there.

World's first railway station
After that, it was good to get some fresh air outside. Then we had a ride on the old steam locomotive "Planet". The ride starts from the oldest railway station in the world.

The Communications Section
After lunch, we had a look round the Communications Section. I really liked that huge old computer, called "Baby". It was built in 1948.

Main Building
The Xperiment Section in the Main Building was also good fun. You could do all sorts of experiments yourself, like lifting a Mini car! But for me the best was going deep down underground in that old Manchester sewer. It smelled so real!

No time for Air and Space Section
So it was a great day. We didn't even have time for the Air and Space Section, so that'll have to wait till next time. I can't wait!

b) Right or wrong?

1. David spent a whole weekend at MOSI.
2. There are five buildings at the museum.
3. Some parts of the museum are very noisy.
4. "Baby" is a very old steam locomotive.
5. You don't have to pay to get into the museum.

Answer the questions.

1. What did David see before lunch?
2. What was his favourite part?
3. Which part wasn't David able to see?
4. Is he going to visit the museum again?

portfolio
I can read

workbook
B1, B2

B2 ● Fantastic inventions?

Here are some inventions that weren't so brilliant.

a) Read the texts and match them with the pictures.

The bicycle shower, that's number …

1

Bicycle shower
One cyclist had a brilliant idea: his "velodouche" combined the morning shower with a bit of exercise. Pedal power was used to pump water into the shower. The more you pedalled, the more powerful the shower!

Eagle power
One of the strangest flying machines was designed in the 19th century. The idea was to use the power of eagles. They were fixed to a metal cage that carried a man. Of course, the idea didn't get off the ground!

2

3

First parachute jump
Frenchman André Garnerin built a 7-metre wide parachute. Then he jumped from a hot-air balloon and made the first ever parachute jump. The problem was, he didn't know he needed to cut a hole in the top to let the air through. So the parachute swung so wildly that André Garnerin was very sick. But at least he landed safely!

Amphicar – the car that swims!
The "Amphicar" was designed by the German Hans Trippel in 1961. It was a boat and a car in one and could travel on land and on water. The trouble was, on land it was like a fish out of water and couldn't go faster than 65 kph. It wasn't exactly a best-seller, as you can imagine!

4

portfolio
I can write

b) Which is your favourite? Say why.

My favourite invention is … because …

LiF
15

workbook
B3–B6

c) Look at the texts and the pictures again and write about the inventions.

The … → was → invented / designed → by … *(inventor)* in … *(year)*

B3 ● Hit or flop?

CD
2/5

a) Listen to a radio reporter talking to Karen Waterman about her car. What kind of car is it? Where do they drive the car?

portfolio
I can listen

workbook
B7–B9

b) ★ What does Karen think about the Amphicar? Hit or flop? What do you think the reporter thinks about the Amphicar? Hit or flop?

☼ Read the text about the Amphicar in B2. Then listen to the CD again. What new information can you find out about the Amphicar from the CD?

B4 ○ Are you a successful inventor?

Match the inventions and their names.

biscuit baker

cleaning skates

X-ray glasses

Lennie's invention must be the …

Lennie

Claire and Chris

Emma

workbook B10, B11

What can the following inventions do? Can you guess?

close-your-eyes lamp | shrink-and-grow lunchbox | singing toilet roll

B5 ○ Inventions for the future

What new inventions would you like to have for the future? Work in groups.

1. Choose a topic: food, medicine, everyday life …
2. Now collect ideas about your new invention. For example think about:
   - What is it good for?
   - What does it look like?
   - What is it called?
   - Who can use it?
   - What is it made of?
   - …
3. Write short texts about your invention and draw pictures. Make a poster.
4. Present your invention to the class. Have a vote: which invention is the most original? Which is the most useful?

project

wordbank science

how to … present

portfolio I can work with words, dossier

B6 ○ The techno trousers

In the film "The wrong trousers" Wallace gives Gromit a pair of "techno trousers" as a birthday present. The techno trousers are Wallace's invention. Watch the scene (0:00:00 – 0:05:35) and answer the questions.

1. What are the techno trousers for?
2. How do they work?
3. What does Gromit do with them?
4. Does Gromit like his birthday present?

film

P1 Say it in English

Match the sentences.

1. Wie sagt man, dass man Strom zum Fernsehen braucht?
2. Wie kannst du sagen, dass du etwas im Internet nachgeschaut hast?
3. Wie sagt man, dass man sich für Flugzeuge interessiert?
4. Wie fragt der Fahrkartenkontrolleur nach Fahrkarten?
5. Was kannst du sagen, wenn du jemandem etwas gibst?
6. Wie sagt man, dass das Amphicar Boot und Auto in einem war?

a. Any more tickets, please?
b. Here you are.
c. I'm interested in planes.
d. You need electricity for watching TV.
e. The Amphicar was a boat and a car in one.
f. I checked it out on the Internet.

P2 Mssng vwls

portfolio
I can work with words

a) **What are these words? Add the missing vowels. They are all to do with science and technology.**

dscvry msm lcmtv

rpln scntst lctrcty prcht nvntn shwr xprmnt

CD 2/1

b) **Listen to the CD and check your words.**

c) **Now write down more words with missing vowels and ask your classmates to find the words.**

P3 Have you ever …?

Work with a partner. Ask and answer questions.

LiF 2R

Have you ever …	
	been to a … museum?
	travelled on a steam train?
	invented anything?
	heard a singing toilet roll?
	seen …?
	…?

Yes, I have.

No, I haven't.

P4 Rhyme words

CD 2/2

a) **Listen to the CD and repeat what you hear.**

b) **Find the rhyme words.**

CD 2/3

c) **Listen to the CD and check your rhyme words.**

light	satellite	sign
boat	rule	Liverpool
time	need	about
train	without	rhyme
ride	note	aeroplane
design	hide	read
air	wear	

P5 May I?

a) Match the phrases which mean the same.

I'm not allowed to | Must I? | I needn't | I mustn't | Do I have to? | Am I allowed to? | I must | I don't have to | May I? | I have to

LiF 14

b) Write down six sentences about what you are allowed to do, what you have to do, …

I'm allowed to come home after 8 o'clock in the evening.
I have to clean my room once a week.

P6 When was it opened?

LiF 15

a) Copy these sentences into your exercise book. Complete them with a past participle from the box.

opened	powered
designed	born
eaten	built
played	checked

1. My brother was … in 1990.
2. The first machines in the cotton mills were … by water.
3. The first parachute was … by a Frenchman called André Garnerin.
4. The Avro Shackleton aeroplane was … in 1954.
5. Basketball is … by ten players.
6. Cornflakes are usually … with milk.

b) Listen to the CD and check your sentences.

CD 2/4

P7 What, who, when?

1. were – 1908 – Dog biscuits – in – invented – .
2. The – was – first – in – teddy bear – 1902 – made – .
3. invented – hot-air balloon – was – 1783 – The – in – .
4. Levi Strauss – by – designed – were – Blue jeans – .
5. 1895 – first – The – were – cornflakes – made – in – .
6. 2000 – was – London Eye – in – opened – The – .
7. was – Eiffel Tower – The – 1889 – in – built – .

a) Unscramble the sentences.

LiF 12, 15

b) Listen to the CD and check your sentences.

CD 2/5

P8 Sound check

a) Listen to the CD and repeat the words.

CD 2/6

sent	passenger	gas	many
website	check	invention	adult
travel	technology	champions	
any	regular	back	

b) Listen again and fill in your lists.

c) Listen and check your lists.

CD 2/7

[æ]	[e]
travel	*sent*

A spiky story

Go for a summer walk in the country, and when you come back you'll often find spiky little balls on your clothes or on your dog's fur. They're called burrs in English, and they're a special kind of seed. They stick to people or animals and are carried to other places. So they can fall off and grow somewhere else.

For most people they're just irritating. But they gave a Swiss engineer called George de Mestral the idea for a really cool invention. Can you guess what he invented?

Well, in 1948 he arrived home after a walk one day. Some of these spiky burrs stuck to his clothes. He pulled one off and looked at it under his microscope. What he saw were hundreds of thin spikes with little hooks on the ends. These hooks made the burrs stick to his clothes.

This gave him a brilliant idea for a clever new invention for holding things together. He worked for eight years on his design before he got it right. In the end he had the perfect material to make his invention work. The material was called nylon, and he made two different strips from it. There were thousands of small hooks on one strip, and thousands of small loops on the other strip. When the two strips were pressed together, they stuck together very strongly. Yes, this clever Swiss had invented the "hook and loop fastener", or Velcro®, as we now call it.

The Velcro® fastener has been very successful and is used in lots of different products – on clothing, shoes and rucksacks, for example. It has replaced many buttons, zips or other fasteners. How many Velcro® fasteners can you find in your home?

Velcro® is a good example of how a problem can be turned into a solution. And some of the best inventions, like Velcro®, are made when we copy nature.

Explain in German how the hook and loop fastener works.

Cash in hand 6

In diesem *Theme* …

- unterhältst du dich über Taschengeld und was du damit machst.
- beschäftigst du dich mit Kaufen und Verkaufen.
- erfährst du etwas über Wohltätigkeitsveranstaltungen in Großbritannien.
- erfährst du etwas über den *London Marathon*.
- lernst du Bedingungen aufzustellen: was wird, wenn …

A1 Pocket money

a) Interview your partner:

portfolio
I can talk

- Do you get pocket money every week or every month?
- Do you get money for good marks at school?
- Do you do jobs in the house for extra pocket money?
- What jobs do you do to earn money?

b) Now report to the class.

Marcus gets …

He doesn't get extra pocket money for jobs in the house.

c) What do you spend your money on?

clothes

I spend my pocket money on things like CDs or clothes.

I spend my money on …

tickets for a football match

class trips

cinema

make-up

things for school

…

workbook
A1

A2 Short of money

a) What can young people do to earn extra money? What are your ideas? Talk to your partner.

wordbank
jobs and money

- sell things at a flea market
- do the shopping for someone
- do a paper round
- babysit
- take someone's dog for a walk
- do some gardening
- make …
- …

You could sell things at a flea market.

If you are short of money, you can do the shopping for someone.

Perhaps you can …

Why don't you …?

workbook
A2

b) Tell the class about your ideas.

A3 Earn some money

What can you do to earn some money? What will you be able to do? Write sentences.

LiF
16

workbook
A3

If I	do sell take …	a paper round, my old toys at a flea market, someone's dog for a walk, …	I can I can't I will be able to I won't be able to	buy get …	…

A4 A car boot sale

a) **Look at the photo. What are the people doing?**

b) **Now listen to the conversation. What are the girls talking about?**

CD 2/8 2/8

Gillian and Vanessa are going on a class trip to France. It's very expensive, so they decide to sell some things at a car boot sale. If they sell enough, they'll have some extra money for the trip. They found some old things in their rooms. Their friends gave them some, too.

how to … listen

Gillian: Wow! We have so many old clothes here. And this vase! And look at all these books.
Vanessa: And here are some plates. And some pictures.
Gillian: Oh, look! Here's our first customer. Hi, Rosemary!
Rosemary: Hello, you two. What are you doing here?
Gillian: We're trying to sell some things to make some money for our class trip to France next month. And you?
Rosemary: I'm looking for a present for my aunt. Have you got anything really old?
Vanessa: Well, there are some really old plates here, see.
Gillian: And lots of old books. Does she like detective stories?
Rosemary: I'm not sure. Oh! But can I have a look at that old picture over there?
Vanessa: Yes, here you are. Now that's something very special, don't you think?
Gillian: Yes, if you buy her that, you'll make her very happy.
Rosemary: Mhm, it looks interesting. I've never seen anything like that before.
Gillian: Between you and me, I'm sure it's a Picasso, you know!
Rosemary: You're joking!
Vanessa: Err, what's a Pi … ?
Rosemary: Picasso. Never heard of him? He was a famous Spanish painter, Vanessa. His pictures are worth lots of money. Thousands of pounds.
Vanessa: Really? And you say this is …
Gillian: Yes, it's very special. And just for you, Rosemary, a very special offer. Just £3!
Rosemary: OK, Mrs Art Expert, I'll take it. Even if it's not a Picasso, I'm sure my aunt will like it.
Gillian: Yes, and if she keeps it long enough, she'll be rich one day.
Rosemary: Well, you never know.

A5 Special offer

CD 2/8 2/8

a) Listen to Gillian, Vanessa and Rosemary again and read along. Then answer at least three of these questions.

1. Why do the girls need the money?
2. Who gave them some old things to sell?
3. Who is Gillian and Vanessa's first customer?
4. Who does Rosemary need a present for?
5. Does Rosemary's aunt like detective stories?
6. How much is the picture that Rosemary buys?

b) Match the sentence parts.

1. Gillian and Vanessa are going
2. If they sell enough,
3. I'm looking for
4. I've never seen
5. If you buy her that,
6. His pictures are worth
7. If she keeps it long enough,

a. she'll be rich one day.
b. lots of money.
c. anything like that before.
d. they'll have some pocket money for the trip.
e. on a class trip to France.
f. you'll make her very happy.
g. a present for my aunt.

Match the words and their definitions.

1. car boot sale
2. expensive
3. vase
4. present
5. plate
6. famous
7. aunt
8. rich
9. painter
10. customer

a. when a thing costs a lot of money
b. when you have a lot of money
c. a person who buys something
d. a place to sell old things
e. this is what a lot of pop stars are
f. he or she paints pictures
g. something you give or get at Christmas, for example
h. your mother's sister or your father's sister
i. you put flowers in this
j. you put bread or cake on this

workbook A4–A8

A6 At the flea market

CD 2/9

a) Listen to the four dialogues. What are the people trying to buy or sell at the flea market?

portfolio I can listen

a hockey stick

comics

a pair of shoes

DVDs

a pair of trousers

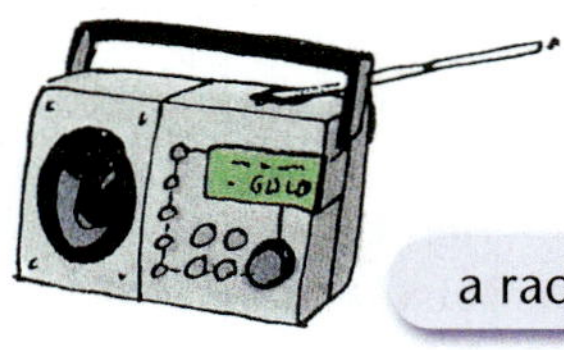
a radio

b) Listen again. How much do the customers pay in the end?

A7 ● Buying and selling

a) Look at these phrases and write them in the table.

customer	seller
How much is it?	It's £9.

- Oh, that's too expensive.
- It's a special offer.
- Have you got anything cheaper?
- Have you got any …?
- How much is it?
- What do you want for that?
- Here's your change.
- Does it work?
- What do you think about this?
- It's £9.
- What's on offer?
- I need something for my friend's birthday.
- I think I'll take it.
- What size are they?
- Sorry, I don't have any … but I have some …
- OK. Let's say £8.

LiF 17, 18R

portfolio I can work with words

Can you think of more phrases? Write them in your table.

b) Work with a partner or in a small group. Try to buy or sell one of these things. Write down your dialogue and practise it.

portfolio I can write, I can talk, I can learn English

portfolio dossier

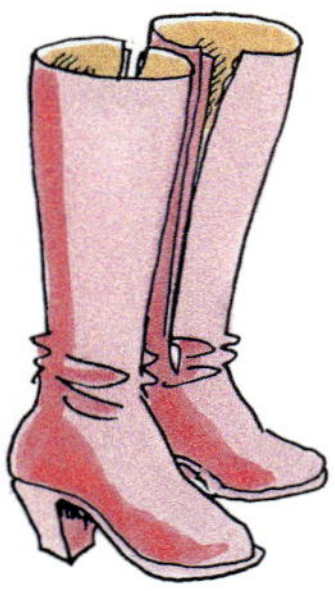

- a pair of pink boots
- an old plate with flowers on it
- a pair of skis
- a mobile phone
- a model train from 1932
- …

workbook A9–A12

A8 ○ Choose

1. Act out your dialogue from A7 b) and record it (audio or video). Present your dialogue and decide: who is the best seller in your class? Who is the cleverest customer?

wordbank jobs and money

2. Work with a partner. Go back to page 73, pick one of the inventions and try to sell it at a flea market. Act out the scene and record it (audio or video). Then present it and decide: who is the best seller in your class? Who is the cleverest customer?

how to … talk

3. Have you ever sold things at a flea market? What was it like? Tell the class. Think about:

- When did you have to be there?
- When did the flea market finish?
- Did you sell a lot?
- What did you sell?
- Did you have a table or did you sit on the ground?
- …

portfolio I can talk

portfolio dossier

A9 Money, money, money

CD 2/10 2/12

a) Listen to the song.

I work all night, I work all day
To pay the bills I have to pay
Ain't it sad
And still there never seems to be
A single penny left for me
That's too bad
In my dreams I have a plan
If I got me a wealthy man
I wouldn't have to work at all
I'd fool around and have a ball …

Chorus:
Money, money, money
Must be funny
In the rich man's world
Money, money, money
Always sunny
In the rich man's world
Aha-ahaaa
All the things I could do
If I had a little money
It's a rich man's world
It's a rich man's world

A man like that is hard to find
But I can't get him off my mind
Ain't it sad
And if he happens to be free
I bet he wouldn't fancy me
That's too bad
So I must leave, I'll have to go
To Las Vegas or Monaco
And win a fortune in a game
My life will never be the same …

Chorus (2x)

Music and lyrics:
Benny Andersson / Björn Ulvaeus

b) What do you think:
who is the woman in the song?
What does she look like? What is she wearing? Where does she live?

What are the woman's dreams? Why does she want to go to Las Vegas?

workbook B1

B1 ● The London Marathon

a) Talk about the photos.

b) Read about the marathon and find out: what do the runners collect money for?

Once a year, on a Sunday in April, the streets of London are closed to cars and buses. About 33,000 people run in the London Marathon and thousands more stand at the sides of the streets to watch them. The marathon starts near Greenwich and finishes 26 miles later in front of Buckingham Palace. Most runners have one or more sponsors – they run as many miles as they can and their sponsors pay money for each mile. The more miles they run, the more money they collect. Then the money is given to a charity.

B2 ● Not just one race

a) Read the article. Where does the marathon start? Where does it end?

Tipp
In Großbritannien schreibt man 2,500 aber man sagt *two thousand five hundred*. Man schreibt 42.195 und man sagt *forty-two point one nine five*. Man schreibt 2:15:25 aber man sagt *two hours, fifteen minutes and twenty-five seconds*. Bei Uhrzeiten schreibt man 9.30 und sagt *nine thirty*.

portfolio
I can read

Ready for the marathon

In just a few days, on 26th April, one of the world's biggest marathons will take place. There are three starting points for the 33,000 runners at Blackheath and Greenwich Park. The race finishes in the Mall in front of Buckingham Palace, 26 miles and 385 yards or 42.195 kilometres later.

The London Marathon is not just one race. There is:

- **The Elite Race:** Women start at 9.00 from the Blue Start in Blackheath. Men start at 9.30 from the same place. The women's world record is 2:15:25 at the moment; the men's is 2:03:59.
- **The Mass Race:** This race starts at 9.45 from the Red Start in Greenwich Park. The runners dress up for the race and they find sponsors – they collect money for every mile they run. In this race fun is more important than time.
- **The Wheelchair London Marathon:** This race starts at 9.25 from the Green Start. It is open to wheelchair athletes from all over the world.
- **The Mini Marathon:** This race is much shorter – it is run over the last 3 miles of the marathon. It starts at 9.00 from Southwark Bridge. More than 2,500 young people between the ages of 11 and 17 will run in it.

This year the runners will collect money for *The Children's Trust* and other charities.

CD
2/11

portfolio
I can listen

b) Listen to the radio report and look at the map. Follow the route with your finger.

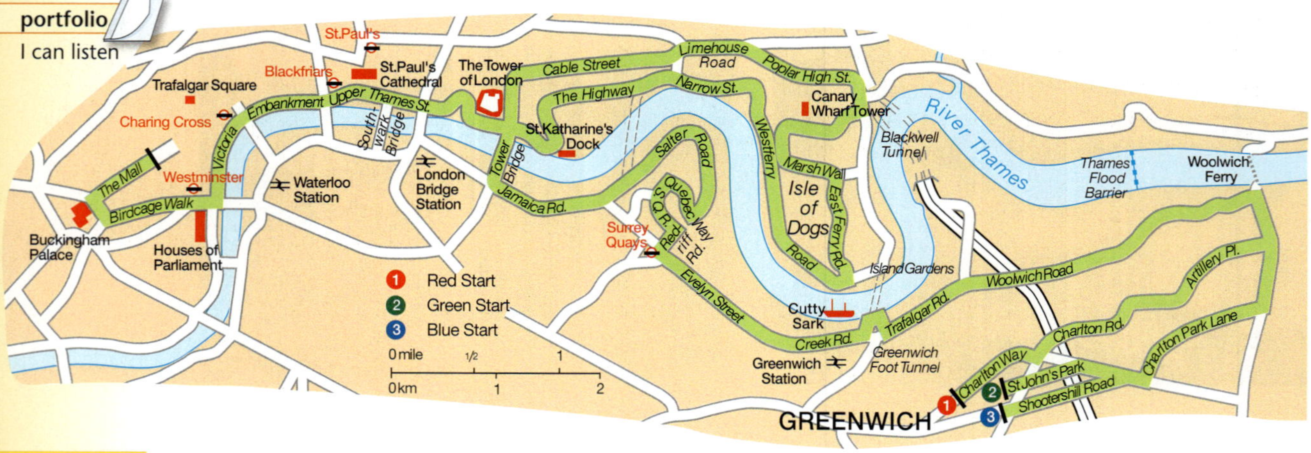

c) Find out from the article what these numbers stand for. Copy the table and fill in the numbers.

3 · 42.195 · 9.45 · 9.00 · 2,500 · 33,000 · 26

when?	how many?	how long?

Read the article again and make up a quiz for the class or your group.

What is more important for the runners in the mass race than the time? ...

d) Look at the article again and write sentences.

If you	are a woman and fit, want to collect money for charity, are in a wheelchair, are a man and a fast runner, are between 11 and 17, want to dress up for the marathon,	you	can must	start at ... from ...

LiF 16

workbook B2–B8

B3 An article for a school newspaper

Write an article for a magazine or make a podcast about the marathon.

how to ... write

portfolio I can write, I can learn English, dossier

Land & Leute 5

Fundraising

Es kommt immer wieder vor, dass Vereine, Organisationen oder Privatpersonen zusätzliches Geld brauchen: Im Krankenhaus soll ein Spielzimmer für Kinder eingerichtet werden, jemand benötigt dringend eine teure Operation, eine Betreuungsstation für alte und kranke Menschen soll eingerichet werden oder ein Projekt in einem „Entwicklungsland" braucht besondere Unterstützung.

Für solche gemeinnützige Vorhaben Geld zu beschaffen, nennt man im Englischen fundraising. Man kann ein Konzert veranstalten, ein Fußballturnier organisieren, einen Flohmarkt durchführen, zu einem Sponsorenlauf aufrufen ...

Es gibt viele Ideen für Fundraising-Aktionen. Eine besonders erfolgreiche und witzige hatte die britische Wohltätigkeitsorganisation *Comic Relief*, die in den achtziger Jahren mit besonders originellen Spendenaktionen begann. Sie rief auch den *Red Nose Day* ins Leben: Wer an diesem Tag selbst spendet und zum Spenden ermuntern will, trägt eine rote Plastiknase zum Zeichen der Unterstützung. So kam zum Beispiel am *Red Nose Day* im Jahr 2007 die beachtliche Summe von £67.726.409 zusammen.
www.comicrelief.com

Auch bei uns in Deutschland gibt es mehr und mehr Sponsoren-Veranstaltungen. Hast du schon einmal an einer teilgenommen oder in der Nachbarschaft eine Veranstaltung erlebt? Berichte darüber.

workbook B9–B11

P1 Say it in English

Match the sentences.

1. Wie kannst du zwei Freunde oder Freundinnen begrüßen?
2. Wie sagst du, dass du so etwas noch nie gesehen hast?
3. Wie sagst du, dass etwas ein ganz besonderes Angebot ist?
4. Wie sagst du, dass du nicht glaubst, dass jemand das ernst meint?
5. Wie fragst du nach der Größe eines Kleidungsstücks?
6. Wie sagst du, dass du dich zum Kauf entschlossen hast?

a. OK, I'll take it.
b. What size is it?
c. You're joking!
d. Hello, you two.
e. I've never seen anything like that before.
f. It's a very special offer.

P2 Odd one out

Find the ending that does not fit.

1. I spend my money on …
a. make-up.
b. clothes.
c. things for school.
d. all day.

2. For extra money I do …
a. the shopping for my neighbour.
b. some gardening for my neighbour.
c. my old toys.
d. the dishes for my mother.

3. At a car boot sale you can buy …
a. car boots.
b. old books.
c. second-hand clothes.
d. pictures.

4. A customer sometimes says:
a. "Special offer."
b. "OK, I'll take it."
c. "What's on offer?"
d. "Do you have a smaller size?"

5. A seller sometimes says:
a. "We've got lots of good things."
b. "That's nine pounds."
c. "Here's your change."
d. "That is very expensive."

P3 If you are clever …

LiF 16

… you will find four sentences. Look through A4 again and find all the sentences with "if". Explain them in German to a partner.

P4 More ifs

LiF 16

Match the sentence parts and finish the sentences that have no ending.

1. If Tom goes out tonight …
2. If it rains this weekend …
3. If it's sunny this weekend …
4. If we go to the cinema tonight …
5. If Dad cooks tonight …
6. If the pupils forget their homework again …
7. If Colin helps his mother in the garden …
8. If the weather is nice tomorrow …

a. I know what he will make.
b. what film will we see?
c. I will ride my bike.
d. I'll go with him.
e. Jack will stay at home.
f. the teacher will be really angry!
…
…

P5 Something to do

a) Match the sentences and write them down.

LiF 17

1. Is there anything left?
2. I'm looking for something interesting to read.
3. Stop talking, please!
4. Have you got anything more to say?
5. I'd like something hot and spicy.
6. What's for lunch today?
7. Have you got anything a bit cheaper?

a. Well, this T-shirt costs only 50 pence.
b. No, we've sold everything.
c. No, I think I've said enough already!
d. What about this Harry Potter book?
e. Something special. I'm sure you'll like it.
f. Why not try this Indian curry, then?
g. I didn't say anything!

b) Listen to the CD and check your answers.

CD 2/15

P6 Two stalls

Work with a partner. What can you get at the two stalls?

You can get something to eat at stall two.

You can't get anything to eat at stall one.

LiF 17

portfolio
I can work with grammar

eat · drink · wear · read · listen to · put on the wall · play with

P7 Figure it out?

Listen to the CD and write down the numbers you hear.

CD 2/16

The face behind Facebook

Mark Elliot Zuckerberg was born on 14th May, 1984. He is an American computer programmer and a very good businessman. When he was a student, he started the website Facebook with the help of three other students. On Facebook a group of people can contact each other and chat online.

When he was at school, Mark and his friend Adam D'Angelo worked on different projects. They designed an MP3 player that learned what its different listeners liked to listen to. Several companies wanted to buy the MP3 player, but the friends said no.

After high school, Mark went to Harvard University and did more projects. He started Facebook from his Harvard bedroom on 4th February, 2004. It quickly became very popular at Harvard. More than two-thirds of the students joined in the first two weeks.

Mark then decided to let other universities use Facebook and his friend, Dustin Moskovitz, helped him. By the beginning of the summer almost 30 universities were using Facebook.

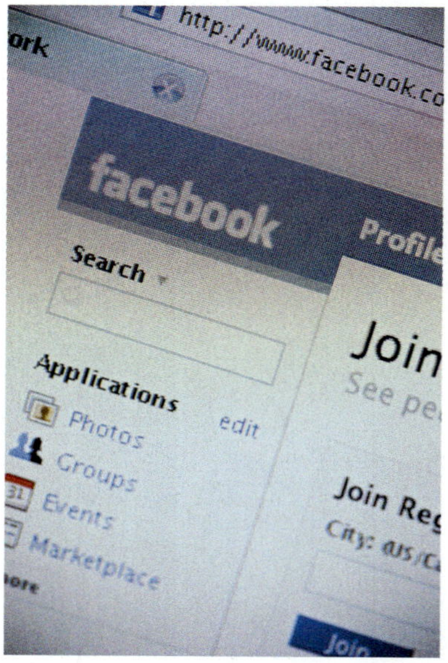

Mark moved to Palo Alto, California, with Dustin and some other friends during the summer of 2004. They rented a small house for their first office. Today, the company has four buildings in Palo Alto.

> **Tipp**
> $ = amerikanischer Dollar

In September 2006, Yahoo offered the boys about $1 billion for Facebook. The boys said no. Google offered them $2.3 billion. The boys again said no. In October 2007, Microsoft offered them $240 million for 1.6 % of Facebook. This time the boys said yes.

But there is also a big problem. Some other Harvard students who went to the university at the same time as Mark say that they had the idea for Facebook first. They claim that Mark stole their idea.

Check the Internet for the latest news about the face behind Facebook.
What do you think about Facebook or similar websites?

Art and music 7

In diesem *Theme* …

- unterhältst du dich über deine Lieblingsmusik.
- übst du, Texte zu überfliegen und gezielt Informationen zu finden.
- beschäftigst du dich mit Kunstwerken und äußerst deine Meinung dazu.
- lernst du wiederzugeben, was jemand anderes sagt.

A1 ● Your favourite music

portfolio
I can talk

a) What is your favourite group or singer at the moment? Talk about it in small groups.

b) In class make a list of your favourite groups and singers. Who is the most favourite?

I listen a lot to …

I think … is cool.

My favourite … is …

I like … because …

A2 ● Pink

a) What do you know about the singer Pink? Talk about her in class.

b) What else would you like to know about her? Collect questions.

portfolio
I can read

c) Read this page about Pink from a magazine and try and find answers to your questions.

Has she got … ?

Can she … ?

Does she like … ?

Is she … ?

Pink was born on 8th September 1979 in Doylestown, Pennsylvania, USA.

Pink doesn't like horror movies.

Pink's favourite colours are green and pink.

Pink is a musician and an actress.

P!nk

Some of Pink's tattoos:
- a guardian angel on her shoulder
- "what goes around comes around" on her wrist
- a red star on her hand
- a bar code for her album M!ssundaztood on the back of her neck

Famous songs:
Dear Mr. President,
Stupid Girls,
Sober

Pink's real name is Alecia Beth Moore.

Pink has won two Grammys.

Pink is a big supporter of animal rights organizations. She is a strict vegetarian.

Pink began writing her own songs at the age of 14. She didn't want to sing love songs that didn't mean anything to her.

Pink's father taught her to play the guitar.

d) What do you think is most interesting? What is surprising?

portfolio
I can write

e) Make a fact sheet about Pink.

Make a fact sheet for Pink and *your* favourite star and compare them.

Name: Pink (Alecia Beth Moore)
Birthday: 8th September 1979
Born in: …
Likes: …
…

workbook A1, A2

A3 ○ Your star

a) Work in a small group. Choose a film or pop star. Collect information and photos. Make a collage like the one about Pink.

b) Present your work. Have an exhibition of all the posters in your class.

how to … present

portfolio I can talk, I can learn English

portfolio dossier

A4 ● Radio Junior Europe

Listen to the reporter Tony Denims and his two interview partners.

- Where is Tony Denims?
- Who is he talking to?
- What is the interview about?

CD 2/13

portfolio I can listen

workbook A3

A5 ○ Portobello Road

a) Listen to the CD.

CD 2/14 2/17

Portobello Market is my favourite place
to meet
You can see all kinds of people walking
down the street
Sometimes there's a pop star or an actor
that I know
Always something interesting on
Portobello Road

And the people are all friendly
And the music always loud
And you can hear all kinds of conversation,
walking through the crowd
And the food looks so delicious
I wish I didn't have to go

Always something interesting on
Portobello Road

CD 2/15 2/18

b) Use the karaoke version and sing the song.

c) Write your own verses about your favourite place and present them to the class. Find help with your song in your workbook.

Write your own verses about your favourite place and present them to the class.

how to … present

workbook A4

A6 ● Sabrina and the Gatecrashers

a) Look at the pictures with a partner. What is the comic about? Who are the people?

b) Read the comic.

portfolio
I can read

CD
2/16 2/19

c) What happens in the comic? Write a short summary. The sentence parts will help you.

Sabrina The Gatecrashers Half of the roadies Gillian and Susan	are wants have to pay have got have	a break. gone home. exams every day next week. tired. a lot for new instruments.

It is the day after the concert. What do Susan and Gillian tell their friends? Make notes.

A7 ● Who's speaking?

Who says what?

1. We could do with a break.

1. Sabrina says that they could do with a break.

2. We have to pay a lot for the new instruments.
3. We've got exams at school next week.
4. Ten kids will be outside the Electric Theatre.
5. We're helping Sabrina.
6. I've booked the Electric Theatre for a gig.
7. Half of the roadies have gone home.
8. We'll get free tickets for the concert.
9. I'm tired.

workbook A5

LiF 19

portfolio I can work with grammar

Tipp
I → he / she
We → they

workbook A6–A10

B1 What's on in London?

These pages are from a magazine called *What's on for kids*.

a) What do you expect to find in a magazine like this? Discuss in a small group.

how to ... read

b) Skim through the two magazine pages and find out if you were right.

portfolio I can read

c) Look again. What do you find most interesting? Choose one of the adverts and talk about it in German.

how to ... help out in English

The Kids' Cookery School

107 Gunnersbury Lane, Acton, W3 8HQ (020 8992 8882)
www.thekidscookeryschool.co.uk
Acton Town tube
Open Office 9 am–5.30 pm Mon-Fri.
Fees £15/75 minutes; £30/2.5 hours; £50/5 hours.
Do you want to find out how to cook delicious food? This is the place to go. It's a project for children of all ages. You can touch, smell, taste and feel different foods. There is a maximum number of 12 children in each cookery class.

Children's bookshop
Helpful staff
Lots of titles – from comics to young adult fiction
Discounts on school books

Children's Bookshop
29 Fortis Green Road,
Muswell Hill, London N10 3HP
020 8444 5500

Explore Your World

African masks,
historic instruments,
Egyptian mummies,
a giant walrus
and much more

HORNIMAN MUSEUM

FREE admission

Train Forest Hill
(just 13 minutes from London Bridge)

London Road • Forest Hill • London SE23
Tel 020 8699 1872
www.horniman.ac.uk

Museum of Childhood

Cambridge Heath Road, E2 9PA (020 8983 5200)
www.museumofchildhood.org.uk
Bethnal Green tube/rail
Open 10 am - 5.50 pm Mon-Thur, Sat, Sun.
Closed 1 Jan, 24-26 Dec.
Admission free.

The Museum is now the UK's biggest collection of toys. You can enjoy board games, early electronic toys, puppets from all over the world and children's clothes from former times. Raid the huge dressing up box filled with 19th century clothing and use everything that's in there.

Young Pavement Artists Competition

Tate Britain, Millbank, SW1P 4RG (01304 611428)
pavementart.muscular-dystrophy.org/
Pimlico tube
Date *Exhibition 1.30–5.50 pm, 14–16 July.*
This year's competition has a "rainforest" theme.
Children aged four to 18 can compete. It costs £1.

families BRITAIN **TATE**
... have great days out at Tate

A visit to Tate is child's play ...

There's lots to do for FREE at Tate. Fun activities, creative workshops and special holiday events.
The BP British Art Displays are also free and there are reduced family tickets to all exhibitions.

Open daily 10.00–17.50; every first Friday of every month until 22.00
Closed 24–26 December
Call 020 7887 8888

Tate Britain,
Millbank,
London SW1P 4RG
Pimlico tube

www.tate.org.uk/families

London Transport Museum
Covent Garden Piazza,
WC2E 7BB
(020 7379 6344)
www.ltmuseum.co.uk
Covent Garden tube
Open *Sat-Thur 10.00–18.00, Fri 11.00–21.00.*
Admission *adults £10, under 16s free.*
Looking for cool games or somewhere to go for a great day out? The LTM is the place for you. You can drive a bus or tube train or play some brilliant online games.

Drama Classes and Holiday Courses for ages 4-16
in Fulham, Kensington, Hampstead & Queen's Park

For a free class information pack:
020 8969 3249/020 8871 4987
info@allsortsdrama.com
www.allsortsdrama.com

WESTWAY Sports Centre

SPORT & FUN FOR EVERYONE AT WESTWAY SPORTS CENTRE

CLIMBING, TENNIS, FOOTBALL, HORSE-RIDING, BASKETBALL, NETBALL, GYM

Largest climbing centre in the UK
8 indoor tennis courts and 4 outdoor
6 all-weather football pitches
... and MUCH MORE!

Whatever you want, Westway can help. Courses, group hire, lessons, kids parties, tournaments, special events ...

Call 020 8969 0992 for details

1 Crowthorne Road, London W10
Tube – Latimer Road
(Hammersmith & City Line)
www.westwaysportscentre.org.uk/

d) Look at these questions. How many can you answer in eight minutes?

1. How much does it cost to take part in the Young Pavement Artists Competition?
2. What street is the Museum of Childhood on?
3. In which museum can you look at an African mask?
4. What books can you buy more cheaply at the Children's Bookshop?
5. Where can you go climbing?
6. What is the nearest underground station to Tate Britain?
7. How many hours of cooking can you get for £50 at the Kids' Cookery School?
8. What number do you ring when you want to do a drama course?
9. What does LTM stand for?
10. How long is the train journey from London Bridge to Forest Hill?
11. On which day of the week is the Museum of Childhood closed?
12. How old do you have to be to take part in a drama class?

Work with a partner. Ask and answer more questions.

wordbank
time out

workbook
B1, B2

how to … use the Internet

workbook B3

B2 ○ Choose

1. Draw an advertising poster for the Young Pavement Artists Competition or the Kids' Cookery School or the Museum of Childhood.
2. Choose one of the adverts and find out more on the Internet. Present your results to the class.

portfolio I can talk

wordbank time out

B3 ● What's on in your area?

a) You have an English-speaking visitor. Find out what's on in your area at the moment. Bring a programme or make notes in German.

Zoo: Giraffenbaby
Zirkus
Neuer James Bond Film

b) What do you say to your visitor? What can you do? Work with a partner.

Let's go to the zoo and have a look at the new baby giraffe.

No, that's boring.

There's a circus in town. Why don't we go there?

That's a good idea!

portfolio I can talk

B4 ○ Two pictures from the Tate Gallery

a) Look at the pictures A and B and talk to a partner. Describe what you can see.

In the centre of picture A I can see …

on the left | on the right | at the top | at the bottom | in the centre

wordbank art

A

L. S. Lowry (1927)

B

Marc Chagall (1950)

b) What do you like about the pictures? What don't you like?

I like picture A because …

I don't like the colours in picture B because …

The colours are …

In the picture there are no …

…

boring	fantastic
bright	interesting
colourful	realistic
dark	strange
depressing	unrealistic
dreamlike	…

c) With a partner give the pictures a title. Share your ideas with two more pupils and agree on a title.

B5 In the picture

a) Describe a person from one of the pictures.

My person is a man / woman / boy / girl.
His / Her hair is …
He / She is wearing …
I think he / she is a …

In a group, write about a person from one of the pictures. You can write down what the person thinks, what the person is going to do … You can also write a little story. Read your text to another group and ask them for feedback.

Our person is a man / woman / boy / girl.
His / Her hair is …
He / She is wearing …
We think he / she is a …
They are talking about …
He / She / They has / have just …
Perhaps …
…

b) Do you want to know what title the painters gave their picture? Listen to the audio guides and find out more about the pictures.

portfolio
I can write

how to …
give feedback

portfolio
dossier

CD
2/22
2/23

workbook
B4 – B8

P1 Say it in English

Match the sentences.

1. Wie sagst du, dass du eine Pause gebrauchen könntest?
2. Wie kannst du vorschlagen, in ein Konzert zu gehen?
3. Wie kannst du sagen, dass du etwas langweilig findest?
4. Wie kannst du sagen, dass du erschöpft bist?
5. Wie sagst du, dass du die Farben in dem Bild nicht magst?
6. Wie fragst du jemanden, was mit ihm los ist?

a. That's boring.
b. What's the matter with you?
c. I could do with a break.
d. I don't like the colours in the picture.
e. Let's go to a concert.
f. I'm exhausted.

P2 Odd one out

a) Find the odd one out.

1. concert – gig – instrument – show
2. cool – boring – interesting – exciting
3. actor – musician – singer – waiter
4. cinema – album – CD – song
5. exhibition – museum – advert – gallery
6. at the top – on Monday – at the bottom – in the centre

b) Why is it the odd one out?

c) Write a new odd one out for your partner.

Instrument is the odd one out because you can't go to it.

P3 Sound check

CD 2/29

a) Listen to the words from Theme 7 and repeat them. Is the stress on the first, second or third syllable? Write a list.

favourite · surprising · vegetarian · information · equipment · exhibition · professional · instruments · museum · competition · realistic · admission

first syllable	second syllable	third syllable
favourite	surprising	vegetarian
...	...	...

CD 2/30

b) Listen again and check your list.

P4 ○ What does she say?

a) Jake wants to go to a concert. He asks his sister to ring up her friend who has already been to the concert in another town. What does Jake's sister tell Jake?

1. It was fantastic.
2. I had a seat in the front row.
3. There were hundreds of people in the audience.
4. My sister thought it was great, too.
5. They played for two hours.
6. Your brother should get there early to get a good seat.
7. I hope he has a good time.

1. It was fantastic. → She says it was fantastic.

b) Listen to the CD and check your sentences.

LiF 19

portfolio I can work with grammar

CD 2/31

P5 ○ A nice person

Write a short text about someone you know. Use at least six of the following verbs:

come · live · like · hate · want · work · have · be · prefer · do · make · play · look

My best friend comes from Afghanistan but she lives in Hamburg. She ...

portfolio I can write

P6 ○ My star

Write a poem about your favourite star.

POP STAR
MY IDOL
NO MEAT
PINK

Pink

Famous musician
Tough person
Great songs
Strict vegetarian
Pink

model

portfolio dossier

1 Picasso and the children

Children in different countries of the world looked at this picture by Picasso.

Pablo Picasso: Goat, 1946

Then they made a copy of it and "finished" it. Afterwards they thought about a story to go with their picture. Here's what two of them wrote:

A day with the coolest camel in New York
This is Joey, the coolest camel in New York. After eating breakfast in the morning, Joey goes to the store called "Game Land". In "Game Land" Joey plays video games for five hours. He usually wins every game that he plays. Joey wears sunglasses, a cool T-shirt with many rockets on it and shoes!

Joey can drive cars, dance, sing and talk. He left his family in the deserts of Africa and came to New York to have fun. He eats hot dogs and pizza for lunch. After lunch Joey goes to work in a show. There he dances, sings and tells jokes to his audience. Joey has many fans. Everyone in New York knows him! Sometimes the newcomers are very surprised when they see Joey, the camel.

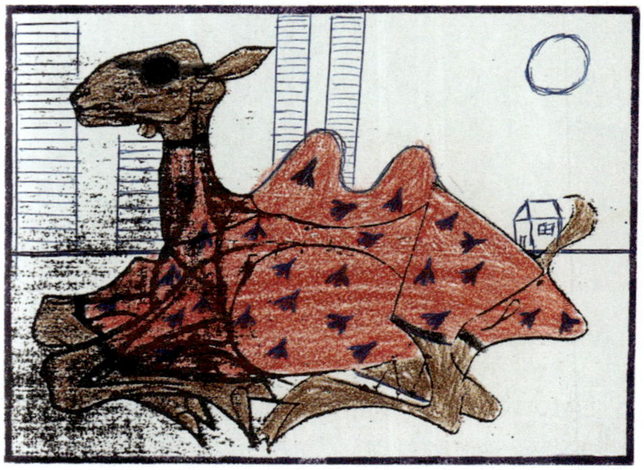

Rubayet: Joey, the coolest camel in New York.
Rubayet, 10, comes from Bangladesh and now lives in New York, USA.

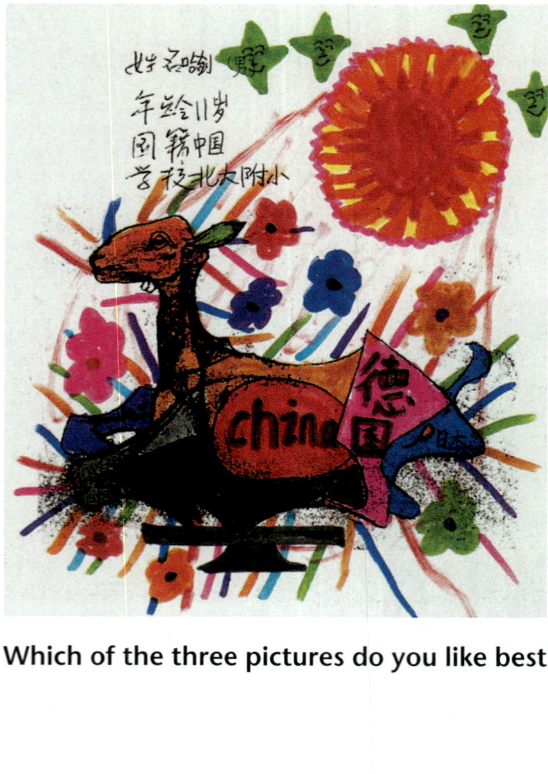

On the back of the little deer
On the back of this little deer there are lots of countries. The sun and a group of stars come to this little coloured deer and bring sunshine and warmth to China, Japan, America, Germany.
The world is then warmed by the sunshine and friendship. And the stars in the sky are smiling.

Ha Tien: On the back of the little deer.
Ha Tien, 11, lives in Beijing, China.

Which of the three pictures do you like best? Say why.

2 Empire of light

What is special about this picture?

CD 2/18 2/32

3 Conversations with my 13-year-old self

Conversations with my thirteen-year-old self
Conversations with my thirteen-year-old self

You're angry
I know this
The world couldn't care less
You're lonely
I feel this
And you wish you were the best
No teachers
Or guidance
And you always walk alone
You're crying
At night when
Nobody else is home

Come over here and let me hold your hand and hug you darling
I promise you that it won't always feel this bad
There are so many things I want to say to you
You're the girl I used to be
You little heartbroken thirteen-year-old me

You're laughing
But you're hiding
God I know that trick too well
You forget
That I've been you
And now I'm just the shell

I promise
I love you and
Everything will work out fine
Don't try to
Grow up yet
Oh just give it some time

The pain you feel is real you're not asleep but it's a nightmare
But you can wake up anytime
Oh don't lose your passion or the fighter that's inside of you
You're the girl I used to be
The pissed off complicated thirteen-year-old me

Conversations with my thirteen-year-old self
Conversations with my thirteen-year-old self

Until we meet again
Oh I wish you well oh
I wish you well
Little girl
Until we meet again
Oh
I wish you well
Little girl
I wish you well
Until we meet again
My little thirteen-year-old me

Music and lyrics: Pink / Billy Mann

What is the song about?

Going places 8

In diesem *Theme* ...

- unterhältst du dich über Reisepläne und Ferienaktivitäten.
- erfährst du etwas über Englisch als Weltsprache.
- hörst du Lieder, in denen es um das Thema Verreisen geht.
- lernst du, wie man Interviews vorbereiten und durchführen kann.

A1 ● Plans! Plans! Plans!

portfolio
I can talk

The summer holidays are almost here. What are you going to do? Talk about your plans in small groups.

In the summer holidays I'm going to …

stay … | meet … | see … | visit … | fly to … | go to … | have a good time in … | …

workbook
A1, A2

A2 ○ Travelling

wordbank
travelling

Do you have friends or family in other countries or cities? Write about them.

- Do they come to visit you?
- How do they travel?
- Have you ever visited them?

LiF
3

portfolio
I can write

model

I have an aunt, an uncle and two cousins in Russia. My aunt is a cook and my uncle is a bus driver. They have never visited us but I have visited them once. I went there with my parents. We went by plane and the flight to Moscow took three hours. We stayed for two weeks.

portfolio
dossier

A3 I just want to see the world

a) Listen to the song and find out: where does the singer want to go? Which places does he want to see?

CD 2/20 2/33

I was looking through a magazine
At all the countries I've never seen
If I could raise the money and book a flight
I'd be on that plane tonight!

If I could go to Canada I'd see Niagara Falls
In China I could walk along the wall
But anywhere really would be OK
Because I just want to see the world

I was looking through a magazine
At all the countries I've never seen
If I could raise the money and book a flight
I'd be on that plane tonight!

If I could go to Cairo I would see the pyramids
It would be the best thing that I ever did
I could travel to all kinds of foreign lands
Because I just want to see the world
See the world

portfolio
I can listen

b) Listen to the song again and complete the sentences in your exercise book.

If I could book a flight I would be on ...
If I could go to Canada I would ...
If I could go to Cairo ...

workbook
A3

A4 Your phrase book for travelling

When you travel to a foreign country it is a good idea to have a phrase book. In small groups make a German-English phrase book with typical situations.

how to ...
write

a) Start with "asking for and giving directions".

b) Here are some more typical situations for your phrase book. Choose one or more.

- going shopping
- at the restaurant
- making friends
- ...

- at the doctor's
- asking for help with the language
- ...

c) Choose one of the situations. Write a mini dialogue with your partner and act it out.

A: Excuse me, can you tell me the way to the station, please?
B: Yes, of course. Go ...

Asking for directions

Entschuldigung, wie komme ich zum Bahnhof?	Excuse me, how can I get to the station?

Giving directions

Gehen Sie / Gehe geradeaus.	Go straight on.

portfolio
I can work with words

portfolio
dossier

workbook
A4–A6

A5 Summer camps

a) Look at the web page. What is it about?

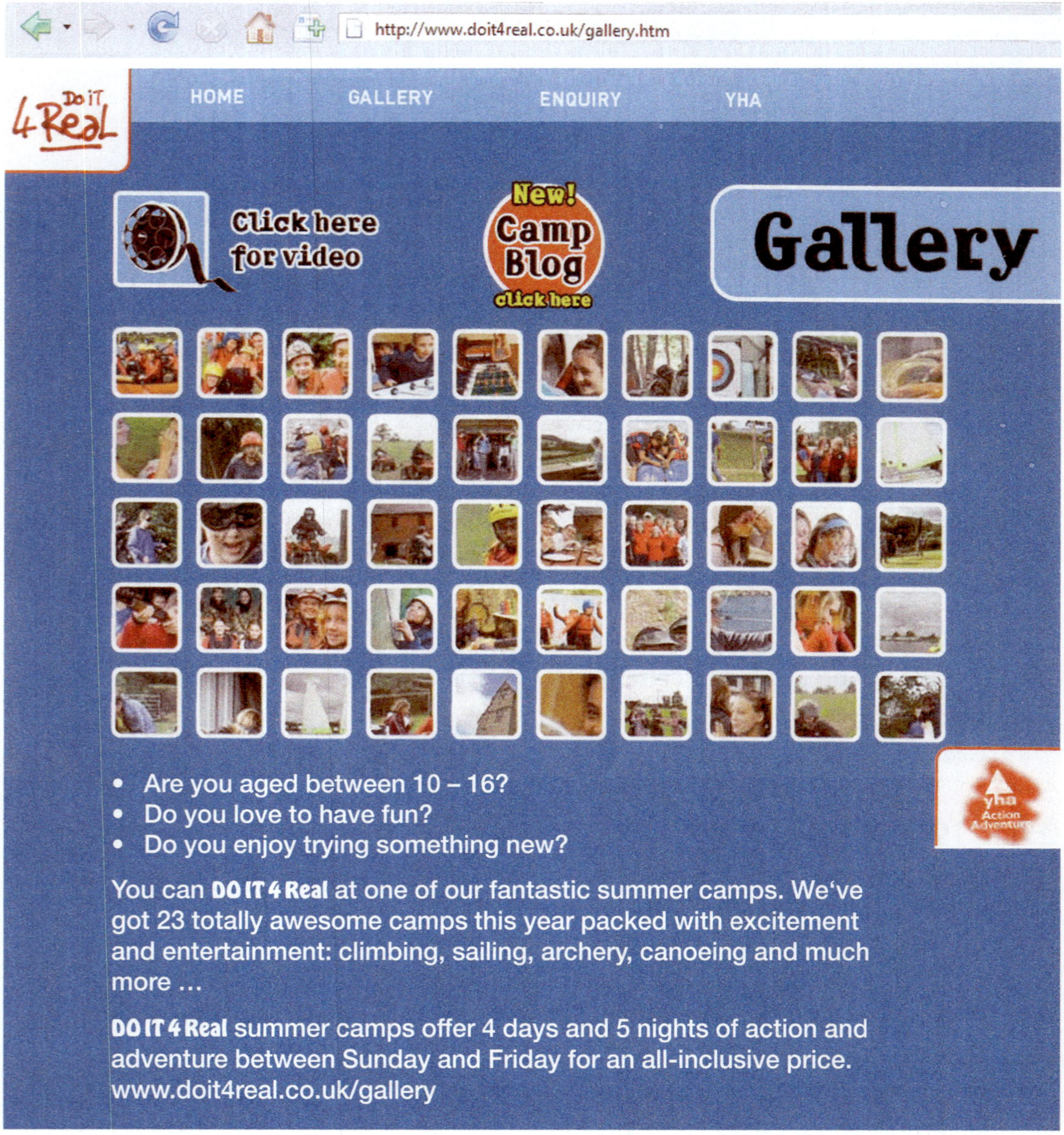

portfolio
I can read

workbook
A7

b) Have a look at the web page. What activities can you find?

LiF
2R

Work with a partner and look at the summer activities.
Ask your partner:

Have you ever tried climbing?

Have you ever been to …

No, but I would like to …

Which activities have you done before?

I have tried …

I've taken part in …

A6 Choosing a camp

David and Rajiv want to go to a summer camp.

CD 2/23

a) **Listen to David and Rajiv on the telephone. Write down in which order they talk about the camps.**

First they talk about …
Then they talk about …

Water Sports Plus

Climbing Club

portfolio
I can listen

Football and Rugby Camp

Musical Star Club

b) **Which camp do David and Rajiv both like?**

c) **Which camp would you like to go to? Say why.**

workbook A8–A10

A7 Holidays without parents

a) **Look up these words in your dictionary.**

Nachtwanderung · Zeltplatz · Ferienlager · Jugendherberge · Lagerfeuer · Taschenlampe · Gruppenreise · Betreuer/in · Heimweh haben

portfolio
I can work with words

b) **Look at the picture. What is happening?**

c) **Talk about the people.**

- What are the parents thinking? How do they feel?
- What are the children thinking? How do they feel?

sad · happy · excited · glad · tired · worried · …

wordbank
travelling, feelings

Have you ever been away from home without your parents? Talk about it with a partner.

Last year I went …

I felt homesick.

I have never been away from home without my parents.

I wouldn't like to …

portfolio
I can talk

workbook A11

B1 ● Different types of English

CD 2/24 2/39

how to ... listen

wordbank travelling

Listen to the travellers talking about their trips. Take notes.

- What are their names?
- Where do they come from?
- What are they going to do?
- What other information do they give?

name	comes from	is going to	other information

Land & Leute 6

Englisch – eine Weltsprache

Englisch wird von ungefähr 350 Millionen Menschen in Großbritannien, Nordamerika, Australien, Neuseeland und weiteren Ländern als Muttersprache gesprochen.

Für mehr als eine Milliarde Menschen ist Englisch eine zweite Sprache. Sie sprechen Englisch in Schulen und an Universitäten; Englisch dient als Sprache in Geschäftsbeziehungen und Verwaltung. Nur zu Hause benutzen diese Menschen ihre Muttersprache. Beispiele dafür sind Indien, Pakistan, Hong Kong, Zimbabwe und Trinidad und Tobago.

Nahezu überall auf der Welt sprechen Menschen Englisch, wenn sie die Muttersprache des anderen nicht verstehen. Ein deutscher Tourist kommt z.B. in Schweden mit Englisch gut zurecht und ein japanischer Geschäftsmann kann sich mit seinen deutschen Geschäftspartnern auf Englisch verständigen.

Dennoch unterscheidet sich das Englisch, insbesondere in der Aussprache. Man sagt dann, dass jemand einen amerikanischen, einen indischen oder einen deutschen Akzent hat. Unterschiede gibt es aber auch in der Wortwahl und sogar der Grammatik. Hier spricht man von unterschiedlichen Dialekten. Dialekte können sich von Stadt zu Stadt, sogar von Dorf zu Dorf unterscheiden.

Aber überall wird ein Standardenglisch verstanden. Dieses Englisch hören wir im britischen und amerikanischen Radio und Fernsehen. Und wenn du lernst, dieses Standardenglisch zu sprechen, werden dich Menschen überall auf der Welt verstehen.

Schau dir die Karte hinten im Buch an. Welche englischsprachigen Länder kannst du noch finden?

workbook B1

B2 ○ At Heathrow Airport

CD 2/25 2/40

a) Charlie, Vanessa and her father are at the airport. They are waiting for Vanessa's cousin Cheryl to arrive from New York. Listen to the CD. What countries and cities can you hear?

workbook B2–B4

b) Have **you** ever been to an airport to pick someone up? What was it like? Talk about it in class.

B3 Going to an airport – a project

You can meet interesting people at an airport: travellers, pilots and people who work there. Many of them speak English. So why not visit your nearest international airport?

1. **First collect ideas. Write lists:**
   - What people can you meet at the airport?
   - What can you see there?

People at the airport:
- *tourists*
- *flight attendants*
- *…*

Tipp
plan it
do it
check it
present it

2. **Then think about your project and what you can do at the airport:**

We could talk to travellers.

We could interview people who work at the airport.

We could record some announcements.

We could …

Places and things at the airport:
- *shops*
- *signs*
- *…*

We could collect information about …

how to … work on a project

3. **Now get together in groups. Decide: who wants to do what? Do you want to do interviews? Then write down questions you want to ask. Don't forget to practise doing interviews. Also look at B4 for help.**
4. **At the airport: record and collect information.**
5. **After the trip: make a presentation or a class exhibition about your trip.**

wordbank travelling

portfolio dossier

B4 Interviews

a) **Imagine you are going to do an interview with someone at the airport. It could be:**

- a passenger who is going somewhere
- a passenger who has just arrived
- …

- a pilot
- a flight attendant
- a famous person
- …

Choose one person and write down questions for an interview. You can ask questions about his or her holiday or plans:

What's your name?
Where are you …?
Why are you …?
Do you …?

b) **Work in small groups and write an interview together.**

1. Agree on one person you want to interview.
2. Compare your questions from a).
3. Agree on the ten best questions.
4. Put them in order.
5. Write down one complete interview with questions and answers. Start like this:

A: Excuse me. We are pupils from … school. Can we do an interview with you in English?
B: Yes, of course. What would you like to know?
…

how to … do an interview

portfolio I can talk, I can write

c) **Act out the interview in class.**

workbook B5

P1 Say it in English

Match the sentences.

1. Wie kannst du sagen, dass du einen Onkel in Russland hast?
2. Wie erkundigst du dich nach dem Weg zum Bahnhof?
3. Wie sagst du jemandem, dass er geradeaus gehen soll?
4. Wie sagst du, dass du Heimweh hattest?
5. Wie fragt man jemanden höflich, ob er Englisch spricht?
6. Wie fragt man, ob der Flug pünktlich ankommt?
7. Wie sagst du, dass du mit dem Flugzeug verreist bist?

a. I felt homesick.
b. Excuse me, please, do you speak English?
c. Is the flight on time?
d. I have an uncle in Russia.
e. I went by plane.
f. Excuse me, how can I get to the station?
g. Go straight on.

P2 After school

a) What are you going to do this afternoon? What are you going to do this evening?

This afternoon I'm going to meet a friend. Then I'm going to … This evening I'm going to …

help at home · go shopping · watch TV · do my homework · have … training · chat with friends · meet a friend · visit a cousin · …

b) Talk to five other pupils. Guess your partners' plans. Ask questions.

Are you going to chat with friends?

No, I'm not.

Are you going to …?

Yes, I am.

P3 FAQ – Frequently asked questions

LiF 12

a) You have just arrived at your summer camp. There is so much you want to know. Unscramble the questions.

1. time – get – do – what – we – up – ?
2. toilets – the – where – are – ?
3. we – have – do – breakfast – when – ?
4. have – we – free – do – time – ?
5. in – can – our – rooms – stay – we – ?
6. when – start – do – campfire – we – our – ?
7. my – where – I – bag – can – put – ?
8. next – sleep – friend – my – can – to – I – ?
9. not – are – we – swimming – allowed – to – why – go – ?

What time do we get up?

Where are …?

Tipp
Schreibe deine Satzanfänge groß.

CD 2/41

b) Listen to the CD and check your questions.

P4 Pack your bag

a) Copy the grid. Put the words into your grid. Look up the words you don't know in your dictionary.

portfolio
I can learn English, I can work with words

skateboard · toothpaste · trousers · helmet · games · comb · ball · camera · soap · swimming costume · socks · pyjamas · sweatshirts · T-shirts · torch · water bottle · sleeping bag · guitar · raincoat · pocket knife

clothes	toiletries	sports equipment	other things
trousers	*toothpaste*	*skateboard*	*games*

b) Match the words and the information.

swimming costume
clothes
camera
a warm jacket
raincoat

- to take photos of new friends and activities
- to stay dry in the rain
- take at least two so you do not have to wear a wet one
- for warm and cool weather
- because the nights can get cool

swimming costume – take at least two so you do not have to wear a wet one

P5 Sound check

Listen to the CD and read the names of the places, cities and countries. Repeat what you hear.

CD 2/42

Niagara Falls	Canada	China
Cairo	Melbourne	Australia
Manchester	Bala	Wales
Hungary	Houston	Texas
Birmingham	Dartford	London
New York	Kerry	Ireland
the Himalayas	Madrid	Tunis

CD 2/27 2/43

Leaving on a jet plane

All my bags are packed, I'm ready to go
I'm standing here outside your door
I hate to wake you up to say goodbye
But the dawn is breakin' it's early morn
The taxi's waitin' he's blowin' his horn
Already I'm so lonesome I could die

Chorus
So kiss me and smile for me
tell me that you'll wait for me
Hold me like you'll never let me go
'Cause I'm leavin' on a jet plane
Don't know when I'll be back again
Oh, babe, I hate to go

There's so many times I let you down
So many times I played around
And I tell you now, they don't mean a thing
Every place I go, I'll think of you
Every song I sing, I'll sing for you
When I come back I'll bring your wedding ring

Chorus

Now the time has come to leave you
One more time, let me kiss you
Close your eyes, I'll be on my way
Dream about the days to come
When I won't have to leave alone
About the times I won't have to say:

Chorus

Music and lyrics: John Denver

What can you find out about the people in the song and their feelings?

BS1 Kieran

Kieran can't walk like the rest of us.
He comes to school on the special bus.
He has to use crutches to get about
And he's fast, but he can't keep up
when we run
When we race in the wind and fight
and have fun
He can't keep up, he has to shout
"Wait for me, everyone, wait for me."
And sometimes we wait, and sometimes we
Run off and hide, and that's when he
Sits in the yard with his sticks on the ground
Sits by himself until he's found
By Sir, or Miss, and they sit and talk
And we watch them laugh in a special way
And we'd love to know what he has to say
About the ones who ran away.
The ones who forgot that he can't walk.
And then we remember to ask him to play
And we kick the ball and he hits it back;
He's quick with those sticks, he has the knack
Of whamming the ball right into the goal.
And if he falls over he doesn't fuss,
We hoist him back up and we laugh at the soil
On his hands and his face, and give him his sticks.
He's strong when he fights us, but he never kicks –
He can't use his legs like the rest of us.
He comes to school on the special bus.

Berlie Doherty

BS2 Hearing the ball

Being a teenager can be tough. Sometimes it seems the world is against you. But have you ever wondered what it must be like to have a disability, too? We spoke to Joe Harrison about living with disabilities.

Joe Harrison, 19, is visually impaired and plays cricket with other visually impaired and blind teens for the Sussex Sharks and for England.

Question: Tell us about your disability, Joe.
Answer: I have no sight in my left eye and tunnel vision in my right eye. I can't see much at all. It's been like that since I was three. I can't remember what it's like to see normally.

Question: How do you get around?
Answer: I try to be as independent as possible. If I know the route, I can walk on my own. I use a cane in crowded places, like railway stations. My neighbour is one of my best friends and he often walks with me. A lot of my friends drive, so I can go with them.

Question: What have you found most difficult?
Answer: Some of my friends are learning to drive now. It's a bit unfair that I can't learn to drive.

Question: How do you play blind cricket?
Answer: A normal cricket ball would be too small to see. We play with a small football that has ball-bearings inside, so the fully blind players can hear it. The other equipment, like the bat, is also bigger than in normal cricket. At least four players in a team must be totally blind. It's fantastic what the fully blind players can do.

Question: Do you travel with the English team?
Answer: Yes, I've been to Barbados and Sri Lanka. I hope I'll be going to Australia to play next year.

Question: How should other people treat you?
Answer: The same as everyone else – when people need help, they usually ask for it. I've never been treated differently and don't want to be treated differently.

BS3 Summer sports

DIRTSURFING

What can snowboarders do to stay fit in summer? What can windsurfers do when they don't live near the sea? Dirtsurfing is the answer! It is the latest trend for people who love summer sports in nature. A dirtsurfer board is a combination of a skateboard and a BMX bike. You can use it in the mountains. You can also use a sail with your dirtsurfer board and go windsurfing on the land!

ROLLERSOCCER

Rollersoccer is football on skates! It is an international sport. You play rollersoccer with a standard football and about five players in each team. The rules are the same as with normal football. But roller soccer is very fast and exciting – like ice hockey!
And because you wear skates when you play, you need a lot of body control!

ULTIMATE FRISBEE

You haven't played ultimate frisbee yet? Ultimate frisbee is an exciting team sport. It is a bit like American football with a frisbee. In the game you win points when you get the frisbee into one of the end zones of the playing field. But players are not allowed to run with the frisbee. You must pass the frisbee from teammate to teammate. If someone doesn't catch the frisbee, the other team gets it. The rules are so simple that anyone can quickly learn how to play. The best players are very fast and can do a lot of tricks with the frisbee.

SLACKLINING

Slacklining is a balance sport. When you are slacklining, you are walking on a strip of webbing stretched tight between two points, for example between two trees. In contrast with tightrope walking, you use a line which is flat and not pulled tight.
This sport comes from California. In the 1980 climbers started walking on their climbing webbing to develop a version of tightrope walking. Slacklining helped climbers to improve reflexes and to develop a good sense of balance. When slacklining is done close to the ground, it is known as lowlining. Because they are not very high up many people feel relatively safe and learn a variety of tricks.
Whether practised a few feet or a few thousand feet from the ground, slacklining helps to improve balance and concentration – and is really great fun!

BS4 ○ The blue lagoon

Dick and Emmeline land on an island in the South Pacific with Paddy Button, a sailor, after their ship is destroyed by a fire. They are happy and live from day to day.

But Dick was beginning to think of tomorrow.

"Mr Button," he said one day, "what will we do when we have eaten all the potatoes?"

"Eat something else," said Paddy. "There are bananas."

"We"ll get very tired of bananas. How do potatoes grow? From seeds?"

"No! No!"

"Well, how?"

"You dig holes in the ground and put bits of potato in them, and the bits grow into plants, and then the plants die and you find lots of potatoes in the ground where the plant was."

Dick used a flat stone for digging. Paddy showed him how to cut the potatoes, leaving an "eye" in each bit.

So they did their first gardening. Paddy did not like work, but he sat smoking his pipe and told Dick what to do.

...

There was a cloud in the sky.

"Mr Button!"

"Yes, my boy?"

"Doesn't it ever rain here?"

"Oh, yes; there are months in the year when it rains all the time; and then for the rest of the year it hardly rains at all."

"Which months?" asked Dick.

"It might be soon."

"If the rain will soon be coming, we ought to have a better house."

"Yes," said Paddy, rather unhappily; "yes, we should. But it's a lot of work building a house."

"Draw a picture in the sand," said Dick, "and show me what sort of house we can build."

So Paddy drew. "You get those long sticks – bamboos – and fix them together at the top. You must use thin rope and tie them together. But we have no thin rope."

"There are long plants like rope growing down from the trees," said Dick.

"Yes, we can use those. You get them while I cut the bamboos."

It was Dick who thought of cutting a hole in the side of one bamboo so as to fix the two together more strongly. Three weeks passed before the house began to be ready, and even then there was a lot more to be done to the roof. Paddy was tired.

"Let's rest now," he said. "I'll tell you a story about fairies."

"I don't want a story," answered Dick. "Let's get on with the work." So Dick drove Paddy on till the house was ready.

Emmeline, Dick and Paddy live on the island for several years. If you want to read on, this is the book to look for:
"The blue lagoon" by H. de Vere Stacpoole.

BS5 The class trip thief

Meet Steve, Emma, Martin and Sally. The four friends do lots of things together. Here they are on a class trip to Brighton.

Steve

Emma

Martin

Sally

And this is Colin. He has problems. No one really likes him much and he's a bit of a loner.

What do you think happens next? Choose your favourite ending.

Or:

Or:

BS6 The history of jeans

16th century

The earliest known forerunner to jeans is known as *dungarees*. The thick cotton cloth is sold in India. It is usually dyed with indigo, a dark blue colour taken from a plant.

17th century

Jeans are also made in Italy. The navy requires trousers for its sailors that can be worn wet or dry and whose legs can easily be rolled up while the sailors are cleaning the deck.

Many people think the name jeans comes from *bleu de Genes*, i. e. *blue of Genoa*. The material comes from the city of Nîmes in France: *de Nîmes* became *denim*.

18th century

This is the century of trade, slave labour and cotton plantations in North America. Workers wear jeans because the material is strong and it does not wear out easily.

1848

Gold is found in California and the famous Gold Rush begins. Like the sailors and the workers, gold miners also need clothes that are strong and do not tear easily.

1853

The German immigrant Levi Strauss founds the firm Levi Strauss & Company in San Francisco. There he sells blue jeans to the gold miners of California.

1873

A big problem with the clothes of the gold miners is that the pockets tear away easily from the jeans. A man called Jacob Davis has the idea of using metal rivets to hold the pockets and the jeans together. Strauss likes Davis' idea. From now on the two men work together.

1930s

The image of the jeans-wearing cowboy becomes popular. Many Americans who lived in the eastern states go on vacation to ranches in the West and take pairs of denim back home with them.

1940s	During the time of World War II fewer jeans are made. But they are introduced to the world by American soldiers, who wear them when they are off duty. After the war new companies like Wrangler and Lee also produce jeans.
1950s	Now everyone can buy a pair of original Levi's Jeans, as they are now called. They become a popular fashion for teenagers and young adults. The popularity is also helped by the film and music industry. Rock and roll music is very influential and so are two actors, who represent the teenage rebel: Marlon Brando and James Dean.
1960s	Many university and college students wear jeans. When fashion changes, the style of jeans changes. In many non-western countries, such as East Germany, blue jeans become a symbol of "western decadence" on the one hand and freedom on the other.
1970s	The hippie movement starts. Flower power people start to personalize and decorate denim. A pair of jeans is the only uniform to wear to a 1970s pop concert. Bell-bottom jeans are a symbol for love, peace and harmony.
1980s	Jeans finally become fashion clothing, when famous designers like Armani, Versace and Calvin Klein start making their own styles of jeans with their own labels.
1990s	Although teenagers still wear denim, the worldwide recession of the 1990s stops the growing sales of jeans.
The new millennium	Denim is everywhere and in all forms: low rise, boot-cut, straight cut, Bermudas, mini-skirts … The history of blue jeans goes on …

BS7 ○ A car accident

It was just before 8 pm when they collided. It was the cyclist's fault. He now stood beside his broken bicycle, swearing in a low voice.

The car driver was looking at the car's shattered indicator and the scratches on its wing. The cyclist grumbled: "You needn't act as if it were all my fault. It was just as much yours." Robert Kessing, the driver of the car, looked at the cyclist and said, "I would let the police decide whose fault it was. But one thing is for sure," he went on, "you shot out of that entrance like a madman without looking left or right."

"That's what you say," the cyclist shouted. "There was nobody else around." He gazed up and down the street, but it was not a main road and there was little traffic. The few people who had paused earlier had all gone away by now. "Well, where are your witnesses?" the cyclist asked aggressively, with a quick look at the block of flats opposite.

At that moment the police patrol car came round the corner.

"You've taken your time, I must say!" were Mr Kessing's first words to the two officers.

"Sorry, sir," replied Sergeant Horn. "There was a hold-up in the tunnel under the river and we couldn't get through."

The officers took statements, measured the skidmarks and estimated the damage, which was not very serious. The cyclist seemed happy when he was allowed to go. He snatched up his wreck of a bike, shouldered it and made off.

Sergeant Horn turned to the driver. "You see, Mr … " – here he looked quickly at his notebook – "Mr Kessing, it's your word against his. But you said something about a witness a moment ago."

"Yes, there was a woman who saw what happened, sergeant. As I got out of the car, I saw her looking out of a window across the road. From that big block of flats – on the second floor, the end window on the left."

The sergeant nodded. "Let's try our luck."

The woman turned away grumbling. "You'd better ask him, not me. In any case, I've been far too busy today to stand there staring out of the window."
"She's telling lies," declared Mr Kessing angrily.
For a moment it looked as if the woman would throw something at Robert Kessing. Then she thought better of it. She replied in a coarse voice: "We'll soon see who's telling lies."
At this, Sergeant Horn drew himself up to his full height.
"We know that already, madam," he corrected her. "You're the one who's lying."
"But ... "

The name on the door was Marquand. They had to ring three times before the door was opened. An elderly grey-haired woman stood before them. She gave Kessing a very unfriendly look, and allowed the men to enter only after protesting.
"Well? What do you want?" she asked harshly.
"It's about the accident," explained the officer.
"What accident?"
Mr Kessing was beginning to feel helpless. "But you saw what happened from your window. You even shook your head," he stammered.
"You must be mistaken. You've mixed me up with someone else."
Mr Kessing took a deep breath. "But I recognize you perfectly," he insisted.

At this point Sergeant Horn took over. "Are you saying you've never seen this gentleman before?"
"Never!"
"Nor the other man who was in the accident?"
"No. I didn't know the cyclist either."
The policeman in his turn seemed as helpless as Kessing had been.
"Now look here, Mrs Marquand," he said sharply. "Why should this gentleman say that he saw you at the window if it isn't true?"

How did Sergeant Horn know Mrs Marquand wasn't speaking the truth?

How to talk / How to listen

Do you remember?

Zu den Themen *How to talk, How to listen, How to read* und *How to write* hast du in Klasse 5 und 6 schon einiges erfahren. Hier deshalb zur Erinnerung eine kurze Zusammenfassung der wichtigsten Punkte:

How to talk

- Wenn du einen Vortrag, ein Interview oder ein Gespräch zu einem bestimmten Thema vorbereiten willst, kann es dir helfen, wenn du dir vorher auf Kärtchen Notizen dazu machst.
- Versuche aber immer, frei zu sprechen und nicht einfach deine Notizen abzulesen.
- Achte dabei auch auf deine Aussprache, Betonung und die Satzmelodie, damit das, was du sagst, lebendig klingt und nicht eintönig.
- Das Sprechen wird dir leichter fallen, wenn du ein Gespräch oder einen Vortrag gut vorbereitest und übst.
- Achte beim Sprechen auch auf deine Körpersprache, deinen Gesichtsausdruck und deine Gesten.
- Schau deine Zuhörer beim Sprechen an.
- Hab keine Angst vor Fehlern!
- Nutze jede Gelegenheit, Englisch zu sprechen, dann wirst du mit der Zeit immer sicherer.

How to listen

- Wenn du einem Gesprächspartner zuhörst, schau ihn dabei an. Es hilft nämlich, beim Zuhören auch die Lippenbewegungen zu sehen, wenn der andere spricht. Achte im Gespräch auf Körpersprache, Gesichtsausdruck und Gesten. Dies hilft dir zu verstehen, was der andere sagen will.
- Wenn du dir eine Geschichte oder einen Bericht z. B. von CD anhörst, können dir folgende Fragewörter helfen, um die wichtigsten Informationen herauszuhören:
  - **who?**: Um wen geht es, wer ist beteiligt?
  - **what?**: Worum geht es? Was passiert?
  - **where?**: Wo spielt sich das Gehörte oder die Geschichte ab?
  - **when?**: Wann passiert etwas?
  - **why?**: Warum passiert etwas?
- Also: Mache dir Notizen zu *who, what, where, when* und *why*.

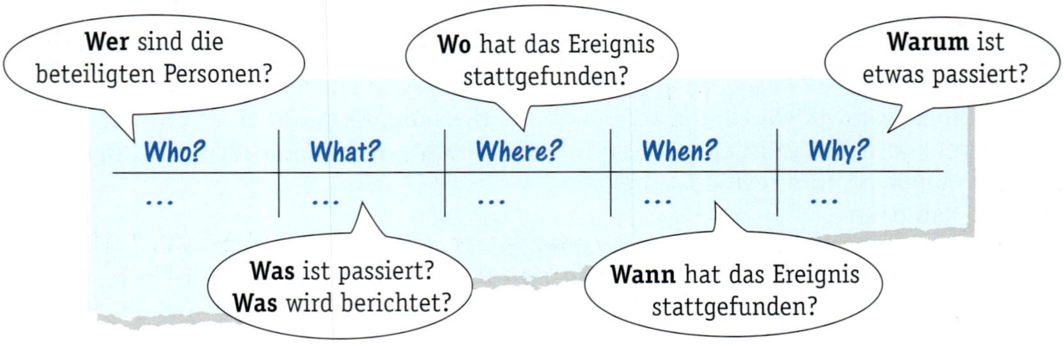

How to read

- Bevor du anfängst zu lesen, achte auf Überschriften und – falls vorhanden – Bilder zum Text. Sie können dir helfen zu erfassen, um welches Thema es gehen könnte.
- Überfliege dann zunächst den Text (*skimming*). Du musst dabei nicht jedes Wort verstehen. Achte auf die Wörter, die du schon kennst. Sie können dir Hinweise auf den Inhalt des Textes geben.
- Wie beim Zuhören helfen die Fragewörter *who, what, where, when* und *why* auch beim Lesen von Texten. So kannst du dich besser auf die wichtigsten Informationen konzentrieren und dir gezielt Notizen machen.
- Achte auch auf Schlüsselwörter (*keywords*), die verdeutlichen, worum es in dem Text geht. Bei einem Text im *workbook* oder auf einem Arbeitsblatt kannst du diese Wörter auch farbig markieren.

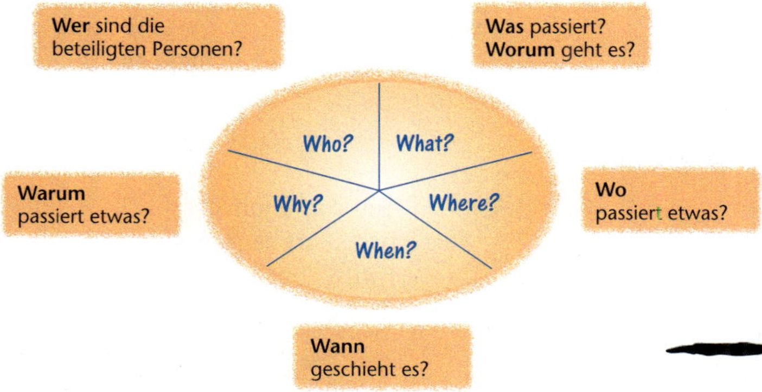

How to write

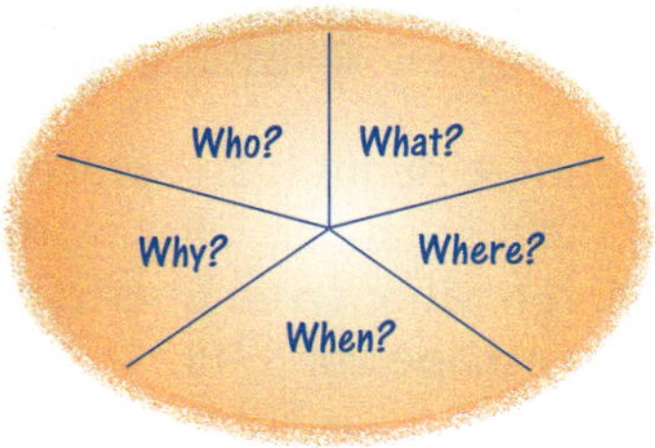

- Wenn du eine Geschichte schreiben willst, kannst du mit Hilfe von *who, what, where, when* (und eventuell auch *why*) Ideen sammeln und die Geschichte planen.
- Außerdem kann es helfen, in einem *word web* relevante Wörter zu sammeln. Du kannst auch in den *wordbanks* im Buch oder in einem Wörterbuch nachschauen, um noch mehr passende Wörter zu finden.
- Überlege dir eine Reihenfolge für deine Geschichte: Was sollte am Anfang stehen, wie weckst du Interesse? Was folgt darauf? Wie könnte das Ende der Geschichte aussehen?
- Bei jeder Art von Texten gilt, dass du zunächst einen Entwurf schreiben solltest (*draft*).
- Dann solltest du deinen Text überarbeiten und verbessern (*edit*). Du kannst ihn auch jemand anderem zu lesen geben und ihn nach seiner Meinung und nach Verbesserungsvorschlägen fragen.
- Ist dein Text fertig, sollte er „veröffentlicht" werden (*publish*). Stelle ihn aus und bewahre ihn z. B. in deinem Portfolio auf.
- Merke dir also beim Schreiben von Texten folgende Vorgehensweise: *draft – edit – publish*.

Einem Partner Feedback geben

Im Englischunterricht gibt es viele Gelegenheiten, sich beim Lernen gegenseitig zu helfen. So kannst du einen Text deines Partners lesen und ihm Feedback dazu geben. Bei **6B3 An article for a school newspaper** auf S. 85 kannst du dies einmal ausprobieren. Hierzu ein paar Tipps:

- Versuche immer etwas Positives über den Text deines Partners zu sagen.
- Korrigiere den Text mit einem Bleistift, damit dein Partner entscheiden kann, ob er deine Vorschläge übernehmen möchte.
- Versuche nicht nur Fehler zu korrigieren, sondern auch Vorschläge zu machen, wie der Text interessanter sein könnte.

Diese Sätze können euch beim gegenseitigen Korrigieren helfen:

Um Klärung bitten:

I don't quite understand this. Can you explain it?

I'm not sure what you mean here.

Fehler finden und korrigieren:

I think this is wrong – but I'm not sure how to write it.

I think you spell … with a small letter.

Den Text verbessern:

Why don't you use a different word here?

Try to write a better ending.

You could join these two short sentences with "but".

Zwischen zwei Sprachen vermitteln

Stell dir vor, du bist mit deinen Eltern oder Großeltern in London und ihr plant einen Ausflug. Eine Broschüre bietet zwar eine Menge Tipps, aber vielleicht verstehen ja nicht alle deine Mitreisenden, was da steht. Dann kannst du ihnen helfen, indem du das Wesentliche auf Deutsch zusammenfasst.

Diese Übertragung von Informationen von einer Sprache in eine andere nennt man Sprachmittlung. Das ist etwas anderes als Übersetzung, denn es kommt nicht darauf an, alles wortgetreu wiederzugeben, sondern möglichst knapp die wesentlichen Informationen zu übertragen. Eine weitere Sprachmittlungssituation findest du bei **3B1 A narrow escape** auf S. 45.

Es kann aber auch vorkommen, dass du in deiner Stadt einen englischsprachigen Reisenden triffst, der deine Hilfe beim Lesen eines Fahrplans braucht. Ihm kannst du auf Englisch erklären, wie er zu seinem Ziel kommt. Hab dabei keine Angst vor Fehlern. Es kommt darauf an, verstanden zu werden – der andere freut sich auf jeden Fall über deine Hilfe. Hier nun noch einmal das Wichtigste zur Sprachmittlung zusammengefasst:

- Gib in deinen eigenen Worten das Wesentliche in der anderen Sprache wieder.
- Übersetze nicht Wort für Wort.
- Benutze kurze, einfache Sätze.
- Versuche Wörter, die dir fehlen, mit anderen Worten auszudrücken.
- Verwende auch Gesten.
- Hab keine Angst vor Fehlern.
- Bei der Sprachmittlung ist alles erlaubt, was irgendwie die Verständigung ermöglicht!

Internetrecherchen

Auf den ersten Blick ist es sehr leicht, im Internet an Informationen zu kommen: Du trägst ein Suchwort in das dafür vorgesehene Feld [1] einer Suchmaschine ein und drückst die Eingabetaste. Aber dann beginnt erst die Arbeit, denn oft findet die Suchmaschine viel mehr Webseiten als du dir anschauen kannst. In **Theme 3** geht es z. B. um den Notting Hill Carnival. Wenn du nun als Suchwort „Notting Hill Carnival" eintippst, erhältst du ungefähr 270.000 „Treffer", also 270.000 Dokumente, die irgendetwas mit dem Suchbegriff zu tun haben. Nur was?

- Es ist unmöglich, alle diese „Treffer" durchzusehen. Aber du kannst davon ausgehen, dass gute Suchmaschinen die wichtigsten Dokumente auch zuerst in der „Trefferliste" anzeigen; also genügt es meistens, die ersten 10 bis 20 Suchergebnisse anzuschauen.
- Oft reicht schon ein Blick auf die kurzen Zeilen, die die Suchmaschine von jeder Fundstelle anzeigt [2], um zu entscheiden, ob hier wichtige Informationen enthalten sein könnten. Wenn du nicht sicher bist, klickst du den Link an. Überfliege zunächst die Webseite, um zu sehen, ob sie nützliche Informationen enthält. Im Zweifel kannst du sie speichern oder ausdrucken und in einem zweiten Durchgang gezielt durchgehen.
- Hilfreich ist es auch, nach den Internet-Adressen [3] der Fundstücke zu schauen, die die Suchmaschine anzeigt. Schon die erste Internet-Adresse (www.nottinghillcarnival.org.uk) zeigt, dass du dich hier auf einer speziellen Website zum Karneval befindest. Die zweite Adresse (de.wikipedia.org/wiki/Notting_Hill_Carnival) verrät dir, dass es sich bei diesem Ergebnis um das Stichwort „Notting Hill Carnival" in Wikipedia handelt, also um einen Artikel im Internetlexikon [4].
- Denke aber daran, dass Wikipedia ein Lexikon ist, das von Tausenden Menschen auf der ganzen Welt gemeinsam erstellt wird. Dabei sind nicht alle auch Experten auf dem Gebiet, über das sie in Wikipedia schreiben. Es ist also immer gut, Informationen aus Wikipedia zusätzlich zu überprüfen – aber das gilt eigentlich für alle Infos, die man aus dem Internet fischt!
- Übrigens: Wikipedia gibt es in vielen Sprachen. Die meisten Einträge hat jedoch die englische Version. Es gibt auch eine einfachere Fassung in *simple English*. Du findest sie unter der Adresse http://simple.wikipedia.org/wiki/Main_Page.

Präsentieren leicht gemacht

Wenn du eine Präsentation (wie z. B. bei **5B5 Inventions for the future** auf S. 73) vor der Klasse hältst, solltest du Folgendes bedenken: Deine Zuhörer werden sich nicht alles merken können, was du vorträgst. Am besten behalten sie sich, was besonders hervorgehoben und betont wird. Deswegen solltest du dir bei der Vorbereitung deiner Präsentation genau überlegen: „Was sollten sich meine Zuhörer unbedingt merken? 1. ..., 2. ..., 3. ..." Denn wenn sie diese Punkte behalten sollen, musst du sie immer wieder anders formulieren, wiederholen und zusammenfassen.

Vielleicht kannst du Stichworte und/oder Bilder auf einem Poster, an der Tafel, am Overheadprojektor oder in einer Computerpräsentation zeigen, um das, was du sagen willst, zu unterstreichen.

So kannst du im Einzelnen vorgehen:

1. Wähle drei Hauptpunkte aus.
2. Mache Notizen zur Einleitung: Nenne das Thema und zähle die Hauptpunkte kurz auf.
3. Überlege dir, welche Hilfsmittel du einsetzen möchtest (z. B. Poster, Overheadprojektor, Computer mit Beamer).
4. Überlege, was deine Zuhörer schon wissen. Dann redest du weder über die Köpfe hinweg, noch langweilst du sie.
5. Fertige Notizen zum Hauptteil deiner Präsentation an. Versuche jeden Hauptpunkt dreimal anders darzustellen durch Beispiele und unterschiedliche Formulierungen.
6. Notiere für die Zusammenfassung noch einmal klar deine Hauptpunkte.

Eins solltest du auf jeden Fall versuchen: Halte deine Präsentation möglichst frei und lies nicht einfach nur deinen Text vor. Dein Spickzettel sollte höchstens ein paar Stichworte enthalten, sonst läufst du Gefahr, dass du nur auf deinen Text achtest und dein Publikum kaum anschaust – das kommt ganz schlecht an bei den Zuhörern.

Hier ein paar sprachliche Tipps:

Für die Einleitung:

- *First of all, I'm going to ...*
- *Then I'll talk about ...*
- *Finally I'll ...*

Etwas Neues einleiten:

- *So let's start with ...*
- *OK, my first / next / last point is ...*

Auf Hilfsmittel hinweisen:

- *If you look at the poster / overhead transparency / handout / screen, you'll see ...*

Etwas anders ausdrücken:

- *In other words, ...*
- *That is to say ...*
- *What I'm saying is ...*

Aufmerksamkeit aufrechterhalten:

- *You see?*
- *Don't you agree?*
- *What do you think?*

Zum Schluss kommen:

- *So my main points are ...*
- *Thank you for listening.*

Englische Wörter im Wörterbuch nachschlagen

Das *dictionary* hinten in diesem Buch hilft dir, Wörter zu verstehen, die in *Notting Hill Gate* vorkommen. Was machst du aber, wenn du ein englisches Wort, beispielsweise in einem Songtext oder im Internet, nicht verstehst und du findest es nicht im Schulbuch?
Dafür gibt es größere zweisprachige Wörterbücher (*dictionaries*). Vielleicht besitzt du bereits eines, sonst wird dich deine Englischlehrerin oder dein Englischlehrer gerne beraten. Englisch-deutsche Wörterbücher sind wie andere Wörterbücher auch aufgebaut:

- Sie sind alphabetisch sortiert.
- Sie haben auf jeder Seite oben Leitwörter, die verraten, welche Wörter auf der jeweiligen Seite zu finden sind.
- Nach dem fett gedruckten Wort gibt es Erklärungen und Übersetzungen.

Bei einem *English-German dictionary* geht es vor allem um die Übersetzung ins Deutsche, und deshalb gibt es einige wichtige Besonderheiten. Schau dir folgendes Beispiel an:

In **Theme 7** geht es um die Sängerin Pink. Auf ihrer Homepage bedankte sie sich nach der Trennung von ihrem Mann in einem Brief bei ihren Fans mit folgenden Worten: „Thanks for the concern and caring." Wenn du nun *concern* in einem Wörterbuch nachschlägst, findest du mehrere Einträge:

Substantiv / Nomen

Lautschrift — Verb

con·cern [kən'sɜːn] **I.** *vt* **1.** betreffen, angehen, interessieren; wichtig sein für **2.** beunruhigen; **be ~ed about** sich Gedanken, Sorgen machen um; **~ o.s. about** sich bemühen, sich Mühe machen um; **~ o.s. with** sich befassen, zu tun haben, sich abgeben mit; **as ~s** was ... betrifft, betreffend, betreffs; **as far as I am ~ed** was mich angeht, von mir aus; **to whom it may ~** an die zuständige Stelle **II.** *s* **1.** Beziehung *f,* Bezug *m* **2.** Interesse *nt,* Anteil *m* **3.** Sorge, Besorgnis, Beunruhigung *f* (*over* wegen) **4.** Angelegenheit, Sache *f* **5.** Geschäft, Unternehmen *nt,* Betrieb *m;* **with deep ~** sehr besorgt; **have a ~ in** interessiert sein, Anteil haben an; **that is no ~ of yours** das geht Sie nichts an; **business ~s** Geschäftsinteressen *ntpl;* **going ~** gutgehendes Geschäft, Unternehmen; **con·cerned** [kən'sɜːnd] *adj* **1.** betroffen (*in* von), beteiligt (*in* an) **2.** besorgt, in Unruhe (*at, for s.o.* um jdn, *about s.th.* wegen einer S); **all ~** alle Beteiligten *mpl;* **the persons ~** die Interessenten *mpl,* die Betroffenen *mpl;* **con·cern·ing** [-ɪŋ] *prep* betreffend, betreffs; bezüglich, in Bezug auf
con·cert ['kɒnsət] *s* Konzert *nt;* **in ~** im

Schau dir das Zitat von Pink noch einmal an: Welche Übersetzung könnte hier passen?

Wie du siehst, werden zunächst einige Verben genannt, also „betreffen", „interessieren" und andere. Allerdings kann es sich bei *concern* in diesem Beispiel nicht um ein Verb handeln. Erst weiter unten findest du als Übersetzung mehrere Nomen.

Überlege nun: Welches Nomen passt in diesem Zusammenhang am besten? Es reicht nicht, nur den ersten Eintrag zu lesen. Erst unter 3. wirst du in diesem Fall fündig: *concern* kann unter anderem Sorge oder Besorgnis heißen.

Doch du kannst aus diesem Wörterbucheintrag noch mehr herauslesen als die Wortart und die Übersetzung: die Aussprache zum Beispiel. Du findest die Lautschrift direkt hinter dem englischen Wort.

Interessante Projekte

Projekte außerhalb der Schule sind besonders spannend, weil ihr hier Menschen begegnen könnt, die im Alltag Englisch sprechen, zum Beispiel in einer Jugendherberge, an einem Fährhafen oder an einem größeren Bahnhof.

Nehmen wir an, ihr möchtet wie bei **8B3 Going to an airport** auf S. 113 einen internationalen Flughafen besuchen. Auch bei diesem Projekt geht ihr in vier Schritten vor.

1. Plan it

- Stellt euch die Situation am Flughafen vor: Wie sieht es dort aus? Was gibt es zu sehen? Wen könntet ihr treffen?
- Überlegt, welche Menschen ihr auf dem Flughafen treffen werdet, die ihr interviewen könntet: Passagiere, Flugbegleiterinnen, Verkäufer, …
- Überlegt euch interessante Fragen, die möglichst nicht nur mit „yes" oder „no" beantwortet werden können. Mehr Hinweise dazu findet ihr bei „How to do an interview".
- Sortiert die Fragen und übt die Interviews. Schreibt zur Sicherheit eure Fragen auf, lest sie aber möglichst nicht ab.
- Was könnte noch von Interesse sein? Zum Beispiel englischsprachige Hinweisschilder, Durchsagen, Zeitungen, …
- Ihr könnt Materialien und Aufnahmen sammeln und diese für eure Präsentation verwenden.
- Bedenkt, was ihr an Material benötigt: Kamera, Aufnahmegerät, Notizblock, Stifte, …

2. Do it

- Prüft, ob ihr alle benötigten Materialien zusammen habt und ob alles funktioniert.
- Seid freundlich, wenn ihr Menschen um ein Interview bittet!
- Zurück vom Flughafen: Wertet euer gesammeltes Material aus. Entscheidet, was ihr für eure Präsentation benutzen möchtet.
- Entscheidet euch für eine Präsentationsform (Mappe, Poster, Powerpoint, …).

3. Check it

- Prüft, ob die wichtigsten Ergebnisse berücksichtigt sind.
- Überprüft noch einmal, ob ihr Fehler gemacht habt und ob die Texte gut zu lesen sind.

4. Present it

- Übt die Präsentation bevor ihr sie in der Klasse haltet.
- Hinweise zu Präsentationen findet ihr auch bei „How to present".

Interviews durchführen

Ein Interview gelingt dir am besten, wenn du es vorher gut vorbereitest. Bevor du also z.B. im Rahmen des Flughafen-Projekts bei **8B3 Going to an airport** oder bei **8B4 Interviews** (S. 113) Leute interviewst, solltest du folgende Tipps beachten.

Vor dem Interview

1. Bereite eine Liste mit Themen vor, die dich besonders interessieren, also z. B. Reiseziel der Person, Beruf, Familie, …
2. Bereite 6–7 Fragen vor. Tipp: Stelle offene Fragen, die mehr als nur ein einziges Wort als Antwort erfordern. Sie beginnen meistens mit einem Fragewort wie z. B. *What? Where? Who? How much? How long?* Vermeide Fragen, die mit Ja oder Nein beantwortet werden können. Bei diesen geschlossenen Fragen hat dein Interviewpartner wenig Möglichkeit, über sich selbst zu erzählen.
3. Fertige eine Tabelle an und trage die Fragen ein. Rechts lässt du Platz für deine Notizen.

Where are you from?
Where are you travelling to?
Why are you going there?
…

Während des Interviews

1. Sprich die Person höflich an und frage sie, ob sie Englisch spricht.

Excuse me, please, do you speak English?

2. Frage, ob er oder sie bereit ist, dir ein Interview auf Englisch zu geben. Erkläre auch, von welcher Schule du kommst und warum du ihn oder sie interviewen möchtest.

Can I do an interview with you?

My name is … and I'm a pupil from … school.

I'm working on a project …

3. Wenn du das Interview auch aufnehmen willst, bitte vorher deinen Interviewpartner um sein Einverständnis.

Can I record the interview?

4. Fange erst mit deinen Fragen an, wenn dein Interviewpartner einverstanden ist.
5. Wenn etwas unklar ist oder du nicht richtig verstanden hast, was gesagt wurde, solltest du weitere Fragen stellen oder um Wiederholung bitten.

Did you say that you …?

Could you repeat …?

6. Höre deinem Interviewpartner genau zu. Er erzählt dir viel mehr, wenn er das Gefühl hat, dass du aktiv zuhörst.

I think Hamburg is a very interesting city.

Really?

Oh yes! …

7. Bedanke dich am Ende für das Interview.

Nach dem Interview

1. Stelle die Informationen zusammen und ordne sie am besten auf Karteikarten.
2. Anhand dieser Notizen kannst du einen mündlichen oder schriftlichen Bericht vorbereiten.

Jane comes from Sydney, Australia. She is travelling to London. She is a nurse and she is going to start a new job in a hospital in London. …

Food and drink

at the restaurant:

read the menu
choose a meal
have a starter
order a main course
have ice cream for dessert
call the waiter
ask for the bill

eat from a plate
use knife and fork
eat with chopsticks
put it in a bowl
sit around the table

dishes:

soup
salad
roast lamb
roast beef
fish
lasagna
sausage
baked potato

Indian food:

chicken curry
banana raita
samosa
chapati
spice
chilli paste
cinnamon
cardamom

cut onions
put cheese on pizza
make a curry
use spices
help with the cooking
mash the potatoes
add the salt
mix with the yoghurt

food can be:

spicy · hot · cold · mild · delicious · sweet · healthy · fresh · old · good · bad · wonderful · terrible · awful

Sport

You play ...	You go ...	You do ...
basketball	swimming	karate
hockey	dancing	judo
football	skating	gymnastics
volleyball	in-line skating	aerobics
table tennis	cycling	
rugby	running	

people in sport:

basketball player
football team
goalkeeper
swimmer
dancer
cheerleader
athlete

people can be:

fit
fast
successful
strong
skilful
sporty

activities:

jump up and down
defend oneself
do press-ups
hop on one foot
touch one's toes
practise often
go to lessons
be in a race
break the world record

Health

health problems:

be ill
have a cold
have a headache
have a stomach ache
have a broken arm
have a sore leg
have backache

What you can say:	What the doctor says:
That hurts.	What's the problem?
I can't move my arm.	Where does it hurt?
My finger is swollen.	We'll take an X-ray.
I've broken my finger.	You need a bandage.
I have a bad cold.	You have to stay in bed.
My throat hurts.	Do you have a temperature?
I've cut my foot.	
I feel really bad.	

Keep fit and healthy!

Walk to school.
Eat healthy food.
Drink lots of water.
Do sport regularly.
Get enough sleep.

Festivals

steel bands

parade

floats

carnival

party

masks

COSTUMES

PROGRAMME

street festival

what you can do:

celebrate carnival
watch a parade (on TV)
dress up
wear colourful costumes
wear a mask
take photos
make videos
have a party
sing and dance in the street
play music
have a drink
spend money

famous · colourful · great · big · loud

people in the street:

the police
police officer
tourists
pick pockets
fire brigade
crowds of people

everyday life in the streets:

steal wallets
be careful
set up stalls
fine weather
organize an event
drive a car
watch a match
sit outside

Feelings

feel sad
feel glad
feel good
feel wonderful
feel great
feel terrible
feel lonely
feel safe
feel homesick

be happy / unhappy
be friendly / unfriendly
be excited
be angry
be bored
be frightened
be tired
be down
be desperate
be surprised
be knackered
be complicated
be exhausted
be shy
be aggressive
be sick

verbs that express feelings: love · like · hate · enjoy · miss · cry · feel

Don't worry so much.
Poor you!
You must be joking!
It's not your fault.
I couldn't care less.
She's always worried.

I felt terribly homesick.
I like ice hockey. It's most exciting.
Just give it some time.
Stay cool!
I missed my home and my family.

friends and relationships:

teach someone
go out with someone
hold someone's hand
hug someone
rescue someone
wait for someone
agree with someone

fall in love with someone
ask for help
be back home
make friends
live alone
write a message
break up

invite a friend
go red in the face
run away
understand a problem
solve a problem
make a decision
make a promise

Wordbank

Places

restaurant · pub · island · pyramid · wall · rainforest · children's home · forest · beach · park · cinema · supermarket · camp · hospital · airport · library · museum · zoo · boat · garden · earth · bookshop · castle · house · hut · shop · bridge · field · river · mountain · waterfall · lake · factory

Do you like living in a small town?

Yes, I do. It's nice because all my friends live here, too.

places can be:

beautiful
interesting
expensive
quiet
noisy
boring
fantastic
wonderful
dark
amazing
dirty
huge
dry
warm
famous
dangerous
far away

a person can:

live on an island
live in a street
go to a museum
visit a castle
work in a factory
lie on the beach
take a walk in the forest
be cast away
go on a class trip
do a paper round
take the dog for a walk
go on holiday
board a ship

inside / outside
upstairs / downstairs
opposite the bookshop

Science

inventions:

glasses
shower
toaster
dishwasher
light bulb
Velcro®
sewer
medicine
matches
microscope

what we use inventions for:

check out the Internet
go to a website
wash dishes
toast bread
drive a car
travel on a train
play music
cook a meal
listen to the radio
watch TV
do experiments

inventions used for communication:

computer
TV
radio
stereo
Internet
DVD player
MP3 player
mobile phone
telephone

trains:

take a ride
locomotive
passenger
railway station
train ticket
ticket inspector
journey
platform

inventions used for getting around:

train
Amphicar
hot-air balloon
parachute
aeroplane
bicycle / bike
motorbike
car

machine
electricity
noise
discovery
inventor
scientist
engineer
demonstration
factory
cotton mill
industry
sewer

it was built for
it was created by
it was powered by
it was invented by
it was designed in
it was used for

it is practical
it is useful
it is important
it is good to have
it is a brilliant idea
it is a clever idea
it is very successful

Jobs and money

Could we have the bill, please?
Here you are.
I'll take it.
Can I have a look at that?
Let's say £8.
It's free.
What's on offer?
Let me pay.
I'm looking for ...
Here's your change.
How much is it?
Is it for sale?
Have you got any ...?
It's a special offer.

what you can do with money:

- buy a ticket
- be short of money
- get some extra money
- raise money for a good cause
- pay bills
- have enough cash
- win a fortune

verbs that go with money:

pay · raise · spend · win · make · get · have · collect · earn · save · steal

- € euros
- £ pounds
- $ dollars

- rich
- wealthy
- poor

- musician
- doctor
- waiter / waitress
- nurse
- ticket inspector
- bricklayer
- writer
- painter
- engineer
- flight attendant
- baker
- cook
- reporter

- work in a supermarket
- fill up shelves
- sit at a cash-desk
- give up a job
- look for a job
- work a 12-hour shift
- work the early shift
- work the night shift
- be on a business trip

- boss
- seller
- customer
- sponsor
- amateur
- professional

jobs for young people:

- do the shopping for someone
- sell things at a car-boot sale
- help at a gig
- do a paper round
- babysit
- take someone's dog for a walk
- do the gardening

- cheap
- expensive
- worth it
- free tickets
- free admission
- free information pack
- for free
- reduced tickets
- there is a fee
- there is a charge

What do you spend your money on?

I spend my money on telephone bills.

Time out

where to go:

- exhibition
- museum
- drama class
- climbing centre
- picture gallery
- event
- competition
- car-boot sale
- restaurant
- sports centre
- festival
- workshop

Have a great day!

Have a good time!

- actor / actress
- audience
- musician
- artist
- singer
- dancer
- painter
- poet
- roadie
- fan

Enjoy the show!

Have fun!

I can't wait!

- The Tate Gallery
- The Museum of Science and Industry
- The Saturday Roadshow
- The London Marathon
- The Notting Hill Carnival

what to do:

- get tickets
- have guests
- have a day out
- help at a gig
- go to a flea market
- spend the weekend with friends
- go to a party
- look at pictures
- go to the theatre
- listen to the singers
- have a rehearsal
- enjoy a concert
- fly the London Eye
- pick up a friend
- do some sightseeing
- visit relatives
- watch a competition
- watch the parade
- dance in the streets

- my favourite band
- my favourite restaurant
- my favourite place to meet

Art

pictures:

The picture shows a room.

painting
drawing
portrait
photo
photograph
comic
cartoon

art can be:

exciting
interesting
boring
depressing
fantastic
dreamlike
realistic
unrealistic
strange
beautiful

in the centre
in the background
on the left
on the right
at the top
at the bottom
above
next to
in front of
behind
between

There is a …

I can see a …

In the centre there is …

at the top

on the left

on the right

at the bottom

in the centre

colours can be:

dark · light · bright · warm · cold · soft · strong

museum
gallery
exhibition

music:

Listen to the music.
What instruments can you hear?
Who is singing?
What is he or she singing about?

song
music
lyrics
rhythm

rock
pop
rap
hip hop
R & B
country
ballet
steel band music
techno
reggae

band
group
singer
star
concert
gig
rehearsal
equipment
instrument
microphone

poems:

Read the poem.
What is the poem about?
What does the poem mean?
What does … stand for …?

rhyme
line
verse
chorus

films:

Watch the film.
What is the title of the film?
What kind of film is it?
Who is playing in the film?
Where was it filmed?

cinema
actor / actress
audience
dialogue
play a role
act out
act a scene

Travelling

Get home safely!

Have a great time!

Come back soon!

Enjoy your trip!

Thank you for travelling with Deutsche Bahn.

Welcome to London!

holiday
flight
trip
journey
arrival
airport
ticket
station

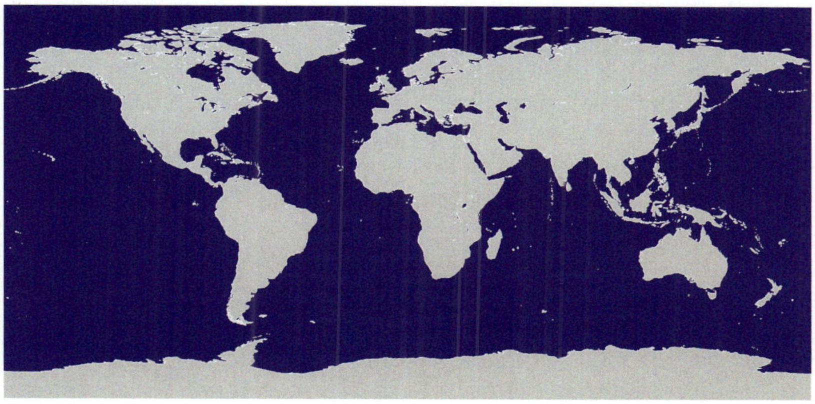

people:

pilot
flight attendant
ticket inspector
tourist
visitor

travel to foreign countries:

book a flight
pack one's bag
say goodbye
the taxi is waiting
ask at the tourist information
go sightseeing
send postcards
take pictures (of famous sights)
buy tickets
buy souvenirs
visit friends
be invited by friends
lie on the beach
eat foreign food

foreign countries:

Australia · Austria · The British Isles · Canada · China · France · Great Britain · Hungary · India · Iran · Ireland · Italy · Japan · Northern Ireland · Poland · Portugal · Russia · Scotland · South Africa · Spain · Turkey · USA · Wales

Africa
North America
South America
Australia
Asia
Europe

how to travel:

take a flight
board a ship
take the train
drive a car
take the bus
go by plane
change trains
get on a bus
get off the bus

asking for directions:

Excuse me, how can I get to the station?
Can you tell me the way to the museum, please?
Can you show it on the map?
Where can I get a bus to Buckingham Palace?

giving directions:

Turn left / right.
Take the second street.
Go straight on.
It is opposite / right next to / around the corner from Big Ben.
You can't miss it.

C Classroom phrases

Allgemeines

Sorry, I'm late.	Tut mir leid, dass ich zu spät bin.
Sorry, I haven't got my exercise book / homework with me.	Tut mir leid, ich habe mein Heft / meine Hausaufgaben nicht dabei.
What's the matter?	Was ist los?
I'm fine. / I feel sick.	Mir geht's gut. / Mir ist schlecht.
I've got a headache.	Ich habe Kopfschmerzen.
Can I open the window, please?	Kann ich bitte das Fenster öffnen?
Can I go to the toilet, please?	Kann ich bitte zur Toilette gehen?

Was der Schüler oder die Schülerin sagt

Can you help me, please?	Können Sie mir bitte helfen?
I've got a question.	Ich habe eine Frage.
I don't understand this.	Ich verstehe das hier nicht.
Could you explain that (again), please?	Können Sie das bitte (noch einmal) erklären?
Could you repeat that, please?	Können Sie das bitte noch einmal sagen?
What's … in English / German?	Was heißt … auf Englisch / Deutsch?
What does … mean?	Was bedeutet …?
Sorry, I don't know.	Tut mir leid, das weiß ich nicht.
What page, please?	Auf welcher Seite bitte?
Can you write it on the board, please?	Können Sie das bitte an die Tafel schreiben?
Can we listen to the CD again?	Können wir die CD bitte noch einmal hören?
Can you turn the volume up / down, please?	Können Sie den Ton bitte lauter / leiser stellen?
I can't see the board / transparency properly.	Ich kann die Tafel / die Folie nicht richtig sehen.
We are almost finished.	Wir sind fast fertig.
Can we have an extra five minutes, please?	Können wir bitte noch fünf Minuten haben?
What's for homework?	Was haben wir als Hausaufgabe auf?

Was die Lehrerin oder der Lehrer sagt

Open your books at page …	Öffnet eure Bücher auf Seite …
Turn to page …	Blättert zu Seite …
Look at the next paragraph / line …	Seht euch den nächsten Absatz / Zeile … an.
Work in pairs / in groups.	Arbeitet zu zweit / in Gruppen.
Listen to track number …	Hör dir / Hört euch Nummer … an.
Make up your own dialogue.	Entwirf / Entwerft selbst ein Dialog.
Change roles.	Tauscht die Rollen.
Take turns.	Wechselt euch ab.

Collect the exercise books, please. — Sammelt bitte die Hefte ein.
Do this exercise at home, please. — Macht diese Aufgabe bitte zu Hause.

Please speak up. — Sprich bitte lauter.
You can do better. — Das kannst du besser.
Try again. — Versuch es noch einmal.
Well done. — Gut gemacht.
That's it. — Das ist alles. / Richtig!

Wenn du mit dem Computer arbeitest

What's your e-mail address? — Wie ist deine E-Mail-Adresse?
You can click on this link. — Du kannst auf diesen Link klicken.
Can I print it out / download it? — Kann ich das ausdrucken / herunterladen?
I saved it. — Ich habe es gespeichert.
My computer has crashed. — Mein Computer ist abgestürzt.

Wenn man zusammen arbeitet

Can I take that chair? — Kann ich den Stuhl haben?
Do you want to work with me? — Möchtest du mit mir arbeiten?
Why don't we do this together? — Wollen wir das nicht zusammen machen?
What are we going to do first? — Was machen wir zuerst?

Let's compare our … — Lass uns unsere … vergleichen.
Let's check my … — Komm, wir überprüfen meine …
Can I help you with …? — Soll ich dir bei … helfen?
Could you please check my spelling? — Kannst du bitte meine Rechtschreibung überprüfen?

What's another word for …? — Wie kann man noch … sagen?
Can you look that word up, please? — Kannst du das Wort bitte nachschauen?
Whose turn is it? — Wer ist dran?
Sorry, that was my fault. — Entschuldigung, das war mein Fehler.
Do you follow me? — Verstehst du, was ich meine?
Say that again, please. — Sag das bitte noch einmal.

We're running out of time. — Unsere Zeit ist fast um.
It's time to finish. — Es ist Zeit aufzuhören.
Don't forget to bring … tomorrow. — Denk dran, morgen … mitzubringen.
Thanks for your help. — Danke für deine Hilfe.

Glossary

Deutscher Begriff	Englischer Begriff mit Aussprache	Beispiele	LiF
Adjektiv (Eigenschaftswort)	adjective ['ædʒɪktɪv]	green, expensive, boring	6
Aussagesatz	statement [steɪtment]	School starts at 9 o'clock.	12
Bedingungssatz	conditional clause [kən'dɪʃənl ˌklə:z]	If I sell my old toys, I will earn some money.	16
Berichtete Rede	reported speech [rɪˌpə:tɪd 'spi:tʃ]	Susan says that they're helping Sabrina.	19
Bestätigungsfrage	question tag ['kwestʃən ˌtæg]	He is a good cook, isn't he?	4
Einfache Gegenwart (Präsens)	simple present [sɪmpl 'preznt]	She lives in my street.	
Einfache Vergangenheit (Präteritum)	simple past [sɪmpl pɑ:st]	I stayed with my uncle.	3, 11
Fragesatz	question ['kwestʃən]	Have we got any milk?	2, 3, 4, 9, 11, 12, 17, 18
Futur mit going to	going to-future ['gəʊɪŋ tu: 'fju:tʃə]	We are going to have a party.	
Futur mit will	will-future [wɪl 'fju:tʃə]	I'll find a good job.	7, 14
Grundform [des Verbs], Infinitiv	infinitive [ɪn'fɪnətɪv]	go, live, be, do, have	5, 7, 13, 14
ing-Form	ing-form [ɪa ən dʒɪ fɔ:m]	playing, looking, having	5, 9, 10
Ja/Nein-Frage	yes/no-question [jes'nəʊkwestʃən]	Can I watch the film at 10 o'clock?	2, 4, 9, 10, 11, 12, 17, 18
Komparativ (1. Vergleichsform)	comparative [kəm'pærətɪv]	bigger, nicer, more interesting, better	6
Kurzantwort	short answer [ʃɔ:t‿'ɑ:nsə]	Yes, I can. / No, I didn't.	
Kurzform	short form [ʃɔ:t fɔ:m]	I'm / she's / we'll	
Langform	long form ['lɒŋ fɔ:m]	I am / she is / we will	
Nomen / Substantiv	noun [naʊn]	house, light, life	
Partizip [Perfekt]	past participle [ˌpɑ:st 'pɑ:tɪsɪpl]	played, been, taken	2, 3, 7
Passiv	passive [ˌpæsɪv]	Matches are used to make fire.	13
Perfekt	present perfect [ˌpreznt 'pɜ:fɪkt]	have gone / has been / has visited	2, 3, 7
Prädikat (Satzaussage)	verb group / predicate [vɜ:b gru:p] / ['predɪkət]	I don't know the way. Have you been there?	12
Pronomen (Fürwort)	pronoun [prəʊnaʊn]	I, you, she, it, they	4
regelmäßiges Verb	regular verb ['regjʊlə vɜ:b]	play, open, want	4, 11
Relativsatz	relative clause [ˌrelətɪv 'klə:z]	There are police officers who help people.	8
Subjekt (Satzgegenstand)	subject ['sʌbdʒekt]	I missed my home. Who speaks Polish?	12
Superlativ (2. Vergleichsform)	superlative [su:'pɜ:lətɪv]	biggest, nicest, most interesting, best	6
Verb (Zeitwort, Tätigkeitswort)	verb [vɜ:b]	play, go, do, talk	3, 4, 5, 9, 10, 11, 13
Vergangenheitsform	past form [ˌpɑ:st fɔ:m]	played, went, did	3, 7, 11
Vergleichsformen (des Adjektivs)	comparison (of the adjective) ['kɒm'pærɪsn] ([əv ðɪ 'ædʒɪktɪv])	tall, taller, tallest muscular, more muscular, most muscular	6
Verlaufsform der Gegenwart	present progressive [ˌpreznt prəʊ'gresɪv]	We are looking at postcards. I'm having a great time.	9
Verlaufsform der Vergangenheit	past progressive [ˌpɑ:st prəʊ'gresɪv]	He was watching the parade.	10
Verneinung	negation [nɪ'geɪʃn]	I don't know. / I won't marry anyone.	2, 9, 10, 11, 12, 17, 18

Theme 1 ● Eating out

Say it in English

So kann man …

fragen, ob jemand hungrig ist.	**Are you hungry?**
fragen, was jemand essen möchte.	**What are you having?**
fragen, wie es jemandem schmeckt.	**What's your food like?**
sagen, dass man die Rechnung haben möchte.	**Could we have the bill, please?**
einen Vorschlag machen.	**We could** try that new pizza place.
sagen, dass man eine Idee hat.	**I've got an idea.**
fragen, was jemand schon gemacht hat.	**Have you ever** eaten snake?
jemanden bedauern.	**Poor you!**
sagen, dass man etwas nicht so schlimm findet.	**It's not that bad.**

Sprachliche Mittel

LiF 1 Mengenangaben ● much / many / a lot of

much, **many** und **a lot of** – alle drei Wörter bedeuten *viel* beziehungsweise *viele* auf Deutsch. Was ist der Unterschied?

- **many** bezeichnet eine große *Anzahl* von etwas. Es steht vor zählbaren Nomen (*count nouns*):

  Many pizzas have a lot of cheese on them.

- **much** bezeichnet eine große *Menge* von etwas. Es steht vor nicht zählbaren Nomen (*uncount nouns*):

  Well, some pizzas don't have much cheese on them.

- **many** und **much** werden vor allem in Fragen und negativen Sätzen verwendet. Sonst kannst du für *viel(e)* auch immer **a lot of** oder auch **lots of** nehmen. Dabei brauchst du nicht zwischen zählbaren und nicht zählbaren Nomen zu unterscheiden:

  I've had a lot of salad this week.
  A lot of restaurants do takeaway food.

  When she came here from India, she brought lots of spices with her.

Tipp Zählbare Nomen erkennst du leicht daran, dass sie fast immer das Mehrzahl-s tragen – aber Vorsicht: Es gibt Ausnahmen wie *children, men, women, mice* usw.! Am besten machst du dir mit anderen aus der Klasse einige Merk-Poster mit „much-words" und „many-words" darauf. Mit den Wörtern aus A6 und dem gesamten Theme 1 könnt ihr gleich anfangen.

LiF 2 Remember? Das Perfekt ● present perfect

present perfect

- drückt aus, dass eine Handlung, die in der Vergangenheit begann, in der Gegenwart noch andauert oder nachwirkt
- wird auch verwendet, wenn man sagen will, was jemand irgendwann schon einmal, schon häufig oder noch nie getan hat

• Signalwörter:	ever, never, yet, already, just, so far
• FORMEL:	*have / has + Partizip Perfekt*
(+)	She **has tried** a lot of interesting food.
(–)	She **hasn't tried** a lot of interesting food.
(Y/N) ?	**Has** she **tried** a lot of interesting food?
(WH-) ?	What **has** she **tried**?
• Partizip Perfekt	(past participle)
regelmäßig:	Infinitiv + **-ed:** cook, cooked, **cooked**; try, tried, **tried**
unregelmäßig:	verschiedene Formen, z. B. eat, ate, **eaten**

Tipp Die drei Formen (*infinitive, past form, past participle*) der unregelmäßigen Verben kannst du dir besser merken, wenn du ähnliche Formen zusammen lernst, z. B. in Reimform:

bring, brought, brought
buy, bought, bought
…

LiF 3 Einfache Vergangenheit oder Perfekt? ● simple past or present perfect?

- Mit dem *present perfect* deckt man im Englischen einen Zeitraum ab, der in der Vergangenheit angefangen hat, aber noch in die Gegenwart reicht:

  Have you ever been to an Italian restaurant? **Yes, I have.**
  (Der Zeitraum reicht von irgendwann damals bis heute.)

- Das *simple past* benutzt man bei Ereignissen und Handlungen, die vergangen und abgeschlossen sind (siehe auch LiF 11 auf Seite 156).

  What was it like? **It was good. I tried three different pizzas.**
  (Das Ereignis begann und endete in der Vergangenheit.)

⚠ Im Deutschen können wir das Präteritum *oder* das Perfekt für ein Ereignis in der Vergangenheit verwenden. Im Englischen *musst* du für Handlungen, die klar in der Vergangenheit stattfanden, das *simple past* benutzen:

Ich habe drei verschiedene Pizzen probiert.	~~I've tried three different pizzas.~~
oder:	nur:
Ich probierte drei verschiedene Pizzen.	**I tried three different pizzas.**

LiF 4 Bestätigungsfragen ● question tags

- Eine Bestätigungsfrage gibt das Signal: Ich möchte, dass du mir zustimmst – wir sind doch einer Meinung, oder? Dazu benutzt man im Englischen Anhängsel wie **… can't you?** oder **… isn't it?**:

  You can read Chinese, can't you?

  He is a good cook, isn't he?

  Auf Deutsch sagen wir normalerweise *nicht wahr?* oder wir benutzen, je nach Gegend, Dialektformen wie zum Beispiel *gell?, woll?, wa?*

- So leicht wie im Deutschen ist das mit den englischen Bestätigungsfragen aber nicht. Du musst die Verbform immer noch einmal wiederholen und dabei **n't** anhängen, die Kurzform von **not**.

  You are chewing gum, aren't you?

  Curry can be very hot, can't it?

  Rajiv has got extra-hot chilli paste, hasn't he?

- Wenn ein Hauptverb allein steht, also nicht von einem Hilfsverb oder Modalverb begleitet wird, musst du für das Anhängsel **do** oder **does** bzw. **did** nehmen:

  You really like spaghetti, don't you?

  Rajiv loves cooking, doesn't he?

  Vanessa helped with the cooking, didn't she?

- Noch eine Schwierigkeit, die wir aus dem Deutschen nicht kennen: Eigennamen und Nomen musst du in der Bestätigungsfrage immer durch das passende Pronomen ersetzen:

  she
  Vanessa likes banana raita, doesn't ~~Vanessa~~?

  they
  Rosemary and Rajiv think the food is delicious, don't ~~Rosemary and Rajiv~~?

  they
  Indian curries are hot, aren't ~~Indian curries~~?

Theme 2 ● Be a sport

Say it in English

So kann man …

fragen, ob jemand regelmäßig Sport treibt. — **Do you do sport regularly?**
sagen, was man einfach / schwierig fand. — Jumping on one foot **was easy / difficult.**
sagen, was man gerne macht. — **I like** playing hockey.
I enjoy playing outside.
sagen, dass man gleicher Meinung ist. — **I think so, too.**
sagen, dass einem etwas weh tut. — **It hurts.**
sagen, dass man seinen Arm nicht bewegen kann. — **I can't move my arm.**
sagen, wozu jemand nicht in der Lage ist. — The boy **is not able to** ride his bike.

Sprachliche Mittel

LiF 5 Die ing-Form als Nomen ● ing-nouns

- Wenn du im Deutschen ein Verb zu einem Nomen umformen willst, brauchst du einfach nur den Infinitiv großzuschreiben. Im Englischen benutzt man dafür die ing-Form des Verbs:

walking	(das) Gehen
jumping	(das) Springen

- Die ing-Form als Nomen kann im Satz dieselben Aufgaben übernehmen wie jedes andere Nomen. Sie kann als Subjekt stehen:

  Stepping on and off a chair ten times was no problem.
  Doing press-ups was difficult.

  Oder als Objekt:

  I love watching football.
  I like playing hockey.

Walking in the forest can be dangerous.

- Bei einigen ing-Formen musst du besonders auf die Schreibweise achten:

  Endet der Infinitiv des Verbs auf **-e**, dann fällt das **-e** in der ing-Form weg.

make	mak**ing**
take	tak**ing**
dance	danc**ing**

  Bei einigen Infinitiven wird der letzte Buchstabe verdoppelt.

sit	sit**ting**
run	run**ning**
hop	hop**ping**

LiF 6 Remember? Vergleichsformen des Adjektivs ● comparison

Vergleichsformen des Adjektivs

Hier kannst du sehen, welche Vergleichsform du wann anwenden musst:

• einsilbige Adjektive:	tall, tall**er**, tall**est**
• zweisilbige Adjektive, wenn sie auf **-y**, **-le**, **-er**, **-ow** enden:	clever, clever**er**, clever**est**
• Adjektive mit zwei oder mehr Silben:	successful, **more** successful, **most** successful
	muscular, **more** muscular, **most** muscular
• Hier wird der Konsonant verdoppelt:	fit, fit**ter**, fit**test**
	big, big**ger**, big**gest**

LiF 7 be able to

- **be able to** drückt die Fähigkeit aus, etwas zu tun; es bedeutet also dasselbe wie **can**.

The boy is able to play football.
The man with the black hair is not able to smell anything.

- Im *simple past* benutzt du **was able to** oder **were able to**. Allerdings kannst du auch **could** verwenden:

Christy's brothers made him a box on wheels, so he was able to play with them.
They built a little house in the garden for him where he could write his stories, read and draw.

- Da **can** nicht in allen Zeitformen stehen kann *musst* du manchmal **be able to** verwenden, so z. B. auch im *will-future*:

The boy will be able to play football again next week.
The old lady won't be able to eat very much.

Du wirst dieses Fahrrad nicht reparieren können.

Tipp Malt euch ein Merk-Poster zu **can / be able to**. So könnte es aussehen:

infinitive	simple past	present perfect	simple present	will-future
can	could	–	can	–
be able to	was able to were able to	have been able to has been able to	am able to are able to is able to	will be able to

Theme 3 ● On the street

Say it in English

So kann man …

sagen, dass man etwas nicht feiert.	**I don't celebrate** carnival.
eine Sache genauer beschreiben.	**There is** a programme **that** tells you what's on.
eine Person genauer beschreiben.	John is the little boy **who** almost had an accident.
beschreiben, was sich jedes Jahr wiederholt.	**Every year** in September **there is** a street festival in our town.
sagen, dass jemand gerade noch einmal davon gekommen ist.	John Scott **had a narrow escape**.
sagen, was jemand zu einem bestimmten Zeitpunkt gerade gemacht hat.	He **was** watch**ing** the parade.

Sprachliche Mittel

LiF 8 Relativsätze ● relative clauses

- Wenn du eine Sache oder eine Person näher beschreiben willst, kannst du einen Relativsatz verwenden:

  There are a lot of dancers and brightly coloured floats that pass by in the parade.
  There are also many tourists who take photos.

  The police put up posters which tell everybody to be careful.

- Englische Relativsätze fangen meistens mit **who**, **which** oder **that** an. **who** kannst du nur für Personen nehmen, **which** geht nur für Dinge. **that** kannst du für Personen und für Dinge verwenden:

There are police officers	**who** **that**	**help people.**
There is a programme	**which** **that**	**tells you what's on.**

Tipp

Mit diesem Spiel könnt ihr die Verwendung von **who** und **which** in Relativsätzen üben: Legt in eurem Klassenraum eine „**who**-Seite" und eine „**which**-Seite" fest. Eine Spielleiterin oder ein Spielleiter eurer Wahl ruft euch dann Nomen zu und ihr müsst schnell auf die richtige Seite laufen.

Beispiel:	"**dancer**"	→	**who**-Seite
	"**band**"	→	**which**-Seite
	usw.		

LiF 9 Remember? Die Verlaufsform der Gegenwart ● present progressive

present progressive

- gibt an, was gerade eben geschieht
- FORMEL: (BE) + (VERB)+**ing**

(+)	He **is watching** the parade.
(–)	He **isn't watching** the parade.
(Y/N) ?	**Is** he **watching** the parade?
(WH-) ?	What **is** he **watching**?

LiF 10 Die Verlaufsform der Vergangenheit ● past progressive

- Das *past progressive* drückt aus, dass eine Handlung in der Vergangenheit über einen längeren Zeitraum im Gange war.

  The boy was watching the parade.

- Wenn zwei Ereignisse in der Vergangenheit gleichzeitig ablaufen, dann bildet das länger andauernde den „Hintergrund" für das kürzere, das sich im „Vordergrund" abspielt. Wir können im Deutschen zum Beispiel sagen: „Ich war gerade am Kochen, als der Briefträger klingelte." Das, was man im Deutschen mit „ich war gerade am Kochen" oder „ich war gerade dabei, zu kochen" ausdrücken kann, das sagt man im Englischen mit dem *past progressive*.

  Vordergrund-Geschehen: **John Scott had a narrow escape yesterday**

  Hintergrund-Geschehen: **while he was watching the carnival parade.**

- Die Formen des *past progressive* werden genauso gebildet wie die Formen des *present progressive*. Nur steht **be** natürlich in der entsprechenden Vergangenheitsform:

FORMEL	**was / were** + (VERB)+**ing**
(+)	**You were stealing wallets.**
(–)	**I wasn't stealing wallets.**
(Y/N)?	**Were you watching TV?**
(WH-)?	**What were you watching?**

While I was taking pictures a man stole my handbag.

Theme 4 ● No man is an island

Say it in English

So kann man …

fragen, was sich verändert hat.	**What has changed** here while you were away?
fragen, was jemand am meisten vermisst hat.	**What did you miss most?**
jemanden nach seiner Meinung fragen.	I think a watch is very important. **What about you?**
sagen, dass man sich nicht sicher ist.	Well, **I'm not sure.**
jemandem zustimmen.	**I think you are right.**
sagen, was man gerne tut.	**I love** read**ing** in my room.
sagen, dass jemand sich weniger sorgen soll.	**Don't worry so much.**
sagen, was jemand am liebsten hätte.	She **would love to have** a dog.
sagen, dass jemand arbeitslos ist.	He **is out of work** at the moment.

Sprachliche Mittel

LiF 11 Remember? Die einfache Vergangenheit ● simple past

simple past

• steht für Ereignisse in der Vergangenheit	
• Signalwörter:	yesterday, last night, last week, last month, last year, a week ago, a month ago, a year ago, …
• FORMEL:	(VERB) + **ed** / *past form*
(+)	I miss**ed** my home and my family.
	I **ate** bananas and potatoes.
(–)	I **didn't miss** my teachers.
	I **didn't eat** any snakes and spiders.
(Y/N) ?	**Did** you **miss** your family?
	Did you **eat** spiders?
(WH-) ?	Who **did** you **miss** most?
	What **did** you **eat**?
• unregelmäßige Verben:	eat ist ein Beispiel für ein unregelmäßiges Verb. Hier gilt die Grundregel *Infinitiv* + **ed** nicht; du musst diese Formen auswendig lernen. Lies dazu auch den Tipp auf S. 150.
• **be**	hat besondere Vergangenheitsformen:
	I **was** / he **was** / she **was** / it **was**
	you **were** / we **were** / they **were**

LiF 12 Die Stellung der Satzglieder ● word order

- In jeder Sprache haben die Sätze einen Bauplan. Der Bauplan englischer Sätze ist ziemlich strikt – aber auch ziemlich klar. Hier ist das Grundmuster für einfache Sätze:

0 (VORFELD)	1 SUBJEKT	2 PRÄDIKAT	3 OBJEKT
	I	missed	my home.
No,	I	didn't brush	my teeth.
Yes,	I	was afraid.	

- Dieser Bauplan bleibt auch in Fragesätzen bestehen. Das ist im Deutschen nicht so. (Deshalb kommen wir manchmal in Schwierigkeiten und verdrehen die Satzglieder.)

0 FRAGESIGNAL	1 SUBJEKT	2 PRÄDIKAT	3 OBJEKT
What did	**you**	**miss?**	
Did	**you**	**brush**	**your teeth?**
Were	**you**	**afraid?**	
Would	**you**	**go back?**	

- Zeitangaben und Ortsangaben stehen immer außerhalb des Kernsatzes. Wenn sie zusammen in einem Satz vorkommen, steht immer „Ort" vor „Zeit":

KERNSATZ (SUBJEKT-PRÄDIKAT-OBJEKT)	ORTSANGABE	ZEITANGABE
Robinson lived	**on the island**	**for many years.**
He and Friday arrived	**in York**	**on 11th June 1687.**

Tipp Wenn dir Merksätze helfen, probier's mit diesem: Like nine before ten, it's "where" before "when".

Eine Zeitangabe kann aber auch *vor* dem Kernsatz stehen:

ZEITANGABE	KERNSATZ (SUBJEKT-PRÄDIKAT-OBJEKT)	ORTSANGABE
On 11th June 1687	**he and Friday arrived**	**in York.**

LiF 13 Der Infinitiv mit to ● to-infinitive

- Nach Verbformen wie **would like**, **would love**, **would hate** musst du immer einen Infinitiv mit **to** verwenden:

He would like to talk to girls in class.

Die Kurzform von **would** lautet **'d**.

He'd like to talk to girls in class.

- Vorsicht! Auch nach **want** steht der Infinitiv mit **to**:

She wants to run away from home.

Theme 5 ● The world of science

Say it in English

So kann man …

sagen, dass ein Vorschlag toll klingt.	**It sounds brilliant.**
jemandem freundlich etwas geben.	**Here you are.**
sagen, dass etwas kostenlos ist.	**It's free.**
eine Entscheidung begründen.	I'd first have a look at the locomotive **because** I've never seen one before.
sagen, was man für besonders wichtig hält.	Matches **are the most important** invention **for me**.
sagen, wofür man etwas braucht.	I **need** electricity **for** my computer.
sagen, dass man etwas kaum erwarten kann.	**I can't wait.**
sagen, was von wem erfunden wurde.	The Amphicar **was invented by** Hans Trippel.

Sprachliche Mittel

LiF 14 have to

- **have to** benutzt man, um eine Notwendigkeit auszudrücken:

  We have to use electricity for cooking.
  When we had no electricity, we had to use candles.

- In den meisten Zeitformen musst du **have to** anstelle von **must** verwenden:

INFINITIVE	SIMPLE PAST	PRESENT PERFECT	SIMPLE PRESENT	WILL-FUTURE
must	–	–	**must**	–
have to	**had to**	**have had to** **has had to**	**have to** **has to**	**will have to**

LiF 15 Das Passiv ● the passive

- Wenn der Urheber einer Handlung nicht von Bedeutung ist, verwendet man oft das Passiv:

  The Amphicar was invented in 1961.

- Verbformen im Passiv bildest du mit **be** und dem Partizip des Hauptverbs. Die Grundform im Passiv lautet bei **invent** zum Beispiel: **be invented** – erfunden werden. Jetzt musst du nur noch **be** in die jeweils passende Zeitform setzen – und fertig:

	(BE)	PARTIZIP	
Matches	**are**	**used**	**to make fire.**
Pedal power	**was**	**used**	**to pump water into the shower.**

- Wenn du in einem Passiv-Satz doch einmal den Urheber nennen willst, musst du ihn mit **by** angeben:

  The Amphicar was designed by Hans Trippel.
  The first machines were powered by water.

Theme 6 ● Cash in hand

Say it in English

So kann man ...

fragen, wofür jemand sein Geld ausgibt. **What do you spend your money on?**

jemandem einen Vorschlag machen, an den eine Bedingung geknüpft ist. **If you** are short of money, **you can** do the shopping for someone.

fragen, was jemand an einem Ort macht. **What are you doing here?**

fragen, was jemand anzubieten hat. **What's on offer?**

ausdrücken, dass man etwas im Vertrauen sagt. **Between you and me,** I'm sure it's a Picasso.

fragen, was etwas kostet. **How much is it? / What do you want for that?**

sagen, dass etwas zu teuer ist. **Oh, that's too expensive.**

Sprachliche Mittel

LiF 16 Bedingungssätze 1 ● conditional clauses 1

- Wenn du sagen willst, was unter bestimmten Bedingungen geschehen wird oder geschehen kann, benutzt du einen Bedingungssatz:

  If I sell my old toys, I can earn some extra money.

  If you are short of money, you can do the shopping for someone.

  If they sell enough, they'll have some extra money for the trip.

- Im if-Satz (*if-clause*) benutzt du ein Verb im *simple present*. Im Hauptsatz (*main clause*) muss ein Modalverb (hier **will, can** oder **must**) mit einem Hauptverb stehen:

IF-CLAUSE	MAIN CLAUSE
If I do a paper round,	**I will earn some extra money.**
If I do a paper round,	**I can earn some extra money.**
If you are in a wheelchair,	**you must start at 9.25 from the Green Start.**

Tipp Die meisten Bedingungssätze fangen mit **if** an, deshalb werden sie auch „if-Sätze" genannt. Du darfst hier niemals **when** statt **if** benutzen, obwohl es vom Deutschen her so vertraut klingt. Wenn du einen deutschen Satz mit „wenn" hast, probiere aus, ob du stattdessen auch „falls" sagen könntest – wenn das geht, benutzt du im Englischen **if**; wenn das nicht geht, benutzt du **when**.

LiF 17 something / anything

- **something** und **anything** bedeuten beide „etwas" auf Deutsch.
  In normalen Aussagesätzen verwendest du **something**:

  Now that's something very special.

- In Fragesätzen nimmst du im Allgemeinen **anything**:

  Have you got anything really old?

- Wenn du etwas anbietest oder um etwas bittest, ist es allerdings besser, **something** zu verwenden, denn damit zeigst du, dass du ein „ja" erwartest:

  Would you like to give something for our car boot sale?

- In negativen Sätzen nimmst du **anything**:

  I didn't find anything interesting.

  I've never seen anything like that before.

LiF 18 Remember? some / (not) any

some / (not) any

• im einfachen Satz:	I need **some milk** for my cornflakes.
	There are **some apples** on the cupboard.
• bei einer Frage:	– Normalfall:
	Have we got **any milk**?
	Are there **any cornflakes** in the cupboard?
	– „ja" wird erwartet:
	Can I have **some milk**, please?
• in Verbindung mit **not**:	No, we have**n't** got **any** cornflakes left.
	There's **never any** milk in this house.

Theme 7 ● Art and music

Say it in English

So kann man …

sagen, dass man eine Pause gebrauchen könnte. **I think we could do with a break.**
jemanden an etwas erinnern. **Don't forget** we're recording a new album next month.
sagen, dass man etwas nicht glauben kann. **You're kidding!**
sagen, dass man müde ist. **I'm tired.**
um Erlaubnis bitten. **Please**, Mum, **can I** go?
sagen, dass man etwas langweilig findet. **That's boring.**
sagen, dass man eine Idee gut findet. **That's a good idea!**

Sprachliche Mittel

LiF 19 Berichtete Rede 1 ● reported speech 1

- Wenn du berichten willst, was jemand gesagt hat, benutzt du die Form der berichteten (indirekten) Rede:

	BEGLEITSATZ *(report clause)*	WIEDERGEGEBENE AUSSAGE *(reported clause)*
"We could do with a break."	**Sabrina says that**	**they could do with a break.**

- Berichtete Rede besteht aus einem Begleitsatz und der wiedergegebenen Aussage. Beide Satzteile können, müssen aber nicht unbedingt durch **that** verbunden werden.
- Wenn die Originalaussage Wörter enthält, die nur aus dem Zusammenhang richtig zu verstehen sind, musst du sie in der wiedergegebenen Aussage anpassen:

"We're helping Sabrina." **Susan says (that) they're helping Sabrina.**

"I'm exhausted." **Sabrina says (that) she's exhausted.**

Theme 8 ● Going places

Say it in English

So kann man …

sagen, was man in den Ferien vorhat. **In the summer holidays I'm going to** visit my friend.
sagen, wie lange man an einem Ort geblieben ist. **We stayed for** two weeks.
sagen, was man in einem unwahrscheinlichen Fall tun würde. **If I could** go to Cairo, **I would** see the pyramids.
nach dem Weg fragen. **Excuse me, can you tell me the way to** the station, please?
sagen, dass man Heimweh hatte. **I felt homesick.**
jemanden fragen, ob er oder sie Englisch spricht. **Excuse me, please, do you speak English?**

So funktionieren die Wortlisten

Es gibt alphabetische Wortlisten und Wortlisten nach Kapiteln.

Alphabetische Wortlisten

Wenn du nicht mehr weißt, wo ein Wort zum ersten Mal vorgekommen ist, kannst du es in der alphabetischen Wortliste (*Dictionary English – German*) ab S. 193 nachschlagen. Dort findest du auch die Wörter, die in den Optionals und im *Book stop* ab Seite 118 vorkommen.
Wörter mit einem ° gehören zu den Texten aus den Optionals.
Wörter, hinter denen „BS“ steht, sind aus den *Book stop*-Texten.

Wortlisten nach Kapiteln

Hier siehst du, wie du diese Wortlisten (ab Seite 165) benutzen kannst.

Die Lautschrift zeigt an, wie man ein Wort ausspricht.

Hier findest du die Übersetzungen.

Links stehen die englischen Wörter mit ihrer Lautschrift.

Fett gedruckte Wörter solltest du dir merken.

(only plural) bedeutet: Dieses Wort wird nur oder gewöhnlich in der Mehrzahl benutzt.

(AE) bedeutet: Dies ist die amerikanische Schreibweise bzw. ein Wort aus dem amerikanischen Englisch.

(informal) bedeutet: Dieses Wort ist umgangssprachlich.

Zu dieser Aufgabe gehören die folgenden Wörter.

(pl) weist auf eine unregelmäßige Mehrzahlform hin.

Kleine Bilder und Beispielsätze helfen dabei, dir Wörter besser einzuprägen.

Hier findest du wichtige Vokabel-Lerntipps.

(no pl) bedeutet: Dieses Wort hat keine Mehrzahl.

W

group [gru:p]	(Musik)gruppe	*group* = band
horror movie ['hɒrə ˌmu:vi]	Horrorfilm	
musician [mju'zɪʃn]	Musiker/in	George Clooney is an *actor*,
actor/actress ['æktə/ 'æktrəs]	Schauspieler/in	Julia Roberts is an *actress*.
be born [bi: 'bɔ:n]	geboren werden	
tattoo [tæ'tu:]	Tattoo, Tätowierung	
guardian angel [ˌgɑ:diən_'eɪndʒl]	Schutzengel	
shoulder ['ʃəʊldə]	Schulter	
What goes around comes around. [wɒt ˌgəʊz_əˌraʊnd 'kʌmz_əˌraʊnd]	Alles rächt sich früher oder später.	
wrist [rɪst]	Handgelenk	
star [stɑ:]	Stern	
bar code ['bɑ: ˌkəʊd]	Strichcode	
album ['ælbəm]	(Musik)album	
stupid ['stju:pɪd]	dumm, blöd	
sober ['səʊbə]	nüchtern	
love song ['lʌv ˌsɒŋ]	Liebeslied	
supporter [sə'pɔ:tə]	Anhänger/in	
animal rights *(only plural)* [ˌænɪml 'raɪts]	*das Recht der Tiere auf Leben und artgerechte Haltung*	
organization [ˌɔ:gənaɪ'zeɪʃn]	Organisation	
strict [strɪkt]	streng	
vegetarian [ˌvedʒə'teəriən]	Vegetarier/in	
be an A-student *(AE)* [bi:_ən 'eɪ ˌstju:dnt]	ein/e Einserschüler/in sein	If you *are an A-student*, you are very good at school.
You're kidding! *(informal)* [jɔ: 'kɪdɪŋ]	Das ist doch nicht dein Ernst!	*You're kidding!* = You're joking!
exam [ɪg'zæm]	Prüfung	
professional [prə'feʃnəl]	Profi	
amateur ['æmətə]	Amateur/in	
rest [rest]	(Ruhe)pause	
just [dʒʌst]	nur, bloß, einfach	I cut the cake
A6 **half** *(pl* **halves)** [hɑ:f, hɑ:vz]	Hälfte	in two *halves*.
equipment [ɪ'kwɪpmənt]	Ausrüstung, Ausstattung	
kid [kɪd]	Kind, Jugendliche(r)	
free ticket [ˌfri: 'tɪkɪt]	Freikarte	
rehearsal [rɪ'hɜ:sl]	Probe	
speaker ['spi:kə]	*hier:* Lautsprecher	There's very loud music coming from the *speakers*.
God! [gɒd]	Oh (mein) Gott!	
be knackered *(informal)* [bi: 'nækəd]	kaputt/fix und fertig sein	
stuff [stʌf]	Zeug	
speak (to/with) [spi:k]	sprechen, reden (mit)	
We could do with … [ˌwi: kəd 'du: wɪð]	Wir könnten … gebrauchen.	*We could do with …* = We need …
What's on? [ˌwɒts_'ɒn]	Was läuft? Was geht ab?	

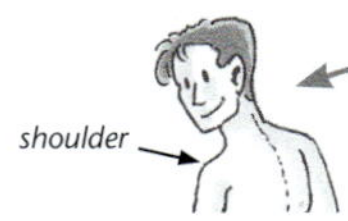

Scrambled words
Arbeite mit einem/r Partner/in. Schreibe Wörter auf ein Blatt Papier. Schreibe anschließend die Buchstaben der Wörter in verdrehter Reihenfolge auf *(scrambled words)*. Dein/e Partner/in muss die „neuen Wörter“ buchstabieren. Dann muss er/sie das ursprüngliche Wort erraten. Wenn er/sie es schafft, ist er/sie an der Reihe. Ihr könnt so eure Rechtschreibung und das englische Alphabet trainieren!

The English alphabet

[eɪ]	[bi:]	[si:]	[di:]	[i:]	[ef]	[dʒi:]	[eɪtʃ]	[aɪ]
a	b	c	d	e	f	g	h	i
[dʒeɪ]	[keɪ]	[el]	[em]	[en]	[əʊ]	[pi:]	[kju:]	[ɑ:]
j	k	l	m	n	o	p	q	r
[es]	[ti:]	[ju:]	[vi:]	['dʌblju:]	[eks]	[waɪ]	[zed]	
s	t	u	v	w	x	y	z	

English sounds

Im Englischen spricht man Wörter oft anders aus, als man sie schreibt. Das ist aber kein Problem. Denn die Aussprache der Wörter ist in jedem Wörterbuch angegeben. So kann man auch neue Wörter richtig aussprechen, ohne sie vorher gehört zu haben.
Dazu nimmt man die Lautschrift zu Hilfe. Das ist eine Schrift, deren Symbole jeden Laut genau bezeichnen. Die Lautschrift wird in jedem Wörterbuch benutzt.
Hier ist eine Liste mit den Symbolen dieser Lautschrift zusammen mit Beispielwörtern, in denen der entsprechende Laut vorkommt.

Vokale

[ɑ:]	**ar**m
[ʌ]	b**u**t
[e]	d**e**sk
[ə]	**a**, **a**n
[ɜ:]	g**ir**l, b**ir**d
[æ]	**a**pple
[ɪ]	**i**n, **i**t
[i]	happ**y**
[i:]	**ea**sy, **ea**t
[ɒ]	**o**range, s**o**rry
[ɔ:]	**a**ll, c**a**ll
[ʊ]	l**oo**k
[u]	Jan**u**ary
[u:]	b**oo**t

Doppellaute

[aɪ]	**eye**, b**y**, b**uy**
[aʊ]	**our**
[eə]	**air**, th**ere**
[eɪ]	t**a**ke, th**ey**
[ɪə]	h**ere**
[ɔɪ]	b**oy**
[əʊ]	g**o**, **o**ld
[ʊə]	t**ou**rist

Konsonanten

[b]	**b**ag, clu**b**
[d]	**d**uck, car**d**
[f]	**f**ish, lau**gh**
[g]	**g**et, do**g**
[h]	**h**ot
[j]	**y**ou
[k]	**c**an, du**ck**
[l]	**l**ot, sma**ll**
[m]	**m**ore, **m**u**m**
[n]	**n**ow, su**n**
[ŋ]	so**ng**, lo**ng**
[p]	**p**resent, to**p**
[r]	**r**ed, a**r**ound
[s]	**s**i**s**ter, cla**ss** (stimmlos)
[z]	no**s**e, dog**s** (stimmhaft)
[t]	**t**ime, ca**t**
[ʒ]	televi**si**on
[dʒ]	sausa**ge**
[ʃ]	fre**sh**
[tʃ]	**ch**ild, **ch**eese
[ð]	**th**ese, mo**th**er (stimmhaft)
[θ]	ba**th**room, **th**ink (stimmlos)
[v]	**v**ery, ha**v**e
[w]	**w**hat, **w**ord

[']	Betonungszeichen für die folgende Silbe (Hauptbetonung)
[ˌ]	Betonungszeichen für die folgende Silbe (Nebenbetonung)

Es gibt auch …

… eine Menge Wörter, die im Englischen wie im Deutschen gleich sind (– außer, dass die meisten von ihnen auf Deutsch groß geschrieben werden). Viele von ihnen sprechen wir auch gleich aus. Mit ihnen kannst du dich schon einmal an die Lautschrift gewöhnen.
Du findest viele dieser Wörter auf dieser Seite. Sie sind nicht in den Wortlisten der einzelnen Kapitel, weil sie dir ja nicht neu sind.
Bei denen, die ein bisschen anders ausgesprochen werden als im Deutschen, haben wir die Lautschrift farbig hervorgehoben.

ABC [ˌeɪ biː ˈsiː]
album [ˈælbəm]
alphabet [ˈælfəˌbet]
American football [əˌmerɪkən ˈfʊtbɔːl]
audio (= audio tape) [ˈɔːdiəʊ (ˈɔːdiəʊ ˌteɪp)]
audio guide [ˈɔːdiəʊ ˌgaɪd]
basketball [ˈbɑːskɪtˌbɔːl]
blog [blɒg]
burger (= hamburger) [ˈbɜːgə]
champion [ˈtʃæmpiən]
cheeseburger [ˈtʃiːzˌbɜːgə]
collage [ˈkɒlɑːʒ]
comic [ˈkɒmɪk]
computer [kəmˈpjuːtə]
cool [kuːl]
cornflakes [ˈkɔːnˌfleɪks]
cowboy [ˈkaʊbɔɪ]
deck [dek]
design [dɪˈzaɪn]
Dr (= doctor) [ˈdɒktə]
DVD [ˌdiː viː ˈdiː]
fair [feə]
fan, fan club [fæn, ˈfæn klʌb]
fast food [ˌfɑːst ˈfuːd]
film, film star [fɪlm, ˈfɪlm stɑː]
form [fɔːm]
frisbee [ˈfrɪzbi]
gas [gæs]
hobby [ˈhɒbi]
hockey [ˈhɒki]
hot dog [ˈhɒt‿ˌdɒg]
information [ˌɪnfəˈmeɪʃn]
instrument [ˈɪnstrʊmənt]
international [ˌɪntəˈnæʃnəl]
interview [ˈɪntəˌvjuː]
karaoke [ˌkæriˈəʊki]
karate [kəˈrɑːti]
laptop [ˈlæpˌtɒp]
make-up [ˈmeɪk‿ʌp]
modern [ˈmɒdən]
muffin [ˈmʌfɪn]
musical [mjuːzɪkəl]
normal [ˈnɔːml]
online [ˈɒnlaɪn]
optional [ˈɒpʃnəl]
parallel [ˈpærəlel]
party [ˈpɑːti]
pizza [ˈpiːtsə]
plan [plæn]
plus [plʌs]
podcast [ˈpɒdˌkɑːst]
pop star [ˈpɒp stɑː]
poster [ˈpəʊstə]
quiz [kwɪz]
radio [ˈreɪdiəʊ]
rest [rest]
roadie *(informal)* [ˈrəʊdi]
rucksack [ˈrʌkˌsæk]
rugby [ˈrʌgbi]
salami [səˈlɑːmi]
sandwich [ˈsænwɪdʒ]
show [ʃəʊ]
skateboard [ˈskeɪtˌbɔːd]
snowboarder [ˈsnəʊbɔːdə]
so [səʊ]
spaghetti [spəˈgeti]
star [stɑː]
super [ˈsuːpə]
sweatshirt [ˈswetˌʃɜːt]
symbol [ˈsɪmbl]
taxi [ˈtæksi]
team [tiːm]
teenager [ˈtiːneɪdʒə]
tennis [ˈtenɪs]
text [tekst]
tourist [ˈtʊərɪst]
trend [trend]
trick [trɪk]
tunnel [ˈtʌnl]
unfair [ʌnˈfeə]
video [ˈvɪdiəʊ]
website [ˈwebˌsaɪt]
windsurfer [ˈwɪndsɜːfə]
workshop [ˈwɜːkˌʃɒp]

L ● Last year in NHG

	cassette [kə'set]	Kassette	
	record ['rekɔ:d]	(Schall)platte	
	all kinds of [ɔ:l 'kaɪndz‿əv]	alle möglichen	
	in-line skating [ˌɪnlaɪn 'skeɪtɪŋ]	Inlineskaten	
	dancing ['dɑ:nsɪŋ]	Tanzen	
	guitar [gɪ'tɑ:]	Gitarre	The boy is playing the *guitar*.
	goldfish (*pl* goldfish) ['gəʊldˌfɪʃ]	Goldfisch	
	president ['prezɪdənt]	Präsident/in	
	travelling ['trævlɪŋ]	Reisen	
	exotic [ɪg'zɒtɪk]	exotisch, fremdländisch	The mango is an *exotic* fruit.

Theme 1 ● Eating out

	eat out [ˌi:t‿'aʊt]	essen gehen	Before we do the shopping we'd better write a shopping *list*.
A1	**list** [lɪst]	Liste	
A2	**menu** ['menju:]	Speisekarte	
	restaurant ['restrɒnt]	Restaurant, Gaststätte	
	bean [bi:n]	Bohne	
	special ['speʃl]	Tagesgericht; *hier:* Spezial	
	chips *(only plural)* [tʃɪps]	Pommes frites	Most children love to eat *chips*.
	soft drink [ˌsɒft‿'drɪŋk]	Softdrink *(alkoholfreies Getränk)*	
	starter ['stɑ:tə]	Vorspeise	You usually eat *soup* with a spoon.
	soup [su:p]	Suppe	
	soup of the day [ˌsu:p‿əv ðə 'deɪ]	Tagessuppe	*Fresh* food is food that has just been made.
	fresh [freʃ]	frisch	
	melon ['melən]	Melone	
	garlic ['gɑ:lɪk]	Knoblauch	
	main course ['meɪn ˌkɔ:s]	Hauptgericht	
	curry ['kʌri]	Curry(gericht)	
	roast lamb [ˌrəʊst 'læm]	gebratenes Lamm	
	mint [mɪnt]	Minze	*mint*
	sauce [sɔ:s]	Soße, Sauce	
	pie [paɪ]	Pastete	*Vegetarian* food is without meat or fish.
	vegetarian [ˌvedʒə'teəriən]	vegetarisch	
	lasagna [lə'zænjə]	Lasagne	
	dessert [dɪ'zɜ:t]	Nachtisch	*Desserts* are usually sweet.
	apple crumble [ˌæpl 'krʌmbl]	Apfelauflauf	
	coffee ['kɒfi]	Kaffee	
	regular ['regjʊlə]	normal(e) (Größe)	There's no *ham* in *vegetarian* food.
	ham [hæm]	Schinken	
	olive ['ɒlɪv]	Olive	

mushrooms

	olive ['ɒlɪv]	Olive	
	chilli (*pl* chillies) ['tʃɪli, 'tʃɪliz]	Chili; Peperoni	
	onion ['ʌnjən]	Zwiebel	
	mushroom ['mʌʃru:m]	Pilz	
	broccoli ['brɒkəli]	Broccoli, Brokkoli	
	Italian [ɪ'tæljən]	Italiener/in; italienisch	
A3	**waiter/waitress** ['weɪtə/ 'weɪtrəs]	Kellner/in	*Waiters* and *waitresses* work in *restaurants*.
	Good evening. [gʊd‿'i:vnɪŋ]	Guten Abend.	

	Are you ready to order? [ɑ: ju: ˌredi tʊ 'ɔ:də]	Möchten Sie schon bestellen?	
	order ['ɔ:də]	bestellen	
	How about you? [ˌhaʊ əˌbaʊt 'ju:]	Wie ist es mit dir/Ihnen?	
	What are you having? ['wɒt‿ɑ: ju: ˌhævɪŋ]	Was nimmst du/nehmen Sie?	
	I'll have … ['aɪl hæv]	Ich werde … nehmen/essen.	
	What is … like? [ˌwɒt ɪz 'laɪk]	Wie ist …?	
	Could we have the bill, please? [kʊd wi: hæv ðə 'bɪl ˌpli:z]	Wir möchten bitte zahlen!, Die Rechnung, bitte!	
	so [səʊ]	also	
A5	meal [mi:l]	Mahlzeit, Essen	
	design [dɪ'zaɪn]	entwerfen, gestalten	

A6	take sb out for a meal [ˌteɪk sʌmbədi ˌaʊt fər‿ə 'mi:l]	jdn zum Essen einladen	*He has taken* her *out for a meal*.
	decide [dɪ'saɪd]	sich entscheiden; beschließen	
	inside [ˌɪn'saɪd]	innen, drinnen	*inside* ≠ outside
	anyway ['eniˌweɪ]	sowieso; überhaupt	
	turn [tɜ:n]	werden	The leaves *turn* yellow in autumn.
	try [traɪ]	*hier:* (aus)probieren	
	so far ['səʊ fɑ:]	bisher	A *takeaway* is a meal that you buy in a restaurant and take home to eat.
	takeaway (food) ['teɪkəˌweɪ]	Essen zum Mitnehmen	
	ring (up) [ˌrɪŋ‿'ʌp]	anrufen; klingeln, läuten	*ring up* = call
	at the same time [ət ðə ˌseɪm 'taɪm]	gleichzeitig, zur gleichen Zeit	
	scene [si:n]	Szene	

A7	detective [dɪ'tektɪv]	Detektiv/in	
A8	lady ['leɪdi]	Frau; Dame	
	bowl [bəʊl]	Schüssel; Schale	These are *bowls*.
	a bowl of soup [ə ˌbəʊl‿əv 'su:p]	eine Tasse Suppe	
	possibly ['pɒsəbli]	möglicherweise, vielleicht	*possibly* = perhaps
	wine [waɪn]	Wein	
	just [dʒʌst]	nur, bloß, einfach	*just* = only
	put (into) [pʊt]	*hier:* gefüllt (in)	
	dish (*pl* dishes) [dɪʃ, 'dɪʃɪz]	Schale, Schüssel; Gericht	

	change one's mind [ˌtʃeɪndʒ wʌnz ˈmaɪnd]	seine Meinung ändern	I've *changed my mind*. I'm going out *some other time*.
	some other time [sʌm‿ˈʌðə ˌtaɪm]	ein anderes Mal	
	sorry about that [ˈsɒri əˌbaʊt ˈðæt]	ich bitte um Entschuldigung, das tut mir leid	
	not at all [ˌnɒt‿ət‿ˈɔ:l]	keine Ursache	
	madam [ˈmædəm]	gnädige Frau *(Anrede)*	
A9	phrase [freɪz]	Satz; Ausdruck; (Rede)wendung	
	sort [sɔ:t]	sortieren	
	guest [gest]	Gast	
	form [fɔ:m]	bilden	
A10	foreign [ˈfɒrɪn]	ausländisch, fremd	
	take sb (somewhere) [ˈteɪk sʌmbədi]	jdn (irgendwohin) mitnehmen	
	surprised [səˈpraɪzd]	überrascht, erstaunt	
	surprise [səˈpraɪz]	überraschen	
	ever [ˈevə]	jemals, schon einmal	Have you *ever* been to Notting Hill? – Yes, I have. – *What was it like?*
	What was it like? [ˌwɒt wəz‿ɪt ˈlaɪk]	Wie war es?	
	taste [teɪst]	schmecken	
	awful [ˈɔ:fl]	furchtbar, schrecklich	
B1	**Indian** [ˈɪndiən]	Inder/in; indisch	
	meal [mi:l]	Mahlzeit, Essen	
	raita [ˈraɪtə]	*indisches Gericht mit Joghurt*	
	grandmother [ˈgrænˌmʌðə]	Großmutter	The woman in the picture is my *grandmother*.
	spice [spaɪs]	Gewürz	
	you [ju:]	man	
	Poor you! [ˌpʊə ˈju:]	Du Arme/r!	She's *holding* her dog in her arms.
	hold [həʊld]	halten	
	sure [ʃɔ:]	sicher	
	extra- [ˈekstrə]	extra-, besonders	*extra* = special
	hot [hɒt]	*hier:* scharf	
	paste [peɪst]	Paste	*Delicious* food tastes very good.
	delicious [dɪˈlɪʃəs]	köstlich, lecker	
	be right [bi: ˈraɪt]	Recht haben	
	Come on! [ˌkʌm‿ˈɒn]	Komm(t) schon!; Mach(t) jetzt!	
	It's not that bad! [ɪtz ˌnɒt ˈðæt ˌbæd]	So schlimm ist es doch nicht!	
	bad [bæd]	schlecht; schlimm	
B2	Guess what! [ˌges ˈwɒt]	Rate mal!; Stell dir vor!	
B3	clever [ˈklevə]	klug, schlau	*clever* = intelligent
	situation [ˌsɪtʃuˈeɪʃn]	Situation, Lage	
	Chinese [ˌtʃaɪˈni:z]	Chinese/Chinesin; chinesisch	
	speech bubble [ˈspi:tʃ ˌbʌbl]	Sprechblase	If you get a letter in *Chinese* and you can't read *Chinese*, you need a *translation*.
	translate [trænsˈleɪt]	übersetzen	
	translation [trænsˈleɪʃn]	Übersetzung	

oh	[əʊ]	oh
er	[ɜ:]	äh(m)
ouch	[aʊtʃ]	aua, autsch
phew	[fju:]	puh
yeah	[jeə]	ja(wohl)
ow	[aʊ]	au

	question tag ['kwestʃn ˌtæg]	Bestätigungsfrage
B4	**check** [tʃek]	überprüfen, kontrollieren
LL1	caste [kɑːst]	Kaste
	Brahmin ['brɑːmɪn]	Brahmane
	untouchable [ʌn'tʌtʃəbl]	Unberührbare/r
	Dalit ['dælɪt]	Unberührbare/r *(ind. Kastensystem)*
B5	traditional [trə'dɪʃnəl]	traditionell
	spicy ['spaɪsi]	würzig; scharf
	recipe ['resəpi]	Rezept
	mild [maɪld]	mild; leicht
	g (= gram, gramme) [græm]	Gramm
	yoghurt ['jɒgət]	Yoghurt, Joghurt
	teaspoon ['tiːˌspuːn]	Teelöffel
	honey ['hʌni]	Honig
	cinnamon ['sɪnəmən]	Zimt
	cardamom ['kɑːdəməm]	Kardamom
	mash [mæʃ]	zerdrücken
	mix [mɪks]	(ver)mischen
	present [prɪ'zent]	präsentieren, vorlegen
B6	**dictionary** ['dɪkʃənri]	Wörterbuch
	task [tɑːsk]	Aufgabe
	milk product ['mɪlk ˌprɒdʌkt]	Milchprodukt
	word snake ['wɜːd ˌsneɪk]	Wortschlange
	hidden word puzzle [ˌhɪdn 'wɜːd ˌpʌzl]	*Suchrätsel*
	puzzle ['pʌzl]	Rätsel
P1	**Practice matters.** [ˌpræktɪs 'mætəz]	*etwa:* Übung macht den Meister.
P5	baked potato [ˌbeɪkt pə'teɪtəʊ]	Ofenkartoffel
	What else …? [wɒt‿'els]	Was sonst …?
P7	similar ['sɪmɪlə]	ähnlich

The teacher *is checking* the pupil's homework.

hot = very *spicy*

mild ≠ *spicy*

honey

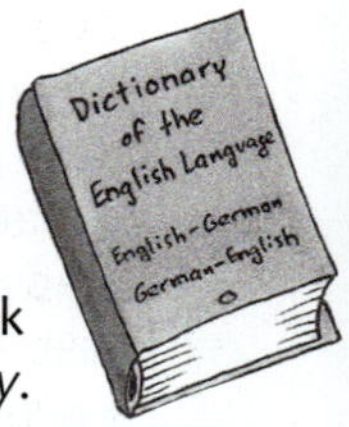

If you don't know the meaning of a word, you can look it up in a *dictionary*.

Sinnvolles Timing
Wann kannst du dich besonders gut konzentrieren? Finde die Zeiten heraus und nutze sie gezielt zum Lernen. Mache ein paar Kniebeugen oder andere Lockerungsübungen, um dich zu entspannen. Plane, was du wann machen willst – denke auch an Pausen, denn jeder braucht Zeit zum „Auftanken"! Abwechslung hilft beim Lernen.
Es gibt viele Möglichkeiten, Vokabeln zu lernen!

Die Vokabeln aus den OPTIONAL-Teilen findest du im englisch-deutschen Dictionary auf den Seiten 193 – 217.

Theme 2 ● Be a sport

I	**Be a sport!** [ˌbiː‿ə ˈspɔːt]	Sei kein/e Spielverderber/in!
A1	lead [liːd]	führen
	healthy [ˈhelθi]	gesund
	free time [ˌfriː ˈtaɪm]	Freizeit
	do sport [duː ˈspɔːt]	Sport treiben
	hang out with sb [ˌhæŋ‿ˈaʊt wɪð sʌmbədi]	Zeit mit jdm verbringen
	regularly [ˈregjʊləli]	regelmäßig
	(every) now and then [ˌnaʊ‿ən ˈðen]	ab und zu
	(twice) a (week) [ˌtwaɪs‿ə ˈwiːk]	(zweimal) pro (Woche)
A2	test [test]	prüfen, testen
	guess [ges]	Vermutung
	be out of breath [bi‿ˌaʊt‿əv ˈbreθ]	außer Atem sein
	not at all [ˌnɒt‿ət‿ˈɔːl]	überhaupt nicht
	step on [ˌstep‿ˈɒn]	steigen auf
	step off [ˌstep‿ ˈɒf]	hinuntersteigen von
	press-up [ˈpres‿ʌp]	Liegestütz
	hop [hɒp]	hüpfen, springen
	the same [ðə ˈseɪm]	der/die/das Gleiche
	Can you do it? [kæn ˈjuː ˌduː ɪt]	Schaffst du das?
	stair [steə]	Treppenstufe
	a little [ə ˈlɪtl]	ein wenig, ein bisschen
	report (to) [rɪˈpɔːt]	berichten
A3	defend oneself [dɪˈfend wʌnˌself]	sich verteidigen
	be good at sth [biː ˈgʊd‿ət ˌsʌmθɪŋ]	etw gut können
	triathlon [traɪˈæθlən]	Triathlon
	part [pɑːt]	Teil
	less [les]	weniger
	break down [ˌbreɪk ˈdaʊn]	kaputtgehen; stehen bleiben
	race [reɪs]	Rennen, Wettkampf
	still [stɪl]	trotzdem
	swimmer [ˈswɪmə]	Schwimmer/in
	even [ˈiːvn]	selbst; sogar
	exciting [ɪkˈsaɪtɪŋ]	aufregend, spannend
	ice hockey [ˈaɪs ˌhɒki]	Eishockey
	clothing [ˈkləʊðɪŋ]	Kleidung
	helmet [ˈhelmɪt]	Helm
	just as [ˈdʒʌst‿əz]	genauso (wie)
	sports hall [ˈspɔːts ˌhɔːl]	Sporthalle
	note [nəʊt]	Notiz
A4	interview [ˈɪntəˌvjuː]	interviewen, befragen

I do sports regularly: every Monday, Wednesday and Friday.

How old are you?
Have a *guess!*

He's doing *press-ups*.

Only use karate to *defend yourself!*

He should eat *less* to stay healthy.

She's a *swimmer*.

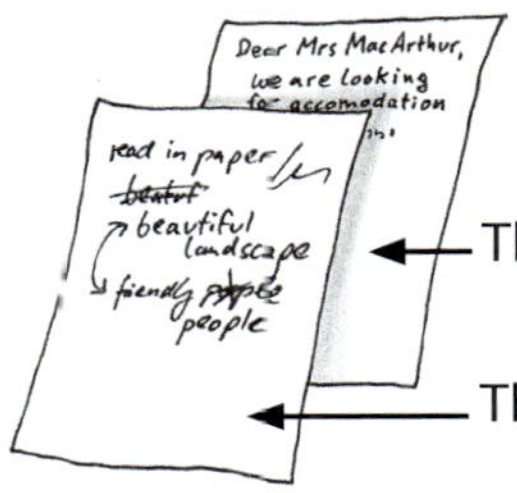

This is a letter.

This is a *note*.

Diese Wörter findest du in den Randspalten:

health	[helθ]	Gesundheit
festival	['festɪvl]	Fest, Festival
travelling	['trævlɪŋ]	Reisen
feeling	['fi:lɪŋ]	Gefühl
time out	[ˌtaɪm‿'aʊt]	Auszeit

	practise ['præktɪs]	üben	
	for help [fə 'help]	zu/als Hilfe	
LL2	term [tɜ:m]	Semester; Trimester	
	house captain ['haʊs ˌkæptɪn]	*Sprecher/in für ein Haus*	
A5	sports [spɔ:ts]	Sport-	
	poem ['pəʊɪm]	Gedicht	
	be (great) fun [bi: 'fʌn]	(viel) Spaß machen	
	breaststroke ['brestˌstrəʊk]	Brustschwimmen	
	stroke [strəʊk]	*hier:* (Schwimm)stil	
	front crawl ['frʌnt ˌkrɔ:l]	Kraulschwimmen, Kraulen	
	the worst [ðə 'wɜ:st]	der/die/das schlechteste	
	burst [bɜ:st]	platzen	
	get out [ˌget‿'aʊt]	herauskommen	
	bye-bye *(informal)* [ˌbaɪ 'baɪ]	tschüs(s)	
	cricket ['krɪkɪt]	Kricket	
	tight [taɪt]	fest	
	thumb [θʌm]	Daumen	
	be about to do sth [bi: əˌbaʊt tə 'du: ˌsʌmθɪŋ]	im Begriff sein, etw zu tun	He's *about* to hit a *cricket* ball.
	release [rɪ'li:s]	freilassen, freigeben	
	spin [spɪn]	rotieren; sausen	
	through [θru:]	durch	The ball was *spinning through* the *air*.
	air [eə]	Luft	
	crowd [kraʊd]	(Menschen)menge	
	sb gives a gasp [ˌsʌmbədi ˌgɪvz‿ə 'gɑ:sp]	jdm bleibt die Luft weg	
	batter ['bætə]	Schlagmann	
	step back [ˌstep 'bæk]	zurücktreten	
	lift [lɪft]	(hoch)heben, anheben	He cannot *lift* it.
	bat [bæt]	Schläger, Schlagholz	
	whack *(informal)* [wæk]	*etwa:* zack	
	better ['betə]	*hier:* lieber	
A6	poet ['pəʊɪt]	Dichter/in	
	player ['pleɪə]	Spieler/in	
	think of ['θɪŋk‿əv]	denken an, sich ausdenken	
	rhyming ['raɪmɪŋ]	Reim-	
	line [laɪn]	Linie; *hier:* Zeile	
A7	**favourite** ['feɪvrət]	Liebling; Favorit/in	She's *looking up* the *meaning* of the word in her dictionary.
	look up [ˌlʊk‿'ʌp]	nachschlagen	
	meaning ['mi:nɪŋ]	Bedeutung	
	successful [sək'sesfl]	erfolgreich	This is a *muscular* man.
	muscular ['mʌskjʊlə]	muskulös	
	clever ['klevə]	klug, schlau	
	powerful ['paʊəfl]	stark, kräftig	
	skilful ['skɪlfl]	geschickt	
	aerobics [eə'rəʊbɪks]	Aerobic	
	have to do sth [ˌhæv tə 'du: ˌsʌmθɪŋ]	etw tun müssen	I *have to do* it. = I must do it.

	hero (*pl* heroes) ['hɪərəʊ, 'hɪərəʊz]	Held
	goalkeeper ['gəʊl,ki:pə]	Tormann/Torfrau
B1	**phone** [fəʊn]	anrufen
	order ['ɔ:də]	Ordnung, Reihenfolge
	surgery ['sɜ:dʒəri]	(Arzt)praxis
	throat [θrəʊt]	Hals
	hurt [hɜ:t]	wehtun, schmerzen
	(bad) cold [kəʊld]	(starke) Erkältung
	wait [weɪt]	(ab)warten, (er)warten
	You're welcome. [ˌjɔ: 'welkəm]	Nichts zu danken!, Gern geschehen!
	Goodbye. [ˌgʊd'baɪ]	Auf Wiedersehen.
	feel bad [ˌfi:l 'bæd]	sich schlecht fühlen
	have a temperature [hæv‿ə 'temprɪtʃə]	Fieber haben
	call [kɔ:l]	(Telefon)anruf
	be wrong with sb [bi: 'rɒŋ wɪð ˌsʌmbədi]	nicht stimmen, los sein
	appointment [ə'pɔɪntmənt]	Termin
B2	**at the doctor's** [ˌæt ðə 'dɒktəz]	beim Arzt/bei der Ärztin
	waiting room ['weɪtɪŋ ˌru:m]	Wartezimmer
	broken ['brəʊkən]	gebrochen
	swollen ['swəʊlən]	geschwollen
	put [pʊt]	*hier:* anlegen
	bandage ['bændɪdʒ]	Verband
	next time ['nekst‿ˌtaɪm]	nächstes Mal
	kick [kɪk]	treten, schießen
	receptionist [rɪ'sepʃnɪst]	Herr/Dame an der Anmeldung
	break [breɪk]	(sich) brechen
	(take an) X-ray ['eksreɪ]	röntgen
	half (*pl* halves) [hɑ:f, hɑ:vz]	Hälfte
	be ready [bi: 'redi]	bereit sein, fertig sein
B3	**patient** ['peɪʃnt]	Patient/in
	stomach ache ['stʌmək‿eɪk]	Magenschmerzen, Bauchschmerzen
	backache ['bækeɪk]	Rückenschmerzen
	cut foot [ˌkʌt 'fʊt]	Schnittwunde am Fuß
	sore [sɔ:]	wund, entzündet
B4	(be) too bad [tu: 'bæd]	wirklich schade (sein)
	blond(e) [blɒnd]	blond
	(pair of) glasses *(only plural)* [ˌpeər‿əv 'glɑ:sɪz]	Brille
	go dancing [ˌgəʊ 'dɑ:nsɪŋ]	tanzen gehen
B5	be about [bi:‿ə'baʊt]	handeln von
	look through [ˌlʊk 'θru:]	durchsehen

Normalerweise sagt man *"hero"* bei einem Mann und *"heroine"* bei einer Frau. Heutzutage hört man jedoch auch *"hero"* in Bezug auf Frauen.

He *has a temperature*.

They are *at the doctor's*. They are sitting in the doctor's *waiting room*.

The doctor has *put* a *bandage* around his head.

The cake has been cut into two *halves*.

When you go to see a doctor you are his *patient*.

When you have a *stomach ache* it is better not to eat anything.

You can *look through glasses*.

	be born [bi: 'bɔ:n]	geboren werden
	bricklayer ['brɪkˌleɪə]	Maurer/in
	notice ['nəʊtɪs]	bemerken
	properly ['prɒpəli]	richtig
	clear [klɪə]	klar
	disabled [dɪs'eɪbld]	behindert
	himself [hɪm'self]	sich (selbst)
	control [kən'trəʊl]	kontrollieren, steuern
	tongue [tʌŋ]	Zunge
	busy ['bɪzi]	beschäftigt; arbeitsreich
	machine [mə'ʃi:n]	Maschine
	housework ['haʊsˌwɜ:k]	Hausarbeit
	intelligent [ɪn'telɪdʒnt]	klug, intelligent
	wheel [wi:l]	Rad
	one day ['wʌn ˌdeɪ]	eines Tages
	clinic ['klɪnɪk]	Klinik
	make money [ˌmeɪk 'mʌni]	*hier:* Geld einbringen
	earn [ɜ:n]	verdienen
	article ['ɑ:tɪkl]	Artikel
	prize [praɪz]	Preis, Auszeichnung
	writer ['raɪtə]	Autor/in
	die [daɪ]	sterben
	be made into a film [bi: ˌmeɪd‿ɪntʊ‿ə 'fɪlm]	verfilmt werden
	called [kɔ:ld]	*hier:* mit dem Titel
B6	summary ['sʌməri]	Zusammenfassung, Inhaltsangabe
	by himself [ˌbaɪ hɪm'self]	ganz allein
P4	in alphabetical order [ɪn‿ælfəˌbetɪkl‿'ɔ:də]	in alphabetische(r) Reihenfolge
	comparative form [kəm'pærətɪv ˌfɔ:m]	Komparativ
	superlative form [sʊ'pɜ:lətɪv ˌfɔ:m]	Superlativ
	comparison [kəm'pærɪsn]	Vergleich
	field [fi:ld]	Feld
	swimming pool ['swɪmɪŋ ˌpu:l]	Schwimmbecken, Schwimmbad
P7	dress sb ['dres‿ˌsʌmbədi]	jdn anziehen

He's a *bricklayer.*

Being *disabled* means that you can't do all the things that other people can.

earn ≠ spend

He's a *writer*. He writes books and *articles*.

Lernwege
Du solltest wissen, dass sich nicht jeder Mensch Dinge auf die gleiche Art und Weise gut einprägen kann. Die Lernmethode, die für deine Freundin oder deinen Freund die beste ist, muss nicht auch für dich die beste sein.
Probiere doch einfach mal verschiedene Methoden aus und entscheide dann selbst, wie du am besten Vokabeln lernen kannst.
Vielleicht findest du ja auch noch andere Methoden, die dir helfen.

Die Vokabeln aus den OPTIONAL-Teilen findest du im englisch-deutschen Dictionary auf den Seiten 193–217.

Theme 3 ● On the street

I	**carnival** ['kɑ:nɪvl]	Karneval, Volksfest
A1	dancer ['dɑ:nsə]	Tänzer/in
	mask [mɑ:sk]	Maske
	costume ['kɒstju:m]	Kostüm
	witch (*pl* witches) [wɪtʃ, 'wɪtʃɪz]	Hexe
	parade [pə'reɪd]	Parade, Umzug
	any ['eni]	(irgend)ein(e); jede(r, s)
	dress up [ˌdres‿'ʌp]	sich verkleiden
A2	**thousand** ['θaʊznd]	Tausend
	take photos [ˌteɪk 'fəʊtəʊz]	fotografieren
LL3	steel band [ˌsti:l 'bænd]	Steelband
	steel drum [ˌsti:l 'drʌm]	Steeldrum
	main parade [ˌmeɪn pə'reɪd]	*hier:* großer Umzug
A3	steel drummer [ˌsti:l 'drʌmə]	*Trommler/in auf einer Steeldrum*
	noise [nɔɪz]	Lärm, Geräusch
	doorbell ['dɔ:ˌbel]	Türklingel
	drum [drʌm]	trommeln
	at the beginning [ˌæt ðə bɪ'gɪnɪŋ]	am Anfang, zu Beginn
	hit [hɪt]	schlagen; treffen; stoßen (gegen)
	date [deɪt]	Datum
	midnight ['mɪdˌnaɪt]	Mitternacht
	event [ɪ'vent]	Ereignis, Veranstaltung
	competition [ˌkɒmpə'tɪʃn]	Wettbewerb
	grand [grænd]	prächtig, großartig
	splash (*pl* splashes) [splæʃ, 'splæʃɪz]	Sensation
	title ['taɪtl]	Titel
	queen [kwi:n]	Königin
	male [meɪl]	männlich
	individual [ˌɪndɪ'vɪdʒuəl]	Einzelperson
	female ['fi:meɪl]	weiblich
	festival ['festɪvl]	Fest, Festival
	official [ə'fɪʃl]	offiziell
	opening ['əʊpnɪŋ]	Eröffnung
	location [ləʊ'keɪʃn]	Standort, Lage
A4	business ['bɪznəs]	Geschäft
	band [bænd]	Band; Gruppe
	bright [braɪt]	hell, grell, leuchtend
	float [fləʊt]	Fest(zugs)wagen
	pass by [ˌpɑ:s 'baɪ]	vorbeikommen
	pickpocket ['pɪkˌpɒkɪt]	Taschendieb/in
	steal [sti:l]	stehlen
	purse [pɜ:s]	Portemonnaie

This man is wearing a *mask*, but it's not a nice *costume*.

He likes to *dress up* as a clown.

She is *taking photos*.

Steel drums make a lot of *noise*.

Today's *date* is the 6th of …

She is dressed up as a *queen*.

male individual

female individual

The man *stole* the tourist's bag.

	watch (*pl* **watches**) [wɒtʃ, ˈwɒtʃɪz]	Armbanduhr	*watch* 
	put up [ˌpʊt‿ˈʌp]	aufhängen	
	samosa [səˈməʊsə]	*mit Kartoffeln oder Hackfleisch gefüllte indische Teigtasche*	
	stall [stɔːl]	(Verkaufs)stand	
	the sign says [ðə ˈsaɪn ˌsez]	auf dem Schild steht	*The sign says "ZOO"*
	Don't worry! [ˌdəʊnt ˈwʌri]	Keine Sorge!	
	guess [ges]	(er)raten	
A5	programme [ˈprəʊgræm]	Programm, Plan	
	be on [biː ˈɒn]	auf dem Programm stehen, laufen	
A6	important [ɪmˈpɔːtnt]	wichtig	
A7	be called [biː ˈkɔːld]	heißen	The cat *is called* Socks.
	fire brigade [ˈfaɪə brɪˌgeɪd]	Feuerwehr	
	adult [ˈædʌlt]	Erwachsene/r	
	set up [ˌset‿ˈʌp]	aufschlagen, errichten	You sell and buy second-hand
	flea market [ˈfliː ˌmɑːkɪt]	Flohmarkt	things at a *flea market.*
	choir [ˈkwaɪə]	Chor	A *choir* is a group of singers.
	magician [məˈdʒɪʃn]	Zauberer/Zauberin	Harry Potter is a *magician.*
	profit [ˈprɒfɪt]	Gewinn, Profit	
	children's home [ˈtʃɪldrənz ˌhəʊm]	Kinderheim, Waisenhaus	
	table [ˈteɪbl]	*hier:* Tabelle	
	organize [ˈɔːgənaɪz]	organisieren	
A8	prepare [prɪˈpeə]	vorbereiten	
	talk [tɔːk]	Gespräch; *hier:* Vortrag	
B1	**narrow** [ˈnærəʊ]	eng; knapp	The boy *had a narrow escape.*
	escape [ɪˈskeɪp]	Flucht, *hier:* Entkommen	
	have a narrow escape [hæv‿ə ˌnærəʊ‿ɪˈskeɪp]	gerade noch einmal davongekommen sein	
	incident [ˈɪnsɪdnt]	Vorfall, Ereignis	
	almost [ˈɔːlməʊst]	fast, beinahe	
	accident [ˈæksɪdnt]	Unfall	
	six-year-old [ˈsɪks jɪər‿ˌəʊld]	der/die/das sechsjährige	
	while [waɪl]	während	
	run away [ˌrʌn‿əˈweɪ]	weglaufen	
	knock [nɒk]	stoßen	
	manage [ˈmænɪdʒ]	es schaffen	
	pull away [ˌpʊl‿əˈweɪ]	wegreißen, wegziehen	
	front wheel [ˌfrʌnt ˈwiːl]	Vorderrad	
	run over [ˌrʌn‿ˈəʊvə]	überfahren, *hier:* überrollen	
	question [ˈkwestʃn]	befragen	
	further [ˈfɜːðə]	weiter, (noch) mehr	
	phrase [freɪz]	Satz; Ausdruck; (Rede)wendung	
	finish [ˈfɪnɪʃ]	(be)enden, aufhören	

Verknüpfungen herstellen:
Bei dieser Lernmethode ist alles erlaubt, was mit deiner Vorstellungskraft zu tun hat und was dir hilft, Vokabeln zu behalten. Für Wörter, die überhaupt nicht in deinen Kopf wollen, kannst du beispielsweise:
- dir das Wort bildlich vorstellen,
- ein kleines Bild dazu zeichnen oder etwas Passendes aus einer Zeitschrift ausschneiden,
- an ein Ereignis denken, das du selbst erlebt hast,
- einen Satz, in dem das Wort vorkommt, auswendig lernen,
- dir eine Eselsbrücke (z. B. einen Reim) ausdenken.

B2	**have a drink** [ˌhævˍə ˈdrɪŋk]	etw trinken
	talk on the phone [ˌtɔːkˍɒn ðə ˈfəʊn]	telefonieren
	wallet [ˈwɒlɪt]	Brieftasche, Portemonnaie
B3	interview [ˈɪntəˌvjuː]	*hier:* Verhör
B4	**each other** [ˌiːtʃˍˈʌðə]	einander
B5	around [əˈraʊnd]	in der Nähe, da
P2	pocket [ˈpɒkɪt]	Tasche *(an Kleidungsstücken)*
P3	sound check [ˈsaʊndˍˌtʃek]	Tonprobe, Soundcheck
	is/are spoken [ɪz/ɑː ˈspəʊkən]	wird/werden gesprochen
P4	spelling [ˈspelɪŋ]	Rechtschreibung
P5	MP3 player [ˌem piː ˈθriː ˌpleɪə]	MP3-Spieler
P6	answer the phone [ˌɑːnsə ðə ˈfəʊn]	ans Telefon gehen
	pay [peɪ]	(be)zahlen
	paint [peɪnt]	Farbe

He is looking at her. She is looking at him. They are looking at *each other.*

She *is answering the phone.*

Die Vokabeln aus den OPTIONAL-Teilen findest du im englisch-deutschen Dictionary auf den Seiten 193–217.

Theme 4 ● No man is an island

I	No man is an island. [ˌnəʊ ˌmænˍɪzˍənˍˈaɪlənd]	Niemand ist alleine auf der Welt.
	island [ˈaɪlənd]	Insel
	home [həʊm]	Zuhause; *hier:* Heimat
A1	version [ˈvɜːʃn]	Version, Fassung
	board a ship [ˌbɔːdˍə ˈʃɪp]	ein Schiff besteigen
	rock [rɒk]	Stein; Fels
	raft [rɑːft]	Floß
	wreck [rek]	(Schiffs)wrack
	cannibal [ˈkænɪbl]	Kannibale/Kannibalin, Menschenfresser/in
	prisoner [ˈprɪznə]	Gefangene/r
	rescue [ˈreskjuː]	retten; befreien
	speak (to/with) [spiːk]	sprechen, reden (mit)
	fish [fɪʃ]	fischen, angeln
	medicine [ˈmedsn]	Medizin, Medikamente
	sail by [ˌseɪl ˈbaɪ]	vorbeisegeln
	Home, sweet home! [ˌhəʊm ˌswiːt ˈhəʊm]	Trautes Heim, Glück allein!
A3	**interview** [ˈɪntəˌvjuː]	interviewen, befragen

island

The *prisoners* want to be *rescued.*

	most of all [ˌməʊst‿əv‿ˈɔ:l]	am meisten	
	away [əˈweɪ]	weg	
	about [əˈbaʊt]	*hier:* an	
	brush one's teeth [ˌbrʌʃ wʌnz ˈti:θ]	sich die Zähne putzen	He'*s brushing* his *teeth.*
	stick [stɪk]	Zweig, Stock	
	point (at/to) [pɔɪnt]	zeigen (auf)	
A4	people [ˈpi:pl]	*hier:* Volk	
	toil [tɔɪl]	hart arbeiten, schuften	*toil* = work very hard
	may [meɪ]	können, mögen	
	sail [seɪl]	segeln	
	many a [ˈmeni‿ə]	manch ein/e	
	shore [ʃɔ:]	Küste, Ufer, Strand	
	chorus (*pl* choruses) [ˈkɔ:rəs, ˈkɔ:rəsɪz]	Refrain	
	willed [ˈwɪld]	vererbt, vermacht	
	sing in praise [ˌsɪŋ‿ɪn ˈpreɪz]	ein Loblied singen	
	waters [ˈwɔ:təz]	Gewässer	
	shine [ʃaɪn]	scheinen, glänzen	The sun *is shining.*
	break [breɪk]	*hier:* anbrechen	
	heav'n (= heaven) [ˈhevn]	Himmel	
	on high [ɒn ˈhaɪ]	in der Höhe	He's carrying a heavy *load.*
	load [ləʊd]	Ladung; Last	
	burning [ˈbɜ:nɪŋ]	brennend, glühend	
	glow [gləʊ]	Leuchten, Scheinen	
	mingle [ˈmɪŋgl]	mischen	
	sweat [swet]	Schweiß	
	earth [ɜ:θ]	Erde, Boden	
	on bended knee(s) [ɒn ˌbendɪd ˈni:z]	auf Knien	
	cane [keɪn]	Rohr, Stock; *hier:* Zuckerrohr	
	waterside [ˈwɔ:təˌsaɪd]	Strand	
	cast a net [ˌkɑ:st‿ə ˈnet]	ein Netz auswerfen	He'*s casting a net.*
	surge [sɜ:dʒ]	branden, wogen	
	tide [taɪd]	Gezeiten	
	awake [əˈweɪk]	aufwachen, erwachen	A *sound* is something that you can hear.
	sound [saʊnd]	Geräusch	
	drum [drʌm]	Trommel	
	philosophical [ˌfɪləˈsɒfɪkl]	abgeklärt, gelassen	
	lyrics *(only plural)* [ˈlɪrɪks]	(Lied)text	
A5	ocean [ˈəʊʃn]	Ozean, Meer	*ocean* = sea
	breeze [bri:z]	Brise	
	fan [fæn]	Luft zufächeln	
	lure [ljʊə]	(an)locken	
	seas *(only plural)* [si:z]	Wellen, Wogen	
	illustrate [ˈɪləstreɪt]	illustrieren, bebildern	
A6	survival kit [səˈvaɪvl ˌkɪt]	Überlebensausrüstung	
	lonely [ˈləʊnli]	einsam	
	first aid kit [ˌfɜ:st‿ˈeɪd ˌkɪt]	Verbandskasten	

	rope [rəʊp]	Seil, Strick	You can make music with a *trumpet*. 
	trumpet ['trʌmpɪt]	Trompete	
	packet ['pækɪt]	Packung, Tüte	
	seed [si:d]	Same, Korn	
	soap [səʊp]	Seife	You brush your teeth with a *toothbrush*.
	toothbrush ['tu:θˌbrʌʃ]	Zahnbürste	
	a pair of scissors [ə ˌpeər‿əv 'sɪzəz]	Schere	*a pair of scissors* 
	plastic bag [ˌplæstɪk 'bæg]	Plastiktüte	
	spade [speɪd]	Spaten	
	sweets *(only plural)* [swi:ts]	Süßigkeiten	If you eat too many *sweets* you'll get bad teeth!
	match (*pl* matches) [mætʃ, 'mætʃɪz]	Streichholz	This is a box of *matches*. 
	top [tɒp]	oberste(r,s); beste(r, s)	
	rather ['rɑ:ðə]	*hier:* eher, lieber	
A7	waterfall ['wɔ:təˌfɔ:l]	Wasserfall	
A8	imagine [ɪ'mædʒɪn]	sich vorstellen	
	be stranded [bi: 'strændɪd]	gestrandet sein, festsitzen	
	survive [sə'vaɪv]	überleben, am Leben bleiben	
	hut [hʌt]	Hütte	
	message in a bottle [ˌmesɪdʒ‿ɪn‿ə 'bɒtl]	Flaschenpost	
	be cast away [bi: ˌkɑ:st‿ə'weɪ]	gestrandet sein	
	package ['pækɪdʒ]	Paket	
	useful ['ju:sfl]	nützlich, praktisch	
A9	heart [hɑ:t]	Herz	
	castle ['kɑ:sl]	Burg, Schloss	My home is my *castle*.
	east [i:st]	Osten	*east* ≠ *west*
	west [west]	Westen	
	acrostic [ə'krɒstɪk]	Akrostichon	
B1	**bullying** ['bʊliɪŋ]	Mobbing	
	share [ʃeə]	teilen; *hier:* weitergeben	
	since [sɪns]	seit	
	receive [rɪ'si:v]	erhalten, bekommen	
	beat up [ˌbi:t‿'ʌp]	verprügeln	
	desperate ['desprət]	verzweifelt	
	remember [rɪ'membə]	*hier:* daran denken	
	fault [fɔ:lt]	Schuld	
	like this/that [ˌlaɪk 'ðɪs/'ðæt]	solche(r, s)	
	love [lʌv]	Liebe	A *secret* is something you don't tell or show anybody.
	secret ['si:krət]	Geheimnis	
	go out with sb *(informal)* [ˌgəʊ‿'aʊt wɪð ˌsʌmbədi]	mit jdm gehen	
	keep a secret [ˌki:p‿ə 'si:krət]	für sich behalten	*keep a secret* = not tell anybody
	break up [ˌbreɪk‿'ʌp]	sich trennen, Schluss machen	When a pair *breaks up* they stop *going out with each other*.

	a way out [ə ˌweɪ‿ˈaʊt]	Ausweg	
	concentrate (on) [ˈkɒnsnˌtreɪt]	sich konzentrieren (auf)	
	schoolwork [ˈskuːlˌwɜːk]	Schularbeiten	
	decision [dɪˈsɪʒn]	Entscheidung	
	solve [sɒlv]	lösen	
	cool down [ˌkuːl ˈdaʊn]	abkühlen, sich beruhigen	
	sort out [ˌsɔːt‿ˈaʊt]	ordnen, sortieren	
	shy [ʃaɪ]	schüchtern	
	go red [ˌgəʊ ˈred]	rot werden	
	take a (deep) breath [ˌteɪk‿ə ˈbreθ]	(tief) Luft holen	
	stay cool [ˌsteɪ ˈkuːl]	ruhig bleiben	She's *going out with him.*
	girlfriend [ˈgɜːlˌfrend]	Freundin *(Partnerin)*	She's his *girlfriend.*

	reaction [riˈækʃn]	Reaktion	
	third [θɜːd]	dritte (r,s)	
	advice [ədˈvaɪs]	Rat	
	quite [kwaɪt]	ziemlich	
	helpful [ˈhelpfl]	hilfreich, nützlich; hilfsbereit	
	lover [ˈlʌvə]	Liebhaber/in	
	useful [ˈjuːsfl]	nützlich, praktisch	
	sad [sæd]	traurig	He is *sad.*

	flat [flæt]	(Etagen)wohnung, Mietwohnung	
	walk the dog [ˌwɔːk ðə ˈdɒg]	den Hund ausführen	
	leave [liːv]	*hier:* zurücklassen	
B2	engineer [ˌendʒɪˈnɪə]	Ingenieur/in	
	be out of work [biː‿ˌaʊt‿əv ˈwɜːk]	arbeitslos sein	
	do the cooking [duː ðə ˈkʊkɪŋ]	kochen	His job is to *do the cooking.*

	check [tʃek]	*hier:* nachsehen (in)	
	normally [ˈnɔːmli]	normalerweise	
	early shift [ˈɜːli ˌʃɪft]	Frühschicht	
	fill up [ˌfɪl‿ˈʌp]	(voll) füllen, *hier:* auffüllen	
	cash desk [ˈkæʃ ˌdesk]	Kasse	She's sitting at the *cash desk.*

	give up [ˌgɪv‿ˈʌp]	aufgeben	
	trainee nurse [ˌtreɪniː ˈnɜːs]	Krankenpflegeschüler/in	
	hospital [ˈhɒspɪtl]	Krankenhaus	
	shift [ʃɪft]	Schicht	*girlfriend ≠ boyfriend*
	boyfriend [ˈbɔɪˌfrend]	Freund *(Partner)*	
	worried [ˈwʌrid]	beunruhigt, besorgt	
	go back [ˌgəʊ ˈbæk]	zurückgehen	She is *ballet* dancing.
	ballet [ˈbæleɪ]	Ballett	
	school report [ˌskuːl rɪˈpɔːt]	(Schul)zeugnis	
	fact [fækt]	Tatsache	
	member [ˈmembə]	Angehörige(r), Mitglied	

B3	ask for help [ˌɑːsk fə ˈhelp]	um Hilfe bitten
B4	world [wɜːld]	Welt
	biology [baɪˈɒlədʒi]	Biologie
	do [duː]	*hier als Verstärkung*
	trigonometry [ˌtrɪgəˈnɒmətri]	Trigonometrie
	algebra [ˈældʒɪbrə]	Algebra
	slide rule [ˈslaɪd ˌruːl]	Rechenschieber
	claim [kleɪm]	behaupten
	be an A-student *(AE)* [biː‿ən ˈeɪ ˌstjuːdnt]	ein/e Einserschüler/in sein
	for [fɔː]	denn
	by [baɪ]	*hier:* indem
P2	parrot [ˈpærət]	Papagei
P4	opposite [ˈɒpəzɪt]	Gegenteil
	unfriendly [ʌnˈfrenli]	unfreundlich
	combine [kəmˈbaɪn]	verbinden, kombinieren
P5	scramble [ˈskræmbl]	durcheinander bringen
	unscramble [ʌnˈskræmbl]	wieder ordnen
P6	far away [ˌfɑːr‿əˈweɪ]	fern; weit entfernt
	take turns [ˌteɪk ˈtɜːnz]	sich abwechseln
P8	is/are stressed [ɪz/ɑː ˈstrest]	wird/werden betont
	syllable [ˈsɪləbəl]	Silbe
	American [əˈmerɪkən]	Amerikaner/in; amerikanisch

You learn something about animals and plants in *biology*.

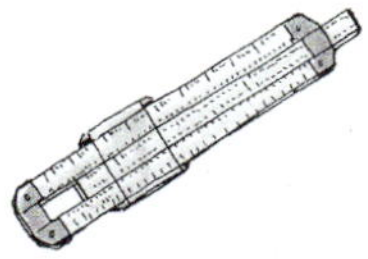

slide rule

If you *are an A-student*, you are very good at school.

Scrambled words
Arbeite mit einem/r Partner/in. Schreibe Wörter auf ein Blatt Papier. Schreibe anschließend die Buchstaben der Wörter in verdrehter Reihenfolge auf *(scrambled words)*. Dein/e Partner/in muss die „neuen Wörter" buchstabieren. Dann muss er/sie das ursprüngliche Wort erraten. Wenn er/sie es schafft, ist er/sie an der Reihe. Ihr könnt so eure Rechtschreibung und das englische Alphabet trainieren!

Die Vokabeln aus den OPTIONAL-Teilen findest du im englisch-deutschen Dictionary auf den Seiten 193 – 217.

Theme 5 ● The world of science

I	**world** [wɜːld]	Welt
A1	go up [ˌgəʊ‿ˈʌp]	hoch fahren
	north [nɔːθ]	Norden; *hier:* in nördliche Richtung
	Have you? [hæv ˈjuː]	*hier:* Und du?
	play sb [ˈpleɪ ˌsʌmbədi]	gegen jdn spielen
	check out *(informal)* [ˌtʃek‿ˈaʊt]	sich ansehen
	industry [ˈɪndəstri]	Industrie
	flyer (= flier) [ˈflaɪə]	Flugblatt; *hier:* Broschüre
	ticket inspector [ˈtɪkɪt‿ɪnˌspektə]	(Fahrkarten)kontrolleur/in
	ticket [ˈtɪkɪt]	(Fahr)karte
	any more [ˌeni ˈmɔː]	noch (mehr)
	Here you are! [ˌhɪə juː‿ˈɑː]	Hier, bitte!, Bitte schön!

north ≠ south

Excuse me, sir, but I've got a *ticket* for this seat.

	(for) free [friː]	gratis, umsonst	Buy two, get one *free*!
	though *(nachgestellt)* [ðəʊ]	(je)doch	The food is very good. The dessert is even better *though*.
	power ['paʊə]	*hier:* Strom, Elektrizität	
	hall [hɔːl]	Halle, Saal	A *hall* is a large room.
	cotton mill ['kɒtn mɪl]	Baumwollspinnerei	
	meet [miːt]	*hier:* abholen	
	journey ['dʒɜːni]	Reise; Fahrt	
	shall [ʃæl]	sollen	
	far [fɑː]	weit	
	about [ə'baʊt]	ungefähr	
	get [get]	*hier:* nehmen	
	train [treɪn]	Zug	*train*
A2	welcome (to) ['welkəm]	willkommen (in)	
	decide [dɪ'saɪd]	sich entscheiden; beschließen	
	visit ['vɪzɪt]	Besuch	
	brochure ['brəʊʃə]	Broschüre	In a *brochure* you can find information.
	crawl [krɔːl]	krabbeln; kriechen	Babies *crawl* before they walk.
	underground [ˌʌndə'graʊnd]	*hier:* unter die Erde	
	spooky ['spuːki]	unheimlich, gespenstisch	
	sewer ['suːə]	Abwasserkanal	
	smell [smel]	Geruch	
	worse [wɜːs]	schlechter; schlimmer	
	locomotive [ˌləʊkə'məʊtɪv]	Lokomotive	
	start [stɑːt]	*hier:* losfahren	
	noisy ['nɔɪzi]	laut	*noisy* = very loud
	cotton ['kɒtn]	Baumwoll-, Baumwolle	
	cover ['kʌvə]	bedecken, abdecken; *hier:* zuhalten	
	ghost [gəʊst]	Geist	
	famous ['feɪməs]	berühmt	
	scientist ['saɪəntɪst]	Wissenschaftler/in	The teacher *is explaining* something to the class.
	explain [ɪk'spleɪn]	erklären	
	discovery [dɪ'skʌvri]	Entdeckung	
	invention [ɪn'venʃn]	Erfindung	
	see [siː]	ansehen, anschauen	
	aeroplane (= plane) ['eərəˌpleɪn]	Flugzeug	
	designed [dɪ'zaɪnd]	entworfen, konzipiert	
	look like ['lʊk ˌlaɪk]	aussehen	
	be interested in [biː‿'ɪntrəstɪd‿ɪn]	sich interessieren für	
	It sounds fun. [ɪt ˌsaʊndz 'fʌn]	Es klingt gut.	
A4	everyday life [ˌevrideɪ 'laɪf]	Alltagsleben	
	Velcro® ['velkrəʊ]	Klettverschluss	
	light bulb ['laɪt ˌbʌlb]	Glühbirne	This is a *light bulb*.
	TV set [ˌtiː 'viː ˌset]	Fernsehgerät	
	decide [dɪ'saɪd]	entscheiden, bestimmen	
A5	**electricity** [ɪˌlek'trɪsəti]	Elektrizität, Strom	
	imagine [ɪ'mædʒɪn]	sich vorstellen	

	candle ['kændl]	Kerze	
A6	give [gɪv]	*hier:* nennen, angeben	
	no longer [nəʊ 'lɒŋgə]	nicht mehr	*Candles are no longer in use* very often.
	be in use [bi:‿ɪn‿'ju:s]	in Gebrauch sein	
LL4	Viking ['vaɪkɪŋ]	Wikinger/in; wikingisch	
	Tourist Information Centre [ˌtʊərɪst ˌɪnfə'meɪʃn ˌsentə]	Touristeninformation	A *leaflet* is a sheet of paper that gives you information about something.
A7	get there ['get ðeə]	hinkommen	
	leaflet ['li:flət]	Prospekt	
	English-speaking ['ɪŋglɪʃˌspi:kɪŋ]	englischsprachig	to visit / *visitor* / a visit
	visitor ['vɪzɪtə]	Besucher/in, Gast	
	exhibition [ˌeksɪ'bɪʃn]	Ausstellung	
B1	amazing [ə'meɪzɪŋ]	erstaunlich, toll	
	day out [ˌdeɪ‿'aʊt]	Tagesausflug	
	report [rɪ'pɔ:t]	Bericht	*mention* = say something but not discuss it
	mention ['menʃn]	erwähnen	
	hot tip [ˌhɒt‿'tɪp]	heißer Tipp	
	hard [hɑ:d]	*hier:* schwierig	*"Hard"* can mean "difficult".
	terrific [tə'rɪfɪk]	gewaltig, ungeheuer	
	water-powered ['wɔ:tə ˌpaʊəd]	*von Wasserkraft angetriebene(r/s)*	
	steam-powered ['sti:m ˌpaʊəd]	*von Dampf angetriebene(r/s)*	
	engine ['endʒɪn]	Maschine, Motor	
	were powered [wɜ: 'paʊəd]	wurden angetrieben	
	even ['i:vn]	*hier:* (sogar) noch	
	spinning machine ['spɪnɪŋ məˌʃi:n]	Spinnmaschine	With the help of *spinning* and *weaving machines* you can make clothes.
	weaving machine ['wi:vɪŋ məˌʃi:n]	Webmaschine	
	after that ['ɑ:ftə ðæt]	danach	
	air [eə]	Luft	
	ride [raɪd]	Fahrt	
	steam locomotive ['sti:m ləʊkəˌməʊtɪv]	Dampflokomotive	
	communications *(only plural)* [kəˌmju:nɪ'keɪʃnz]	Fernmeldewesen, Telekommunikation	
	section ['sekʃn]	Teil; Abteilung	
	have a look round [ˌhæv‿ə lʊk 'raʊnd]	sich umsehen	
	huge [hju:dʒ]	riesig, riesengroß	
	called [kɔ:ld]	*hier:* genannt	
	The computer was built in … [ðə kəm'pju:tə wəz 'bɪlt‿ɪn]	Der Computer wurde … gebaut.	
	main [meɪn]	Haupt-	
	be good fun [bi: ˌgʊd 'fʌn]	viel Spaß machen	I like *all sorts of* music: punk, rock and pop.
	all sorts of [ɔ:l 'sɔ:ts‿əv]	alle möglichen	

	experiment [ɪk'sperɪmənt]	Experiment, Versuch	
	deep [di:p]	tief	*deep* ≠ high
	real [rɪəl]	wirklich, echt	Museums can be *real* fun!
	space [speɪs]	Raum; *hier:* Weltraum	
	not even [nɒt 'i:vn]	noch nicht einmal	
	till (= until) [tɪl]	bis	
	whole [həʊl]	ganz, gesamt	
	pay [peɪ]	(be)zahlen	
	get into [ˌget‿'ɪntu:]	*hier:* hineinkommen	
B2	fantastic [fæn'tæstɪk]	fantastisch, super	
	shower ['ʃaʊə]	Dusche	Ken is having a *shower.*
	cyclist ['saɪklɪst]	Radfahrer/in	A *cyclist* rides a bike.
	exercise ['eksəsaɪz]	Bewegung, Übung	
	pedal power ['pedl ˌpaʊə]	Pedalkraft	
	pump [pʌmp]	pumpen	
	the … the … [ðə ðə]	je …, desto …	
	pedal ['pedl]	in die Pedale treten	
	eagle ['i:gl]	Adler	
	power ['paʊə]	*hier:* Kraft, Stärke	She'*s pumping* water.
	flying machine ['flaɪɪŋ məˌʃi:n]	Flugmaschine	
	century ['sentʃəri]	Jahrhundert	We are living in the 21st *century.*
	fix [fɪks]	festmachen	
	metal ['metl]	aus Metall	
	get off the ground *(informal)* [ˌget‿ɒf ðə 'graʊnd]	abheben; *hier:* verwirklicht werden	If an idea *gets off the ground* you can make it come true.
	parachute jump ['pærəʃu:t‿ˌdʒʌmp]	Fallschirmsprung	
	Frenchman ['frentʃmən]	Franzose	
	metre ['mi:tə]	Meter	100 centimetres = 1 *metre*
	wide [waɪd]	breit	
	parachute ['pærəˌʃu:t]	Fallschirm	
	hot-air balloon [ˌhɒt‿'eə bəˌlu:n]	Heißluftballon	He's jumping out of a *hot-air balloon.*
	the first ever *(informal)* [ðə ˌfɜ:st‿'evə]	der/die/das Allererste	
	need [ni:d]	*hier:* müssen	
	hole [həʊl]	Loch	
	top [tɒp]	*hier:* Spitze	*top*
	swing [swɪŋ]	(hin- und her)schwingen; sich drehen	
	wildly ['waɪldli]	*hier:* stark	
	be sick [bi: 'sɪk]	sich erbrechen; sich elend fühlen	He *is being sick.*
	land [lænd]	landen	
	safely ['seɪfli]	sicher, gefahrlos	
	travel ['trævl]	reisen; fahren	*travel* = to go on a journey
	land [lænd]	Land	
	trouble ['trʌbl]	Ärger, Problem	
	like a fish out of water [laɪk‿ə ˌfɪʃ‿aʊt‿əv 'wɔ:tə]	wie ein Fisch auf dem Trockenen	

	kph (= kilometres per hour) [ˌkeɪ piː‿ˈeɪtʃ (= kɪˌlɒmɪtəz pɜr‿ˈaʊə)]	km/h
	not exactly [nɒt ɪgˈzækli]	nicht gerade
	best-seller [ˌbestˈselə]	Bestseller *(Artikel mit großem Verkaufserfolg)*
	invent [ɪnˈvent]	erfinden
	inventor [ɪnˈventə]	Erfinder/in
B3	flop [flɒp]	Flop, Reinfall, Pleite
	reporter [rɪˈpɔːtə]	Reporter/in
B4	cleaning [ˈkliːnɪŋ]	Reinigungs-
	skate [skeɪt]	Schlittschuh, Rollschuh, Inliner
	biscuit [ˈbɪskɪt]	Keks
	baker [ˈbeɪkə]	Bäcker/in
	X-ray [ˈeksreɪ]	Röntgen-
	practical [ˈpræktɪkl]	praktisch
	have fun [hæv‿ˈfʌn]	Spaß haben
	just the thing [ˌdʒʌst ðə ˈθɪŋ]	genau das Richtige
	following [ˈfɒləʊɪŋ]	folgende(r,s)
	close [kləʊs]	schließen, zumachen
	lamp [læmp]	Lampe
	shrink [ʃrɪŋk]	schrumpfen
	grow [grəʊ]	wachsen, größer werden
	lunchbox [ˈlʌntʃˌbɒks]	Brotdose
	toilet roll [ˈtɔɪlət rəʊl]	Rolle Toilettenpapier
B5	topic [ˈtɒpɪk]	Thema
	have a vote [ˌhæv‿ə ˈvəʊt]	abstimmen
	original [əˈrɪdʒnəl]	originell, außergewöhnlich
B6	(pair of) trousers [ˈtraʊzəz]	Hose
	work [wɜːk]	*hier:* funktionieren
P1	be worth a visit [biː ˌwɜːθ‿ə ˈvɪzɪt]	einen Besuch wert sein
	feature [ˈfiːtʃə]	Merkmal, Eigenschaft
P2	missing [ˈmɪsɪŋ]	*hier:* fehlend
	vowel [ˈvaʊəl]	Vokal, Selbstlaut
P3	steam train [ˈstiːm ˌtreɪn]	Dampflok
	anything [ˈeniˌθɪŋ]	(irgend)etwas
P4	rhyme [raɪm]	Reim-
	satellite [ˈsætəlaɪt]	Satellit
P6	past participle [ˌpɑːst ˈpɑːtɪsɪpl]	Partizip Perfekt
	power [ˈpaʊə]	antreiben
P7	teddy bear [ˈtedi ˌbeə]	Teddybär
	open [ˈəʊpən]	*hier:* eröffnen
P8	passenger [ˈpæsɪndʒə]	Fahrgast, Reisende/r

Gedächtnistraining
Schreibe zehn Vokabeln und ihre Übersetzung auf ein Blatt Papier. Auf die Rückseite schreibst du nur die englischen Wörter untereinander. Nimm dir drei Minuten Zeit, dir die Vokabeln und ihre Bedeutung einzuprägen. Drehe das Blatt um und schreibe so viele Übersetzungen wie möglich aus dem Gedächtnis auf. Probiere auch eine Variante: Schreibe auf die Rückseite des Blattes nur die deutsche Bedeutung und ergänze später die englischen Vokabeln.

close ≠ open

He watches the plant *grow*.

steam train

"gone" is the *past participle* of "go".

A *passenger* is someone who travels on a plane or train.

Die Vokabeln aus den OPTIONAL-Teilen findest du im englisch-deutschen Dictionary auf den Seiten 193–217.

Theme 6 ● Cash in hand

I	**cash** [kæʃ]	Bargeld	*cash* = money
	cash in hand [ˌkæʃ‿ɪn ˈhænd]	Guthaben	
A1	mark [mɑːk]	Note, Zensur	Pupils are happy about good *marks.*
	extra [ˈekstrə]	zusätzlich	
	class trip [ˈklɑːs ˌtrɪp]	Klassenfahrt	
A2	**be short of money** *(informal)* [biː ˌʃɔːt‿əv ˈmʌni]	knapp bei Kasse sein	When you don't have much money left then you*'re short of cash.*
	earn [ɜːn]	verdienen	When you *do a paper round,* you take newspapers to the people's houses.
	do a paper round [duː‿ə ˈpeɪpə‿ˌraʊnd]	Zeitungen austragen	
	babysit [ˈbeɪbiˌsɪt]	babysitten	
	take the dog for a walk [ˌteɪk ðə ˈdɒg fəːr‿ə ˈwɔːk]	den Hund ausführen	
	do gardening [duː ˈgɑːdnɪŋ]	Gartenarbeit machen	
A4	car boot [ˌkɑː ˈbuːt]	Kofferraum	
	car boot sale [ˌkɑː ˈbuːt seɪl]	*Verkauf pers. Gegenstände aus einem Kofferraum*	
	conversation [ˌkɒnvəˈseɪʃn]	Gespräch, Unterhaltung	
	France [frɑːns]	Frankreich	Paris is in *France.*
	vase [vɑːz]	(Blumen)vase	
	customer [ˈkʌstəmə]	Kunde/Kundin	
	detective story [dɪˈtektɪv ˌstɔːri]	Kriminalroman	
	between you and me [bɪˌtwiːn ˌjuː‿ən ˈmiː]	unter uns gesagt	
	be joking [biː ˈdʒəʊkɪŋ]	Spaß machen	They *are joking.*
	Spanish [ˈspænɪʃ]	spanisch	
	painter [ˈpeɪntə]	(Kunst)maler/in	
	be worth [biː ˈwɜːθ]	wert sein	
	special offer [ˌspeʃl‿ˈɒfə]	Sonderangebot	
	expert [ˈekspɜːt]	Experte/Expertin	
	You never know. [juː ˌnevə ˈnəʊ]	*etwa:* Das kann man nie wissen.	
A5	definition [ˌdefəˈnɪʃn]	Definition, Erklärung	
	person [ˈpɜːsn]	Person, Mensch	
	paint [peɪnt]	malen	
A6	hockey stick [ˈhɒki ˌstɪk]	Hockeyschläger	
	(pair of) trousers [ˈtraʊzəz]	Hose	
	customer [ˈkʌstəmə]	Kunde/Kundin	
	in the end [ɪn ðiː‿ˈend]	letzten Endes; schließlich	
A7	buying and selling [ˌbaɪɪŋ ənd ˈselɪŋ]	Kaufen und Verkaufen, An- und Verkauf	
	seller [ˈselə]	Verkäufer/in	
	It's … £ (pounds). [ˌɪts … ˈpaʊndz]	Es kostet … Pfund.	
	anything [ˈeniˌθɪŋ]	(irgend)etwas	*anything* ≠ nothing

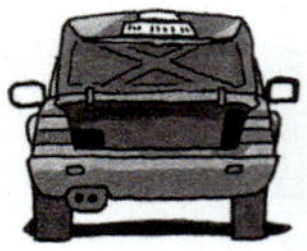
car boot

car boot sale

They *are joking.*

customer *seller*

	work [wɜːk]	*hier:* funktionieren, laufen
	What's on offer? [ˌwɒts‿ɒn‿ˈɒfə]	Was ist im Angebot?
	practise [ˈpræktɪs]	üben
	pink [pɪŋk]	rosa, pink
	boot [buːt]	Stiefel
	a pair of skis [ə ˌpeər‿əv ˈskiːz]	ein Paar Skier
	model train [ˌmɒdl ˈtreɪn]	Modelleisenbahn
A8	pick [pɪk]	aussuchen
	ground [graʊnd]	(Erd)boden; Erde
A9	bill [bɪl]	Rechnung
	ain't it (= isn't it) [ˈeɪnt‿ɪt]	ist es nicht
	single [ˈsɪŋgl]	einzige(r, s)
	be left [biː ˈleft]	übrig bleiben
	That's too bad! [ˌðæts ˌtuː ˈbæd]	Das ist wirklich schade!
	if I got me *(informal)* [ɪf aɪ ˈgɒt miː]	wenn ich bekommen könnte
	wealthy [ˈwelθi]	reich, wohlhabend
	fool around *(informal)* [ˌfuːl‿əˈraʊnd]	*hier:* seine Zeit verschwenden
	have a ball *(informal)* [ˌhæv‿ə ˈbɔːl]	Spaß haben, sich bestens amüsieren
	get sb off one's mind *(informal)* [ˌget ˌsʌmbədi‿ɒf wʌnz ˈmaɪnd]	sich jdn aus dem Kopf schlagen
	happen to be [ˈhæpən tə biː]	zufällig sein
	free *(informal)* [friː]	frei, *hier:* nicht gebunden
	bet [bet]	wetten
	fancy sb *(informal)* [ˈfænsi ˌsʌmbədi]	auf jdn stehen
	fortune [ˈfɔːtʃən]	Vermögen
B1	marathon [ˈmærəθn]	Marathon(lauf)
	runner [ˈrʌnə]	Läufer/in
	once a year [ˌwʌns ə ˈjɪə]	einmal im/pro Jahr
	closed [kləʊzd]	geschlossen, zu; *hier:* gesperrt
	mile [maɪl]	Meile *(= 1,609 km)*
	most [məʊst]	die meisten
	sponsor [ˈspɒnsə]	Sponsor/in
	each [iːtʃ]	jede(r, s)
	the more … the more … [ðə ˈmɔː ðə ˈmɔː]	je mehr …, desto …
	charity [ˈtʃærəti]	Wohltätigkeitsorganisation
B2	end [end]	enden
	ready [ˈredi]	fertig, bereit
	point [pɔɪnt]	Punkt; *hier:* Komma
	take place [ˌteɪk ˈpleɪs]	stattfinden
	starting point [ˈstɑːtɪŋ ˌpɔɪnt]	Ausgangspunkt

Vergiss es einfach
Hast du manchmal Probleme, dir bestimmte Wörter zu merken? Sind es immer wieder dieselben Vokabeln, die dir nicht einfallen? Dann probier es doch mal mit Vergessen! Das geht so: Suche fünf oder sechs schwierige Wörter aus, die du unbedingt vergessen willst. Schreibe sie auf mehrere Zettel und hänge sie neben dein Bett, über deinen Schreibtisch oder an den Badezimmerspiegel. Lies sie bei jeder Gelegenheit durch, damit du dich daran erinnerst, welche Wörter du unbedingt vergessen willst.

Charlie can't get Lisa *off his mind*.

He *fancies* her. That's why he gives her a kiss.

closed ≠ open

A *mile* is longer than a kilometre.

A yard is 91 *point* 44 cms long.

	yard [jɑːd]	Yard (= 91,44 cm)	
	kilometre [kɪˈlɒmɪtə]	Kilometer	1000 metres = 1 *kilometre*
	elite [ɪˈliːt]	Elite	
	world record [ˌwɜːld ˈrekɔːd]	Weltrekord	
	mass [mæs]	Masse; *hier:* Massen-	
	wheelchair [ˈwiːlˌtʃeə]	Rollstuhl	a *wheelchair athlete*
	athlete [ˈæθliːt]	Athlet/in	
	from all over the world [frəm‿ˌɔːl‿əʊvə ðə ˈwɜːld]	aus der ganzen Welt	
	trust [trʌst]	*hier:* Stiftung	
	map [mæp]	(Land)karte	
	route [ruːt]	Strecke, Route	
B3	school newspaper [ˌskuːl ˈnjuːzˌpeɪpə]	Schülerzeitung	
LL5	fundraising [ˈfʌndreɪzɪŋ]	*Sammeln von Geld/Spenden*	
P1	You're joking! [jʊə ˈdʒəʊkɪŋ]	Das ist doch nicht dein Ernst!	
P2	the odd one out [ðiˌ‿ɒd wʌn‿ˈaʊt]	*das Wort, das nicht zu den anderen passt*	
	ending [ˈendɪŋ]	Ende; *hier:* Endung	
	fit [fɪt]	passen	
	do the dishes [ˌduː ðə ˈdɪʃɪz]	(ab)spülen, abwaschen	
	second-hand [ˌsekənd ˈhænd]	gebraucht	*second-hand* = not new
P6	put on [ˌpʊt‿ˈɒn]	*hier:* hängen	
	wall [wɔːl]	Wand, Mauer	
P7	figure out sth *(informal)* [ˌfɪgər‿ˈaʊt ˌsʌmθɪŋ]	etw herausfinden	If you *figure out something*, you find it out.

Die Vokabeln aus den OPTIONAL-Teilen findest du im englisch-deutschen Dictionary auf den Seiten 193 – 217.

Theme 7 ● Art and media

A1	**group** [gruːp]	(Musik)gruppe	*group* = band
A2	horror movie [ˈhɒrə ˌmuːvi]	Horrorfilm	
	musician [mjuˈzɪʃn]	Musiker/in	George Clooney is an *actor*, Julia Roberts is an *actress*.
	actor/actress [ˈæktə/ˈæktrəs]	Schauspieler/in	
	be born [biː ˈbɔːn]	geboren werden	
	tattoo [tæˈtuː]	Tattoo, Tätowierung	
	guardian angel [ˌgɑːdiən‿ˈeɪndʒl]	Schutzengel	
	shoulder [ˈʃəʊldə]	Schulter	

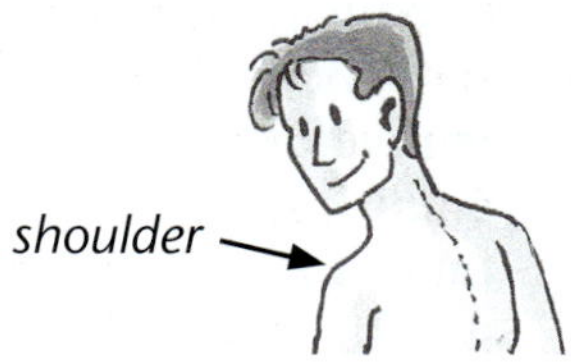

	What goes around comes around. [wɒt ˌɡəʊz‿əˌraʊnd ˈkʌmz‿əˌraʊnd]	Alles rächt sich früher oder später.	
	wrist [rɪst]	Handgelenk	He is reaching for the *stars*.
	star [stɑː]	Stern	
	bar code [ˈbɑː ˌkəʊd]	Strichcode	
	album [ˈælbəm]	(Musik)album	
	stupid [ˈstjuːpɪd]	dumm, blöd	*stupid* ≠ clever
	sober [ˈsəʊbə]	nüchtern	
	love song [ˈlʌv ˌsɒŋ]	Liebeslied	
	supporter [səˈpɔːtə]	Anhänger/in	
	animal rights *(only plural)* [ˌænɪml ˈraɪts]	*das Recht der Tiere auf Leben und artgerechte Haltung*	
	organization [ˌɔːɡənaɪˈzeɪʃn]	Organisation	*organization* = a group of people who are interested in the same topic
	strict [strɪkt]	streng	
	vegetarian [ˌvedʒəˈteəriən]	Vegetarier/in	Someone who doesn't eat meat or fish is a *vegetarian*.
	guitar [ɡɪˈtɑː]	Gitarre	He's playing the *guitar*. 
	surprising [səˈpraɪzɪŋ]	überraschend	
	fact sheet [ˈfækt ˌʃiːt]	Informationsblatt	
A5	walk down the street [ˌwɔːk daʊn ðə ˈstriːt]	die Straße entlanggehen	
	verse [vɜːs]	Strophe, Vers	
	present [prɪˈzent]	*hier:* vortragen	
	help [help]	Hilfe	
A6	pop group [ˈpɒp ˌɡruːp]	Popgruppe	A *pop group* makes pop music.
	just [dʒʌst]	*hier:* gerade (eben)	
	come back [ˌkʌm ˈbæk]	zurückkommen	*come back* = return
	concert [ˈkɒnsət]	Konzert	
	exhausted [ɪɡˈzɔːstɪd]	erschöpft	*exhausted* = very tired
	sb could do with sth *(informal)* [ˌsʌmbədi kʊd‿ˈduː wɪð ˌsʌmθɪŋ]	jd könnte etw gebrauchen/vertragen	
	book [bʊk]	reservieren, buchen	
	gig [ɡɪɡ]	Gig *(Auftritt einer Band)*	
	You're kidding! *(informal)* [jɔː ˈkɪdɪŋ]	Das ist doch nicht dein Ernst!	*You're kidding*! = You're joking!
	exam [ɪɡˈzæm]	Prüfung	
	professional [prəˈfeʃnəl]	Profi	
	amateur [ˈæmətə]	Amateur/in	
	rest [rest]	(Ruhe)pause	
	just [dʒʌst]	nur, bloß, einfach	I cut the cake
	half (*pl* halves) [hɑːf, hɑːvz]	Hälfte	in two *halves*.
	equipment [ɪˈkwɪpmənt]	Ausrüstung, Ausstattung	
	kid [kɪd]	Kind, Jugendliche(r)	
	free ticket [ˌfriː ˈtɪkɪt]	Freikarte	
	rehearsal [rɪˈhɜːsl]	Probe	
	speaker [ˈspiːkə]	*hier:* Lautsprecher	There's very loud music
	God! [ɡɒd]	Oh (mein) Gott!	coming from the *speakers*.
	be knackered *(informal)* [biː ˈnækəd]	kaputt/fix und fertig sein	*be knackered* = be very tired

	stuff [stʌf]	Zeug	
A7	**speak (to/with)** [spiːk]	sprechen, reden (mit)	*to speak* = to talk
	We could do with … [ˌwiː kəd ˈduː wɪð]	Wir könnten … gebrauchen.	*We could do with …* = We need …
B1	**What's on?** [ˌwɒts‿ˈɒn]	Was läuft? Was geht ab?	
	expect [ɪkˈspekt]	erwarten, mit etwas rechnen	
	skim through [ˈskɪm θruː]	überfliegen	
	advert (= advertisement) [ˈædvɜːt, ədˈvɜːtɪsmənt]	Anzeige, Inserat	
	cookery [ˈkʊkri]	Koch-	
	office [ˈɒfɪs]	Büro	
	fee [fiː]	Gebühr	
	the place to go [ðə ˌpleɪs tə ˈgəʊ]	*etwa: hier ist man genau richtig*	
	of all ages [əv ˈɔːl‿ˌeɪdʒɪz]	aller Altersstufen	
	maximum [ˈmæksɪməm]	maximal, Höchst-	
	bookshop [ˈbʊkˌʃɒp]	Buchladen	A *bookshop* is a shop where you can buy books.
	staff [stɑːf]	Personal, Mitarbeiter	
	adult [ˈædʌlt]	Erwachsene/r	baby → child → teenager → *adult*
	fiction [ˈfɪkʃn]	Erzählliteratur, Roman	
	discount [ˈdɪsˌkaʊnt]	Rabatt, Preisnachlass	
	explore [ɪkˈsplɔː]	erforschen, untersuchen	
	African [ˈæfrɪkən]	Afrikaner/in; afrikanisch	
	historic [hɪˈstɒrɪk]	historisch	*historic* ≠ modern
	Egyptian mummy [iˌdʒɪpʃən ˈmʌmi]	ägyptische Mumie	
	giant [ˈdʒaɪənt]	riesig	
	walrus (*pl* walrus *or* walruses) [ˈwɔːlrəs, ˈwɔːlrəsɪz]	Walross	A *walrus* is a *giant* animal.
	admission [ədˈmɪʃn]	Eintritt	
	childhood [ˈtʃaɪldˌhʊd]	Kindheit	
	rail [reɪl]	Bahn	
	closed [kləʊzd]	geschlossen, zu	
	board game [ˈbɔːd ˌgeɪm]	Brettspiel	
	electronic [ˌelekˈtrɒnɪk]	elektronisch	
	puppet [ˈpʌpɪt]	(Hand)puppe, Marionette	
	former [ˈfɔːmə]	ehemalige(r, s), frühere(r, s)	
	raid [reɪd]	plündern	
	dressing up box [ˌdresɪŋ‿ˈʌp‿ˌbɒks]	Verkleidungskiste	
	pavement artist [ˈpeɪvmənt‿ˌɑːtɪst]	Pflastermaler/in	
	Tate Britain [ˌteɪt ˈbrɪtn]	*Nationalgalerie für britische Kunst*	
	rainforest [ˈreɪnˌfɒrɪst]	Regenwald	
	aged [eɪdʒd]	im Alter von	
	compete (for) [kəmˈpiːt]	wetteifern, (gegen einander) antreten (um)	

Mon = Monday
Tue = Tuesday
Wed = Wednesday
Thur = Thursday
Fri = Friday
Sat = Saturday
Sun = Sunday

They are playing a *board game.*

Max *is exploring* the *rainforest.*

	be child's play [biː ˈtʃaɪəldz ˌpleɪ]	ein Kinderspiel sein	
	fun [fʌn]	lustig	*fun*, funny ≠ sad
	activity [ækˈtɪvəti]	Aktivität, Unternehmung	
	creative [kriˈeɪtɪv]	kreativ, schöpferisch	
	display [dɪˈspleɪ]	Auslage *(Museum)*	
	reduced [riˈdjuːst]	reduziert, heruntergesetzt	discount = *reduced* price
	daily [ˈdeɪli]	jeden Tag, täglich	
	information pack [ˌɪnfəˈmeɪʃn ˌpæk]	Informationspaket	
	sports centre [ˈspɔːts‿ˌsentə]	Sportcenter	
	climbing [ˈklaɪmɪŋ]	Bergsteigen; *hier:* Klettern	He loves *climbing.*
	horse-riding [ˈhɔːsˌraɪdɪŋ]	Reiten	
	netball [ˈnetˌbɔːl]	Korbball	
	gym (= gymnastics) [dʒɪm]	Turnen	
	indoor [ˈɪndɔː]	Innen-; *hier:* Hallen-	outdoor ≠ indoor
	tennis court [ˈtenɪs ˌkɔːt]	Tennisplatz	
	outdoor [ˌaʊtˈdɔː]	Freiluft-	
	all-weather [ˌɔːl ˈweðə]	Allwetter-, wetterfest	
	pitch [pɪtʃ]	(Spiel)feld, Platz	*pitch* = playing field
	group [gruːp]	Gruppen-	
	hire [ˈhaɪə]	Vermietung	
	tournament [ˈtʊənəmənt]	Turnier	
B2	advertising [ˈædvəˌtaɪzɪŋ]	Werbung, Reklame	
	result [rɪˈzʌlt]	Ergebnis	
B3	**English-speaking** [ˈɪŋglɪʃ ˌspiːkɪŋ]	englischsprachig	
	circus [ˈsɜːkəs]	Zirkus	
B4	at the top [ət ðə ˈtɒp]	oben	
	at the bottom [ət ðə ˈbɒtəm]	unten	
	in the centre [ɪn ðə ˈsentə]	im Zentrum, in der Mitte	
	in the picture [ˌɪn ðə ˈpɪktʃə]	auf dem Bild	
	colourful [ˈkʌləfl]	farbenfroh, bunt	
	depressing [dɪˈpresɪŋ]	deprimierend	
	dreamlike [ˈdriːmˌlaɪk]	traumhaft	*dreamlike* = like a dream
	fantastic [fænˈtæstɪk]	fantastisch; *hier:* Fantasie-	
	realistic [ˌrɪəˈlɪstɪk]	realistisch	
	unrealistic [ˌʌnrɪəˈlɪstɪk]	unrealistisch, wirklichkeitsfremd	*unrealistic* ≠ realistic
	agree on [əˈgriː‿ɒn]	sich einigen auf	
B5	feedback [ˈfiːdbæk]	Feedback, Rückmeldung	a *feedback* on something = a kind of reaction to something
P2	gallery [ˈgæləri]	Galerie	
P3	stress [stres]	Betonung, Akzent	
P4	seat [siːt]	(Sitz)platz	The *seats* in the *front row* are very good. The *audience* there can see the actors and musicians well.
	front [frʌnt]	vorderste(r, s)	
	row [rəʊ]	Reihe	
	audience [ˈɔːdiəns]	Publikum	
P5	prefer [priˈfɜː]	vorziehen, bevorzugen	

Was passt zusammen?
Damit du dir all die englischen Verben besser einprägen kannst, versuche doch einmal, sie bestimmten Hauptwörtern zuzuordnen. Zum Beispiel:
clothes: *wear, put on, take off, buy, …*
book: *read, collect, …*
bike: *ride, …*
car: …

P6	idol ['aɪdl]	Idol	For many teenagers, pop stars or actors are *idols*.
	tough [tʌf]	robust, zäh	

Die Vokabeln aus den OPTIONAL-Teilen findest du im englisch-deutschen Dictionary auf den Seiten 193–217.

Theme 8 ● Going places

I	go places ['gə ˌpleɪsɪz]	Ausflüge machen, herumreisen	
A2	**travelling** ['trævlɪŋ]	Reisen	
	Russia ['rʌʃə]	Russland	
	bus driver ['bʌs ˌdraɪvə]	Busfahrer/in	
	flight [flaɪt]	Flug, Fliegen	
	Moscow ['mɒskəʊ]	Moskau	He delivers newspapers to *raise money*.
	take [teɪk]	*hier:* dauern	
A3	raise money [ˌreɪz 'mʌni]	Geld aufbringen	
	Canada ['kænədə]	Kanada	
	the Niagara Falls *(only plural)* [ðə naɪˌægərə 'fɔːlz]	die Niagarafälle	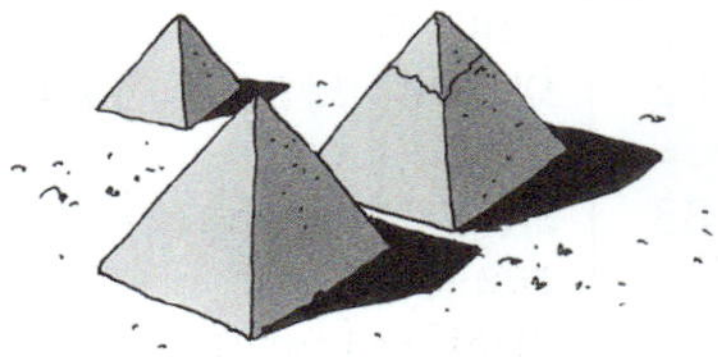
	wall [wɔːl]	*hier:* die Chinesische Mauer	
	anywhere ['eniˌweə]	überall	
	Cairo ['kaɪərəʊ]	Kairo	
	pyramid ['pɪrəmɪd]	Pyramide	These are *pyramids*.
A4	phrase book ['freɪz ˌbʊk]	Sprachführer	If you go to a *foreign* country and don't speak the language, a *phrase book* is useful.
	foreign ['fɒrɪn]	ausländisch, fremd	
	typical ['tɪpɪkl]	typisch; charakteristisch	
	ask for directions [ˌɑːsk fə dɪ'rekʃnz]	nach dem Weg fragen	
	give (sb) directions [gɪv dɪ'rekʃnz]	(jdm) den Weg beschreiben	
	get [get]	*hier:* kommen	
	make friends [meɪk 'frendz]	sich anfreunden, Freundschaften schließen	
	ask for help [ˌɑːsk‿fə 'help]	um Hilfe bitten	She's not just *asking for help*, she's shouting for help.
	way [weɪ]	Weg	
A5	camp [kæmp]	(Zelt)lager	
	web page ['webˌpeɪdʒ]	Webseite, Internetseite	A *web page* is a page that you can read on a website.
	What is … about? [ˌwɒt‿ɪs ə'baʊt]	Worum geht es in/bei …?	
	for real *(informal)* [fə‿'rɪəl]	echt, wahr	
	click [klɪk]	(an)klicken	
	totally ['təʊtli]	völlig, total	*totally* = completely

	awesome *(AE, informal)* ['ɔ:sm]	spitze, super	
	packed with ['pækt wɪð]	voll gepackt mit	
	excitement [ɪk'saɪtmənt]	Aufregung	
	entertainment [ˌentə'teɪnmənt]	Unterhaltung	
	sailing ['seɪlɪŋ]	Segeln	She loves *sailing*.
	archery ['ɑ:tʃəri]	Bogenschießen	
	canoeing [kə'nu:ɪŋ]	Paddeln, Kanufahren	*Canoeing*, *archery* and *sailing* are outdoor sports.
	offer ['ɒfə]	anbieten, bieten	
	all-inclusive [ɔ:l ɪn'klu:sɪv]	pauschal	
	take part (in) [ˌteɪk 'pɑ:t]	teilnehmen (an)	
A6	water sports *(only plural)* ['wɔ:tə ˌspɔ:tz]	Wassersport	If you do *water sports* you must be able to swim.
	both [bəʊθ]	beide	
A7	excited [ɪk'saɪtɪd]	aufgeregt, begeistert	
	glad [glæd]	glücklich	*glad* = happy
	feel homesick [fi:l 'həʊmˌsɪk]	Heimweh haben	When you miss home while you are away you *feel homesick*.
B1	type [taɪp]	Art	
	traveller ['trævlə]	Reisende/r	
	trip [trɪp]	Reise, Fahrt	
	G'day! = Good day! [gə‿'deɪ]	Tag, hi, hallo	
	business trip ['bɪznəs trɪp]	Geschäftsreise	
	flight [flaɪt]	Flug, Fliegen	
	Hungary ['hʌŋgəri]	Ungarn	
	see [si:]	*hier:* treffen	
	relative ['relətɪv]	Verwandte(r)	
	pilot ['paɪlət]	Pilot/in	
	British Airways (BA) [ˌbrɪtɪʃ‿'eəweɪz]	brit. Luftfahrtgesellschaft	
	southwest [ˌsaʊθ'west]	Südwesten	
	be on one's way [bi:‿ˌɒn wʌnz 'weɪ]	*hier:* unterwegs sein	
	trekking ['trekɪŋ]	Trekking, Wandern	
	(the) Himalayas *(only plural)* [ˌhɪmə'leɪəz]	Himalaya	
B2	wait for sb to do sth [ˌweɪt fɔ: ˌsʌmbədi tu: 'du: ˌsʌmθɪŋ]	darauf warten, dass jd etw tut	She is *waiting for* her son to stop shouting.
	on time [ɒn 'taɪm]	pünktlich	Don't be late! You've got to be *on time*!
	gate [geɪt]	Tor; Flugsteig, Gate	
	sir [sɜ:]	Herr *(Anrede)*	
	right [raɪt]	völlig, ganz	
	kangaroo [ˌkæŋgə'ru:]	Känguru	 *kangaroo*
	pick up sb/sth [ˌpɪk‿'ʌp ˌsʌmbədi/ˌsʌmθɪŋ]	jdn./etw. abholen	
B3	flight attendant ['flaɪt‿əˌtendənt]	Flugbegleiter/in, Steward/Stewardess	*Pilots* and *flight attendants* work on planes.

Vokabel-Kartei
Schreibe einzelne Vokabeln auf Kärtchen – auf der einen Seite auf Deutsch, auf der anderen Seite auf Englisch. Du kannst die Wörter mal Englisch-Deutsch und mal Deutsch-Englisch üben. Außerdem kannst du die Kärtchen immer wieder neu sortieren, zum Beispiel nach Themen, Wortarten (Verben, Adjektive, etc.) und Schwierigkeitsgrad.

	announcement [əˈnaʊnsmənt]	Durchsage	
	presentation [ˌpreznˈteɪʃn]	Präsentation, Vortrag	
B4	put sth in order [ˌpʊt ˌsʌmθɪŋ‿ɪn‿ˈɔːdə]	etw in eine Reihenfolge bringen	
	complete [kəmˈpliːt]	vollständig, komplett	
P1	miss [mɪs]	verfehlen	The neighbours *are chatting with* each other.
P2	chat with/to [ˈtʃæt wɪð/‿tʊ]	plaudern mit, chatten mit	
P3	FAQ (= frequently asked questions) [ˌef‿ˌeɪ ˈkjuː]	oft gestellte Fragen	
	toilet [ˈtɔɪlət]	Toilette	
	campfire [ˈkæmpˌfaɪə]	Lagerfeuer	*campfire* 
P4	pack [pæk]	packen	
	toothpaste [ˈtuːθˌpeɪst]	Zahnpasta	
	comb [kəʊm]	Kamm	
	camera [ˈkæmrə]	Fotoapparat	
	swimming costume [ˈswɪmɪŋ ˌkɒstjuːm]	Badeanzug	*swimming costume* 
	pyjamas *(only plural)* [pəˈdʒɑːməz]	Schlafanzug	
	torch *(pl* torches) [tɔːtʃ, ˈtɔːtʃɪz]	Taschenlampe	
	sleeping bag [ˈsliːpɪŋ ˌbæg]	Schlafsack	
	raincoat [ˈreɪnˌkəʊt]	Regenmantel	*raincoat*
	pocket knife [ˈpɒkɪt ˌnaɪf]	Taschenmesser	
	toiletries *(only plural)* [ˈtɔɪlətriz]	Toilettenartikel	A toothbrush and *toothpaste*, a *comb* and soap are *toiletries*.
	dry [draɪ]	trocken	
	wet [wet]	nass; feucht	*wet* ≠ dry
	cool [kuːl]	kühl; kalt	*cool* ≠ hot

Die Vokabeln aus den OPTIONAL-Teilen findest du im englisch-deutschen Dictionary auf den Seiten 193–217.

A

a/an [ə, ən] ein(e) I/W
once a year [ˌwʌns ə ˈjɪə] einmal im/pro Jahr III/6B1
(twice) a (week) [ˌtwaɪs‿ə ˈwiːk] (zweimal) pro (Woche) III/2A1
be an A-student *(AE)* [biː‿ən ˈeɪ ˌstjuːdnt] ein/e Einserschüler/in sein III/4B4
be able to do sth [be‿ˈeɪbl tə ˈduː: ˌsʌmθɪŋ] etw tun können II/5C2
about [əˈbaʊt] über I/1A4; ungefähr III/5A1
about [əˈbaʊt] *hier:* an III/4A3
be about [biː‿əˈbaʊt] handeln von III/2B5
°it's about [ɪts‿əˈbaʊt] *hier:* es geht um III/BS7
What about …? *(informal)* [wɒt‿əˈbaʊt] Was ist mit …? II/1B2
be about to do sth [biː əˌbaʊt tə ˈduː: ˌsʌmθɪŋ] im Begriff sein, etw zu tun III/2A5
above [əˈbʌv] oberhalb; *hier:* oben II/4A5; über II/3C1
accident [ˈæksɪdnt] Unfall III/3B1
across [əˈkrɒs] über II/2C1
°across the road [əˌkrɒs ðə ˈrəʊd] *hier:* auf der gegenüberliegenden Straßenseite III/BS7
acrostic [əˈkrɒstɪk] Akrostichon III/4A9
°act as if [ˌækt‿əz‿ˈɪf] so tun, als ob … III/BS7
act out [ˌækt‿ˈaʊt] nachspielen II/2A3
activity [ækˈtɪvəti] Aktivität, Unternehmung III/7B1
actor/actress [ˈæktə/ˈæktrəs] Schauspieler/in III/7A2
add [æd] hinzufügen I/5C3
adjective [ˈædʒɪktɪv] Adjektiv II/1A3
admission [ədˈmɪʃn] Eintritt III/7B1
adult [ˈædʌlt] Erwachsene/r III/7B1
adventure [ədˈventʃə] Abenteuer, Erlebnis II/1B6
advert (= advertisement) [ˈædvɜːt, ədˈvɜːtɪsmənt] Anzeige, Inserat III/7B1
advertising [ˈædvəˌtaɪzɪŋ] Werbung, Reklame III/7B2
advice [ədˈvaɪs] Rat III/4B1
aerobics [eəˈrəʊbɪks] Aerobic III/2A7
aeroplane (= plane) [ˈeərəˌpleɪn] Flugzeug III/5A2
be afraid (of) [be‿əˈfreɪd] Angst haben (vor) II/5C2
°Africa [ˈæfrɪkə] Afrika III/7O1
African [ˈæfrɪkən] Afrikaner/in; afrikanisch III/7B1
after [ˈɑːftə] nach I/2C6
°after [ˈɑːftə] nachdem III/2O
after that [ˈɑːftə ðæt] danach III/5B1
afternoon [ˌɑːftəˈnuːn] Nachmittag I/2C1
in the afternoon [ˌɪn ðiː‿ɑːftəˈnuːn] am Nachmittag I/6A3
this afternoon [ðɪs‿ˌɑːftəˈnuːn] heute Nachmittag II/2A3
afterwards [ˈɑːftəwədz] später; danach, anschließend II/2C3
again [əˈgen] wieder; noch (ein)mal I/1C2
against [əˈgenst] gegen I/3A3
age [eɪdʒ] Alter II/4C3
aged [eɪdʒd] im Alter von III/7B1
of all ages [əv ˈɔːl ˌeɪdʒɪz] aller Altersstufen III/7B1
°aggressive [əˈgresɪv] aggressiv III/BS7
(long) ago [əˈgəʊ] vor (langer Zeit) I/5A1
agree [əˈgriː] zustimmen II/5C3
agree on [əˈgriː‿ɒn] sich einigen auf III/7B4
ain't it (= isn't it) [ˈeɪnt ɪt] ist es nicht III/6A9
air [eə] Luft III/5B1
airport [ˈeəˌpɔːt] Flughafen II/2C1
album [ˈælbəm] (Musik)album III/7A2
algebra [ˈældʒɪbrə] Algebra III/4B4
be alive [bi‿əˈlaɪv] leben, am Leben sein II/6B2
all day [ˌɔːl ˈdeɪ] den ganzen Tag II/6A4
all kinds of [ɔːl ˈkaɪndz‿əv] alle möglichen III/L
from all over the world [frəm‿ɔːl‿əʊvə ðə ˈwɜːld] aus der ganzen Welt III/6B2
all sorts of [ɔːl ˈsɔːts‿əv] alle möglichen III/5B1
All the best! [ˌɔːl ðə‿ˈbest] Alles Gute! II/4B9
all (the) [ɔːl] alle(s); der/die/das ganze I/1A3
all-inclusive [ɔːl ɪnˈkluːsɪv] pauschal III/8A5
all-weather [ˌɔːl ˈweðə] Allwetter-, wetterfest III/7B1
°allow [əˈlaʊ] erlauben, gestatten III/BS7
be allowed to do sth [bi‿əˈlaʊd tə ˈduː: ˌsʌmθɪŋ] etw tun dürfen II/5A3
almost [ˈɔːlməʊst] fast, beinahe III/3B1
alone [əˈləʊn] allein II/3C1
in alphabetical order [ɪn‿ælfəˌbetɪkl‿ˈɔːdə] in alphabetische(r) Reihenfolge III/2P4
already [ɔːlˈredi] schon, bereits II/3A1
also [ˈɔːlsəʊ] auch, außerdem I/5A1
°although [ɔːlˈðəʊ] obwohl III/BS6
always [ˈɔːlweɪz] immer I/1C1
am (= ante meridiem) [ˌeɪ ˈem, ˌænti məˈrɪdiəm] morgens, vormittags *(nur hinter Uhrzeit zwischen Mitternacht und 12 Uhr mittags)* I/2B7
amateur [ˈæmətə] Amateur/in III/7A6
amazing [əˈmeɪzɪŋ] erstaunlich, toll III/5B1
°America [əˈmerɪkə] Amerika III/7O1
American [əˈmerɪkən] Amerikaner/in; amerikanisch III/4P8
and [ænd] und I/1A2
angry [ˈæŋgri] verärgert; zornig; wütend II/3B2
be angry about [bi‿ˈæŋgri əˈbaʊt] sich ärgern über II/5A3
animal [ˈænɪml] Tier I/1A4
animal rights *(only plural)* [ˌænɪml ˈraɪts] *das Recht der Tiere auf Leben und artgerechte Haltung* III/7A2
announcement [əˈnaʊnsmənt] Durchsage III/8B3
another [əˈnʌðə] *hier:* ein(e) andere(r, s) II/3C1; noch eine(r, s) I/3C2
answer [ˈɑːnsə] (be)antworten I/2A7; Antwort II/1B5
answer the phone [ˌɑːnsə ðə ˈfəʊn] ans Telefon gehen III/3P6
any [ˈeni] (irgend)ein(e); jede(r, s) III/3A1
not any [nɒt‿ˈeni] kein/keine II/3A9
not … any [nɒt‿ˈeni] keine(r, s) II/6A4
any more [ˌeni ˈmɔː] noch (mehr) III/5A1
anybody [ˈeniˌbɒdi] jede(r); jemand I/5C4
not anymore [nɒt‿ˌeniˈmɔː] nicht mehr II/5C2
°anyone [ˈeniˌwʌn] jede(r, s) III/BS3
not anyone [ˌnɒt‿ˈeniwʌn] niemand II/3A1
anything [ˈeniˌθɪŋ] (irgend)etwas III/6A7
not anything [ˌnɒt‿ˈeniθɪŋ] nichts II/3C5
anything else [ˌeniθɪŋ‿ˈels] (irgend)etwas anderes II/5C3
°anytime [ˈeniˌtaɪm] jederzeit III/7O3
anyway [ˈeniˌweɪ] sowieso; überhaupt III/1A6
anywhere [ˈeniˌweə] überall III/8A3
not … anywhere [ˌnɒt‿ˈeniweə] nirgendwo(hin) II/6A2
apple [ˈæpl] Apfel I/1C1

apple crumble [ˌæpl ˈkrʌmbl] Apfelauflauf III/1A2
appointment [əˈpɔɪntmənt] Termin III/2B1
April [ˈeɪprəl] April I/5C2
archery [ˈɑːtʃəri] Bogenschießen III/8A5
Are you ready to order? [ɑː juː ˌredi tʊ‿ˈɔːdə] Möchten Sie schon bestellen? III/1A3
area [ˈeəriə] Gebiet, Region; *hier:* Viertel, Gegend II/6B6
arm [ɑːm] Arm I/2A4
around [əˈraʊnd] um (… herum) I/1B1
around [əˈraʊnd] in der Nähe, da III/3B5
arrive [əˈraɪv] ankommen II/5B1
art [ɑːt] (bildende) Kunst I/5A1
article [ˈɑːtɪkl] Artikel III/2B5
as [æz] als; wie; da II/6B3
°as if [əz‿ˈɪf] als ob III/BS7
°act as if [ˌækt‿əz‿ˈɪf] so tun, als ob … III/BS7
as … as [əz ... əz] (genau)so … wie … II/4B2
ask [ɑːsk] fragen; bitten I/2A7
ask for directions [ˌɑːsk fə dɪˈrekʃnz] nach dem Weg fragen III/8A4
ask for help [ˌɑːsk fə ˈhelp] um Hilfe bitten III/8A4
ask questions [ˌɑːsk‿ˈkwestʃnz] Fragen stellen I/2A7
°be asleep [biː‿əˈsliːp] schlafen III/7O3
(shop) assistant [əˈsɪstənt] Verkäufer/in II/4C3
at [æt] auf, an, in, bei I/1C1; *hier:* um I/3A1
not at all [ˌnɒt‿ət‿ˈɔːl] überhaupt nicht III/6A9
at first [ət ˈfɜːst] zuerst II/5C2
at Gillian's [æt ˈdʒɪliənz] bei Gillian (zu Hause) I/3C2
at home [æt ˈhəʊm] zu Hause I/2B1
at last [ət lˈɑːst] endlich, schließlich II/6A2
at least [ət ˈliːst] mindestens, zumindest II/2A6
at night [ət ˈnaɪt] nachts I/3B1
at sb's house [æt ˌsʌmbədiz ˈhaʊs] bei jdm zu Hause II/3A1
at the back (of) [ˌæt ðə ˈbæk] hinten II/1C5
at the beginning [ˌæt ðə bɪˈɡɪnɪŋ] am Anfang, zu Beginn III/3A3
at the doctor's [ˌæt ðə ˈdɒktəz] beim Arzt/bei der Ärztin III/2B2
at the front (of) [ˌæt ðə ˈfrʌnt] vorne II/1C5
at the moment [ˌæt ðə ˈməʊmənt] im Augenblick, momentan II/2A5
at the same time [ət ðə ˌseɪm ˈtaɪm] gleichzeitig, zur gleichen Zeit III/1A6
at the weekend [æt ðə ˌwiːkˈend] am Wochenende II/6A1
°at this point [ət ˌðɪs ˈpɔɪnt] an dieser Stelle III/BS7
athlete [ˈæθliːt] Athlet/in III/6B2
audience [ˈɔːdiəns] Publikum III/7P4
August [ˈɔːɡəst] August I/5C2
aunt [ɑːnt] Tante I/W
°Australia [ɒˈstreɪliə] Australien III/BS2
autumn [ˈɔːtəm] Herbst I/4C8
awake [əˈweɪk] aufwachen, erwachen III/4A4
away [əˈweɪ] weg III/4A3
awesome *(AE, informal)* [ˈɔːsm] spitze, super III/8A5
awful [ˈɔːfl] furchtbar, schrecklich III/1A10

B

°babe (= baby) *(informal) (AE)* [beɪb] Baby, Schatz, Liebling III/8O
babysit [ˈbeɪbiˌsɪt] babysitten III/6A2
back [bæk] Rücken; Rückseite I/2A4; zurück I/4C5
at the back (of) [ˌæt ðə ˈbæk] hinten II/1C5
backache [ˈbækeɪk] Rückenschmerzen III/2B3
bad [bæd] schlecht; schlimm III/1B1
feel bad [ˌfiːl ˈbæd] sich schlecht fühlen III/2B1
It's not that bad! [ɪtz ˌnɒt ˈðæt ˌbæd] So schlimm ist es doch nicht! III/1B1
That's too bad! [ˌðæts ˌtuː ˈbæd] Das ist wirklich schade! III/6A9
(bad) cold [kəʊld] (starke) Erkältung III/2B1
bag [bæɡ] Tasche II/1C1
baked potato [ˌbeɪkt pəˈteɪtəʊ] Ofenkartoffel III/1P5
baker [ˈbeɪkə] Bäcker/in III/5B4
°balance [ˈbæləns] Gleichgewicht III/BS3
ball [bɔːl] Ball I/3B7
°ball [bɔːl] Ball; *hier:* Kugel III/5O
°ball bearing [ˌbɔːl ˈbeərɪŋ] Kugellager III/BS2
ballet [ˈbæleɪ] Ballett III/4B2
°bamboo [ˌbæmˈbuː] Bambus III/BS4
banana [bəˈnɑːnə] Banane I/2C2
band [bænd] Band; Gruppe III/3A4
bandage [ˈbændɪdʒ] Verband III/2B2
bar code [ˈbɑː ˌkəʊd] Strichcode III/7A2
basket [ˈbɑːskɪt] Korb I/3B4
bat [bæt] Schläger, Schlagholz III/2A5
bath [bɑːθ] Bad(ewanne) I/W
bathroom [ˈbɑːθˌruːm] Bad(ezimmer) I/2A2
batter [ˈbætə] Schlagmann III/2A5
be [biː] sein I/W
be in use [biː‿ɪn‿ˈjuːs] in Gebrauch sein III/5A6
be joking [biː ˈdʒəʊkɪŋ] Spaß machen III/6A4
°be mistaken [biː mɪˈsteɪkən] sich irren III/BS7
°be on one's way [ˌbiː‿ɒn wʌnz ˈweɪ] *hier:* unterwegs sein III/8O
be out of breath [biˌ‿aʊt‿əv ˈbreθ] außer Atem sein III/2A2
be right [biː ˈraɪt] Recht haben III/1B1
be worth [biː ˈwɜːθ] wert sein III/6A4
beach [biːtʃ] Strand II/1A1
bean [biːn] Bohne III/1A2
beat [biːt] schlagen; *hier:* besiegen II/5C4
beat up [ˌbiːt‿ˈʌp] verprügeln III/4B1
beautiful [ˈbjuːtəfl] schön II/2B1
because [bɪˈkɒz] weil, da I/4B1
become [bɪˈkʌm] werden II/6B2
bed [bed] Bett I/W
bedroom [ˈbedruːm] Schlafzimmer I/4C2
before [bɪˈfɔː] bevor I/4C4; vor I/2B2; zuvor, vorher II/6A2
begin [bɪˈɡɪn] anfangen, beginnen II/1B3
beginning [bɪˈɡɪnɪŋ] Anfang, Beginn II/3C2
at the beginning [ˌæt ðə bɪˈɡɪnɪŋ] am Anfang, zu Beginn III/3A3
behind [bɪˈhaɪnd] hinter I/2A2
believe [bɪˈliːv] glauben II/1C4
°bell-bottom jeans [ˌbel bɒtəm ˈdʒiːnz] Schlaghose III/BS6
below [bɪˈləʊ] unten, darunter I/4B1; unter I/2C2
on bended knee(s) [ɒn ˌbendɪd ˈniːz] auf Knien III/4A4
°beside [bɪˈsaɪd] neben III/BS7
best [best] beste(r, s) II/1L
the best [ðə‿ˈbest] der/die/das beste I/1A4
best-seller [ˌbestˈselə] Bestseller *(Artikel mit großem Verkaufserfolg)* III/5B2
bet [bet] wetten III/6A9
better [ˈbetə] besser I/1A5
better [ˈbetə] *hier:* lieber III/2A5
between [bɪˈtwiːn] zwischen I/2C4

between you and me [bɪˌtwiːn ˌjuː‿ən ˈmiː] unter uns gesagt III/6A4
bicycle [ˈbaɪsɪkl] Fahrrad II/6C2
big [bɪg] groß I/W
bike [baɪk] (Fahr)rad I/1A5
bill [bɪl] Rechnung III/6A9
Could we have the bill, please? [kʊd wiː hæv ðə ˈbɪl ˌpliːz] Wir möchten bitte zahlen!, Die Rechnung, bitte! III/1A3
°billion [ˈbɪljən] Milliarde III/6O
bin [bɪn] Mülleimer, Mülltonne I/1C1
biology [baɪˈɒlədʒi] Biologie III/4B4
bird [bɜːd] Vogel II/2B3
birthday [ˈbɜːθdeɪ] Geburtstag I/5B4
Happy birthday (to you)! [ˌhæpi ˈbɜːθdeɪ] Alles Gute zum Geburtstag! I/3C4
biscuit [ˈbɪskɪt] Keks III/5B4
°bit [bɪt] Stück III/BS4
a bit [ə ˈbɪt] ein bisschen II/1A4
black [blæk] schwarz I/W
blackboard [ˈblækˌbɔːd] Tafel I/1C1
°blind [blaɪnd] blind III/2O
°block of flats [ˌblɒk‿əv ˈflæts] Mehrfamilienhaus III/BS7
blond(e) [blɒnd] blond III/2B4
blouse [blaʊz] Bluse II/5B5
°blow one's horn [ˌbləʊ wʌnz ˈhɔːn] hupen III/8O
blue [bluː] blau I/2A5
board [bɔːd] Brett; Tafel I/3C3
board a ship [ˌbɔːd‿ə ˈʃɪp] ein Schiff besteigen III/4A1
board game [ˈbɔːd ˌgeɪm] Brettspiel III/7B1
boat [bəʊt] Boot; Schiff II/2C1
body [ˈbɒdi] Körper I/6C1
book [bʊk] Buch I/1A8
book [bʊk] reservieren, buchen III/7A6
°book stop [ˈbʊk ˌstɒp] *Buch-Haltestelle* III/BS1
bookshop [ˈbʊkˌʃɒp] Buchladen III/7B1
boot [buːt] Stiefel III/6A7
°boot-cut [ˈbuːtkʌt] *Schnitt, bei dem die Hosen unten am Bein weit sind, damit man sie über Stiefel anziehen kann* III/BS6
boring [ˈbɔːrɪŋ] langweilig II/1A2
be born [biː ˈbɔːn] geboren werden III/7A2
both [bəʊθ] beide III/8A6
bottle [ˈbɒtl] Flasche I/2C2
at the bottom [ət ðə ˈbɒtəm] unten III/7B4
bowl [bəʊl] Schüssel; Schale III/1A8
a bowl of soup [ə ˌbəʊl‿əv ˈsuːp] eine Tasse Suppe III/1A8
box [bɒks] Kiste; Schachtel; Kasten I/2P3
boy [bɔɪ] Junge I/1A2
boyfriend [ˈbɔɪˌfrend] Freund *(Partner)* III/4B2
Brahmin [ˈbrɑːmɪn] Brahmane III/1LL1
bread [bred] Brot I/2C2
break [breɪk] (sich) brechen II/2B2; Pause I/5A1
break [breɪk] *hier:* anbrechen III/4A4
break down [ˌbreɪk ˈdaʊn] kaputtgehen; stehen bleiben III/2A3
break up [ˌbreɪk‿ˈʌp] sich trennen, Schluss machen III/4B1
breakfast [ˈbrekfəst] Frühstück I/1A4
°eat breakfast [ˌiːt ˈbrekfəst] frühstücken III/7O1
have breakfast [ˌhæv ˈbrekfəst] frühstücken I/2B2
breaststroke [ˈbrestˌstrəʊk] Brustschwimmen III/2A5
be out of breath [biː ˌaʊt‿əv ˈbreθ] außer Atem sein III/2A2
take a (deep) breath [ˌteɪk‿ə ˈbreθ] (tief) Luft holen III/4B1
breeze [briːz] Brise III/4A5
bricklayer [ˈbrɪkˌleɪə] Maurer/in III/2B5
bridge [brɪdʒ] Brücke II/2C1
bright [braɪt] hell, grell, leuchtend III/3A4
brilliant [ˈbrɪljənt] toll, klasse I/3A1
bring [brɪŋ] (mit)bringen I/1B4
(Great) Britain [ˈbrɪtn] Großbritannien II/1LL1
British Airways (BA) [ˌbrɪtɪʃ‿ˈeəweɪz] *brit. Luftfahrtgesellschaft* III/8B1
the British Isles *(only plural)* [ðə ˌbrɪtɪʃ‿ˈaɪlz] die Britischen Inseln II/1LL1
broccoli [ˈbrɒkəli] Broccoli, Brokkoli III/1A2
brochure [ˈbrəʊʃə] Broschüre III/5A2
broken [ˈbrəʊkən] gebrochen III/2B2; *hier:* kaputt III/BS7
°bronze medal [ˌbrɒnz ˈmedl] Bronzemedaille III/2O
brother [ˈbrʌðə] Bruder I/1A4
brothers and sisters [ˈbrʌðəz‿ændˌsɪstəz] Geschwister I/1A6
brown [braʊn] braun I/2A5
brush one's teeth [ˌbrʌʃ wʌnz ˈtiːθ] sich die Zähne putzen III/4A3
build [bɪld] bauen II/6A1
building [ˈbɪldɪŋ] Gebäude, Bau II/5B1
bullying [ˈbʊliɪŋ] Mobbing III/4B1
burn [bɜːn] (ver)brennen II/3C1
burning [ˈbɜːnɪŋ] brennend, glühend III/4A4
°burr [bɜː] Klette III/5O
burst [bɜːst] platzen III/2A5
bus [bʌs] Bus I/2B7
take the bus [ˌteɪk ðə ˈbʌs] mit dem Bus fahren II/5C2
bus driver [ˈbʌs ˌdraɪvə] Busfahrer/in III/8A2
bus stop [ˈbʌs ˌstɒp] Bushaltestelle II/5C1
business [ˈbɪznəs] Geschäft III/3A4
business trip [ˈbɪznəs trɪp] Geschäftsreise III/8B1
°businessman *(pl* businessmen) [ˈbɪznəsmæn, ˈbɪznəsmen] Geschäftsmann III/6O
busy [ˈbɪzi] beschäftigt; arbeitsreich III/2B5
but [bʌt] aber I/1A3
butter [ˈbʌtə] Butter I/2B1
°button [ˈbʌtn] Knopf III/5O
buy [baɪ] kaufen I/2C1
buying and selling [ˌbaɪɪŋ ənd ˈselɪŋ] Kaufen und Verkaufen, An- und Verkauf I I/6A7
by [baɪ] *hier:* von II/6A4
by [baɪ] *hier:* indem III/4B4; *hier:* bis III/6O
by *(+ Verkehrsmittel)* [baɪ] mit II/6C2
by *(+ Zeitpunkt)* [baɪ] (spätestens) bis II/5A2
by heart [ˌbaɪ ˈhɑːt] auswendig II/4C2
by himself [ˌbaɪ hɪmˈself] ganz allein III/2B6
°by now [baɪ ˈnaʊ] mittlerweile III/BS7
bye-bye *(informal)* [ˌbaɪ ˈbaɪ] tschüs(s) III/2A5
Bye. *(informal)* [baɪ] Tschüss. I/6C6

C

cage [keɪdʒ] Käfig I/3B4
Cairo [ˈkaɪərəʊ] Kairo III/8A3
cake [keɪk] Kuchen; Torte II/4B6
calendar [ˈkælɪndə] Kalender II/4A5
°California [ˌkæləˈfɔːniə] Kalifornien III/BS3
call [kɔːl] (an)rufen; nennen I/2B3; (Telefon)anruf III/2B1
make a call [ˌmeɪk‿ə ˈkɔːl] telefonieren II/5B1
call sb names [ˌkɔːl sʌmbədi ˈneɪmz] jdn beschimpfen II/5C3
called [kɔːld] *hier:* genannt III/5B1
called [kɔːld] *hier:* mit dem Titel III/2B5
be called [biː ˈkɔːld] heißen III/3A7
°camel [ˈkæml] Kamel III/7O1

camera ['kæmrə] Fotoapparat III/8P4
camp [kæmp] (Zelt)lager III/8A5
campfire ['kæmp,faɪə] Lagerfeuer III/8A7
campsite ['kæmp,saɪt] Zeltplatz III/8A7
can [kæn] können I/1A4
Canada ['kænədə] Kanada III/8A3
candle ['kændl] Kerze III/5A5
cane [keɪn] Rohr, Stock; *hier:* Zuckerrohr III/4A4; Rohr, Stock; *hier:* Blindenstock III/BS2
cannibal ['kænɪbl] Kannibale/Kannibalin, Menschenfresser/in III/4A1
canoeing [kə'nu:ɪŋ] Paddeln, Kanufahren III/8A5
car [kɑ:] Auto I/1B5
car boot [,kɑ: 'bu:t] Kofferraum III/6A4
car boot sale [,kɑ: 'bu:t seɪl] *Verkauf pers. Gegenstände aus einem Kofferraum* III/6A4
card [kɑ:d] Pappe, Karton; Karte I/1C4
cardamom ['kɑ:dəməm] Kardamom III/1B5
°care for sb ['keə‿fə ,sʌmbədi] sich um jdn kümmern III/4O
°sb couldn't care less *(informal)* [,sʌmbədi ,kʊdnt ,keə 'les] jdm ist es völlig egal III/7O3
take care of [teɪk‿'keər‿əv] sich kümmern um, versorgen II/3A4
careful ['keəfl] vorsichtig II/3C2
carnival ['kɑ:nɪvl] Karneval, Volksfest III/3I
carrot ['kærət] Möhre, Karotte, Mohrrübe I/1A4
carry ['kæri] tragen I/6C5
cartridge ['kɑ:trɪdʒ] Patrone I/1C4
cash [kæʃ] Bargeld III/6I
cash desk ['kæʃ,desk] Kasse III/4B2
cash in hand [,kæʃ‿ɪn 'hænd] Guthaben III/6I
cassette [kə'set] Kassette III/L
cast a net [,kɑ:st‿ə 'net] ein Netz auswerfen III/4A4
be cast away [bi: ,kɑ:st‿ə'weɪ] gestrandet sein III/4A8
caste [kɑ:st] Kaste III/1LL1
castle ['kɑ:sl] Burg, Schloss III/4A9
cat [kæt] Katze I/1A6
catch [kætʃ] fangen I/6A3
°'cause (= because) [kɒz] weil, da III/8O
celebrate ['selə,breɪt] feiern II/4A1
celebration [,selə'breɪʃn] Feier II/4I
center (*AE* = **centre** *BE*) ['sentə] Zentrum II/6B6
in the centre [ɪn ðə 'sentə] im Zentrum, in der Mitte III/7B4
century ['sentʃəri] Jahrhundert III/5B2
chair [tʃeə] Stuhl I/W
change [tʃeɪndʒ] (ver)ändern; austauschen I/3B6; *hier:* umsteigen I/4B1; Wechselgeld I/5B6
change one's mind [,tʃeɪndʒ wʌnz 'maɪnd] seine Meinung ändern III/1A8
°chapati (*pl* chapatis *or* chapaties) [tʃə'pɑ:ti, tʃə'pɑ:tiz] Chapatti *(indisches Fladenbrot)* III/1O
charity ['tʃærəti] Wohltätigkeitsorganisation III/6B1
°have a chat [,hæv‿ə 'tʃæt] sich unterhalten III/BS5
chat with/to ['tʃæt wɪð/‿tʊ] plaudern mit, chatten mit III/8P2
cheap [tʃi:p] billig, preiswert II/4B2
check [tʃek] überprüfen, kontrollieren III/1B4
check [tʃek] *hier:* nachsehen (in) III/4B2
check out *(informal)* [,tʃek‿'aʊt] sich ansehen III/5A1
cheese [tʃi:z] Käse I/2B1
chest of drawers [,tʃest‿əv 'drɔ:z] Kommode I/4A1
chew [tʃu:] kauen II/5A5
chewing gum ['tʃu:ɪŋ gʌm] Kaugummi II/5B1
chicken ['tʃɪkɪn] Huhn I/2C2
child (*pl* **children**) [tʃaɪld, 'tʃɪldrən] Kind I/1A6
be child's play [bi: 'tʃaɪəldz ,pleɪ] ein Kinderspiel sein III/7B1
childhood ['tʃaɪld,hʊd] Kindheit III/7B1
children's home ['tʃɪldrənz ,həʊm] Kinderheim, Waisenhaus III/3A7
chilli (*pl* chillies) ['tʃɪli, 'tʃɪliz] Chili; Peperoni III/1A2
Chinese [,tʃaɪ'ni:z] Chinese/Chinesin; chinesisch III/1B3
chips *(only plural)* [tʃɪps] Pommes frites III/1A2
chocolate ['tʃɒklət] Schokolade I/2C1
choir ['kwaɪə] Chor III/3A7
choose [tʃu:z] wählen; sich entscheiden II/1A3
°chopstick ['tʃɒp,stɪk] (Ess)stäbchen III/10
chorus (*pl* choruses) ['kɔ:rəs, 'kɔ:rəsɪz] Refrain III/4A4
Christmas ['krɪsməs] Weihnachten I/6P7
Christmas Day [,krɪsməs 'deɪ] erster Weihnachtsfeiertag II/4A4
Christmas Eve [,krɪsməs‿'i:v] Heiligabend II/4A4
church [tʃɜ:tʃ] Kirche II/4A4
cinema ['sɪnəmə] Kino II/1A4
cinnamon ['sɪnəmən] Zimt III/1B5
circus ['sɜ:kəs] Zirkus III/7B3
city ['sɪti] (Groß)stadt I/6B1
claim [kleɪm] behaupten III/4B4
class [klɑ:s] (Schul)klasse I/1A6; *hier:* Unterricht(sstunde) II/5B1
class trip ['klɑ:s ,trɪp] Klassenfahrt III/6A1
classmate ['klɑ:s,meɪt] Klassenkamerad/in, Mitschüler/in II/2A1
classroom ['klɑ:s,ru:m] Klassenzimmer I/1C2
clean [kli:n] sauber I/3B4; sauber machen I/4B2
cleaning ['kli:nɪŋ] Reinigungs- III/5B4
clear [klɪə] klar III/2B5
clever ['klevə] klug, schlau III/2A7
click [klɪk] (an)klicken III/8A5
climb (up) [klaɪm] (hinauf)steigen; klettern (auf) II/2C1
°climber ['klaɪmə] Bergsteiger/in, Kletterer/Kletterin III/BS3
climbing ['klaɪmɪŋ] Bergsteigen; *hier:* Klettern III/7B1
clinic ['klɪnɪk] Klinik III/2B5
clock [klɒk] Uhr I/2B6
close [kləʊs] schließen, zumachen III/5B4; nah(e) III/BS3
closed [kləʊzd] geschlossen, zu; *hier:* gesperrt III/6B1
°cloth [klɒθ] Tuch, Stoff III/1O
clothes *(only plural)* [kləʊðz] Kleider, Kleidung I/1A8
clothing ['kləʊðɪŋ] Kleidung III/2A3
°cloud [klaʊd] Wolke III/BS4
club [klʌb] Klub, Verein; Schul-AG I/3A1
°in a coarse voice [ɪn‿ə ,kɔ:s 'vɔɪs] *hier:* mit rauer Stimme III/BS7
coat [kəʊt] Mantel II/4C3
coffee ['kɒfi] Kaffee III/1A2
cold [kəʊld] kalt I/1C1
(bad) cold [kəʊld] (starke) Erkältung III/2B1
collect [kə'lekt] sammeln I/3A1
collection [kə'lekʃn] Sammlung I/3A1
°college ['kɒlɪdʒ] Gymnasium, College III/BS6
°collide [kə'laɪd] zusammenstoßen III/BS7
colour ['kʌlə] Farbe I/1A8
°coloured ['kʌləd] farbig, bunt III/7O1
colourful ['kʌləfl] farbenfroh, bunt III/7B4

comb [kəʊm] Kamm III/8P4
°combination [ˌkɒmbɪˈneɪʃn] Kombination III/BS3
combine [kəmˈbaɪn] verbinden, kombinieren III/4P4
come [kʌm] kommen I/1A6
come back [ˌkʌm ˈbæk] zurückkommen III/7A6
°come for a swim [ˌkʌm fər‿ə ˈswɪm] zum Schwimmen kommen III/BS5
come in [ˌkʌm‿ˈɪn] hereinkommen I/5C4
Come on! [ˌkʌm‿ˈɒn] *hier:* Jetzt hör aber auf! II/1A4; Komm(t) schon!; Mach(t) jetzt! III/1B1
°come together [ˌkʌm təˈgeðə] zusammenkommen III/2O
communications *(only plural)* [kəˌmju:nɪˈkeɪʃnz] Fernmeldewesen, Telekommunikation III/5B1
°company [ˈkʌmpni] Firma, Unternehmen III/6O
comparative form [kəmˈpærətɪv ˌfɔ:m] Komparativ III/2P4
compare [kəmˈpeə] vergleichen II/4B2
comparison [kəmˈpærɪsn] Vergleich III/2P4
compete (for) [kəmˈpi:t] wetteifern, (gegen einander) antreten (um) III/7B1
competition [ˌkɒmpəˈtɪʃn] Wettbewerb III/3A3
complete [kəmˈpli:t] vervollständigen II/1A4
complete [kəmˈpli:t] vollständig, komplett III/8B4
°complicated [ˈkɒmplɪˌkeɪtɪd] kompliziert, schwierig III/7O3
concentrate (on) [ˈkɒnsnˌtreɪt] sich konzentrieren (auf) III/4B1
°concentration [ˌkɒnsnˈtreɪʃn] Konzentration III/BS3
concert [ˈkɒnsət] Konzert III/7A6
°contact [ˈkɒntækt] sich in Verbindung setzen mit III/6O
°in contrast [ɪn ˈkɒntrɑ:st] im Gegensatz III/BS3
control [kənˈtrəʊl] kontrollieren, steuern III/2B5; Kontrolle III/BS3
°take control [ˌteɪk kənˈtrəʊl] die Kontrolle übernehmen III/3O
conversation [ˌkɒnvəˈseɪʃn] Gespräch, Unterhaltung III/6A4
cook [kʊk] Koch/Köchin II/3A4; kochen; braten II/3A4
cookery [ˈkʊkri] Koch- III/7B1
do the cooking [du: ðə ˈkʊkɪŋ] kochen III/4B2
cool [ku:l] kühl; kalt III/8P4
stay cool [ˌsteɪ ˈku:l] ruhig bleiben III/4B1
cool down [ˌku:l ˈdaʊn] abkühlen, sich beruhigen III/4B1
copy [ˈkɒpi] abschreiben II/1A4
°copy [ˈkɒpi] Kopie III/7O1; kopieren III/5O
(at the) corner [ˈkɔ:nə] (an der) Ecke II/2B4
correct [kəˈrekt] richtig, korrekt I/5B5
°correct [kəˈrekt] korrigieren III/BS7
cost [kɒst] kosten II/6A4
costume [ˈkɒstju:m] Kostüm III/3A1
cotton [ˈkɒtn] Baumwoll-, Baumwolle III/5A2
cotton mill [ˈkɒtn mɪl] Baumwollspinnerei III/5A1
could [kʊd] könnte(n/st/t) II/4B7
sb could do with sth *(informal)* [ˌsʌmbədi kʊd‿ˈdu: wɪð ˌsʌmθɪŋ] jd könnte etw gebrauchen/vertragen III/7A6
Could we have the bill, please? [kʊd wi: ˌhæv ðə ˈbɪl ˌpli:z] Wir möchten bitte zahlen!, Die Rechnung, bitte! III/1A3
country [ˈkʌntri] Land I/3A1
°in the country [ˌɪn ðə ˈkʌntri] auf dem Land III/5O
cousin [ˈkʌzn] Cousin/e I/5C7
cover [ˈkʌvə] bedecken, abdecken; *hier:* zuhalten III/5A2
cow [kaʊ] Kuh I/6B1
crawl [krɔ:l] krabbeln; kriechen III/5A2
creative [kriˈeɪtɪv] kreativ, schöpferisch III/7B1
cricket [ˈkrɪkɪt] Kricket III/2A5
°cricket ball [ˈkrɪkɪt ˌbɔ:l] Kricketball III/BS2
crisps *(only plural)* [krɪsps] Chips II/4C4
crowd [kraʊd] (Menschen)menge III/2A5
°crowded [ˈkraʊdɪd] überfüllt III/BS2
°crutch [krʌtʃ] Krücke III/BS1
cry [kraɪ] weinen; schreien II/3C3
cup [kʌp] Tasse I/2B3
cupboard [ˈkʌbəd] Schrank II/3A1
°currently [ˈkʌrəntli] zur Zeit III/2O
curry [ˈkʌri] Curry(gericht) III/1A2
customer [ˈkʌstəmə] Kunde/Kundin III/6A6
cut [kʌt] schneiden II/3A4
cut foot [ˌkʌt ˈfʊt] Schnittwunde am Fuß III/2B3
cycle [ˈsaɪkl] Rad fahren II/5A5
cyclist [ˈsaɪklɪst] Radfahrer/in III/5B2

D

dad *(informal)* [dæd] Papa, Vati I/1A3
daily [ˈdeɪli] jeden Tag, täglich III/7B1
Dalit [ˈdælɪt] Unberührbare/r *(ind. Kastensystem)* III/1LL1
°damage [ˈdæmɪdʒ] Schaden III/BS7
dance [dɑ:ns] tanzen I/4C5
dancer [ˈdɑ:nsə] Tänzer/in III/3A1
dancing [ˈdɑ:nsɪŋ] Tanzen III/L
go dancing [ˌgəʊ ˈdɑ:nsɪŋ] tanzen gehen III/2B4
dangerous [ˈdeɪndʒərəs] gefährlich II/2B5
dark [dɑ:k] dunkel II/3A1
°darling [ˈdɑ:lɪŋ] Liebling, Schatz III/7O3
date [deɪt] Datum III/3A3
daughter [ˈdɔ:tə] Tochter I/5C7
°dawn [dɔ:n] (Morgen)dämmerung III/8O
day [deɪ] Tag I/4I
one day [ˈwʌn ˌdeɪ] eines Tages III/2B5
day off [ˌdeɪ‿ˈɒf] freier Tag III/7A6
day out [ˌdeɪ‿ˈaʊt] Tagesausflug III/5B1
°days to come [ˌdeɪz tə ˈkʌm] *hier:* Zukunft I I/8O
dear [dɪə] Sehr geehrte(r) …, *hier:* Liebe(r, s) II/5A3
°decadence [ˈdekədəns] Dekadenz, Verfall III/BS6
°deceive [dɪˈsi:v] betrügen, täuschen III/4O
December [dɪˈsembə] Dezember I/5C2
decide [dɪˈsaɪd] sich entscheiden; beschließen III/5A2
decide [dɪˈsaɪd] entscheiden, bestimmen III/5A4
decision [dɪˈsɪʒn] Entscheidung III/4B1
°declare [dɪˈkleə] verkünden III/BS7
°decorate [ˈdekəreɪt] schmücken III/BS6
deep [di:p] tief III/5B1
°deer [dɪə] Hirsch III/7O1
°defend [dɪˈfend] verteidigen III/2O
defend oneself [dɪˈfend wʌnˌself] sich verteidigen III/2A3
definition [ˌdefəˈnɪʃn] Definition, Erklärung III/6A5
delicious [dɪˈlɪʃəs] köstlich, lecker III/1B1
°denim [ˈdenɪm] blauer Jeansstoff III/BS6
department store [dɪˈpɑ:tmənt ˌstɔ:] Kaufhaus II/4B2
depressing [dɪˈpresɪŋ] deprimierend III/7B4
describe [dɪˈskraɪb] beschreiben II/3C2

°desert ['dezət] Wüste III/7O1
design [dɪ'zaɪn] entwerfen, gestalten III/1A5
designed [dɪ'zaɪnd] entworfen, konzipiert III/5A2
°designer [di'zaɪnə] Designer/in III/BS6
desk [desk] Schreibtisch I/1C1
desperate ['desprət] verzweifelt III/4B1
dessert [dɪ'zɜ:t] Nachtisch III/1A2
°destroy [dɪ'strɔɪ] zerstören III/BS4
detective [dɪ'tektɪv] Detektiv/in III/1A7
detective story [dɪ'tektɪv ˌstɔ:ri] Kriminalroman III/6A4
°develop [di'veləp] erarbeiten, entwickeln III/BS3
dialogue ['daɪəlɒg] Gespräch, Dialog II/1A1
dictionary ['dɪkʃənri] Wörterbuch III/1B6
die [daɪ] sterben III/2B5
difference ['dɪfrəns] Unterschied II/5B6
different ['dɪfrənt] anders, andere(r, s); unterschiedlich, verschieden I/4A5
°differently ['dɪfrəntli] verschieden, unterschiedlich III/BS2
difficult ['dɪfɪklt] schwierig, schwer II/1B5
°dig [dɪg] graben III/BS4
dinner ['dɪnə] Abendessen; Mittagessen I/4A4
dinosaur ['daɪnəˌsɔ:] Dinosaurier II/6B1
ask for directions [ˌɑ:sk fə dɪ'rekʃnz] nach dem Weg fragen III/8A4
give (sb) directions [gɪv dɪ'rekʃnz] (jdm) den Weg beschreiben III/8A4
°dirtsurfing ['dɜ:tˌsɜ:fɪŋ] *Funsportart* III/BS3
dirty ['dɜ:ti] dreckig, schmutzig II/2A2
°disability [ˌdɪsə'bɪləti] Behinderung III/BS2
disabled [dɪs'eɪbld] behindert III/2B5
discount ['dɪsˌkaʊnt] Rabatt, Preisnachlass III/7B1
discovery [dɪ'skʌvri] Entdeckung III/5A2
discuss [dɪ'skʌs] besprechen, diskutieren II/4B5
discussion [dɪ'skʌʃn] Diskussion, Erörterung II/5B6
dish (*pl* dishes) [dɪʃ, 'dɪʃɪz] Schale, Schüssel; Gericht III/1A8
do the dishes [ˌdu: ðə 'dɪʃɪz] (ab)spülen, abwaschen III/6P2
display [dɪ'spleɪ] Auslage *(Museum)* III/7B1
do [du:] tun, machen I/1B5
do [du:] *hier als Verstärkung* III/4B4
do a paper round [du:‿ə 'peɪpə‿ˌraʊnd] Zeitungen austragen III/6A2
do gardening [du: 'gɑ:dnɪŋ] Gartenarbeit machen III/6A2
Can you do it? [kæn 'ju: ˌdu: ɪt] Schaffst du das? III/2A2
do sport [du: 'spɔ:t] Sport treiben III/2A1
do the dishes [ˌdu: ðə 'dɪʃɪz] (ab)spülen, abwaschen III/6P2
do the shopping [ˌdu: ðə 'ʃɒpɪŋ] einkaufen (gehen) I/4B3
do the washing up [ˌdu: ðə ˌwɒʃɪŋ‿'ʌp] abspülen I/4B6
°do well [ˌdu: 'wel] *hier:* erfolgreich sein III/2O
doctor ['dɒktə] Arzt/Ärztin II/3C1
dog [dɒg] Hund I/1A6
walk the dog [ˌwɔ:k ðə 'dɒg] den Hund ausführen III/4B1
take the dog for a walk [ˌteɪk ðə 'dɒg fə:r‿ə 'wɔ:k] den Hund ausführen III/6A2
door [dɔ:] Tür I/W
doorbell ['dɔ:ˌbel] Türklingel III/3A3
dos and don'ts [ˌdu:z‿ənd 'dəʊnts] was man tun und was man nicht tun sollte II/5I
dossier ['dɒsieɪ] Dossier, Akte II/2B1
°double ['dʌbl] doppelt, Doppel-, III/4O
down [daʊn] hinunter, hinab I/5B4
walk down the street [ˌwɔ:k daʊn ðə 'stri:t] die Straße entlanggehen III/7A5
drama ['drɑ:mə] Theater(kurs); Schauspielerei I/5A2
draw [drɔ:] zeichnen I/1B6
°draw oneself up to one's full height [ˌdrɔ: wʌnself‿'ʌp tʊ wʌnz ˌfʊl 'haɪt] sich zu seiner vollen Größe aufrichten III/BS7
dream [dri:m] Traum I/1B5; träumen II/3B1
dreamlike ['dri:mˌlaɪk] traumhaft III/7B4
dress [dres] Kleid I/2C7; sich anziehen I/4C4
dress sb ['dres‿ˌsʌmbədi] jdn anziehen III/2P7
dress up [ˌdres‿'ʌp] sich verkleiden III/3A1
dressing up box [ˌdresɪŋ‿'ʌp‿ˌbɒks] Verkleidungskiste III/7B1
drink [drɪŋk] Getränk II/5A4; trinken I/2B1
have a drink [ˌhæv‿ə 'drɪŋk] etw trinken III/3B2
drive [draɪv] fahren II/3A4
°drive sb on [draɪv sʌmbədi‿'ɒn] jdn antreiben III/BS4
°driver ['draɪvə] (Auto)fahrer/in III/BS7
drum [drʌm] Trommel III/4A4; trommeln III/3A3
dry [draɪ] trocken III/8P4
°during ['djʊərɪŋ] während III/6O
°dye [daɪ] färben III/BS6

E

each [i:tʃ] jede(r, s) III/6B1
each other [ˌi:tʃ‿'ʌðə] einander III/3B4
eagle ['i:gl] Adler III/5B2
ear [ɪə] Ohr I/2A2
early ['ɜ:li] früh II/4A3
°early ['ɜ:li] *hier:* erste(r, s), frühe(r, s) III/8O
early shift ['ɜ:li ˌʃɪft] Frühschicht III/4B2
earn [ɜ:n] verdienen III/6A2
earth [ɜ:θ] Erde, Boden III/4A4
east [i:st] Osten III/4A9
°East Germany [ˌi:st 'dʒɜ:məni] Ostdeutschland III/BS6
°eastern ['i:stən] östlich, Ost- III/BS6
easy ['i:zi] leicht, einfach I/4C1
eat [i:t] essen I/1A4
°eat breakfast [ˌi:t 'brekfəst] frühstücken III/7O1
eat out [ˌi:t‿'aʊt] essen gehen III/1I
°eating habits *(only plural)* ['i:tɪŋ ˌhæbɪts] Essgewohnheiten III/1O
egg [eg] Ei I/2B1
Egyptian mummy [iˌdʒɪpʃən 'mʌmi] ägyptische Mumie III/7B1
eight [eɪt] acht I/2A2
°not … either [nɒt‿'aɪðə] auch nicht III/BS7
°elderly ['eldəli] ältere(r,s) III/BS7
electricity [ɪˌlek'trɪsəti] Elektrizität, Strom III/5A5
electronic [ˌelek'trɒnɪk] elektronisch III/7B1
elephant ['elɪfənt] Elefant I/3B4
eleven [ɪ'levn] elf I/1A4
elite [ɪ'li:t] Elite III/6B2
°everyone else [ˌevriwʌn‿'els] *hier:* alle anderen III/BS2
°nobody else [ˌnəʊbədi‿'els] niemand anderes III/7O3
°someone else [ˌsʌmwʌn‿'els] jemand anderes III/BS7
°something else [ˌsʌmθɪŋ‿'els] etwas anderes III/BS4
What else …? [wɒt‿'els] Was sonst …? III/7A2
°empire ['empaɪə] Imperium, Reich III/7O2
empty ['empti] leer II/3C2

end [end] Ende II/1A4
end [end] enden III/6B2; *hier:* das letzte III/BS7
in the end [ɪn ðiː‿ˈend] letzten Endes; schließlich III/6A6
ending [ˈendɪŋ] Ende, Schluss II/3C2
ending [ˈendɪŋ] Ende; *hier:* Endung III/6P2
engine [ˈendʒɪn] Maschine, Motor III/5B1
engineer [ˌendʒɪˈnɪə] Ingenieur/in III/4B2
England [ˈɪŋɡlənd] England II/1LL1
English [ˈɪŋɡlɪʃ] englisch; Englisch I/1C4
English-speaking [ˈɪŋɡlɪʃ ˌspiːkɪŋ] englischsprachig III/7B3
enjoy [ɪnˈdʒɔɪ] genießen II/1B2
enough [ɪˈnʌf] genug I/5C5
°enter [ˈentə] hineingehen, eintreten III/BS7
entertainment [ˌentəˈteɪnmənt] Unterhaltung III/8A5
°entrance [ˈentrənts] Eingang; Einfahrt III/BS7
equipment [ɪˈkwɪpmənt] Ausrüstung, Ausstattung III/7A6
eraser [ɪˈreɪzə] Radiergummi II/1C1
escape [ɪˈskeɪp] Flucht, *hier:* Entkommen III/3B1
have a narrow escape [hæv‿ə ˌnærəʊ‿ɪˈskeɪp] gerade noch einmal davongekommen sein III/3B1
°estimate [ˈestɪmeɪt] (ein)schätzen III/BS7
Europe [ˈjʊərəp] Europa II/6C2
even [ˈiːvn] selbst; sogar III/2A3
even [ˈiːvn] *hier:* (sogar) noch III/5B1
not even [nɒt‿iːvn] noch nicht einmal III/5B1
evening [ˈiːvnɪŋ] Abend I/4B3
in the evening [ˌɪn ði‿ˈiːvnɪŋ] am Abend I/4B4
this evening [ðɪs‿ˈiːvnɪŋ] heute Abend II/5A2
event [ɪˈvent] Ereignis, Veranstaltung III/3A3
ever [ˈevə] jemals, schon einmal III/1A10
the first ever *(informal)* [ðə ˌfɜːst ˈevə] der/die/das Allererste III/5B2
every [ˈevri] jede(r, s) I/4A6
(every) now and then [ˌnaʊ‿ən ˈðen] ab und zu III/2A1
everybody [ˈevriˌbɒdi] jede(r); alle I/1A4
everyday life [ˌevrideɪ ˈlaɪf] Alltagsleben III/5A4
everyone [ˈevriˌwʌn] jede(r); alle I/4B2
°everyone else [ˌevriwʌn‿ˈels] *hier:* alle anderen III/BS2
everything [ˈevriˌθɪŋ] alles II/4B6
not exactly [nɒt ɪɡˈzækli] nicht gerade III/5B2
exam [ɪɡˈzæm] Prüfung III/7A6
°example [ɪɡˈzɑːmpl] Beispiel III/5O
excited [ɪkˈsaɪtɪd] aufgeregt, begeistert III/8A7
excitement [ɪkˈsaɪtmənt] Aufregung III/8A5
exciting [ɪkˈsaɪtɪŋ] aufregend, spannend III/2A3
Excuse me! [ɪkˈskjuːz ˌmiː] Entschuldigen Sie bitte!, Entschuldigung! I/5B6
exercise [ˈeksəsaɪz] Bewegung, Übung III/5B2
exercise book [ˈeksəsaɪz ˌbʊk] Heft I/1A4
exhausted [ɪɡˈzɔːstɪd] erschöpft III/7A6
exhibition [ˌeksɪˈbɪʃn] Ausstellung III/5A7
expect [ɪkˈspekt] erwarten, mit etwas rechnen III/7B1
expensive [ɪkˈspensɪv] teuer II/2B2
experiment [ɪkˈsperɪmənt] Experiment, Versuch III/5B1
exotic [ɪɡˈzɒtɪk] exotisch, fremdländisch
expert [ˈekspɜːt] Experte/Expertin III/6A4
explain [ɪkˈspleɪn] erklären III/5A2
explore [ɪkˈsplɔː] erforschen, untersuchen III/7B1
extra [ˈekstrə] zusätzlich III/6A1
extra- [ˈekstrə] extra-, besonders III/1B1
eye [aɪ] Auge I/2A2

F

face [feɪs] Gesicht I/2A2
fact [fækt] Tatsache III/4B2
fact sheet [ˈfækt ˌʃiːt] Informationsblatt III/7A2
°fairy [ˈfeəri] Fee III/BS4
fall [fɔːl] fallen I/4C9
fall in love (with) [ˌfɔːl‿ɪn ˈlʌv] sich verlieben (in) II/3A8
fall off [ˌfɔːl‿ˈɒf] abfallen, herunterfallen III/5O
°fall over [ˌfɔːl‿ˈəʊvə] hinfallen III/BS1
family [ˈfæmli] Familie I/5C2
famous [ˈfeɪməs] berühmt III/5A2
fan [fæn] Luft zufächeln III/4A5
fancy sb *(informal)* [ˈfænsi ˌsʌmbədi] auf jdn stehen III/6A9
fantastic [fænˈtæstɪk] fantastisch, super III/5B2; fantastisch; *hier:* Fantasie- III/7B4
FAQ (= frequently asked questions) [ˌef‿eɪ ˈkjuː] oft gestellte Fragen III/8P3
far [fɑː] weit III/5A1
°far [fɑː] *hier:* weitaus III/BS7
far away [ˌfɑːr‿əˈweɪ] fern; weit entfernt III/4P6
farm [fɑːm] Bauernhof I/3B8
°fashion [ˈfæʃn] Mode III/BS6
fast [fɑːst] schnell II/1B2
°fastener [ˈfɑːsnə] Verschluss III/5O
father [ˈfɑːðə] Vater I/1B2
fault [fɔːlt] Schuld III/4B1
favourite [ˈfeɪvrət] Liebling; Favorit/in III/2A7; Lieblings- I/W
feature [ˈfiːtʃə] Merkmal, Eigenschaft III/5P1
February [ˈfebruəri] Februar I/3A1
fee [fiː] Gebühr III/7B1
feed [fiːd] zu essen geben, füttern I/3B8
feedback [ˈfiːdbæk] Feedback, Rückmeldung III/7B5
feel [fiːl] (sich) fühlen I/4B5
feel bad [ˌfiːl ˈbæd] sich schlecht fühlen III/2B1
feel homesick [fiːl ˈhəʊmˌsɪk] Heimweh haben III/8A7
feel safe [fiːl ˈseɪf] sich sicher fühlen II/5C4
feeling [ˈfiːlɪŋ] Gefühl III/2A4
felt-tip [ˌfelt ˈtɪp] Filzstift II/1C1
female [ˈfiːmeɪl] weiblich III/3A3
festival [ˈfestɪvl] Fest, Festival III/2A4
a few [ə ˈfjuː] einige; wenige II/3C1
fiction [ˈfɪkʃn] Erzählliteratur, Roman III/7B1
field [fiːld] Feld III/2P4
°fiesta [fɪˈestə] Fiesta, (Volks)fest III/3O
°fight [faɪt] kämpfen III/BS1
°fighter [ˈfaɪtə] Kämpfer/in III/7O3
figure out sth *(informal)* [ˌfɪɡər‿ˈaʊt ˌsʌmθɪŋ] etw herausfinden III/6P7
fill [fɪl] füllen I/6A2
fill in [fɪl‿ˈɪn] ausfüllen I/2A4; eintragen I/5A1
fill up [ˌfɪl‿ˈʌp] (voll) füllen, *hier:* auffüllen III/4B2
be made into a film [biː ˌmeɪd‿ɪntʊ‿ə ˈfɪlm] verfilmt werden III/2B5
°finally [ˈfaɪnli] schließlich, endlich III/2O
find [faɪnd] finden I/1A4
find out [faɪnd‿ˈaʊt] herausfinden I/1B1

find out about [faɪnd‿'aʊt‿əˌbaʊt] sich informieren über I/3B4
fine [faɪn] in Ordnung, gut I/2B4
I'm fine. [aɪm 'faɪn] Es geht mir gut. I/4B5
finger ['fɪŋgə] Finger I/2A4
finish ['fɪnɪʃ] (be)enden, aufhören III/3B1; *hier:* fertig stellen; den letzten Schliff geben III/7O1
fire ['faɪə] Feuer; Brand II/3C1
fire brigade ['faɪə brɪˌgeɪd] Feuerwehr III/3A7
firework ['faɪəˌwɜ:k] Feuerwerkskörper II/4C3
°firm [fɜ:m] Firma, Unternehmen III/BS6
first [fɜ:st] erste(r, s) I/3A1; zuerst, als Erstes I/4B1
first aid kit [ˌfɜ:st‿'eɪd ˌkɪt] Verbandskasten III/4A6
the first ever *(informal)* [ðə ˌfɜ:st‿'evə] der/die/das Allererste III/5B2
fish [fɪʃ] fischen, angeln III/4A1
like a fish out of water [laɪk‿ə ˌfɪʃ‿aʊt‿əv 'wɔ:tə] wie ein Fisch auf dem Trockenen III/5B2
fish (*pl* fish *or* fishes) [fɪʃ, fɪʃ, fɪʃɪz] Fisch I/4A6
fit [fɪt] passen III/6P2
five [faɪv] fünf I/1A4
fix [fɪks] festmachen III/5B2
flat [flæt] (Etagen)wohnung, Mietwohnung III/4B1
°flat [flæt] flach III/BS3
flea market ['fli: ˌmɑ:kɪt] Flohmarkt III/3A7
flight [flaɪt] Flug, Fliegen III/8B1
flight attendant ['flaɪt‿əˌtendənt] Flugbegleiter/in, Steward/Stewardess III/8B3
float [fləʊt] Fest(zugs)wagen III/3A4
floor [flɔ:] (Fuß)boden I/4A1
°floor [flɔ:] Stock, Stockwerk III/BS7
flop [flɒp] Flop, Reinfall, Pleite III/5B3
flower ['flaʊə] Blume I/4B2
°flower power ['flaʊə ˌpaʊə] *Slogan der Hippie-Bewegung* III/BS6
fly [flaɪ] fliegen I/6A3
flyer (= flier) ['flaɪə] Flugblatt; *hier:* Broschüre III/5A1
flying machine ['flaɪɪŋ məˌʃi:n] Flugmaschine III/5B2
follow ['fɒləʊ] folgen II/1B5
following ['fɒləʊɪŋ] folgende(r,s) III/5B4
food [fu:d] Essen I/5C4
food technology [ˌfu:d tek'nɒlədʒi] Ernährungslehre I/5A2
fool around *(informal)* [ˌfu:l‿ə'raʊnd] *hier:* seine Zeit verschwenden III/6A9
foot (*pl* feet) [fʊt, fi:t] Fuß I/2A2
football ['fʊtˌbɔ:l] Fußball I/1A4
for [fɔ:] für; *hier:* zu(m) I/1A4
for [fɔ:] denn III/4B4
for an hour [fər‿ən 'aʊr] eine Stunde lang II/5A2
for example [ˌfɔ:r‿ɪg'zɑ:mpl] zum Beispiel II/2B8
for real *(informal)* [fə‿'rɪəl] echt, wahr III/8A5
for sale [fə 'seɪl] zu verkaufen I/3A1
°for sure *(informal)* [fə 'ʃɔ:] ganz sicher III/BS7
for ... (+ *Zeitraum*) [fə] für ..., ... lang II/1A4
foreign ['fɒrɪn] ausländisch, fremd III/8A4
°forerunner ['fɔ:ˌrʌnə] Vorläufer/in III/BS6
forest ['fɒrɪst] Wald II/3B1
°forever [fər'evə] ewig III/3O
forget [fə'get] vergessen I/1C5
fork [fɔ:k] Gabel I/2B3
form [fɔ:m] bilden III/1A9
former ['fɔ:mə] ehemalige(r, s), frühere(r, s) III/7B1
fortune ['fɔ:tʃən] Vermögen III/6A9
°found [faʊnd] gründen III/BS6
four [fɔ:] vier I/1B1
France [frɑ:ns] Frankreich III/6A4
(for) free [fri:] gratis, umsonst III/5A1
free *(informal)* [fri:] frei, *hier:* nicht gebunden III/6A9
free ticket [ˌfri: 'tɪkɪt] Freikarte III/7A6
free time [ˌfri: 'taɪm] Freizeit III/2A1
°freedom ['fri:dəm] Freiheit III/BS6
French [frentʃ] Franzose/Französin; französisch; *hier:* Französisch I/5A2
Frenchman ['frentʃmən] Franzose III/5B2
fresh [freʃ] frisch III/1A2
Friday ['fraɪdeɪ] Freitag I/2B7
fridge *(informal)* [frɪdʒ] Kühlschrank II/4B6
friend [frend] Freund/in I/1I
friendly ['frendli] freundlich I/1B2
make friends [meɪk 'frendz] sich anfreunden, Freundschaften schließen III/8A4
°friendship ['frenʃɪp] Freundschaft III/7O1
from [frəm] von, aus I/W
from all over the world [frəm‿ɔ:l‿əʊvə ðə 'wɜ:ld] aus der ganzen Welt III/7B1
front [frʌnt] vorderste(r, s) III/7P4
front crawl ['frʌnt ˌkrɔ:l] Kraulschwimmen, Kraulen III/2A5
in front of [ɪn 'frʌnt‿əv] vor I/2C2
at the front (of) [ˌæt ðə 'frʌnt] vorne II/1C5
front wheel [ˌfrʌnt 'wi:l] Vorderrad III/3B1
fruit [fru:t] Frucht; Obst I/2B1
full [fʊl] voll I/4B1
°fully ['fʊli] völlig III/BS2
fun [fʌn] Spaß II/4A6
fun [fʌn] lustig III/7B1
be (great) fun [bi: 'fʌn] (viel) Spaß machen III/2A5
be good fun [bi: ˌgʊd 'fʌn] viel Spaß machen III/5B1
have fun [hæv‿'fʌn] Spaß haben III/5B4
It sounds fun. [ɪt ˌsaʊndz 'fʌn] Es klingt gut. III/5A2
fundraising ['fʌndreɪzɪŋ] *Sammeln von Geld/Spenden* III/6LL5
funny ['fʌni] lustig, witzig, komisch I/6B3
°fur [fɜ:] Fell III/5O
further ['fɜ:ðə] weiter, (noch) mehr III/3B1
°fuss [fʌs] Wirbel machen III/BS1
future ['fju:tʃə] Zukunft II/3A1

G

g (= gram, gramme) [græm] Gramm III/1B5
G'day! = Good day! [gə'deɪ] Tag, hi, hallo III/8B1
gallery ['gæləri] Galerie III/7P2
game [geɪm] Spiel II/1B8
garden ['gɑ:dn] Garten I/1B2
do gardening [du: 'gɑ:dnɪŋ] Gartenarbeit machen III/6A2
garlic ['gɑ:lɪk] Knoblauch III/1A2
sb gives a gasp [ˌsʌmbədi ˌgɪvz‿ə 'gɑ:sp] jdm bleibt die Luft weg III/2A5
gate [geɪt] Tor; Flugsteig, Gate III/8B2
°gaze [geɪz] *hier:* schauen III/BS7
°gentleman (*pl* gentlemen) ['dʒentlmən] Gentleman, Herr III/BS7
geography [dʒi:'ɒgrəfi] Erdkunde, Geografie I/5A2
German ['dʒɜ:mən] Deutsche/r; deutsch II/1C6
in German [ɪn 'dʒɜ:mən] auf Deutsch II/1B6
Germany ['dʒɜ:məni] Deutschland I/1A8

get [get] erhalten, bekommen I/2C1; *hier:* holen, kaufen I/2C7; werden II/3C1
get [get] *hier:* kommen III/8A4; *hier:* nehmen III/5A1
°get about [ˌget‿əˈbaʊt] herumkommen III/BS1
get around [ˌget‿əˈraʊnd] herumkommen II/2B2
°get by [ˌget ˈbaɪ] auskommen; *hier:* zurechtkommen III/4O
get into [ˌget‿ˈɪntuː] *hier:* hineinkommen III/5B1
get off the ground *(informal)* [ˌget‿ɒf ðə ˈgraʊnd] abheben; *hier:* verwirklicht werden III/5B2
°get on with [ˌget‿ˈɒn wɪð] vorankommen mit III/BS4
°get one's hands on sb [ˌget wʌnz ˈhændz‿ɒn ˌsʌmbədi] jdn zu fassen kriegen III/BS5
get out [ˌget‿ˈaʊt] herauskommen III/2A5
get sb off one's mind *(informal)* [ˌget ˌsʌmbədi‿ɒf wʌnz ˈmaɪnd] sich jdn aus dem Kopf schlagen III/6A9
°get started [ˌget ˈstɑːtəd] beginnen III/3O
°get sth right [ˌget ˌsʌmθɪŋ ˈraɪt] etw richtig machen III/5O
get there [ˈget ðeə] hinkommen III/5A7
°get through [ˌget ˈθruː] durchkommen III/BS7
°get tired of sth [ˌget‿ˈtaɪəd‿əv sʌmθɪŋ] etw satt bekommen III/BS4
get up [ˌget‿ˈʌp] aufstehen I/4C4
get well card [get ˈwel ˌkɑːd] Genesungskarte II/6A5
ghost [gəʊst] Geist III/5A2
giant [ˈdʒaɪənt] riesig III/7B1
gig [gɪg] Gig *(Auftritt einer Band)* III/7A6
giraffe [dʒəˈrɑːf] Giraffe II/2B3
girl [gɜːl] Mädchen I/1A6
girlfriend [ˈgɜːlˌfrend] Freundin; Partnerin III/4B1
give [gɪv] geben I/2B4
give [gɪv] *hier:* nennen, angeben III/5A6
°give sb an unfriendly look [ˌgɪv sʌmbədi‿ən‿ʌnˌfrenli ˈlʊk] jdm einen unfreundlichen Blick zuwerfen III/BS7
give (sb) directions [gɪv dɪˈrekʃnz] (jdm) den Weg beschreiben III/8A4
give up [ˌgɪv‿ˈʌp] aufgeben III/4B2
sb gives a gasp [ˌsʌmbədi ˌgɪvz‿ə ˈgɑːsp] jdm bleibt die Luft weg III/2A5

glad [glæd] glücklich III/8A7
glass [glɑːs] Glas I/1A4
(pair of) glasses *(only plural)* [ˌpeər‿əv ˈglɑːsɪz] Brille III/2B4
glove [glʌv] Handschuh I/4C7
glow [gləʊ] Leuchten, Scheinen III/4A4
glue *(no pl)* [gluː] Klebstoff II/1C1
go [gəʊ] gehen I/1A2; *hier:* fahren I/5A3
°go away [ˌgəʊ‿əˈweɪ] weggehen, fortgehen III/BS7
go back [ˌgəʊ ˈbæk] zurückgehen III/4B2
go dancing [ˌgəʊ ˈdɑːnsɪŋ] tanzen gehen III/2B4
°go home [ˌgəʊ ˈhəʊm] nach Hause gehen III/2O
°go on [ˌgəʊ‿ˈɒn] *hier:* weiterreden III/BS7; weitergehen III/2O
go on holiday [ˌgəʊ‿ɒn ˈhɒlɪdeɪ] in Urlaub gehen/fahren II/1A1
go out [gəʊ‿ˈaʊt] ausgehen; weggehen II/3A1
go out with sb *(informal)* [ˌgəʊ‿ˈaʊt wɪð ˌsʌmbədi] mit jdm gehen III/4B1
go places [ˈgə ˌpleɪsɪz] Ausflüge machen, herumreisen III/8I
go red [ˌgəʊ ˈred] rot werden III/4B1
go shopping [ˌgəʊ ˈʃɒpɪŋ] einkaufen gehen I/2C1
go swimming [ˌgəʊ ˈswɪmɪŋ] schwimmen gehen II/6A2
go up [ˌgəʊ‿ˈʌp] hoch fahren III/5A1
go with [ˈgəʊ wɪð] passen zu II/4A4
goal [gəʊl] Ziel; Tor I/3A5
goalkeeper [ˈgəʊlˌkiːpə] Tormann/Torfrau III/2A7
°goat [gəʊt] Ziege III/7O1
God! [gɒd] Oh (mein) Gott! III/7A6
°gold [gəʊld] Gold, Gold- III/2O
°gold medal [ˌgəʊld ˈmedl] Goldmedaille III/2O
°gold miner [ˈgəʊld ˌmaɪnə] Goldgräber/in III/BS6
°gold rush [ˈgəʊld rʌʃ] Goldrausch III/BS6
goldfish *(pl* goldfish) [ˈgəʊldˌfɪʃ] Goldfisch III/L
good [gʊd] gut I/1A4
be good at sth [biː ˈgʊd‿ət ˌsʌmθɪŋ] etw gut können III/2A3
Good evening. [gʊd‿ˈiːvnɪŋ] Guten Abend. III/1A3
be good fun [biː ˌgʊd ˈfʌn] viel Spaß machen III/5B1
good luck [gʊd ˈlʌk] viel Glück II/4A3

have a good time [ˌhæv‿ə gʊd ˈtaɪm] sich amüsieren I/6A6
°say goodbye [ˌseɪ ˌgʊdˈbaɪ] auf Wiedersehen sagen, sich verabschieden III/8O
Goodbye. [ˌgʊdˈbaɪ] Auf Wiedersehen. III/2B1
grammar [ˈgræmə] Grammatik II/4B2
grand [grænd] prächtig, großartig III/3A3
grandma *(informal)* [ˈgrænˌmɑː] Oma, Omi I/W
grandmother [ˈgrænˌmʌðə] Großmutter III/1B1
grandpa *(informal)* [ˈgrænˌpɑː] Opa, Opi I/5C5
grandparents *(only plural)* [ˈgrænˌpeərənts] Großeltern II/1A1
grass [grɑːs] Gras I/6A2
great [greɪt] groß, riesig; großartig I/1A3
green [griːn] grün I/2A4
grey [greɪ] grau I/2A7
°grey-haired [ˌgreɪˈheəd] grauhaarig III/BS7
grid [grɪd] Gitter; *hier:* Tabelle II/1A4
ground [graʊnd] (Erd)boden; Erde III/6A8
get off the ground *(informal)* [ˌget‿ɒf ðə ˈgraʊnd] abheben; *hier:* verwirklicht werden III/5B2
group [gruːp] (Musik)gruppe III/7A1; Gruppe I/4B4
group [gruːp] Gruppen- III/7B1
group travel [ˈgruːp trævl] Gruppenreise III/8A7
in groups [ɪn ˈgruːpz] in Gruppen, gruppenweise II/1B6
grow [grəʊ] wachsen, größer werden III/5B4
grow up [ˌgrəʊ‿ˈʌp] erwachsen werden II/3A4
°grumble [ˈgrʌmbl] murren, meckern III/BS7
guardian angel [ˌgɑːdiən‿ˈeɪndʒl] Schutzengel III/7A2
guess [ges] (er)raten III/3A4
guess [ges] Vermutung III/2A2
Guess what! [ˌges ˈwɒt] Rate mal!; Stell dir vor! III/1B2
guest [gest] Gast III/1A9
°guidance [ˈgaɪdns] Beratung, (An)leitung III/7O3
guitar [gɪˈtɑː] Gitarre III/7A2
(chewing) gum [gʌm] Kaugummi II/5B1
gym (= gymnastics) [dʒɪm] Turnen III/7B1

H

hair *(no pl)* [heə] Haar(e) I/2A2
half an hour [ˌhɑːf‿ən‿ˈaʊə] eine halbe Stunde II/2B1
half past ten [ˈhɑːf ˌpɑːst ˈten] halb elf I/2B6
half (*pl* halves) [hɑːf, hɑːvz] Hälfte III/7A6
hall [hɔːl] Halle, Saal III/5A1
sports hall [ˈspɔːts ˌhɔːl] Sporthalle III/2A3
ham [hæm] Schinken III/1A2
hamster [ˈhæmstə] Hamster I/3B4
hand [hænd] Hand I/2A2
°on the one hand ..., on the other hand ... [ɒn ðə ˈwʌn ˌhænd ..., ɒn ði‿ˈʌðə ˌhænd] einerseits ... andererseits ... III/BS6
°handicap [ˈhændiˌkæp] Handicap, Behinderung III/2O
°get one's hands on sb [ˌget wʌnz ˈhændz‿ɒn ˌsʌmbədi] jdn zu fassen kriegen III/BS5
hang out with sb [ˌhæŋ‿ˈaʊt wɪð sʌmbədi] Zeit mit jdm verbringen III/2A1
happen [ˈhæpən] geschehen, passieren II/3A6
happen to be [ˈhæpən tə biː] zufällig sein III/6A9
happy [ˈhæpi] glücklich; zufrieden; fröhlich I/3B3
Happy birthday (to you)! [ˌhæpi ˈbɜːθdeɪ] Alles Gute zum Geburtstag! I/3C4
Happy New Year! [ˌhæpi njuː ˈjɪə] Gutes/Frohes neues Jahr! II/4A2
hard [hɑːd] hart; *hier:* anstrengend II/2A1; hart; schwer II/3B1; *hier:* schwierig III/5B1
°hardly at all [ˌhɑːdli‿ət‿ˈɔːl] so gut wie nie III/BS4
°harmony [ˈhɑːməni] Harmonie III/BS6
°harsh [hɑːʃ] rau; hart III/BS7
hat [hæt] Hut; Mütze I/4C7
hate [heɪt] hassen, nicht ausstehen können I/1A5
have [hæv] haben I/W; *hier:* essen, trinken I/2B1
have a ball *(informal)* [ˌhæv‿ə ˈbɔːl] Spaß haben, sich bestens amüsieren III/6A9
°have a chat [ˌhæv‿ə ˈtʃæt] sich unterhalten III/BS5
have a drink [ˌhæv‿ə ˈdrɪŋk] etw trinken III/3B2
have a good time [ˌhæv‿ə gʊd ˈtaɪm] sich amüsieren I/6A6
°have a knack [hæv‿ə ˈnæk] den Bogen raus haben III/BS1
have a look (at) [ˌhæv‿ə ˈlʊk] sich ansehen II/2C1
have a look round [ˌhæv‿ə lʊk ˈraʊnd] sich umsehen III/5B1
have a party [ˌhæv‿ə ˈpɑːti] eine Party machen II/4A2
have a temperature [hæv‿ə ˈtemprɪtʃə] Fieber haben III/2B1
have a vote [ˌhæv‿ə ˈvəʊt] abstimmen III/5B5
have breakfast [hæv ˈbrekfəst] frühstücken I/2B2
have fun [hæv‿ˈfʌn] Spaß haben III/5B4
have got [hæv ˈgɒt] haben I/W
have tea [hæv ˈtiː] Tee trinken II/2C1
have to do sth [ˌhæv tə ˈduː ˌsʌmθɪŋ] etw tun müssen III/2A7
Have you? [hæv ˈjuː] *hier:* Und du? III/5A1
he [hi] er I/1A4
head [hed] Kopf I/2A4
°shake one's head [ˌʃeɪk wʌnz ˈhed] den Kopf schütteln III/BS7
health [helθ] Gesundheit III/2A4
healthy [ˈhelθi] gesund III/2A1
hear [hɪə] hören I/1A1
heart [hɑːt] Herz III/4A9
by heart [ˌbaɪ ˈhɑːt] auswendig II/4C2
°heartbroken [ˈhɑːtˌbrəʊkən] todunglücklich, untröstlich III/7O3
heav'n (= heaven) [ˈhevn] Himmel III/4A4
heavy [ˈhevi] schwer; stark I/4C10
hedgehog [ˈhedʒˌhɒg] Igel I/3B2
°draw oneself up to one's full height [ˌdrɔː wʌnself‿ˈʌp tʊ wʌnz ˌfʊl ˈhaɪt] sich zu seiner vollen Größe aufrichten III/BS7
Hello. [həˈləʊ] Hallo. I/1A2
helmet [ˈhelmɪt] Helm III/2A3
help [help] helfen I/1B2
help [help] Hilfe III/7A5
ask for help [ˌɑːsk fə ˈhelp] um Hilfe bitten III/8A4
for help [fə ˈhelp] zu/als Hilfe III/2A4
help out [help ˈaʊt] (aus)helfen, unterstützen II/2B8
Help! [help] (Zu) Hilfe! II/3B2
helpful [ˈhelpfl] hilfreich, nützlich; hilfsbereit III/4B1
°helpless [ˈhelpləs] hilflos, machtlos III/BS7
her [hɜː] sie; ihr(e, n) I/1A4
here [hɪə] hier(her) I/1B2
Here you are! [ˌhɪə juː‿ˈɑː] Hier, bitte!, Bitte schön! III/5A1
hero (*pl* heroes) [ˈhɪərəʊ, ˈhɪərəʊz] Held III/2A7
hidden word puzzle [ˌhɪdn ˈwɜːd ˌpʌzl] *Suchrätsel* III/1B6
hide [haɪd] verstecken II/4A6
high [haɪ] hoch I/6C1
°high school *(AE)* [ˈhaɪ ˌskuːl] High-school *(weiterführende Schule)* III/6O
him [hɪm] ihm, ihn I/3B4
(the) Himalayas *(only plural)* [ˌhɪməˈleɪəz] Himalaya III/8B1
himself [hɪmˈself] sich (selbst) III/2B5
by himself [ˌbaɪ hɪmˈself] ganz allein III/2B6
hire [ˈhaɪə] Vermietung III/7B1
his [hɪz] sein(e, r) I/1A2
historic [hɪˈstɒrɪk] historisch III/7B1
history [ˈhɪstri] Geschichte I/5A1
hit [hɪt] schlagen; treffen; stoßen (gegen) III/3A3
hockey stick [ˈhɒki ˌstɪk] Hockeyschläger III/6A6
°hoist [hɔɪst] (hoch)heben III/BS1
hold [həʊld] halten III/1B1
°hold together [ˌhəʊld təˈgeðə] zusammenhalten III/5O
°hold-up [ˈhəʊldʌp] *hier:* Stau III/BS7
hole [həʊl] Loch III/5B2
holiday [ˈhɒlɪdeɪ] Urlaub, Ferien I/6A1
be on holiday [ˌbi ɒn ˈhɒlɪdeɪ] Urlaub/Ferien haben I/6A3
go on holiday [ˌgəʊ‿ɒn ˈhɒlɪdeɪ] in Urlaub gehen/fahren II/1A1
holiday camp [ˈhɒlɪdeɪ ˌkæmp] Ferienlager III/8A7
home [həʊm] Zuhause I/3A1; Zuhause; *hier:* Heimat III/4I; zuhause; *hier:* nach Hause I/5A3
°home [həʊm] *hier:* Haus, Wohnung III/5O
at home [ət ˈhəʊm] zu Hause I/2B1
°go home [ˌgəʊ ˈhəʊm] nach Hause gehen III/2O
Home, sweet home! [ˌhəʊm ˌswiːt ˈhəʊm] Trautes Heim, Glück allein! III/4A1
feel homesick [fiːl ˈhəʊmˌsɪk] Heimweh haben III/8A7
homework *(no pl)* [ˈhəʊmˌwɜːk] Hausaufgaben I/1C1
honey [ˈhʌni] Honig III/1B5
°hook [hʊk] Haken III/5O

°hook and loop fastener [ˌhʊk‿ən 'lu:p ˌfɑ:snə] *Klettverschluss* III/5O
hop [hɒp] hüpfen, springen III/2A2
hope [həʊp] hoffen I/3A4
°blow one's horn [ˌbləʊ wʌnz 'hɔ:n] hupen III/8O
horror movie ['hɒrə ˌmu:vi] Horrorfilm III/7A2
horse [hɔ:s] Pferd I/3A7
horse-riding ['hɔ:sˌraɪdɪŋ] Reiten III/7B1
hospital ['hɒspɪtl] Krankenhaus III/4B2
hot [hɒt] heiß I/4A6; *hier:* scharf III/1B1
hot tip [ˌhɒt‿'tɪp] heißer Tipp III/5B1
hot-air balloon [ˌhɒt‿'eə bəˌlu:n] Heißluftballon III/5B2
hour ['aʊə] Stunde I/6A6
house [haʊs] Haus I/W
at sb's house [æt ˌsʌmbədiz 'haʊs] bei jdm zu Hause II/3A1
house captain ['haʊs ˌkæptɪn] *Sprecher/in für ein Haus* III/2LL2
housework ['haʊsˌwɜ:k] Hausarbeit III/2B5
how [haʊ] wie I/W
How about you? [ˌhaʊ əˌbaʊt 'ju:] Wie ist es mit dir/Ihnen? III/1A3
How are you? [haʊ‿'ɑ: ju:] Wie geht es dir/Ihnen/euch? I/4B5
how many [haʊ 'meni] wie viele II/1B8
How much is/are ...? [ˌhaʊ mʌtʃ‿'ɪz/ɑ:] Was kostet/kosten ...? I/2C5
How old are you? [haʊ‿'əʊld‿ə jʊ] Wie alt bist du/seid ihr? I/W
how to ['haʊ tə] wie man II/1A1
°hug [hʌg] umarmen III/7O3
huge [hju:dʒ] riesig, riesengroß III/5B1
Hungary ['hʌŋgəri] Ungarn III/8B1
hungry ['hʌŋgri] hungrig I/1A3
hurry up [ˌhʌri‿'ʌp] sich beeilen II/3B2
hurt [hɜ:t] wehtun, schmerzen III/2B1
husband ['hʌzbənd] Ehemann I/5C7
hut [hʌt] Hütte III/4A8

I

I [aɪ] ich I/W
I'd like (to) ... [aɪd 'laɪk] Ich hätte/würde gern ... I/5B6
I'll have ... ['aɪl hæv] Ich werde ... nehmen/essen. III/1A3
I'm fine. [aɪm 'faɪn] Es geht mir gut. I/4B5
I'm (from ...) [aɪm] Ich bin/komme (aus ...) I/W
°i. e. (= id est) [ˌaɪ 'i:] d. h. (= das heißt) III/BS6
ice cream [ˌaɪs 'kri:m] Eiskrem, Eis I/2C1
ice hockey ['aɪs ˌhɒki] Eishockey III/2A3
idea [aɪ'dɪə] Idee I/1A3; Vorstellung II/3A1
idol ['aɪdl] Idol III/7P6
if [ɪf] wenn, falls; ob I/5A3
if I got me *(informal)* [ɪf aɪ 'gɒt mi:] wenn ich bekommen könnte III/6A9
ill [ɪl] krank II/3A4
illustrate ['ɪləstreɪt] illustrieren, bebildern III/4A5
°image ['ɪmɪdʒ] *hier:* Vorstellung III/BS6
imagine [ɪ'mædʒɪn] sich vorstellen III/5A5
°immigrant ['ɪmɪgrənt] Einwanderer/in III/BS6
important [ɪm'pɔ:tnt] wichtig III/3A6
°improve [ɪm'pru:v] verbessern III/BS3
in [ɪn] in I/W
°in a low voice [ɪn‿ə ˌləʊ 'vɔɪs] mit leiser Stimme III/BS7
°in any case [ɪn‿'eni ˌkeɪs] auf jeden Fall III/BS7
°in contrast [ɪn 'kɒntrɑ:st] im Gegensatz III/BS3
in English [ɪn‿'ɪŋglɪʃ] auf Englisch II/1A1
in front of [ɪn 'frʌnt‿əv] vor I/2C2
in German [ɪn 'dʒɜ:mən] auf Deutsch II/1B6
in groups [ɪn 'gru:pz] in Gruppen, gruppenweise II/1B6
in the afternoon [ˌɪn ði:‿ɑ:ftə'nu:n] am Nachmittag I/6A3
°in the country [ˌɪn ðə 'kʌntri] auf dem Land III/5O
in the evening [ˌɪn ði‿'i:vnɪŋ] am Abend I/4B4
in the middle ['ɪn ðə 'mɪdl] in der Mitte; mitten in/auf II/1C5
in the morning [ˌɪn ðə 'mɔ:nɪŋ] am Morgen I/4C4
in the picture [ˌɪn ðə 'pɪktʃə] auf dem Bild III/7B4
in the street [ˌɪn ðə 'stri:t] auf der Straße II/2A1
°in turn [ɪn 'tɜ:n] wiederum III/BS7
in-line skating [ˌɪnlaɪn 'skeɪtɪŋ] Inlineskaten III/L
incident ['ɪnsɪdnt] Vorfall, Ereignis III/3B1
°independent [ˌɪndɪ'pendənt] unabhängig, selbständig III/BS2
India ['ɪndiə] Indien II/1L
Indian ['ɪndiən] Inder/in; indisch III/1B1
°indicator ['ɪndɪˌkeɪtə] Blinker III/BS7
°indigo ['ɪndɪgəʊ] Indigo(blau) III/BS6
individual [ˌɪndɪ'vɪdʒuəl] Einzelperson III/3A3
indoor ['ɪndɔ:] Innen-; *hier:* Hallen- III/7B1
industry ['ɪndəstri] Industrie III/5A1
°influential [ˌɪnflu'enʃl] einflussreich III/BS6
information pack [ˌɪnfə'meɪʃn ˌpæk] Informationspaket III/7B1
information technology [ɪnfəˌmeɪʃn tek'nɒlədʒi] Informationstechnologie; *hier:* Informatik I/5A2
inside [ˌɪn'saɪd] innen, drinnen III/1A6
°insist [ɪn'sɪst] bestehen III/BS7
intelligent [ɪn'telɪdʒnt] klug, intelligent III/2B5
be interested in [bi:‿'ɪntrəstɪd‿ɪn] sich interessieren für III/5A2
interesting ['ɪntrəstɪŋ] interessant I/5A2
on the Internet [ˌɒn ði‿'ɪntənet] im Internet II/1B7
search the Internet [ˌsɜ:tʃ ði‿'ɪntənet] im Internet suchen II/6B4
surf the Internet [ˌsɜ:f ði‿'ɪntənet] im Internet surfen II/6A6
interview ['ɪntəˌvju:] interviewen, befragen III/4A3
interview ['ɪntəˌvju:] *hier:* Verhör III/3B3
into ['ɪntʊ] in I/2A4
°introduce [ˌɪntrə'dju:s] vorstellen III/2O; vorstellen; *hier:* einführen III/BS6
invent [ɪn'vent] erfinden III/5B2
invention [ɪn'venʃn] Erfindung III/5A2
inventor [ɪn'ventə] Erfinder/in III/5B2
invite [ɪn'vaɪt] einladen II/4B9
(Republic of) Ireland ['aɪələnd] (Republik) Irland II/1LL1
°irritating ['ɪrɪˌteɪtɪŋ] ärgerlich, lästig III/5O
island ['aɪlənd] Insel III/4I
No man is an island. [ˌnəʊ ˌmæn‿ɪz‿ən‿'aɪlənd] Niemand ist alleine auf der Welt. III/4I
it [ɪt] es I/1A4
It's ... £ (pounds). [ˌɪts ... 'paʊndz] Es kostet ... Pfund. III/6A7
Italian [ɪ'tæljən] Italiener/in; italienisch III/1A2

°Italy ['ɪtəli] Italien III/BS6
its [ɪts] sein(e), ihr(e) I/3B2

J

jacket ['dʒækɪt] Jacke I/4C7
°jam [dʒæm] frei improvisieren, jammen *(Musik)* III/3O
January ['dʒænjuəri] Januar I/5C2
°jet plane ['dʒet ˌpleɪn] Düsenflugzeug III/8O
job [dʒɒb] Arbeit, Stelle, Aufgabe I/4C1
°join [dʒɔɪn] *hier:* beitreten, Mitglied werden III/6O; *hier:* sich gesellen zu III/3O
°tell jokes [ˌtel 'dʒəʊks] Witze reißen III/7O1
be joking [biː 'dʒəʊkɪŋ] Spaß machen III/6A4
You must be joking! [jʊ ˌmʌst bi 'dʒəʊkɪŋ] Das meinst du doch nicht im Ernst!, Das soll wohl ein Witz sein! II/3A1
You're joking! [jʊə 'dʒəʊkɪŋ] Das ist doch nicht dein Ernst! III/6P1
journey ['dʒɜːni] Reise; Fahrt III/5A1
juice [dʒuːs] Saft I/1A4
July [dʒʊ'laɪ] Juli I/5C2
jump [dʒʌmp] springen II/1B2
June [dʒuːn] Juni I/2P3
just [dʒʌst] *hier:* gerade (eben) III/7A6; nur, bloß, einfach III/7A6
just as ['dʒʌst‿əz] genauso (wie) III/2A3
°just before [ˌdʒʌst bɪ'fɔː] kurz vor III/BS7
just the thing [ˌdʒʌst ðə 'θɪŋ] genau das Richtige III/5B4

K

kangaroo [ˌkæŋgə'ruː] Känguru III/8B2
°Karamu [kæ'rɑːmuː] *Festessen* III/3O
keep [kiːp] aufbewahren; behalten I/4A6
keep a secret [ˌkiːp‿ə 'siːkrət] für sich behalten III/4B1
°keep up (with sb) [ˌkiːp‿'ʌp] (mit jdm) mithalten III/BS1
kick [kɪk] treten, schießen III/2B2
kid [kɪd] Kind, Jugendliche(r) III/7A6
You're kidding! *(informal)* [jɔː 'kɪdɪŋ] Das ist doch nicht dein Ernst! III/7A6
kilo ['kiːləʊ] Kilo I/5B1
kilometre [kɪ'lɒmɪtə] Kilometer III/6B2
kind [kaɪnd] Art, Sorte I/3C2
all kinds of [ɔːl 'kaɪndz‿əv] alle möglichen III/3A7
king [kɪŋ] König II/4C1
kiss [kɪs] küssen II/5A5
kitchen ['kɪtʃən] Küche I/2B3
°have a knack [hæv‿ə 'næk] den Bogen raus haben III/BS1
be knackered *(informal)* [biː 'nækəd] kaputt/fix und fertig sein III/7A6
knee [niː] Knie I/2A4
on bended knee(s) [ɒn ˌbendɪd 'niːz] auf Knien III/4A4
knife (*pl* knives) [naɪf, naɪvz] Messer I/2B3
knock [nɒk] stoßen III/3B1
know [nəʊ] wissen; kennen I/1A6
°known [nəʊn] bekannt III/BS6
kph (= kilometres per hour) [ˌkeɪ piː‿'eɪtʃ (= kɪˌlɒmɪtəz pɜr‿'aʊə)] km/h III/5B2

L

°label ['leɪbl] Etikett; Marke III/BS6
lady ['leɪdi] Frau; Dame III/1A8
°lagoon [lə'guːn] Lagune III/BS4
lake [laɪk] See II/2C1
lamp [læmp] Lampe III/5B4
land [lænd] Land III/5B2
land [lænd] landen III/5B2
language ['læŋgwɪdʒ] Sprache II/4A1
large [lɑːdʒ] groß II/2C1
lasagna [lə'zænjə] Lasagne III/1A2
last [lɑːst] letzte(r, s) I/5A1
at last [ət l'ɑːst] endlich, schließlich II/6A2
(too) late [leɪt] (zu) spät II/1B5
later ['leɪtə] später II/1A4
°the latest [ðə 'leɪtɪst] der/die/das jüngste, letzte III/6O
laugh [lɑːf] lachen I/6C5
lead [liːd] führen III/2A1
leaf (*pl* leaves) [liːf, liːvz] Blatt II/2B3
leaflet ['liːflət] Prospekt III/5A7
learn [lɜːn] lernen I/1C6
least [liːst] am wenigsten II/5B1
leave [liːv] (weg)gehen; abfahren II/5A2; verlassen II/5B1
leave [liːv] *hier:* zurücklassen III/4B1
left [left] linke(r, s) I/2A4
(turn) left [left] links (abbiegen) II/2B4
be left [biː 'left] übrig bleiben III/6A9
on the left [ˌɒn ðə 'left] links, auf der linken Seite II/1C5
leg [leg] Bein I/2A4
lemon ['lemən] Zitrone I/5B1
less [les] weniger III/2A3
lesson ['lesn] Stunde I/3C4
let [let] lassen I/1A2
°let sb down [ˌlet ˌsʌmbədi 'daʊn] jdn enttäuschen III/8O
let's (= let us) … [lets, 'let‿əs] lass(t) uns … I/1A2
letter ['letə] Brief; Buchstabe I/3C3
library ['laɪbrəri] Bibliothek, Bücherei II/6B4
lie [laɪ] liegen; sich hinlegen II/3C1
°tell lies [ˌtel 'laɪz] Lügen erzählen III/BS7
life (*pl* lives) [laɪf, laɪvz] Leben I/4C1
lift [lɪft] (hoch)heben, anheben III/2A5
light [laɪt] Licht I/4A4
light bulb ['laɪt ˌbʌlb] Glühbirne III/5A4
like [laɪk] mögen I/W; wie I/4A6
°like [laɪk] *hier:* als ob III/8O
like a fish out of water [laɪk‿ə ˌfɪʃ‿aʊt‿əv 'wɔːtə] wie ein Fisch auf dem Trockenen III/5B2
like best [ˌlaɪk 'best] am liebsten mögen II/4A4
like this/that [ˌlaɪk 'ðɪs/'ðæt] so; auf diese Weise II/1B1
like this/that [ˌlaɪk 'ðɪs/'ðæt] solche(r, s) III/4B1
I'd like (to) … [aɪd 'laɪk] Ich hätte/würde gern … I/5B6
What was it like? [ˌwɒt wəs‿ɪt 'laɪk] Wie war es? III/8B2
°liming [laɪmɪŋ] *Nichtstun, Faulenzen* III/3O
line [laɪn] Linie; *hier:* Zeile III/2A6; *hier:* Leine, Schnur III/BS3
lion ['laɪən] Löwe II/2B3
list [lɪst] Liste III/1A1
listen (to) ['lɪsn] (zu)hören I/1A1
°listener ['lɪsənə] Zuhörer/in III/6O
little ['lɪtl] klein I/4C6
°little ['lɪtl] *hier:* wenig III/BS7
a little [ə 'lɪtl] ein wenig, ein bisschen III/2A2
live [lɪv] leben, wohnen I/W
living room ['lɪvɪŋ ˌruːm] Wohnzimmer I/4B2
load [ləʊd] Ladung; Last III/4A4
location [ləʊ'keɪʃn] Standort, Lage III/3A3
locomotive [ˌləʊkə'məʊtɪv] Lokomotive III/5A2
lonely ['ləʊnli] einsam III/4A6
°be a bit of a loner [biː‿ə ˌbɪt‿əv‿ə 'ləʊnə] ein/e ziemliche/r Einzelgänger/in sein III/BS5
°lonesome ['ləʊnsm] einsam III/8O
long [lɒŋ] lang I/2A5
look [lʊk] *hier:* aussehen I/3B8; sehen, schauen I/1A2
°look [lʊk] Blick III/BS7
°give sb an unfriendly look [ˌgɪv sʌmbədi‿ən‿ʌnˌfrenli 'lʊk] jdm einen

unfreundlichen Blick zuwerfen III/BS7
look after [lʊk‿'ɑ:ftə] sich kümmern um II/1A4
look at ['lʊk‿ət] betrachten, sehen I/1C1
have a look (at) [ˌhæv‿ə 'lʊk] sich ansehen II/2C1
look for ['lʊk ˌfə] suchen nach II/2A1
look like ['lʊk ˌlaɪk] aussehen III/5A2
have a look round [ˌhæv‿ə lʊk 'raʊnd] sich umsehen III/5B1
look through [ˌlʊk 'θru:] durchsehen III/2B5
look up [ˌlʊk‿'ʌp] nachschlagen III/2A7
°loop [lu:p] Schleife; Schlinge III/5O
lose [lu:z] verlieren II/3C1
lose one's way ['lu:z wʌnz 'weɪ] sich verirren II/6A8
a lot (of) [ə 'lɒt] viel(e) I/1A1
lots *(informal)* [lɒts] viel, jede Menge II/1A4
lots of ['lɒts‿əv] viel, jede Menge I/3A6
loud [laʊd] laut I/1C5
love [lʌv] Liebe III/4B1; lieben; sehr gern mögen I/1A4
love *(in Briefen)* [lʌv] alles Liebe, viele Grüße II/6C6
love song ['lʌv ˌsɒŋ] Liebeslied III/7A2
fall in love (with) [ˌfɔ:l‿ɪn 'lʌv] sich verlieben (in) II/3A8
lovely ['lʌvli] schön, hübsch; *hier:* herrlich I/4C5
lover ['lʌvə] Liebhaber/in III/4B1
°low rise [ˌləʊ 'raɪz] *Schnitt* III/BS6
°in a low voice [ɪn‿ə ˌləʊ 'vɔɪs] mit leiser Stimme III/BS7
°try one's luck [ˌtraɪ wʌnz 'lʌk] sein Glück versuchen III/BS7
be lucky [bi: 'lʌki] Glück haben II/3C1
lunch [lʌntʃ] Mittagessen I/5A1
lunchbox ['lʌntʃˌbɒks] Brotdose III/5B4
lure [ljʊə] (an)locken III/4A5
°luv (= love) *(informal)* [lʌv] Liebe III/4O
lyrics *(only plural)* ['lɪrɪks] (Lied)text III/4A4

M

°m (= metre) ['mi:tə] Meter III/2O
machine [mə'ʃi:n] Maschine III/2B5
madam ['mædəm] gnädige Frau *(Anrede)* III/1A8
°madman ['mædmən] Irrer, Verrückter III/BS7
magazine [ˌmægə'zi:n] Zeitschrift, Magazin II/3B1
magician [mə'dʒɪʃn] Zauberer/Zauberin III/3A7
main [meɪn] Haupt- III/5B1
main course ['meɪn ˌkɔ:s] Hauptgericht III/1A2
main parade [ˌmeɪn pə'reɪd] *hier:* großer Umzug III/3LL3
°main road [ˌmeɪn 'rəʊd] Hauptstraße III/BS7
make [meɪk] machen I/1A8
make a call [ˌmeɪk‿ə 'kɔ:l] telefonieren II/5B1
make friends [meɪk 'frendz] sich anfreunden, Freundschaften schließen III/8A4
make money [ˌmeɪk 'mʌni] Geld verdienen II/3B1
make money [ˌmeɪk 'mʌni] *hier:* Geld einbringen III/2B5
make notes (on) [ˌmeɪk 'nəʊts] (sich) Notizen machen (über) II/3A4
°make off *(informal)* [ˌmeɪk‿'ɒf] verschwinden, abhauen III/BS7
°make sb think of sth [ˌmeɪk sʌmbədi 'θɪŋk‿əv ˌsʌmθɪŋ] jdn an etw denken lassen III/3O
make up [meɪk‿'ʌp] erfinden, (sich) ausdenken II/6B2
male [meɪl] männlich III/3A3
man *(pl* **men)** [mæn, men] Mann I/2A7; Mensch II/3B1
manage ['mænɪdʒ] es schaffen III/3B1
many ['meni] viele I/3B1
many a ['meni‿ə] manch ein/e III/4A4
map [mæp] (Land)karte III/6B2
marathon ['mærəθn] Marathon(lauf) III/6B1
March [mɑ:tʃ] März I/3B7
mark [mɑ:k] Note, Zensur III/6A1
market ['mɑ:kɪt] Markt I/1B1
married ['mærid] verheiratet I/5C7
mash [mæʃ] zerdrücken III/1B5
mask [mɑ:sk] Maske III/3A1
mass [mæs] Masse; *hier:* Massen- III/6B2
match [mætʃ] Spiel I/3A3
match *(pl* matches) [mætʃ, 'mætʃɪz] Streichholz III/4A6
match (with/to) [mætʃ] zuordnen I/3B3
°mate [meɪt] Freund/in, Kumpel III/4O
°material [mə'tɪəriəl] Material III/5O
maths [mæθs] Mathe I/5A1
What's the matter? [ˌwɒts ðə 'mætə] Was ist los? II/2A1
maximum ['mæksɪməm] maximal, Höchst- II /7B1
May [meɪ] Mai I/5C2
may [meɪ] können, mögen III/4A4
maybe ['meɪbi] vielleicht, möglicherweise I/4B3
me [mi:] mir, mich; *hier:* ich I/1A3
meal [mi:l] Mahlzeit, Essen III/1B1
take sb out for a meal [ˌteɪk sʌmbədi‿'aʊt fər‿ə 'mi:l] jdn zum Essen einladen III/1A6
mean [mi:n] bedeuten; meinen I/4B5
°they don't mean a thing [ˌðeɪ dəʊnt ˌmi:n‿ə 'θɪŋ] *hier:* sie bedeuten gar nichts III/3O
meaning ['mi:nɪŋ] Bedeutung III/2A7
°measure ['meʒə] (ab)messen III/BS7
meat [mi:t] Fleisch II/2B3
medicine ['medsn] Medizin, Medikamente III/4A1
meet [mi:t] (sich) treffen I/1B5
meet [mi:t] *hier:* abholen III/5A1; treffen, kennen lernen III/BS5
melon ['melən] Melone III/1A2
member ['membə] Angehörige(r), Mitglied II/4B2
mention ['menʃn] erwähnen III/5B1
menu ['menju:] Speisekarte III/1A2
°merry-go-round ['merigəʊˌraʊnd] Karussell III/3O
message in a bottle [ˌmesɪdʒ‿ɪn‿ə 'bɒtl] Flaschenpost III/4A8
metal ['metl] aus Metall III/5B2
metre ['mi:tə] Meter III/5B2
°microscope ['maɪkrəˌskəʊp] Mikroskop III/5O
in the middle ['ɪn ðə 'mɪdl] in der Mitte; mitten in/auf II/1C5
midnight ['mɪdˌnaɪt] Mitternacht III/3A3
might [maɪt] könnte(st, n) II/2A4
°mighty *(AE, informal)* ['maɪti] sehr III/4O
mild [maɪld] mild; leicht III/1B5
mile [maɪl] Meile *(= 1,609 km)* III/6B1
milk [mɪlk] Milch I/2B1
milk product ['mɪlk ˌprɒdʌkt] Milchprodukt II/1B6
°millennium [mɪ'leniəm] Jahrtausend III/BS6
change one's mind [ˌtʃeɪndʒ wʌnz 'maɪnd] seine Meinung ändern III/1A8
mingle ['mɪŋgl] mischen III/4A4
°miniskirt ['mɪniskɜ:t] Minirock III/BS6
mint [mɪnt] Minze III/1A2
minute ['mɪnɪt] Minute II/2B1
miss [mɪs] vermissen; verpassen II/6A5

miss [mɪs] verfehlen III/8P1
°Miss [mɪs] Miss; Fräulein; Frau Lehrerin III/BS1
missing ['mɪsɪŋ] verschwunden; *hier:* fehlend III/5P2
°be mistaken [bi: mɪ'steɪkən] sich irren III/BS7
mix [mɪks] (ver)mischen III/1B5
°mix up sb [ˌmɪks‿'ʌp ˌsʌmbədi] jdn verwechseln III/BS7
mobile (phone) ['məʊbaɪl] Mobiltelefon, Handy II/5B1
model (text) ['mɒdl] Mustertext II/1C6
model train [ˌmɒdl 'treɪn] Modelleisenbahn III/6A7
°moment ['məʊmənt] Moment, Augenblick III/BS7
at the moment [ˌæt ðə 'məʊmənt] im Augenblick, momentan II/2A5
Monday ['mʌndeɪ] Montag I/2B7
money ['mʌni] Geld II/2B8
make money [ˌmeɪk 'mʌni] Geld verdienen II/3B1
make money [ˌmeɪk 'mʌni] *hier:* Geld einbringen III/2B5
raise money [ˌreɪz 'mʌni] Geld aufbringen III/8A3
be short of money *(informal)* [bi: ˌʃɔ:t‿əv 'mʌni] knapp bei Kasse sein III/6A2
monkey ['mʌŋki] Affe I/6C1
month [mʌnθ] Monat I/5C1
moon [mu:n] Mond II/3A1
more [mɔ:] mehr I/1C4; noch mehr; weitere(r, s) II/6A7
°morn (= morning) [mɔ:n] Morgen III/8O
morning ['mɔ:nɪŋ] Morgen, Vormittag I/2A2
in the morning [ˌɪn ðə 'mɔ:nɪŋ] am Morgen I/4C4
this morning [ðɪs 'mɔ:nɪŋ] heute Morgen I/5B2
Moscow ['mɒskəʊ] Moskau III/8A2
most [məʊst] am meisten II/5B1; die meisten III/6B1
most of all [ˌməʊst‿əv‿'ɔ:l] am meisten III/4A3
mother ['mʌðə] Mutter I/2B3
mountain ['maʊntɪn] Berg II/1A4
mouse (*pl* mice) [maʊs, maɪs] Maus I/3B1
mouth [maʊθ] Mund I/2A2
move [mu:v] (sich) bewegen II/3C1
°movement ['mu:vmənt] Bewegung III/BS6
MP3 player [ˌem pi: 'θri: ˌpleɪə] MP3-Spieler III/3P5
Mr ['mɪstə] Herr *(Anrede)* I/W
Mrs ['mɪsɪz] Frau *(Anrede)* I/W
much [mʌtʃ] *hier:* häufig, oft II/5A5; viel; sehr I/1A5
mum *(informal)* [mʌm] Mama, Mutti I/1A3
muscular ['mʌskjʊlə] muskulös III/2A7
museum [mju:'zi:əm] Museum II/2C5
mushroom ['mʌʃru:m] Pilz III/1A2
music ['mju:zɪk] Musik I/6C6
musician [mju'zɪʃn] Musiker/in III/7A2
must [mʌst] müssen I/4A4
must not [ˌmʌst 'nɒt] nicht dürfen II/5A3
my [maɪ] mein(e) I/W

N

name [neɪm] Name I/W
call sb names [ˌkɔ:l sʌmbədi 'neɪmz] jdn beschimpfen II/5C3
narrow ['nærəʊ] eng; knapp III/3B1
have a narrow escape [hæv‿ə ˌnærəʊ‿ɪ'skeɪp] gerade noch einmal davongekommen sein III/3B1
°nature ['neɪtʃə] Natur III/5O
°the navy [ðə 'neɪvi] die Marine III/BS6
near [nɪə] nahe (bei) I/1B1
nearly ['nɪəli] fast, beinahe II/3C1
neck [nek] Hals; Nacken I/2A2
need [ni:d] brauchen II/1B5
need [ni:d] *hier:* müssen III/5B2
neighbour ['neɪbə] Nachbar/in II/4A2
cast a net [ˌkɑ:st‿ə 'net] ein Netz auswerfen III/4A4
netball ['netˌbɔ:l] Korbball III/7B1
never ['nevə] nie(mals) I/4C1
new [nju:] neu I/1A2
New Year [ˌnju: 'jɪə] Neujahr II/4A3
Happy New Year! [ˌhæpi nju: 'jɪə] Gutes/Frohes neues Jahr! II/4A2
°newcomer ['nju:ˌkʌmə] Neuankömmling III/7O1
news *(no pl)* [nju:z] Neuigkeit; Nachrichten II/1B4
newspaper ['nju:zˌpeɪpə] Zeitung I/4C10
next [nekst] nächste(r, s) I/2B7
°next [nekst] *hier:* als Nächstes III/BS5
next time ['nekst‿ˌtaɪm] nächstes Mal III/2B2
next to ['nekst‿tə] neben I/2C2
the Niagara Falls *(only plural)* [ðə naɪˌægərə 'fɔ:lz] die Niagarafälle III/8A3
nice [naɪs] schön; nett I/1B2
Nice to meet you. [ˌnaɪs tə 'mi:t jə] Es freut mich, Sie/dich kennen zu lernen. I/4B5
night [naɪt] Nacht II/3C2
at night [ət 'naɪt] nachts I/3B1
night hike ['naɪt ˌhaɪk] Nachtwanderung III/8A7
°nightmare ['naɪtˌmeə] Albtraum III/7O3
nine [naɪn] neun I/2B4
no [nəʊ] kein(e) I/1A6; nein I/W
no longer [nəʊ 'lɒŋgə] nicht mehr III/5A6
No man is an island. [ˌnəʊ ˌmæn‿ɪz‿ən‿'aɪlənd] Niemand ist alleine auf der Welt. III/4I
°no one ['nəʊ wʌn] keiner, niemand III/BS5
nobody ['nəʊbɒdi] niemand I/5C4
°nobody else [ˌnəʊbədi‿'els] niemand anderes III/BS7
°nod [nɒd] nicken III/BS7
noise [nɔɪz] Lärm, Geräusch III/3A3
noisy ['nɔɪzi] laut III/5A2
°non-western [ˌnɒn 'westən] nicht westlich III/BS6
°nor [nɔ:] und auch nicht, noch III/BS7
normally ['nɔ:mli] normalerweise III/4B2
north [nɔ:θ] Norden I/4C10; Norden; *hier:* in nördliche Richtung III/5A1
°North America [ˌnɔ:θ‿ə'merɪkə] Nordamerika III/BS6
Northern Ireland [ˌnɔ:ðn‿'aɪələnd] Nordirland II/1LL1
nose [nəʊz] Nase I/2A2
not [nɒt] nicht I/1A4
not … any [ˌnɒt‿'eni] keine(r, s) II/6A4
not … anywhere [ˌnɒt‿'eniweə] nirgendwo(hin) II/6A2
not any [nɒt‿'eni] kein/keine II/3A9
not anymore [nɒt‿ˌeni'mɔ:] nicht mehr II/5C2
not anyone [ˌnɒt‿'eniwʌn] niemand II/3A1
not anything [ˌnɒt‿'eniθɪŋ] nichts II/3C5
not at all [ˌnɒt‿ət‿'ɔ:l] keine Ursache III/1A8; überhaupt nicht III/2A2
not even [nɒt 'i:vn] noch nicht einmal III/5B1
note [nəʊt] Notiz III/2A3
°notebook ['nəʊtbʊk] Notizbuch III/BS7
take/make notes (on) [ˌteɪk/ˌmeɪk 'nəʊts] (sich) Notizen machen (über) II/3A4

nothing ['nʌθɪŋ] nichts II/6B2
notice ['nəʊtɪs] bemerken III/2B5
noun [naʊn] Hauptwort, Substantiv II/1A3
November [nəʊ'vembə] November I/3B7
now [naʊ] jetzt I/1B2
(every) now and then [ˌevri naʊ‿ən 'ðen] ab und zu III/2A1
number ['nʌmbə] Zahl; Ziffer, Nummer I/1A6
nurse [nɜːs] (Kranken)schwester, (Kranken)pfleger II/3A4
°nylon ['naɪlɒn] Nylon III/5O

O

(eight) o'clock [ə'klɒk] (acht) Uhr I/2A2
ocean ['əʊʃn] Ozean, Meer III/4A5
October [ɒk'təʊbə] Oktober I/3A1
the odd one out [ðiˌ‿ɒd wʌn‿'aʊt] *das Wort, das nicht zu den anderen passt* III/6P2
of [əv] von II/1A2
of all ages [əv 'ɔːl‿ˌeɪdʒɪz] aller Altersstufen III/7B1
of course [əv 'kɔːs] natürlich II/1A4
day off [ˌdeɪ‿'ɒf] freier Tag III/3P1; 7A6
°off duty [ˌɒf 'djuːti] nicht im Dienst III/BS6
get sb off one's mind *(informal)* [ˌget ˌsʌmbədi‿ɒf wʌnz 'maɪnd] sich jdn aus dem Kopf schlagen III/6A9
offer ['ɒfə] anbieten, bieten III/8A5
What's on offer? [ˌwɒts‿ɒn‿'ɒfə] Was ist im Angebot? III/6P2
office ['ɒfɪs] Büro III/7B1
°(police) officer ['ɒfɪsə] (Polizei)-beamte(r)/-beamtin III/BS7
official [ə'fɪʃl] offiziell III/3A3
often ['ɒfn] oft, häufig I/1A7
old [əʊld] alt I/W
olive ['ɒlɪv] Olive III/1A2
°Olympic [ə'lɪmpɪk] olympisch III/2O
°(the) Olympic Games (= Olympics) [əˌlɪmpɪk 'geɪmz] (die) Olypmischen Spiele III/2O
on [ɒn] auf, an, in I/1A8
be on [biː 'ɒn] auf dem Programm stehen, laufen III/3A5
on high [ɒn 'haɪ] in der Höhe III/4A4
be on holiday [ˌbi‿ɒn 'hɒlɪdeɪ] Urlaub/Ferien haben I/6A3
°on one's own [ˌɒn wʌnz‿'əʊn] (ganz) allein(e) III/BS2
on the Internet [ˌɒn ði‿'ɪntənet] im Internet II/1B7
on the left [ˌɒn ðə 'left] links, auf der linken Seite II/1C5
°on the one hand …, on the other hand … [ɒn ðə 'wʌn ˌhænd ..., ɒn ði‿'ʌðə ˌhænd] einerseits … andererseits … III/BS6
on the right [ˌɒn ðə 'raɪt] rechts, auf der rechten Seite II/1C5
on time [ɒn 'taɪm] pünktlich III/8B2
once [wʌns] einmal II/1A4
°once [wʌns] sobald III/3O
once a year [ˌwʌns ə 'jɪə] einmal im/pro Jahr III/6B1
one [wʌn] eins; ein(e) I/1P7
one day ['wʌn ˌdeɪ] eines Tages III/2B5
°one more time [ˌwʌn mɔː 'taɪm] noch einmal III/8O
onion ['ʌnjən] Zwiebel III/1A2
only ['əʊnli] nur I/6A3
°onto ['ɒntə] auf III/1O
open ['əʊpən] aufmachen, öffnen I/1C1; offen, geöffnet I/6B1; sich öffnen, aufgehen II/2C1
open ['əʊpən] *hier:* eröffnen III/5P7
opening ['əʊpnɪŋ] Eröffnung III/3A3
opposite ['ɒpəzɪt] gegenüber I/2C2
opposite ['ɒpəzɪt] Gegenteil III/4P4
or [ɔː] oder I/1A2
orange ['ɒrɪndʒ] orange I/5C5; Orange, Apfelsine I/1A4
order ['ɔːdə] bestellen III/1A3; Ordnung, Reihenfolge III/2B1
in alphabetical order [ɪn ælfə'betɪkl ˌɔːdə] in alphabetische(r) Reihenfolge III/2P4
put sth in order [ˌpʊt ˌsʌmθɪŋ‿ɪn‿'ɔːdə] etw in eine Reihenfolge bringen III/8B4
Are you ready to order? [ɑː juː ˌredi tʊ 'ɔːdə] Möchten Sie schon bestellen? III/1A3
organization [ˌɔːgənaɪ'zeɪʃn] Organisation III/7A2
organize ['ɔːgənaɪz] organisieren III/3A7
original [ə'rɪdʒnəl] originell, außergewöhnlich III/5B5; original, echt III/BS6
other ['ʌðər] andere(r, s) I/2A7
°ought [ɔːt] sollte(st, n, t) III/BS4
our [aʊə] unser(e) I/1A2
°out of [aʊt‿əv] aus III/BS7
be out of work [biː‿ˌaʊt‿əv 'wɜːk] arbeitslos sein III/4B2
outdoor [ˌaʊt'dɔː] Freiluft- III/7B1
outside [ˌaʊt'saɪd] außen, außerhalb; *hier:* draußen II/3C3
over ['əʊvə] über I/2C3
over there [ˌəʊvə 'ðeə] dort drüben I/2C2
own [əʊn] eigene(r, s) I/6A2
°on one's own [ˌɒn wʌnz‿'əʊn] (ganz) allein(e) III/BS2

P

p (= penny; *pl* -nies *or* pence) ['peni] Penny I /6A4
pack [pæk] packen III/8P4
package ['pækɪdʒ] Paket III/4A8
packed with ['pækt wɪð] voll gepackt mit III/6A5
packet ['pækɪt] Packung, Tüte III/4A6
page [peɪdʒ] Seite I/2A7
°pain [peɪn] Schmerz III/7O3
paint [peɪnt] Farbe III/3P6; malen III/6A5
painter ['peɪntə] (Kunst)maler/in III/6A4
pair [peə] Paar I/6A6
a pair of scissors [ə ˌpeər‿əv 'sɪzəz] Schere III/4A6
a pair of skis [ə ˌpeər‿əv 'skiːz] ein Paar Skier III/6A7
a pair of trousers [ə ˌpeər‿əv 'traʊzəz] eine Hose III/6A6
paper ['peɪpə] Papier I/4B7
do a paper round [duː‿ə 'peɪpə‿ raʊnd] Zeitungen austragen III/6A2
parachute ['pærəˌʃuːt] Fallschirm III/5B2
parachute jump ['pærəʃuːt‿ˌdʒʌmp] Fallschirmsprung III/5B2
parade [pə'reɪd] Parade, Umzug III/3A1
°Paralympic [ˌpærə'lɪmpɪk] paralympisch III/2O
°(the) Paralympics [ˌpærə'lɪmpɪks] *Olympische Spiele für Behinderte* III/2O
parents *(only plural)* ['peərənts] Eltern I/1A6
parrot ['pærət] Papagei III/4P2
part [pɑːt] Teil III/2A3
take part (in) [ˌteɪk 'pɑːt] teilnehmen (an) III/8A5
partner ['pɑːtnə] Partner/in I/1A6
have a party [ˌhæv‿ə 'pɑːti] eine Party machen II/4A2
°pass [pɑːs] *hier:* abgeben III/BS3; *hier:* vergehen III/BS4
pass by [ˌpɑːs 'baɪ] vorbeikommen III/3A4
passenger ['pæsɪndʒə] Fahrgast, Reisende/r III/5P8
°passion ['pæʃn] Leidenschaft III/7O3

past [pɑ:st] Vergangenheit II/2C1; vorbei an; hinter, nach I/2B6
past participle [ˌpɑ:st ˈpɑ:tɪsɪpl] Partizip Perfekt III/5P6
paste [peɪst] Paste III/1B1
patient [ˈpeɪʃnt] Patient/in III/2B3
°patrol car [pəˈtrəʊl ˌkɑ:] Streifenwagen III/BS7
°pause [pɔ:z] *hier:* anhalten III/BS7
pavement artist [ˈpeɪvmənt‿ɑ:tɪst] Pflastermaler/in III/7B1
pay [peɪ] (be)zahlen III/5B1
PE (= physical education) [ˌpi: ˈi:, ˌfɪzɪkl‿edjuˈkeɪʃn] Sport(unterricht) II/5B1
°pea [pi:] Erbse III/1O
°peace [pi:s] Frieden, Ruhe III/BS6
pedal [ˈpedl] in die Pedale treten III/5B2
pedal power [ˈpedl ˌpaʊə] Pedalkraft III/5B2
pen [pen] Stift I/1A8
pencil [ˈpensl] Bleistift I/1A8
pencil case [ˈpensl ˌkeɪs] Federmäppchen I/1C4
penguin [ˈpeŋgwɪn] Pinguin II/2B3
people [ˈpi:pl] Leute, Menschen I/1B6
people [ˈpi:pl] *hier:* Volk III/4A4
perfect [ˈpɜ:fɪkt] vollkommen, perfekt II/2C1
°perfect [ˈpɜ:fɪkt] perfektionieren, vervollkommnen III/5O; vollkommen, perfekt; *hier:* genau III/BS7
perhaps [pəˈhæps] vielleicht II/2A1
person [ˈpɜ:sn] Person, Mensch III/6A5
person who looks after sb [ˈpɜ:sn hu ˌlʊks‿ɑ:ftə ˈsʌmbədi] Betreuer/in III/8A7
°personalize [ˈpɜ:sənəlaɪz] persönlich gestalten III/BS6
pet [pet] Haustier I/1A4
philosophical [ˌfɪləˈsɒfɪkl] abgeklärt, gelassen III/4A4
phone [fəʊn] anrufen III/2B1
(on the) phone [ɒn ðə ˈfəʊn] (am) Telefon II/4C3
answer the phone [ˌɑ:nsə ðə ˈfəʊn] ans Telefon gehen III/3P6
talk on the phone [ˌtɔ:k‿ɒn ðə ˈfəʊn] telefonieren III/3B2
photo [ˈfəʊtəʊ] Foto I/1A8
take photos [ˌteɪk ˈfəʊtəʊz] fotografieren III/3A2
phrase [freɪz] Satz; Ausdruck; (Rede-)wendung III/3B1
phrase book [ˈfreɪz ˌbʊk] Sprachführer III/8A4

physical education [ˌfɪzɪkl‿edjʊˈkeɪʃn] Sport(unterricht) I/5A2
pick [pɪk] aussuchen III/6A8
°pick up [ˌpɪk‿ˈʌp] aufheben; *hier:* aufnehmen III/1O
pick up sb/sth [ˌpɪk‿ˈʌp ˌsʌmbədi/ˌsʌmθɪŋ] jdn./etw. abholen III/8B2
pickpocket [ˈpɪkˌpɒkɪt] Taschendieb/in III/3A4
picture [ˈpɪktʃə] Bild I/1A7
in the picture [ɪn ðə ˈpɪktʃə] auf dem Bild III/7B4
pie [paɪ] Pastete III/1A2
piece [pi:s] Stück I/6C4
pillow [ˈpɪləʊ] (Kopf)kissen, Polster II/5A5
pilot [ˈpaɪlət] Pilot/in III/8B1
pink [pɪŋk] rosa, pink III/6A7
°pipe [paɪp] Pfeife III/BS4
°pissed off *(informal)* [ˌpɪst‿ˈɒf] stinksauer III/7O3
pitch [pɪtʃ] (Spiel)feld, Platz III/7B1
place [pleɪs] Ort; Platz I/3A8
the place to go [ðə ˌpleɪs tə ˈgəʊ] *etwa: hier ist man genau richtig* III/7B1
go places [ˈgə ˌpleɪsɪz] Ausflüge machen, herumreisen III/8I
plan [plæn] planen; vorbereiten II/2B4
plane [pleɪn] Flugzeug I/5B1
plant [plɑ:nt] Pflanze II/2B3
°plantation [plɑ:nˈteɪʃən] Plantage III/BS6
plastic bag [ˌplæstɪk ˈbæg] Plastiktüte III/4A6
plate [pleɪt] Teller I/2B3
play [pleɪ] (Theater)stück I/3A1; spielen I/1A6
be child's play [bi: ˈtʃaɪəldz ˌpleɪ] ein Kinderspiel sein III/7B1
°play around *(informal)* [ˌpleɪ‿əˈraʊnd] fremdgehen III/8O
°play on [ˌpleɪ‿ˈɒn] weiterspielen III/3O
play sb [ˈpleɪ ˌsʌmbədi] gegen jdn spielen III/5A1
player [ˈpleɪə] Spieler/in III/2A6
°playing field [ˈpleɪɪŋ ˌfi:ld] Sportplatz; *hier:* Spielfeld III/BS3
please [pli:z] bitte I/1C1
°plenty *(informal)* [ˈplenti] genug III/4O
pm (= post meridiem) [ˌpi: ˈem, ˌpəʊst məˈrɪdiəm] nachmittags, abends *(nur hinter Uhrzeit zwischen 12 Uhr mittags und Mitternacht)* I/2B7
pocket [ˈpɒkɪt] Tasche *(an Kleidungsstücken)* III/3P2

pocket knife [ˈpɒkɪt ˌnaɪf] Taschenmesser III/8P4
pocket money [ˈpɒkɪt ˌmʌni] Taschengeld II/6A4
poem [ˈpəʊɪm] Gedicht III/2A5
poet [ˈpəʊɪt] Dichter/in III/2A6
point [pɔɪnt] Punkt; *hier:* Komma III/6B2
°point [pɔɪnt] Punkt III/BS3
point (at/to) [pɔɪnt] zeigen (auf) III/4A3
the police [ðə pəˈli:s] die Polizei II/2A1
police officer [pəˈli:s ˌɒfɪsə] Polizeibeamter/-beamtin II/3A4
polite [pəˈlaɪt] höflich II/4B6
°pool [pu:l] (Schwimm)becken, (Schwimm)bad III/BS5
poor [pɔ:] arm II/1B2
Poor you! [ˌpʊə ˈju:] Du Arme/r! III/1B1
pop group [ˈpɒp ˌgru:p] Popgruppe III/7A6
°popular [ˈpɒpjʊlə] beliebt, populär III/6O
°popularity [ˌpɒpjuˈlærəti] Beliebtheit, Popularität III/BS6
portfolio [pɔ:tˈfəʊliəʊ] (Akten)mappe II/1A2
°possible [ˈpɒsəbəl] möglich III/BS2
possibly [ˈpɒsəbli] möglicherweise, vielleicht III/1A8
potato (*pl* potatoes) [pəˈteɪtəʊ, pəˈteɪtəʊz] Kartoffel I/5B1
pound [paʊnd] Pfund *(engl. Währung)* II/3B1
power [ˈpaʊə] antreiben III/5P6; *hier:* Kraft, Stärke III/5B2; *hier:* Strom, Elektrizität III/5A1
powerful [ˈpaʊəfl] stark, kräftig III/2A7
practical [ˈpræktɪkl] praktisch III/5B4
Practice matters. [ˌpræktɪs ˈmætəz] *etwa:* Übung macht den Meister. III/1P1
practise [ˈpræktɪs] üben III/6A7
°practise [ˈpræktɪs] *hier:* ausüben III/BS3
sing in praise [ˌsɪŋ‿ɪn ˈpreɪz] ein Loblied singen III/4A4
prefer [priˈfɜ:] vorziehen, bevorzugen III/7P5
prepare [prɪˈpeə] vorbereiten III/3A8
present [ˈpreznt] Geschenk I/5B4
present [prɪˈzent] präsentieren; *hier:* aufführen II/4A6
present [prɪˈzent] *hier:* vortragen III/7A5; präsentieren, vorlegen III/1B5
presentation [ˌpreznˈteɪʃn] Präsentation, Vortrag III/8B3

president ['prezɪdənt] Präsident/in III/L
°press [pres] drücken III/1O
press-up ['pres‿ʌp] Liegestütz III/2A2
pretty ['prɪti] hübsch I/6A3
price [praɪs] Preis I/5B6
prisoner ['prɪznə] Gefangene/r III/4A1
prize [praɪz] Preis, Auszeichnung III/2B5
problem ['prɒbləm] Problem I/3A4
°produce [prə'dju:s] herstellen, produzieren III/BS6
°product ['prɒdʌkt] Produkt, Erzeugnis III/5O
professional [prə'feʃnəl] Profi III/7A6
profit ['prɒfɪt] Gewinn, Profit III/3A7
programme ['prəʊgræm] Programm, Plan III/3A5
°programmer ['prəʊ,græmə] Programmierer/in III/6O
project ['prɒdʒekt] Projekt II/2B7
°promise ['prɒmɪs] versprechen III/7O3
properly ['prɒpəli] richtig III/2B5
°protest [prə'test] protestieren III/BS7
°pull [pʊl] ziehen III/BS3
pull away [,pʊl‿ə'weɪ] wegreißen, wegziehen III/3B1
°pull off [,pʊl‿'ɒf] ausziehen; *hier:* abziehen III/5O
pump [pʌmp] pumpen III/5B2
pupil ['pju:pl] Schüler/in I/1C2
puppet ['pʌpɪt] (Hand)puppe, Marionette III/7B1
purse [pɜ:s] Portemonnaie III/3A4
put [pʊt] setzen, legen, stellen I/2C5
put [pʊt] *hier:* anlegen III/2B2
put in [,pʊt‿'ɪn] hineinsetzen/-legen/-stellen I/6C4
put (into) [pʊt] *hier:* gefüllt (in) III/1A8
put on [,pʊt‿'ɒn] anziehen II/5B4
put on [,pʊt‿'ɒn] *hier:* hängen III/6P6
put sth in order [,pʊt ,sʌmθɪŋ‿ɪn‿'ɔ:də] etw in eine Reihenfolge bringen III/8B4
put up [,pʊt‿'ʌp] aufhängen III/3A4
puzzle ['pʌzl] Rätsel III/1B6
pyjamas *(only plural)* [pə'dʒa:məz] Schlafanzug III/8P4
pyramid ['pɪrəmɪd] Pyramide III/8A3

Q

quarter (to/past) ['kwɔ:tə] Viertel (vor/nach) I/2A2
queen [kwi:n] Königin III/3A3
question ['kwestʃn] Frage II/1B8
question ['kwestʃn] befragen III/3B1
question tag ['kwestʃn ,tæg] Bestätigungsfrage III/1B3
ask questions [ɑ:sk‿'kwestʃnz] Fragen stellen I/2A7
quick [kwɪk] schnell I/3B2
quiet ['kwaɪət] leise, ruhig II/3C1
quite [kwaɪt] ziemlich III/4B1

R

race [reɪs] Rennen, Wettkampf III/2A3; Rennen laufen; rennen III/BS1
raft [rɑ:ft] Floß III/4A1
raid [reɪd] plündern III/7B1
rail [reɪl] Bahn III/7B1
rain [reɪn] Regen I/4C9; regnen II/3A1
rainbow ['reɪn,bəʊ] Regenbogen I/3B8
raincoat ['reɪn,kəʊt] Regenmantel III/8P4
rainforest ['reɪn,fɒrɪst] Regenwald III/7B1
rainy ['reɪni] regnerisch I/4C8
raise money [,reɪz 'mʌni] Geld aufbringen III/8A3
°raise the roof [,reɪz ðə 'ru:f] ausrasten, vor Begeisterung toben III/3O
raita ['raɪtə] *indisches Gericht mit Joghurt* III/1B1
°ranch [ræntʃ] Farm III/BS6
rather ['rɑ:ðə] *hier:* eher, lieber III/4A6; ziemlich III/BS4
reaction [ri'ækʃn] Reaktion III/4B1
read [ri:d] lesen I/1A4
read along [,ri:d‿ə'lɒŋ] mitlesen I/1B2
°read on ['ri:d‿ɒn] weiterlesen III/BS4
ready ['redi] fertig, bereit III/6B2
be ready [bi: 'redi] bereit sein, fertig sein III/2B2
°be ready to do sth [bi: ,redi tə 'du: ,sʌmθɪŋ] bereit sein, etw zu tun III/8O
real [rɪəl] wirklich, echt III/5B1
realistic [,rɪə'lɪstɪk] realistisch III/7B4
really ['rɪəli] wirklich I/6B2
°rebel ['rebl] Rebell/in III/BS6
receive [rɪ'si:v] erhalten, bekommen III/4B1
receptionist [rɪ'sepʃnɪst] Herr/Dame an der Anmeldung III/2B2
°recession [ri'seʃn] Rezession, Konjunkturrückgang III/BS6
recipe ['resəpi] Rezept III/1B5
°recognize ['rekəgnaɪz] erkennen III/BS7
record [rɪ'kɔ:d] aufzeichnen; *hier:* aufnehmen II/3B4
record ['rekɔ:d] (Schall)platte III/L; Rekord I I/2O
red [red] rot I/1A6
reduced [ri'dju:st] reduziert, heruntergesetzt III/7B1
°reflex ['ri:fleks] Reflex III/BS3
regular ['regjʊlə] normal(e) (Größe) III/1A2
regularly ['regjʊləli] regelmäßig III/2A1
rehearsal [rɪ'hɜ:sl] Probe III/7A6
relative ['relətɪv] Verwandte(r) III/8B1
°relatively ['relətɪvli] relativ III/BS3
release [rɪ'li:s] freilassen, freigeben III/2A5
religious education [re,lɪdʒəs‿edjʊ'keɪʃn] Religionslehre I/5A2
remember [rɪ'membə] sich erinnern (an) II/4C2
remember [rɪ'membə] *hier:* daran denken II/4B1
°rent [rent] mieten, vermieten III/6O
repeat [rɪ'pi:t] wiederholen II/6C2
°replace [rɪ'pleɪs] ersetzen III/5O
°reply [ri'plaɪ] antworten, erwidern III/BS7
report [rɪ'pɔ:t] Bericht III/5B1
report (to) [rɪ'pɔ:t] berichten III/2A2
reporter [rɪ'pɔ:tə] Reporter/in III/5B3
°represent [,reprɪ'zent] repräsentieren; darstellen III/BS6
rescue ['reskju:] retten; befreien III/4A1
rest [rest] (Ruhe)pause III/7A6; (aus)ruhen III/BS4
restaurant ['restrɒnt] Restaurant, Gaststätte III/1A2
result [rɪ'zʌlt] Ergebnis III/7B2
rhyme [raɪm] Reim- III/5P4
rhyme *(no pl)* [raɪm] Reim II/4C2
rhyming ['raɪmɪŋ] Reim- III/2A6
°rhythm ['rɪðəm] Rhythmus III/3O
rich [rɪtʃ] reich II/3A1
ride [raɪd] fahren (mit); reiten I/3A7; Fahrt III/5B1
right [raɪt] rechte(r, s) I/2A4; richtig II/1B3; richtig, in Ordnung I/2B3
right [raɪt] völlig, ganz III/8B2
(turn) right [raɪt] rechts (abbiegen) II/2B4
be right [bi: 'raɪt] Recht haben III/1B1
on the right [,ɒn ðə 'raɪt] rechts, auf der rechten Seite II/1C5
ring (up) [,rɪŋ‿'ʌp] anrufen; klingeln, läuten III/1A6
river ['rɪvə] Fluss II/2C5
°rivet ['rɪvɪt] Niete III/BS6
road [rəʊd] Straße I/5B4

°across the road [əˌkrɒs ðə 'rəʊd] *hier:* auf der gegenüberliegenden Straßenseite III/BS7
roast lamb [ˌrəʊst 'læm] gebratenes Lamm III/1A2
rock [rɒk] Stein; Fels III/4A1
°rocket ['rɒkɪt] Rakete III/7O1
°roll up [ˌrəʊl‿'ʌp] hochrollen, hochkrempeln III/BS6
°rollersoccer ['rəʊləˌsɒkə] *Funsportart* III/BS3
°romance ['rəʊmæns] Romanze, Liebesaffäre III/3O
°raise the roof [ˌreɪz ðə 'ru:f] ausrasten, vor Begeisterung toben III/3O
°roof (*pl* roofs *or* rooves) [ru:f, ru:fs, ru:fvz] Dach III/BS4
room [ru:m] Platz, Raum; Zimmer I/1A5
rope [rəʊp] Seil, Strick III/4A6
rose [rəʊz] Rose I/5B2
°rough [rʌf] rau, hart III/4O
°round [raʊnd] *hier:* um III/BS7
route [ru:t] Strecke, Route III/6B2
row [rəʊ] Reihe III/7P4
rubber ['rʌbə] Gummi; Radiergummi I/1A8
rule [ru:l] Regel II/4B4
ruler ['ru:lə] Lineal I/1A8
run [rʌn] laufen, rennen I/3A4
run away [ˌrʌn‿ə'weɪ] weglaufen III/3B1
°run off *(informal)* [ˌrʌn‿'ɒf] abhauen III/BS1
run over [ˌrʌn‿'əʊvə] überfahren, *hier:* überrollen III/3B1
runner ['rʌnə] Läufer/in III/6B1
Russia ['rʌʃə] Russland III/8A2

S

sad [sæd] traurig III/4B1
safe [seɪf] sicher II/6B2
feel safe [fi:l 'seɪf] sich sicher fühlen II/5C4
safely ['seɪfli] sicher, gefahrlos III/5B2
sail [seɪl] segeln III/4A4
sail by [ˌseɪl 'baɪ] vorbeisegeln III/4A1
sailing ['seɪlɪŋ] Segeln III/8A5
°sailor ['seɪlə] Matrose, Seemann III/BS4
salad ['sæləd] Salat II/4C3
°sale [fə 'seɪl] Verkauf, Absatz III/BS6
for sale [fə 'seɪl] zu verkaufen I/3A1
the same [ðə 'seɪm] der/die/das Gleiche III/2A2; gleich II/2C2
at the same time [ət ðə ˌseɪm 'taɪm] gleichzeitig, zur gleichen Zeit III/5B4
samosa [sə'məʊsə] *mit Kartoffeln oder Hackfleisch gefüllte indische Teigtasche* III/3A4
sand [sænd] Sand I/6A2
satellite ['sætəlaɪt] Satellit III/5P4
Saturday ['sætədeɪ] Samstag I/2B3
sauce [sɔ:s] Soße, Sauce III/1A2
sausage ['sɒsɪdʒ] Wurst, Würstchen II/4C6
say [seɪ] sagen I/1A1
°say goodbye [ˌseɪ ˌgʊd'baɪ] auf Wiedersehen sagen, sich verabschieden III/8O
the sign says [ðə 'saɪn ˌsez] auf dem Schild steht III/3A4
scarf (*pl* scarves) [skɑ:f, skɑ:vz] Schal II/4B2
scene [si:n] Szene III/1A6
school [sku:l] Schule I/1A6
school newspaper [ˌsku:l 'nju:zˌpeɪpə] Schülerzeitung III/6B3
school report [ˌsku:l rɪ'pɔ:t] (Schul)zeugnis III/4B2
schoolbag ['sku:lbæg] Schultasche I/1A8
schoolwork ['sku:lˌwɜ:k] Schularbeiten III/4B1
science ['saɪəns] (Natur)wissenschaft I/5A1
scientist ['saɪəntɪst] Wissenschaftler/in III/5A2
a pair of scissors [ə ˌpeər‿əv 'sɪzəz] Schere III/4A6
score [skɔ:] schießen *(Tor)* I/3A5
Scotland ['skɒtlənd] Schottland II/1LL1
scramble ['skræmbl] durcheinander bringen III/4P5
°scratch [skrætʃ] Kratzer III/BS7
sea [si:] Meer, (die) See I/2A2
search the Internet [ˌsɜ:tʃ ðiˌ'ɪntənet] im Internet suchen II/6B4
seas *(only plural)* [si:z] Wellen, Wogen III/4A5
seat [si:t] (Sitz)platz III/7P4
second ['sekənd] Sekunde II/3A1; zweite(r, s) I/4A4
second-hand [ˌsekənd 'hænd] gebraucht III/6P2
secret ['si:krət] Geheimnis III/4B1
section ['sekʃn] Teil; Abteilung III/5B1
see [si:] *hier:* treffen III/8B1; sehen I/1A1
see [si:] ansehen, anschauen III/5A2
°see you ['si: ju:] *hier:* bis III/BS5
see you (later) [ˌsi: jʊ] bis bald II/6C6
See you soon! [ˌsi: jʊ 'su:n] Bis bald! I/3A4
seed [si:d] Same, Korn III/4A6
seem [si:m] scheinen I/3B1
°self (*pl* selves) [self (selvz)] Selbst, Ich III/7O3
sell [sel] verkaufen I/4B3
seller ['selə] Verkäufer/in III/6A7
send [send] (zu)schicken II/1C4
°sense [sens] Sinn; Gefühl III/BS3
sentence ['sentəns] Satz I/1A5
September [sep'tembə] September I/5C2
°sergeant ['sɑ:dʒnt] Polizeimeister/in; Inspektor III/BS7
°is served [ɪz‿'sɜ:vd] wird serviert III/1O
set the table [ˌset ðə 'teɪbl] den Tisch decken II/4B7
set up [ˌset‿'ʌp] aufschlagen, errichten III/3A7
seven ['sevn] sieben I/2B4
°several ['sevrəl] einige; verschiedene III/BS4
sewer ['su:ə] Abwasserkanal III/5A2
°shake one's head [ˌʃeɪk wʌnz 'hed] den Kopf schütteln III/BS7
shall [ʃæl] sollen III/5A1
share [ʃeə] teilen; *hier:* weitergeben III/4B1
°sharp [ʃɑ:p] scharf III/BS7
°shatter ['ʃætə] zerspringen, zerbrechen III/BS7
she [ʃi:] sie I/1A3
sheep (*pl* sheep) [ʃi:p, ʃi:p] Schaf I/6B2
shelf (*pl* shelves) [ʃelf, ʃelvz] Regal I/4A1
°shell [ʃel] Schale, Panzer III/7O3
shift [ʃɪft] Schicht III/4B2
shine [ʃaɪn] scheinen, glänzen III/4A4
ship [ʃɪp] Schiff II/2C1
board a ship [ˌbɔ:d‿ə 'ʃɪp] ein Schiff besteigen III/4A1
shoe [ʃu:] Schuh I/2C7
°shoot out ['ʃu:t‿aʊt] plötzlich herauskommen, hervorschießen III/BS7
shop [ʃɒp] Geschäft, Laden I/1B1
shop assistant ['ʃɒp‿əˌsɪstənt] Verkäufer/in II/4C3
do the shopping [ˌdu: ðə 'ʃɒpɪŋ] einkaufen (gehen) I/4B3
go shopping [ˌgəʊ 'ʃɒpɪŋ] einkaufen gehen I/2C1
shore [ʃɔ:] Küste, Ufer, Strand III/4A4
short [ʃɔ:t] kurz; klein I/2A5
be short of money *(informal)* [bi: ˌʃɔ:t‿əv 'mʌni] knapp bei Kasse sein III/6A2
should [ʃʊd] sollte/müsste I/3B1
shoulder ['ʃəʊldə] Schulter III/7A2
°shoulder ['ʃəʊldə] schultern III/BS7

shout [ʃaʊt] schreien; rufen I/6A6
show [ʃəʊ] zeigen I/3A1
shower ['ʃaʊə] Dusche III/5B2
shrink [ʃrɪŋk] schrumpfen III/5B4
shy [ʃaɪ] schüchtern III/4B1
be sick [biː 'sɪk] sich erbrechen; sich elend fühlen III/5B2
side [saɪd] Seite II/6B2
°sight [saɪt] Sehvermögen, Sehleistung III/BS2
sight(s) [saɪt] Sehenswürdigkeit(en) II/2B1
sightseeing *(no pl)* ['saɪtˌsiːɪŋ] Besichtigungen, Sightseeing II/2C3
sign [saɪn] Zeichen; (Straßen-/Verkehrs)schild II/5A7
the sign says [ðə 'saɪn ˌsez] auf dem Schild steht III/3A4
silly ['sɪli] albern, dumm II/3A1
°silver medal [ˌsɪlvə 'medl] Silbermedaille III/2O
similar ['sɪmɪlə] ähnlich III/1P7
°simple ['sɪmpl] einfach III/BS3
simple past [ˌsɪmpl 'pɑːst] einfache Vergangenheit II/1B4
since [sɪns] seit III/4B1
sing [sɪŋ] singen I/1A4
°sing along [ˌsɪŋ‿ə'lɒŋ] mitsingen III/3O
singer ['sɪŋə] Sänger/in II/5B9
single ['sɪŋgl] einzige(r, s) III/6A9
sir [sɜː] Herr *(Anrede)* III/8B2
°Sir [sɜː] Herr III/BS1
sister ['sɪstə] Schwester I/1A4
sit [sɪt] sitzen I/5C4
sit down [sɪt ˌdaʊn] sich (hin)setzen II/6B2
situation [ˌsɪtʃu'eɪʃn] Situation, Lage III/1B3
six [sɪks] sechs I/1A2
six-year-old ['sɪks jɪər‿ˌəʊld] der/die/das sechsjährige III/3B1
size [saɪz] Größe I/3A1
skate [skeɪt] Schlittschuh, Rollschuh, Inliner III/5B4
°skid marks *(only plural)* ['skɪd ˌmɑːks] Reifenspuren, Bremsspuren III/BS7
skilful ['skɪlfl] geschickt III/2A7
skim through ['skɪm θruː] überfliegen III/7B1
skirt [skɜːt] Rock I/4C7
a pair of skis [ə ˌpeər‿əv 'skiːz] ein Paar Skier III/6A7
sky [skaɪ] Himmel I/4C9
°slacklining ['slækˌlaɪnɪŋ] *Funsportart* III/BS3
°slave labour [ˌsleɪv 'leɪbə] Sklavenarbeit III/BS6
sleep [sliːp] schlafen I/3B7
sleep over [sliːp‿'əʊvə] über Nacht bleiben, übernachten II/6A1
sleeping bag ['sliːpɪŋ ˌbæg] Schlafsack III/8P4
slide rule ['slaɪd ˌruːl] Rechenschieber III/4B4
slow [sləʊ] langsam II/3C1
small [smɔːl] klein I/1B2
smell [smel] riechen; duften II/4B2
smell [smel] Geruch III/5A2
°smile [smaɪl] lächeln III/2O
°smoke [sməʊk] rauchen III/BS4
snack bar ['snæk ˌbɑː] Imbissstube II/4B2
snake [sneɪk] Schlange II/2B3
°snatch [snætʃ] schnappen, an sich reißen III/BS7
snow [snəʊ] Schnee I/4B3
so [səʊ] also III/1A3; daher, folglich I/3C4
so far ['səʊ fɑː] bisher III/1A6
So what? *(informal)* [səʊ‿'wɒt] Na und?, Na wenn schon! II/6B6
soap [səʊp] Seife III/4A6
sober ['səʊbə] nüchtern III/7A2
sock [sɒk] Socke I/4C7
soft drink [ˌsɒft‿'drɪŋk] Softdrink *(alkoholfreies Getränk)* III/1A2
°soil [sɔɪəl] Erde III/BS1
°soldier ['səʊldʒə] Soldat/in III/BS6
°solution [sə'luːʃn] Lösung III/5O
solve [sɒlv] lösen III/4B1
some [sʌm] einige; etwas I/3B2
some other time [sʌm‿'ʌðə ˌtaɪm] ein anderes Mal III/1A8
someone (= somebody) ['sʌmwʌn] (irgend)jemand, irgendwer II/1C6
something ['sʌmθɪŋ] etwas I/4C5
°something else [ˌsʌmθɪŋ‿'els] etwas anderes III/BS4
sometimes ['sʌmtaɪmz] manchmal I/1B2
somewhere ['sʌmweə] irgendwo II/2A1
son [sʌn] Sohn I/5C7
song [sɒŋ] Lied I/5B2
soon [suːn] bald II/6A5
sore [sɔː] wund, entzündet III/2B3
sorry about that ['sɒri əˌbaʊt 'ðæt] ich bitte um Entschuldigung, das tut mir leid III/1A8
Sorry. ['sɒri] Verzeihung., Entschuldigung. I/1A2
sort [sɔːt] sortieren III/1A9; Sorte, Art III/BS4
sort out [ˌsɔːt‿'aʊt] ordnen, sortieren III/4B1
all sorts of [ɔːl sɔːts‿əv] alle möglichen III/5B1
°soul [səʊl] Seele III/3O
sound [saʊnd] klingen, sich anhören II/4A3
sound [saʊnd] Geräusch III/4A4
sound check ['saʊnd‿ˌtʃek] Tonprobe, Soundcheck III/3P3
It sounds fun. [ɪt ˌsaʊndz 'fʌn] Es klingt gut. III/5A2
soup [suːp] Suppe III/1A2
soup of the day [ˌsuːp‿əv ðə 'deɪ] Tagessuppe III/1A2
south [saʊθ] Süden I/4C10
°South Pacific [ˌsaʊθ pə'sɪfɪk] Südpazifik III/BS4
southwest [ˌsaʊθ'west] Südwesten III/8B1
space [speɪs] Raum; *hier:* Weltraum III/5B1
spade [speɪd] Spaten III/4A6
Spanish ['spænɪʃ] spanisch III/6A4
°speak the truth [ˌspiːk ðə 'truːθ] die Wahrheit sagen III/BS7
speak (to/with) [spiːk] sprechen, reden (mit) III/7A7
speaker ['spiːkə] *hier:* Lautsprecher III/7A6
special ['speʃl] besondere(r, s), spezielle(r, s) II/4A3
special ['speʃl] Tagesgericht; *hier:* Spezial III/1A2
special offer [ˌspeʃl‿'ɒfə] Sonderangebot III/6A4
speech bubble ['spiːtʃ ˌbʌbl] Sprechblase III/1B3
spelling ['spelɪŋ] Rechtschreibung III/3P4
spend [spend] verbringen *(Zeit)*; ausgeben *(Geld)* II/2C3
spice [spaɪs] Gewürz III/1B1
spicy ['spaɪsi] würzig; scharf III/1B5
spider ['spaɪdə] Spinne II/2B3
°spike [spaɪk] Nagel; Stachel III/5O
°spiky ['spaɪki] stachelig, dornig III/5O
spin [spɪn] rotieren; sausen III/2A5
spinning machine ['spɪnɪŋ məˌʃiːn] Spinnmaschine III/5B1
splash *(pl splashes)* [splæʃ, 'splæʃɪz] Sensation III/3A3
is/are spoken [ɪz/ɑː 'spəʊkən] wird/werden gesprochen III/3P3
sponge [spʌndʒ] Schwamm I/1C1
sponsor ['spɒnsə] Sponsor/in III/6B1
spooky ['spuːki] unheimlich, gespenstisch III/5A2
spoon [spuːn] Löffel I/2B3

sport [spɔ:t] Sport(art) I/3A7
do sport [du: 'spɔ:t] Sport treiben III/2A1
Be a sport! [ˌbi:‿ə 'spɔ:t] Sei kein/e Spielverderber/in! III/2I
sports [spɔ:ts] Sport- III/2A5
sports centre ['spɔ:ts‿ˌsentə] Sportcenter III/7B1
sports hall ['spɔ:ts ˌhɔ:l] Sporthalle III/2A3
spring [sprɪŋ] Frühling I/4C8
°stadium (*pl* stadiums *or* stadia) ['steɪdiəm, 'steɪdiəmz, 'steɪdiə] Stadion III/2O
staff [stɑ:f] Personal, Mitarbeiter III/7B1
stair [steə] Treppenstufe III/2A2
stairs *(only plural)* [steəz] Treppe II/2C1
stall [stɔ:l] (Verkaufs)stand III/3A4
°stammer ['stæmə] stottern, stammeln III/BS7
stand [stænd] stehen I/2A4
stand up [ˌstænd‿'ʌp] aufstehen I/5C1
°standard ['stændəd] Standard-; durchschnittlich III/BS3
star [stɑ:] Stern III/7A2
°stare [steə] starren III/BS7
start [stɑ:t] anfangen (mit) I/5A2
start [stɑ:t] *hier:* losfahren III/5A2
°get started [ˌget 'stɑ:təd] beginnen III/3O
starter ['stɑ:tə] Vorspeise III/1A2
starting point ['stɑ:tɪŋ ˌpɔɪnt] Ausgangspunkt III/6B2
statement ['steɪtmənt] Äußerung II/5C3
°take a statement [teɪk‿ə 'steɪtmənt] *hier:* eine Aussage aufnehmen III/BS7
(railway) station ['steɪʃn] Bahnhof II/2C1
stay [steɪ] bleiben I/3B4
stay cool [ˌsteɪ 'ku:l] ruhig bleiben III/4B1
steal [sti:l] stehlen III/3A4
steam locomotive ['sti:m ləʊkəˌməʊtɪv] Dampflokomotive III/5B1
steam train ['sti:m ˌtreɪn] Dampflok III/5P3
steam-powered ['sti:m ˌpaʊəd] *von Dampf angetriebene(r/s)* III/5B1
steel band [ˌsti:l 'bænd] Steelband III/3LL3
steel drum [ˌsti:l 'drʌm] Steeldrum III/3LL3
steel drummer [ˌsti:l 'drʌmə] *Trommler/in auf einer Steeldrum* III/3A3
step back [ˌstep 'bæk] zurücktreten III/2A5
step off [ˌstep‿'ɒf] hinuntersteigen von III/2A2
step on [ˌstep‿'ɒn] steigen auf III/2A2
stick [stɪk] Zweig, Stock III/4A3; *hier:* Krücke III/BS1
°stick (to) [stɪk] kleben, festhängen (an) III/5O
still [stɪl] (immer) noch, noch immer II/3C1; trotzdem III/2A3
stomach ache ['stʌmək‿eɪk] Magenschmerzen, Bauchschmerzen III/2B3
°stone [stəʊn] Stein III/BS4
stop [stɒp] aufhören I/2A4; stehen bleiben; (an)halten II/1B4
°store [stɔ:] Laden, Geschäft III/7O1
storm [stɔ:m] Sturm I/4C10
story ['stɔ:ri] Geschichte, Erzählung I/1A5
°straight cut ['streɪt kʌt] *Schnitt* III/BS6
straight (on) [streɪt] gerade(aus) II/2B4
be stranded [bi: 'strændɪd] gestrandet sein, festsitzen III/4A8
strange [streɪndʒ] sonderbar, merkwürdig II/3C1
street [stri:t] Straße I/1B2
in the street [ˌɪn ðə 'stri:t] auf der Straße II/2A1
walk down the street [ˌwɔ:k daʊn ðə 'stri:t] die Straße entlanggehen III/7A5
stress [stres] Betonung, Akzent III/7P3
is/are stressed [ɪz/ɑ: 'strest] wird/werden betont III/4P8
stretch [stretʃ] (aus)dehnen, straff ziehen III/BS3
strict [strɪkt] streng III/7A2
°strip [strɪp] Streifen III/5O
stroke [strəʊk] *hier:* (Schwimm)stil III/2A5
strong [strɒŋ] stark I/4C10
°strong [strɒŋ] *hier:* stabil III/BS6
°student ['stju:dnt] Student/in III/6O
stuff [stʌf] Zeug III/7A6
stupid ['stju:pɪd] dumm, blöd III/7A2
°style [staɪəl] Stil, Art III/BS6
subject ['sʌbdʒɪkt] Thema; (Schul)fach I/5A1
successful [sək'sesfl] erfolgreich III/2A7
suddenly ['sʌdnli] plötzlich, auf einmal I/6A3
sugar ['ʃʊgə] Zucker I/2B1
suitcase ['su:tˌkeɪs] Koffer II/6C5
summary ['sʌməri] Zusammenfassung, Inhaltsangabe III/2B6
summer ['sʌmə] Sommer I/4C8
sun [sʌn] Sonne I/1A6
Sunday ['sʌndeɪ] Sonntag I/4C1
(on) Sundays ['sʌndeɪz] sonntags II/2C1
sunglasses *(only plural)* ['sʌnˌglɑ:sɪz] Sonnenbrille II/4B2
sunny ['sʌni] sonnig I/4C8
°sunshine ['sʌnˌʃaɪn] Sonnenschein III/7O1
superlative form [sʊ'pɜ:lətɪv ˌfɔ:m] Superlativ III/2P4
supermarket ['su:pəˌmɑ:kɪt] Supermarkt II/2A1
supporter [sə'pɔ:tə] Anhänger/in III/7A2
sure [ʃɔ:] sicher III/1B1
surf the Internet [ˌsɜ:f ði‿'ɪntənet] im Internet surfen II/6A6
surge [sɜ:dʒ] branden, wogen III/4A4
surgery ['sɜ:dʒəri] (Arzt)praxis III/2B1
surprise [sə'praɪz] überraschen III/1A10
surprised [sə'praɪzd] überrascht, erstaunt III/1A10
surprising [sə'praɪzɪŋ] überraschend III/7A2
survival kit [sə'vaɪvl ˌkɪt] Überlebensausrüstung III/4A6
survive [sə'vaɪv] überleben, am Leben bleiben III/4A8
°swear [sweə] fluchen III/BS7
sweat [swet] Schweiß III/4A4
sweet [swi:t] süß I/2B1
sweets *(only plural)* [swi:ts] Süßigkeiten III/4A6
swim [swɪm] schwimmen I/3A7
°come for a swim [ˌkʌm fər‿ə 'swɪm] zum Schwimmen kommen III/BS5
swimmer ['swɪmə] Schwimmer/in III/2A3
swimming ['swɪmɪŋ] Schwimmen I/6A1
go swimming [ˌgəʊ 'swɪmɪŋ] schwimmen gehen II/6A2
swimming costume ['swɪmɪŋ ˌkɒstju:m] Badeanzug III/8P4
swimming pool ['swɪmɪŋ ˌpu:l] Schwimmbecken, Schwimmbad III/2P4
swing [swɪŋ] (hin- und her)schwingen; sich drehen III/5B2
°Swiss [swɪs] Schweizer/in; schweizerisch III/5O
swollen ['swəʊlən] geschwollen III/2B2
syllable ['sɪləbəl] Silbe III/4P8

T

table ['teɪbl] Tisch I/2B3
table ['teɪbl] *hier:* Tabelle III/3A7
set the table [ˌset ðə 'teɪbl] den Tisch decken II/4B7
take [teɪk] bringen; nehmen I/3B5
take [teɪk] *hier:* dauern III/8A2
take a (deep) breath [ˌteɪk‿ə 'breθ] (tief) Luft holen III/4B1
°take a statement [teɪk‿ə 'steɪtmənt] *hier:* eine Aussage aufnehmen III/BS7
(take an) X-ray ['eksreɪ] röntgen III/2B2
take care of [teɪk 'keər‿əv] sich kümmern um, versorgen II/3A4
°take control [ˌteɪk kən'trəʊl] die Kontrolle übernehmen III/3O
take notes (on) [ˌteɪk 'nəʊts] (sich) Notizen machen (über) II/3A4
°take one's time [ˌteɪk wʌnz 'taɪm] sich Zeit lassen III/BS7
°take over [ˌteɪk‿'əʊvə] übernehmen III/BS7
take part (in) [ˌteɪk 'pɑ:t] teilnehmen (an) III/8A5
take photos [ˌteɪk 'fəʊtəʊz] fotografieren III/3A2
take place [ˌteɪk 'pleɪs] stattfinden III/6B2
take sb out for a meal [ˌteɪk sʌmbədi ˌaʊt fər‿ə 'mi:l] jdn zum Essen einladen III/1A6
take sb (somewhere) ['teɪk sʌmbədi] jdn (irgendwohin) mitnehmen III/1A10
take the bus [ˌteɪk ðə 'bʌs] mit dem Bus fahren II/5C2
take the dog for a walk [ˌteɪk ðə 'dɒg fə:r‿ə 'wɔ:k] den Hund ausführen III/6A2
take turns [ˌteɪk 'tɜ:nz] sich abwechseln III/4P6
takeaway (food) ['teɪkəˌweɪ] Essen zum Mitnehmen III/1A6
talk [tɔ:k] Gespräch; *hier:* Vortrag III/3A8
talk on the phone [ˌtɔ:k‿ɒn ðə 'fəʊn] telefonieren III/3B2
talk (to) [tɔ:k] sprechen/reden (mit) I/1A3
tall [tɔ:l] hoch; groß I/2A5
task [tɑ:sk] Aufgabe III/1B6
taste [teɪst] schmecken III/1A10
Tate Britain [ˌteɪt 'brɪtn] *Nationalgalerie für britische Kunst* III/7B1
tattoo [tæ'tu:] Tattoo, Tätowierung III/7A2
tea [ti:] Tee II/5A5
have tea [hæv 'ti:] Tee trinken II/2C1
teach [ti:tʃ] unterrichten; beibringen II/3C1
teacher ['ti:tʃə] Lehrer/in I/1A6
°teammate ['ti:mmeɪt] Mannschaftskamerad/in III/BS3
°tear [teə] (zer)reißen III/BS6
°tear away [ˌteər‿ə'weɪ] abreißen III/BS6
teaspoon ['ti:ˌspu:n] Teelöffel III/1B5
technology [tek'nɒlədʒi] Technologie, Technik I/5A2
teddy bear ['tedi ˌbeə] Teddybär III/5P7
°teenage ['ti:neɪdʒ] jugendlich III/BS6
brush one's teeth [ˌbrʌʃ wʌnz 'ti:θ] sich die Zähne putzen III/4A3
telephone ['telɪˌfəʊn] Telefon I/5C4
tell [tel] sagen; erzählen I/6A4
°tell jokes [ˌtel 'dʒəʊks] Witze reißen III/7O1
°tell lies [ˌtel 'laɪz] Lügen erzählen III/BS7
have a temperature [hæv‿ə 'temprɪtʃə] Fieber haben III/2B1
ten [ten] zehn I/2B4
tennis court ['tenɪs ˌkɔ:t] Tennisplatz III/7B1
term [tɜ:m] Semester; Trimester III/2LL2
terrible ['terəbl] schrecklich, furchtbar I/5A1
terrific [tə'rɪfɪk] gewaltig, ungeheuer III/5B1
test [test] Prüfung, Test; Klassenarbeit II/5B9
test [test] prüfen, testen III/2A2
text message ['tekst ˌmesɪdʒ] SMS II/5C3
textbook ['tekstˌbʊk] Lehrbuch II/1C1
the (River) Thames [ðə 'temz] die Themse II/2C1
than [ðæn] als *(bei Vergleich)* II/2C1
thank you ['θæŋk ju:] danke (schön) II/1B5
Thank you very much. ['θæŋkju: ˌveri 'mʌtʃ] Vielen Dank. I/6B2
thanks [θæŋks] danke I/4B5
Thanks a lot! [ˌθæŋks‿ə 'lɒt] Vielen Dank! I/3C2
that [ðæt] das; der/die/das I/1A2; dass II/2A1
It's not that bad! [ɪtz ˌnɒt 'ðæt ˌbæd] So schlimm ist es doch nicht! III/1B1
That's too bad! [ˌðæts ˌtu: 'bæd] Das ist wirklich schade! III/6A9
the [ðə] der/die/das I/W
the … the … [ðə ðə] je …, desto … III/5B2
The computer was built in … [ðə kəm'pju:tə wəz 'bɪlt‿ɪn] Der Computer wurde … gebaut. III/5B1
the more … the more … [ðə 'mɔ: ðə 'mɔ:] je mehr …, desto … III/6B1
°the one [ðə 'wʌn] derjenige, der/diejenige, die III/BS1
their [ðeə] ihr(e) I/1A5
them [ðem] sie, ihnen I/1C1
theme [θi:m] Thema; *hier:* Lektion, Kapitel II/1I
then [ðen] damals; *hier:* dann I/1C2
there [ðeə] dort(hin) I/1A2
there are [ðeər‿'ɑ:] es gibt, da sind I/1B1
there is [ðeər‿'ɪz] es gibt, da ist I/1A5
these *(pl of* **this)** [ði:z] diese I/1A2
they [ðeɪ] sie I/1A3
°thick [θɪk] dick, dicht III/BS6
°thief *(pl* thieves) [θi:f, θi:vz] Dieb/in III/BS5
thin [θɪn] dünn I/4C9
thing [θɪŋ] Ding, Gegenstand I/1C1
°thing [θɪŋ] *hier:* Sache III/BS5
just the thing [ˌdʒʌst ðə 'θɪŋ] genau das Richtige III/5B4
°they don't mean a thing [ˌðeɪ dəʊnt ˌmi:n‿ə 'θɪŋ] *hier:* sie bedeuten gar nichts III/8O
think [θɪŋk] denken, glauben, meinen I/1A4; *hier:* nachdenken, sich überlegen I/3C4
think about ['θɪŋk‿əˌbaʊt] denken an; nachdenken über II/3A6
°think better of sth [ˌθɪŋk 'betər‿əv ˌsʌmθɪŋ] sich etw anders überlegen III/BS7
think of ['θɪŋk‿əv] denken an, sich ausdenken III/2A6
°make sb think of sth [ˌmeɪk ˌsʌmbədi 'θɪŋk‿əv ˌsʌmθɪŋ] jdn an etw denken lassen III/3O
I don't think so. [aɪ ˌdəʊnt 'θɪŋk səʊ] Ich glaube nicht. II/1C4
third [θɜ:d] dritte (r,s) III/4B1
this [ðɪs] diese(r, s); das I/1A2
this afternoon [ðɪs‿ˌɑ:ftə'nu:n] heute Nachmittag II/2A3
this evening [ðɪs‿'i:vnɪŋ] heute Abend I/5A2
this morning [ðɪs 'mɔ:nɪŋ] heute Morgen I/5B2
those *(pl of* **that)** [ðəʊz] diese; jene I/2C7
though *(nachgestellt)* [ðəʊ] (je)doch III/5A1

thousand ['θaʊznd] Tausend III/3A2
three [θriː] drei I/1C3
throat [θrəʊt] Hals III/2B1
through [θruː] durch III/2A5
throw [θrəʊ] werfen I/4B4
°throw away [ˌθrəʊ əˈweɪ] wegwerfen, beiseite legen III/3O
thumb [θʌm] Daumen III/2A5
Thursday ['θɜːzdeɪ] Donnerstag I/4C5
ticket ['tɪkɪt] (Fahr)karte III/5A1; Karte II/2A2
ticket inspector ['tɪkɪt‿ɪnˌspektə] (Fahrkarten)kontrolleur/in III/5A1
tide [taɪd] Gezeiten III/4A4
tidy ['taɪdi] aufräumen I/4B2
°tie [taɪ] (an)binden III/BS4
tiger ['taɪgə] Tiger II/2A1
tight [taɪt] fest III/2A5
°tightrope walking ['taɪtrəʊp ˌwɔːkɪŋ] Seiltanzen III/BS3
till (= until) [tɪl] bis III/5B1
time [taɪm] (Uhr)zeit I/2B6
at the same time [ət ðə ˌseɪm 'taɪm] gleichzeitig III/1A6; gleichzeitig, zur gleichen Zeit III/5B4
have a good time [ˌhæv‿ə gʊd 'taɪm] sich amüsieren I/6A6
next time ['nekst‿ˌtaɪm] nächstes Mal III/5B1
on time [ɒn 'taɪm] pünktlich III/8B2
some other time [sʌm‿'ʌðə ˌtaɪm] ein anderes Mal III/1A8
°take one's time [ˌteɪk wʌnz 'taɪm] sich Zeit lassen III/BS7
What time is it? [ˌwɒt‿taɪm‿'ɪz‿ɪt] Wie spät ist es? II/3C3
time out [ˌtaɪm‿'aʊt] Auszeit III/2A4
... times [taɪmz] ... Mal II/1A4
timetable ['taɪmˌteɪbl] Stundenplan I/5A1
tip [tɪp] Rat(schlag), Tipp II/5C4
tired ['taɪəd] müde II/2A1
°get tired of sth [ˌget‿'taɪəd‿əv sʌmθɪŋ] etw satt bekommen III/BS4
title ['taɪtl] Titel III/3A3
to [tuː] in, nach, zu I/1C5
°to [tuː] *hier:* um zu III/7O1
°(work) to be done [tə bi 'dʌn] (Arbeit), die getan werden muss III/3O
today [tə'deɪ] heute I/2B3
together [tə'geðə] zusammen, gemeinsam I/3A1
°come together [ˌkʌm tə'geðə] zusammenkommen III/2O
toil [tɔɪl] hart arbeiten, schuften III/4A4

toilet ['tɔɪlət] Toilette III/8P3
toilet roll ['tɔɪlət rəʊl] Rolle Toilettenpapier III/5B4
toiletries *(only plural)* ['tɔɪlətriz] Toilettenartikel III/8P4
tomato (*pl* -es) [tə'mɑːtəʊ, tə'mɑːtəʊz] Tomate I/2B1
tomorrow [tə'mɒrəʊ] morgen I/5C5
tongue [tʌŋ] Zunge III/2B5
tonight [tə'naɪt] heute Abend I/4B5
too [tuː] (all)zu; auch I/1A3
(be) too bad [tuː 'bæd] wirklich schade (sein) III/2B4
tooth (*pl* teeth) [tuːθ, tiːθ] Zahn I/2A2
toothbrush ['tuːθˌbrʌʃ] Zahnbürste III/4A6
toothpaste ['tuːθˌpeɪst] Zahnpasta III/8P4
top [tɒp] *hier:* Spitze III/5B2; oberste(r,s); beste(r, s) III/4A6
at the top [ət ðə 'tɒp] oben III/7B4
topic ['tɒpɪk] Thema III/5B5
torch (*pl* torches) [tɔːtʃ, 'tɔːtʃɪz] Taschenlampe III/8A7
totally ['təʊtli] völlig, total III/8A5
touch [tʌtʃ] berühren II/5A7
tough [tʌf] robust, zäh III/7P6; *hier:* schwierig, hart III/BS2
Tourist Information Centre [ˌtʊərɪst ˌɪnfə'meɪʃn ˌsentə] Touristeninformation III/5LL4
tournament ['tʊənəmənt] Turnier III/7B1
toward(s) [tə'wɔːd(z)] in Richtung II/6B2
towel ['taʊəl] Handtuch I/2A3
town [taʊn] Stadt I/1P4
toy [tɔɪ] Spielzeug II/6B1
°trade [treɪd] Handel III/BS6
°tradition [trə'dɪʃn] Tradition, Brauch III/1O
traditional [trə'dɪʃnəl] traditionell III/1B5
°traditionally [trə'dɪʃnli] traditionell, üblicherweise III/1O
train [treɪn] Zug III/5A1
trainee nurse [ˌtreɪniː 'nɜːs] Krankenpflegeschüler/in III/4B2
training ['treɪnɪŋ] Training I/4C5
translate [træns'leɪt] übersetzen III/1B3
translation [træns'leɪʃn] Übersetzung III/1B3
travel ['trævl] reisen II/1A3; reisen; fahren III/5B2
traveller ['trævlə] Reisende/r III/8B1
travelling ['trævlɪŋ] Reisen III/8A4
tree [triː] Baum I/3P5

trekking ['trekɪŋ] Trekking, Wandern III/8B1
triathlon [traɪ'æθlən] Triathlon III/2A3
trigonometry [ˌtrɪgə'nɒmətri] Trigonometrie III/4B4
trip [trɪp] Ausflug I/3A1; Reise, Fahrt III/8B1
trouble ['trʌbl] Ärger, Problem III/5B2
(pair of) trousers ['traʊzəz] Hose III/6A6
true [truː] wahr II/1B5
trumpet ['trʌmpɪt] Trompete III/4A6
trust [trʌst] *hier:* Stiftung III/6B2
°speak the truth [ˌspiːk ðə 'truːθ] die Wahrheit sagen III/BS7
try [traɪ] *hier:* (aus)probieren III/1A6; versuchen I/6A3
try on [traɪ‿'ɒn] anprobieren II/5B5
°try one's luck [ˌtraɪ wʌnz 'lʌk] sein Glück versuchen III/BS7
the tube [ðə tjuːb] die (Londoner) U-Bahn II/2B1
Tuesday ['tjuːzdeɪ] Dienstag I/4C5
°tuff (= tough) [tʌf] robust, zäh III/4O
tummy *(informal)* ['tʌmi] Bauch I/2A4
°tunnel vision [ˌtʌnəl 'vɪʒn] Tunnelblick III/BS2
turn [tɜːn] werden III/1A6
°turn away [ˌtɜːn‿ə'weɪ] sich abwenden III/BS7
°turn into [ˌtɜːn‿'ɪntʊ] umwandeln in III/5O
turn left/right [tɜːn 'left/'raɪt] links/rechts abbiegen II/2B4
take turns [ˌteɪk 'tɜːnz] sich abwechseln III/4P6
watch TV [ˌwɒtʃ tiː'viː] fernsehen I/4B4
TV (= television) [ˌtiː'viː, 'telɪˌvɪʒn] Fernseher; Fernsehen I/4A6
TV set [ˌtiː 'viː ˌset] Fernsehgerät III/5A4
twelve [twelv] zwölf I/1A6
twice [twaɪs] zweimal II/1A4
two [tuː] zwei I/1A5
°two-thirds [ˌtuː 'θɜːdz] zwei Drittel III/6O
type [taɪp] Art III/8B1
typical ['tɪpɪkl] typisch; charakteristisch III/8A4

U

°ultimate ['ʌltɪmət] beste(r, s), optimal III/BS3
°Ultimate Frisbee [ˌʌltɪmət 'frɪzbi] *Funsportart* III/BS3
uncle ['ʌŋkl] Onkel I/W

under ['ʌndə] unter I/2C3
underground [ˌʌndə'graʊnd] *hier:* unter die Erde III/5A2
understand [ˌʌndə'stænd] verstehen II/3C1
unfriendly [ʌn'frenli] unfreundlich III/4P4
°unhappy [ʌn'hæpi] unglücklich III/BS4
uniform ['ju:nɪfɔ:m] Uniform II/5B1
United Kingdom of Great Britain and Northern Ireland (= UK) [ju:ˌnaɪtɪd ˌkɪŋdəm‿əv greɪt ˌbrɪtn‿ənd ˌnɔ:ðn‿'aɪələnd] das Vereinigte Königreich *(Großbritannien und Nordirland)* II/1LL1
the United States [ðə ju:ˌnaɪtɪd 'steɪts] die Vereinigten Staaten II/6C2
°university [ˌju:nɪ'vɜ:səti] Universität III/6O
unrealistic [ˌʌnrɪə'lɪstɪk] unrealistisch, wirklichkeitsfremd III/7B4
unscramble [ʌn'skræmbl] wieder ordnen III/4P5
until [ən'tɪl] bis I/6A3
untouchable [ʌn'tʌtʃəbl] Unberührbare/r III/1LL1
up [ʌp] nach oben, hinauf II/2C1
up and down [ˌʌp‿ænd 'daʊn] auf und ab II/3C1
upstairs [ʌp'steəz] (nach) oben II/5A5
us [ʌs] uns I/3A1
USA (= United States of America) [ju:es'eɪ, ju:ˌnaɪtɪd ˌsteɪts‿əv‿ə'merɪkə] USA (= Vereinigte Staaten von Amerika) II/4A4
use [ju:z] benutzen II/2B4; *hier:* verwenden, anwenden III/6O
be in use [bi:‿ɪn‿'ju:s] in Gebrauch sein III/5A6
°used to + *Verb* ['ju:st‿tʊ] früher III/7O3
useful ['ju:sfl] nützlich, praktisch III/4B1
usually ['ju:ʒʊəli] gewöhnlich, normalerweise I/4B1

V

°vacation *(AE)* [və'keɪʃən] Ferien, Urlaub III/BS6
°variety [və'raɪəti] Vielfalt III/BS3
vase [vɑ:z] (Blumen)vase III/6A4
vegetable ['vedʒtəbl] Gemüse I/5B1
vegetarian [ˌvedʒə'teəriən] Vegetarier/in III/7A2
vegetarian [ˌvedʒə'teəriən] vegetarisch III/1A2
Velcro® ['velkrəʊ] Klettverschluss III/5A4
°Velcro® (fastener) ['velkrəʊ] Klettverschluss III/5O
verb [vɜ:b] Verb II/1A3
verse [vɜ:s] Strophe, Vers III/7A5
version ['vɜ:ʃn] Version, Fassung III/4A1
very ['veri] sehr I/1A6
°video game ['vɪdiəʊ ˌgeɪm] Videospiel III/7O1
Viking ['vaɪkɪŋ] Wikinger/in; wikingisch III/5LL4
visit ['vɪzɪt] Besuch III/5A2; besuchen I/3A1
be worth a visit [bi: ˌwɜ:θ‿ə 'vɪzɪt] einen Besuch wert sein III/5P1
visitor ['vɪzɪtə] Besucher/in, Gast III/5A7
°visually impaired [ˌvɪʒʊəli ɪm'peəd] sehbehindert III/BS2
°in a coarse voice [ɪn‿ə ˌkɔ:s 'vɔɪs] *hier:* mit rauer Stimme III/BS7
have a vote [ˌhæv‿ə 'vəʊt] abstimmen III/5B5
vowel ['vaʊəl] Vokal, Selbstlaut III/5P2

W

wait [weɪt] (ab)warten, (er)warten III/2B1
Wait a minute! ['weɪt‿ə ˌmɪnɪt] Moment mal! II/1B2
wait for sb to do sth [ˌweɪt fə ˌsʌmbədi tʊ 'du: ˌsʌmθɪŋ] darauf warten, dass jd etw tut III/8B2
wait (for) ['weɪt‿fə] warten auf I/4B2
waiter/waitress ['weɪtə/'weɪtrəs] Kellner/in III/1A3
waiting room ['weɪtɪŋ ˌru:m] Wartezimmer III/2B2
°wake up [ˌweɪk‿'ʌp] aufwachen III/7O3
°wake up sb [ˌweɪk‿'ʌp ˌsʌmbədi] jdn aufwecken III/8O
Wales [weɪlz] Wales II/1LL1
walk [wɔ:k] (zu Fuß) gehen I/2A4; Gehen; Spaziergang I/4B4
take the dog for a walk [ˌteɪk ðə 'dɒg fɔ:r‿ə 'wɔ:k] den Hund ausführen III/6A2
walk down the street [ˌwɔ:k daʊn ðə 'stri:t] die Straße entlanggehen III/7A5
walk the dog [ˌwɔ:k ðə 'dɒg] den Hund ausführen III/4B1
wall [wɔ:l] Wand, Mauer III/6P6; *hier: die Chinesische Mauer* III/8A3
wallet ['wɒlɪt] Brieftasche, Portemonnaie III/3B2
walrus (*pl* walrus *or* walruses) ['wɔ:lrəs, 'wɔ:lrəsɪz] Walross III/7B1
want [wɒnt] wünschen; wollen I/2B3
want sb to do sth [wɒnt ˌsʌmbədi tə du: 'sʌmθɪŋ] wollen, dass jd etw tut I/3C1
wardrobe ['wɔ:drəʊb] (Kleider)schrank I/4A1
warm [wɔ:m] warm I/4C7
°warm [wɔ:m] wärmen III/7O1
°warmth [wɔ:mθ] Wärme; Herzlichkeit III/7O1
wash [wɒʃ] (sich) waschen I/2A2
do the washing up [ˌdu: ðə ˌwɒʃɪŋ‿'ʌp] abspülen I/4B6
watch [wɒtʃ] beobachten; zusehen, zuschauen I/3A3
watch (*pl* watches) [wɒtʃ, 'wɒtʃɪz] Armbanduhr III/3A4
watch TV [ˌwɒtʃ ti:'vi:] fernsehen I/4B4
water ['wɔ:tə] Wasser I/2A2
like a fish out of water [laɪk‿ə ˌfɪʃ‿aʊt‿əv wɔ:tə] wie ein Fisch auf dem Trockenen III/5B2
water sports *(only plural)* ['wɔ:tə ˌspɔ:tz] Wassersport III/8A6
water-powered ['wɔ:tə ˌpaʊəd] *von Wasserkraft angetriebene(r/s)* III/5B1
°waterball ['wɔ:təbɔ:l] Wasserball III/BS5
waterfall ['wɔ:təˌfɔ:l] Wasserfall III/4A7
waters ['wɔ:təz] Gewässer III/4A4
waterside ['wɔ:təˌsaɪd] Strand III/4A4
way [weɪ] Weg III/8A4
° way [weɪ] Art und Weise III/BS1
be on one's way [bi:‿ˌɒn wʌnz 'weɪ] *hier:* unterwegs sein III/8B1
lose one's way [lu:z wʌnz 'weɪ] sich verirren I /6A8
a way out [ə ˌweɪ‿'aʊt] Ausweg III/4B1
we [wi:] wir I/1A3
We could do with … [ˌwi: kəd 'du: wɪð] Wir könnten … gebrauchen. III/7A7
wealthy ['welθi] reich, wohlhabend III/6A9
wear [weə] tragen I/5A1; tragen; anziehen II/5A2
°wear out [ˌweər‿'aʊt] sich abnutzen III/BS6
weather ['weðə] Wetter I/4C8
weaving machine ['wi:vɪŋ məˌʃi:n] Webmaschine III/5B1
web page ['webˌpeɪdʒ] Webseite, Internetseite III/8A5
°webbing ['webɪŋ] Gurtband III/BS3
°wedding ring ['wedɪŋ rɪŋ] Ehering III/8O

Dictionary English – German

Wednesday ['wenzdeɪ] Mittwoch I/3A1
week [wi:k] Woche I/4C5
weekend [ˌwi:k'end] Wochenende I/2B2
at the weekend [æt ðə ˌwi:k'end] am Wochenende II/6A1
welcome (to) ['welkəm] willkommen (in) III/5A2
You're welcome. [ˌjɔ: 'welkəm] Nichts zu danken!, Gern geschehen! III/2B1
well [wel] gut II/3B1; nun (ja), tja I/3A4
°do well [ˌdu: 'wel] *hier:* erfolgreich sein III/2O
°wish sb well [ˌwɪʃ‿ˌsʌmbədi 'wel] jdm alles Gute wünschen III/7O3
Well done! [ˌwel 'dʌn] Gut gemacht! II/1B2
were powered [wɜ: 'paʊəd] wurden angetrieben III/5B1
west [west] Westen III/4A9
wet [wet] nass; feucht III/8P4
whack *(informal)* [wæk] *etwa:* zack III/2A5
°wham *(informal)* [wæm] (hinein)krachen III/BS1
what [wɒt] *hier:* welche(r, s) I/1C1; was I/W
What about ...? *(informal)* [wɒt‿ə'baʊt] Was ist mit ...? II/1B2
What are you having? ['wɒt‿ɑ: ju: ˌhævɪŋ] Was nimmst du/nehmen Sie? III/1A3
What else ...? [wɒt‿'els] Was sonst ...? III/1P5
What goes around comes around. [wɒt ˌɡəʊz‿əˌraʊnd 'kʌmz‿əˌraʊnd] Alles rächt sich früher oder später. III/7A2
What is ... about? [ˌwɒt‿is ə'baʊt] Worum geht es in/bei ...? III/8A5
What is ... like? [ˌwɒt ɪz 'laɪk] Wie ist ...? III/1A3
(at) what time [wɒt‿'taɪm] (um) wie viel Uhr II/1B8
What time is it? [ˌwɒt‿taɪm‿'ɪz‿ɪt] Wie spät ist es? II/3C3
What was it like? [ˌwɒt wəz‿ɪt 'laɪk] Wie war es? III/1A10
What's on offer? [ˌwɒts‿ɒn‿'ɒfə] Was ist im Angebot? III/6A7
What's on? [ˌwɒts‿'ɒn] Was läuft? Was geht ab? III/7B1
What's the matter? [ˌwɒts ðə 'mætə] Was ist los? II/2A1
wheel [wi:l] Rad III/2B5
front wheel [ˌfrʌnt 'wi:l] Vorderrad III/3B1
wheelchair ['wi:lˌtʃeə] Rollstuhl III/6B2
when [wen] als I/5C5; wann; wenn I/1C1
°whenever [wen'evə] jedes Mal, wenn III/2O
where [weə] wo(hin) I/W
°whether ['weðə] ob III/BS3
which [wɪtʃ] welche(r, s) I/3A1
while [waɪl] während III/3B1
white [waɪt] weiß I/2A5
who [hu:] wem, wen II/3A8; wer; der/die/das I/1A1
whole [həʊl] ganz, gesamt III/5B1
whose [hu:z] wessen I/5C7
°whose [hu:z] dessen, deren III/BS6
why [waɪ] warum I/2A4
wide [waɪd] breit III/5B2
wife (*pl* wives) [waɪf, waɪvz] Ehefrau I/5C7
wild [waɪld] wild I/3B2
wildly ['waɪldli] *hier:* stark III/5B2
willed ['wɪld] vererbt, vermacht III/4A4
win [wɪn] gewinnen II/1B2
wind [wɪnd] Wind I/6A2
window ['wɪndəʊ] Fenster I/1B2
°windsurfing ['wɪndˌsɜ:fɪŋ] Windsurfen III/BS3
wine [waɪn] Wein III/1A8
°wing [wɪŋ] Kotflügel III/BS7
winner ['wɪnə] Gewinner/in; Sieger/in I/3A5
winter ['wɪntə] Winter I/4B4
wish [wɪʃ] wünschen II/4B7
°wish sb well [ˌwɪʃ‿ˌsʌmbədi 'wel] jdm alles Gute wünschen III/7O3
witch (*pl* witches) [wɪtʃ, 'wɪtʃɪz] Hexe III/3A1
with [wɪð] mit I/W
without [wɪð'aʊt] ohne II/4C3
°witness ['wɪtnəs] Zeuge/Zeugin III/BS7
woman (*pl* women) ['wʊmən, 'wɪmɪn] Frau I/2A7
°wonder ['wʌndə] sich fragen III/BS2
wonderful ['wʌndəfl] wunderbar, wundervoll II/5B9
wood [wʊd] Holz II/4C4
word [wɜ:d] Wort I/1A4
word snake ['wɜ:d ˌsneɪk] Wortschlange III/1B6
word web ['wɜ:d ˌweb] Wortnetz II/4B9
wordbank ['wɜ:dˌbæŋk] Wortfeld II/1A3
work [wɜ:k] Arbeit I/5A1; arbeiten I/1A6; *hier:* funktionieren, laufen III/6A7
work [wɜ:k] *hier:* funktionieren III/5B6
be out of work [bi:‿ˌaʊt‿əv 'wɜ:k] arbeitslos sein III/4B2
°work out [ˌwɜ:k‿'aʊt] *hier:* sich von allein lösen III/7O3
workbook ['wɜ:kˌbʊk] Arbeitsbuch II/1A2
°worker ['wɜ:kə] Arbeiter/in III/BS6
world [wɜ:ld] Welt III/5I
from all over the world [frəm‿ˌɔ:l‿əʊvə ðə 'wɜ:ld] aus der ganzen Welt III/7B1
world record [ˌwɜ:ld 'rekɔ:d] Weltrekord III/6B2
°world war II [ˌwɜ:ld wɔ: 'tu:] 2. Weltkrieg III/BS6
°world-record [ˌwɜ:ld 'rekɔ:d] Weltrekord- III/2O
°worldwide [ˌwɜ:ld'waɪd] weltweit III/BS6
worried ['wʌrid] beunruhigt, besorgt III/4B2
worry ['wʌri] sich Sorgen machen II/3B2
Don't worry! [ˌdəʊnt 'wʌri] Keine Sorge! III/3A4
worse [wɜ:s] schlechter; schlimmer III/5A2
the worst [ðə 'wɜ:st] der/die/das schlechteste III/2A5
be worth [bi: 'wɜ:θ] wert sein III/6A4
be worth a visit [bi: ˌwɜ:θ‿ə 'vɪzɪt] einen Besuch wert sein III/5P1
would [wʊd] würde(n/st/t) II/4B8
wreck [rek] (Schiffs)wrack III/4A1
wrist [rɪst] Handgelenk III/7A2
write [raɪt] schreiben I/1A4
write down [raɪt 'daʊn] aufschreiben I/1C4
writer ['raɪtə] Autor/in III/2B5
wrong [rɒŋ] falsch I/3P6
be wrong with sb [bi: 'rɒŋ wɪð ˌsʌmbədi] nicht stimmen, los sein III/2B1

X

X-ray ['eksreɪ] Röntgen- III/5B4
(take an) X-ray ['eksreɪ] röntgen III/2B2

Y

yard [jɑ:d] Yard *(= 91,44 cm) III/6B2; Hof III/BS1*
year [jɪə] *hier:* Schuljahr, Klasse I/3A1; Jahr I/W
yellow ['jeləʊ] gelb I/3B8
yes [jes] ja I/1B4
yesterday ['jestədeɪ] gestern II/1B4
°yet [jet] schon; bis jetzt III/7O3

yoghurt ['jɒgət] Yoghurt, Joghurt III/1B5
you [juː] du, dich, dir, Sie, Ihnen; ihr, euch I/W; man III/1B1
You never know. [juː ˌnevə 'nəʊ] *etwa:* Das kann man nie wissen. III/6A4
You're kidding! *(informal)* [jɔː 'kɪdɪŋ] Das ist doch nicht dein Ernst! III/7A6
You're welcome. [ˌjɔː 'welkəm] Nichts zu danken!, Gern geschehen! III/2B1
young [jʌŋ] jung I/3A1
your [jɔː] dein(e); euer/eure; Ihr(e) I/W
yourself (*pl* yourselves) [jə'self, jə'selvz] dich; dir; selbst I/6C6
youth hostel ['juːθ ˌhɒstl] Jugendherberge III/8A7

Z

zebra ['zebrə] Zebra II/2B3
°zip [zɪp] Reißverschluss III/5O
°zone [zəʊn] Zone, Region III/BS3
zoo [zuː] Zoo II/2A1

Dictionary German – English

A

Abend evening
Abendessen; Mittagessen dinner
Abenteuer, Erlebnis adventure
aber but
abschreiben copy
abspülen do the washing up
(ab)warten, (er)warten wait
(acht) Uhr (eight) o'clock
Adjektiv adjective
Affe monkey
(Akten)mappe portfolio
albern, dumm silly
allein alone
alles everything
Alles Gute zum Geburtstag! Happy birthday (to you)!
Alles Gute! All the best!
alles Liebe, viele Grüße love *(in Briefen)*
alle(s); der/die/das ganze all (the)
(all)zu; auch too
als when
als *(bei Vergleich)* than
als; wie; da as
also so
alt old
Alter age
am Abend in the evening
am Anfang, zu Beginn at the beginning
am liebsten mögen like best
am meisten most
am Morgen in the morning
am Nachmittag in the afternoon
(am) Telefon (on the) phone
am wenigsten least
am Wochenende at the weekend
(an der) Ecke (at the) corner
andere(r, s) other
anders, andere(r, s); unterschiedlich, verschieden different
Anfang, Beginn beginning
anfangen (mit) start
anfangen, beginnen begin
Angst haben (vor) be afraid (of)
ankommen arrive
anprobieren try on
anrufen phone
(an)rufen; nennen call
Antwort answer
Anzeige, Inserat advert (= advertisement)
anziehen put on
Apfel apple
April April
Arbeit work
Arbeit, Stelle, Aufgabe job
arbeiten work
Arbeitsbuch workbook
arbeitslos sein be out of work
Arm arm
arm poor
Armbanduhr watch (*pl* watches)
Art, Sorte kind
Arzt/Ärztin doctor
auch, außerdem also
auf der Straße in the street
auf Deutsch in German
auf Englisch in English
auf und ab up and down
Auf Wiedersehen. Goodbye.
auf, an, in on
auf, an, in, bei at
aufbewahren; behalten keep
Aufgabe task
aufgeben give up
aufhören stop
aufmachen, öffnen open
aufräumen tidy
aufregend, spannend exciting
aufschreiben write down
aufstehen get up, stand up
aufzeichnen; *hier:* **aufnehmen** record
Auge eye
August August
Ausflug trip
ausfüllen fill in
ausgehen; weggehen go out
(aus)helfen, unterstützen help out
ausländisch, fremd foreign
hier: **(aus)probieren** try
hier: **aussehen** look
auswendig by heart
Auszeit time out
Auto car
außen, außerhalb; *hier:* **draußen** outside
Äußerung statement

B

babysitten babysit
Bad(ewanne) bath
Bad(ezimmer) bathroom
Bahnhof (railway) station
bald soon
Ball ball
Banane banana
Bargeld cash
Bauch tummy *(informal)*
bauen build
Bauernhof farm
Baum tree
(be)antworten answer
bedeuten; meinen mean
Bedeutung meaning
bei Gillian (zu Hause) at Gillian's
bei jdm zu Hause at sb's house
beim Arzt/bei der Ärztin at the doctor's
Bein leg
benutzen use
beobachten; zusehen, zuschauen watch
Berg mountain
Bericht report
berichten report (to)
berühmt famous
berühren touch
beschreiben describe
Besichtigungen, Sightseeing sightseeing *(no pl)*
besondere(r, s), spezielle(r, s) special
besprechen, diskutieren discuss
besser better
beste(r, s) best
Besuch visit
besuchen visit
betrachten, sehen look at
Betreuer/in person who looks after sb
Bett bed
beunruhigt, besorgt worried
bevor before
Bewegung, Übung exercise
(be)zahlen pay
Bibliothek, Bücherei library
Bild picture
(bildende) Kunst art
billig, preiswert cheap
bis until
bis bald see you (later)
Bis bald! See you soon!
bisher so far
bitte please
Blatt leaf (*pl* leaves)
blau blue
bleiben stay
Bleistift pencil
Blume flower
Bluse blouse
Boot; Schiff boat
brauchen need
braun brown
breit wide
Brett; Tafel board
Brief; Buchstabe letter
Brille (pair of) glasses *(only plural)*
bringen; nehmen take
Broschüre brochure
Brot bread
Brücke bridge
Bruder brother
Buch book
Buchladen bookshop
Burg, Schloss castle
Bus bus
Bushaltestelle bus stop
Butter butter

C

Chips crisps *(only plural)*
Cousin/e cousin

D

daher, folglich so
damals; *hier:* **dann** then
danke thanks
danke (schön) thank you
Das ist doch nicht dein Ernst! You're kidding! *(informal)*
Das meinst du doch nicht im Ernst!, Das soll wohl ein Witz sein! You must be joking!
das Vereinigte Königreich *(Großbritannien und Nordirland)* United

Kingdom of Great Britain and Northern Ireland (= UK)
das; der/die/das that
dass that
Datum date
dein(e); euer/eure; Ihr(e) your
den ganzen Tag all day
den Tisch decken set the table
denken an; nachdenken über think about
denken, glauben, meinen think
der/die/das the
der/die/das beste the best
der/die/das Gleiche the same
der/die/das sechsjährige six-year-old
Deutsche/r; deutsch German
Deutschland Germany
Dezember December
dich; dir; selbst yourself (*pl* yourselves)
die Britischen Inseln the British Isles *(only plural)*
die (Londoner) U-Bahn the tube
die meisten most
die Polizei the police
die Themse the (River) Thames
die Vereinigten Staaten the United States
Dienstag Tuesday
diese these (*pl of* this)
diese; jene those (*pl of* that)
diese(r, s); das this
Ding, Gegenstand thing
Dinosaurier dinosaur
Diskussion, Erörterung discussion
Donnerstag Thursday
dort drüben over there
dort(hin) there
Dossier, Akte dossier
dreckig, schmutzig dirty
du, dich, dir, Sie, Ihnen; ihr, euch you
dumm, blöd stupid
dunkel dark
dünn thin
Dusche shower

E

Ehefrau wife (*pl* wives)
Ehemann husband
Ei egg
eigene(r, s) own
ein bisschen a bit
ein wenig, ein bisschen a little
einander each other
eine halbe Stunde half an hour
eine Hose a pair of trousers
eine Party machen have a party
eine Stunde lang for an hour
ein(e) a/an
hier: **ein(e) andere(r, s)** another
einfache Vergangenheit simple past
einige; etwas some
einige; wenige a few
einkaufen gehen go shopping
einkaufen (gehen) do the shopping
einladen invite
einmal once
einmal im/pro Jahr once a year
eintragen fill in
Eiskrem, Eis ice cream
Elefant elephant
Elektrizität, Strom electricity
Eltern parents *(only plural)*
Ende end
Ende, Schluss ending
endlich, schließlich at last
eng; knapp narrow
England England
englisch; Englisch English
englischsprachig English-speaking
Entschuldigen Sie bitte!, Entschuldigung! Excuse me!
er he
Erdkunde, Geografie geography
Ereignis, Veranstaltung event
erfinden invent
erfinden, (sich) ausdenken make up
Erfinder/in inventor
Erfindung invention
erfolgreich successful
erhalten, bekommen get
(starke) Erkältung (bad) cold
erklären explain
Ernährungslehre food technology
(er)raten guess
erster Weihnachtsfeiertag Christmas Day
erwachsen werden grow up
Erwachsene/r adult
es it
Es freut mich, Sie/dich kennen zu lernen. Nice to meet you.
Es geht mir gut. I'm fine.
es gibt, da ist there is
es gibt, da sind there are
Es kostet… Pfund. It's…£ (pounds).
essen eat
Essen food
essen gehen eat out
hier: **essen, trinken** have
(Etagen)wohnung, Mietwohnung flat
etw trinken have a drink
etw tun dürfen be allowed to do sth
etw tun können be able to do sth
etw tun müssen have to do sth
etwas something
Europa Europe

F

fahren drive
hier: **fahren** go
fahren (mit); reiten ride
(Fahr)karte ticket
(Fahr)rad bike
Fahrrad bicycle
Fahrt ride
fallen fall
falsch wrong
Familie family
fangen catch
Farbe colour
fast, beinahe almost, nearly
Februar February
Federmäppchen pencil case
Feier celebration
feiern celebrate
Fenster window
Ferienlager holiday camp
fernsehen watch TV
Fernseher; Fernsehen TV (= television)
fertig, bereit ready
Fest, Festival festival
Feuer; Brand fire
Feuerwerkskörper firework
Fieber haben have a temperature
Filzstift felt-tip
finden find
Finger finger
Fisch fish (*pl* fish *or* fishes)
Flasche bottle
Fleisch meat
fliegen fly
Flug, Fliegen flight
Flughafen airport
Flugzeug aeroplane (= plane)
Fluss river
folgen follow
Foto photo
fotografieren take photos
Frage question
Fragen stellen ask questions
fragen; bitten ask
Franzose/Französin; französisch; *hier:* **Französisch** French
Frau woman (*pl* women)
Frau *(Anrede)* Mrs
Freitag Friday
Freizeit free time
Freund *(Partner)* boyfriend
Freund/in friend
Freundin *(Partnerin)* girlfriend
freundlich friendly
frisch fresh
Frucht; Obst fruit
früh early
Frühling spring
Frühstück breakfast
frühstücken have breakfast
führen lead
füllen fill
hier: **funktionieren, laufen** work
für …, … lang for … *(+ Zeitraum)*

Dictionary German – English

für; *hier:* **zu(m)** for
furchtbar, schrecklich awful
Fuß foot (*pl* feet)
Fußball football
(Fuß)boden floor

G

Gabel fork
ganz, gesamt whole
Garten garden
Gebäude, Bau building
geben give
Gebiet, Region; *hier:* **Viertel, Gegend** area
geboren werden be born
Geburtstag birthday
gefährlich dangerous
Gefangene/r prisoner
Gefühl feeling
gegen against
gegenüber opposite
gehen go
Gehen; Spaziergang walk
gelb yellow
Geld money
Geld verdienen make money
Gemüse vegetable
hier: **genannt** called
(genau)so … wie … as … as
Genesungskarte get well card
genießen enjoy
genug enough
gerade(aus) straight (on)
hier: **gerade (eben)** just
Geschäft, Laden shop
geschehen, passieren happen
Geschenk present
Geschichte history
Geschichte, Erzählung story
geschlossen, zu; *hier:* **gesperrt** closed
Geschwister brothers and sisters
Gesicht face
Gespräch, Dialog dialogue
gestern yesterday
gesund healthy
Gesundheit health
Getränk drink
gewinnen win
Gewinner/in; Sieger/in winner
gewöhnlich, normalerweise usually
Giraffe giraffe
Gitarre guitar
Gitter; *hier:* **Tabelle** grid
Glas glass
glauben believe
gleich the same
Glück haben be lucky
glücklich; zufrieden; fröhlich happy
Grammatik grammar
Gras grass
gratis, umsonst (for) free
grau grey
groß big, large
groß, riesig; großartig great
Großbritannien (Great) Britain
Größe size
Großeltern grandparents (*only plural*)
Großmutter grandmother
(Groß)stadt city
grün green
Gruppe group
Gruppenreise group travel
Gummi; Radiergummi rubber
gut good, well
Gut gemacht! Well done!
Guten Abend. Good evening.
Gutes/Frohes neues Jahr! Happy New Year!

H

Haar(e) hair (*no pl*)
haben have got, have
halb elf half past ten
Hälfte half (*pl* halves)
hier: **häufig, oft** much
Hallo. Hello.
Hals throat
Hals; Nacken neck
halten hold
Hamster hamster
Hand hand
Handschuh glove
Handtuch towel
hart; *hier:* **anstrengend** hard
hart; schwer hard
hassen, nicht ausstehen können hate
Hauptgericht main course
Hauptwort, Substantiv noun
Haus house
Hausaufgaben homework (*no pl)*
Haustier pet
Heft exercise book
Heiligabend Christmas Eve
Heimweh haben feel homesick
heiß hot
helfen help
herausfinden find out
Herbst autumn
hereinkommen come in
Herr *(Anrede)* Mr
herumkommen get around
heute today
heute Abend this evening, tonight
heute Morgen this morning
heute Nachmittag this afternoon
Hier, bitte!, Bitte schön! Here you are!
hier(her) here
hilfreich, nützlich; hilfsbereit helpful
Himmel sky
(hinauf)steigen; klettern (auf) climb (up)
hineinsetzen/-legen/-stellen put in
hinten at the back (of)
hinter behind
hinunter, hinab down
hinzufügen add
hoch high
hoch; groß tall
hoffen hope
höflich polite
hier: **holen, kaufen** get
Holz wood
hören hear
Hose (pair of) trousers
hübsch pretty
Huhn chicken
Hund dog
hungrig hungry
Hut; Mütze hat

I

ich I
Ich bin/komme (aus …) I'm (from …)
Ich glaube nicht. I don't think so.
Ich hätte/würde gern … I'd like (to) …
Ich werde … nehmen/essen. I'll have …
Idee idea
Igel hedgehog
ihm, ihn him
ihr(e) their
im Alter von aged
im Augenblick, momentan at the moment
im Internet on the Internet
im Internet suchen search the Internet
im Internet surfen surf the Internet
Imbissstube snack bar
immer always
(immer) noch, noch immer still
in in
in into
in der Mitte; mitten in/auf in the middle
in Gruppen, gruppenweise in groups
in Ordnung, gut fine
in Richtung toward(s)
in Urlaub gehen/fahren go on holiday
in, nach, zu to
Inder/in; indisch Indian
Indien India
Informationstechnologie; *hier:* **Informatik** information technology
innen, drinnen inside
Insel island
interessant interesting
interviewen, befragen interview
(irgend)ein(e); jede(r, s) any
(irgend)etwas anything
(irgend)etwas anderes anything else
(irgend)jemand, irgendwer someone, somebody
irgendwo somewhere
Italiener/in; italienisch Italian

J

ja yes
Jacke jacket

Jahr year
Jahrhundert century
Januar January
(jdm) den Weg beschreiben give (sb) directions
jdn beschimpfen call sb names
jeden Tag, täglich daily
jede(r); alle everybody, everyone
jede(r); jemand anybody
jede(r, s) each, every
jemals, schon einmal ever
jetzt now
hier: **Jetzt hör aber auf!** Come on!
Jugendherberge youth hostel
Juli July
jung young
Junge boy
Juni June

K

Käfig cage
Kalender calendar
kalt cold
Karneval, Volksfest carnival
Karte ticket
Kartoffel potato (*pl* -es)
Käse cheese
Katze cat
kauen chew
kaufen buy
Kaufhaus department store
Kaugummi (chewing) gum
kein/keine not any
kein(e) no
keine(r, s) not … any
Kellner/in waiter/waitress
Kilo kilo
Kilometer kilometre
Kind child (*pl* children)
Kino cinema
Kirche church
Kiste; Schachtel; Kasten box
Klassenkamerad/in, Mitschüler/in classmate
Klassenzimmer classroom
Klebstoff glue *(no pl)*
Kleid dress
(Kleider)schrank wardrobe
Kleider, Kleidung clothes *(only plural)*
Kleidung clothing
klein little, small
klingen, sich anhören sound
Klub, Verein; Schul-AG club
klug, schlau clever
km/h kph (= kilometres per hour)
knapp bei Kasse sein be short of money *(informal)*
Knie knee
Koch/Köchin cook
kochen do the cooking
kochen; braten cook
Koffer suitcase
kommen come
Kommode chest of drawers
Komm(t) schon!; Mach(t) jetzt! Come on!
König king
Königin queen
können can
könnte(n/st/t) could
könnte(st, n) might
Konzert concert
Kopf head
(Kopf)kissen, Polster pillow
Korb basket
Körper body
kosten cost
köstlich, lecker delicious
Kostüm costume
krank ill
(Kranken)schwester, (Kranken)pfleger nurse
Küche kitchen
Kuchen; Torte cake
Kuh cow
Kühlschrank fridge *(informal)*
Kunde/Kundin customer
kurz; klein short
küssen kiss

L

lachen laugh
Lagerfeuer campfire
Land country, land
(Land)karte map
lang long
langsam slow
langweilig boring
Lärm, Geräusch noise
lassen let
lass(t) uns … let's (= let us) …
laufen, rennen run
Läufer/in runner
laut loud
Leben life (*pl* lives)
leben, am Leben sein be alive
leben, wohnen live
leer empty
Lehrbuch textbook
Lehrer/in teacher
leicht, einfach easy
leise, ruhig quiet
lernen learn
lesen read
letzte(r, s) last
Leute, Menschen people
Licht light
Liebe love
lieben; sehr gern mögen love
Liebling; Favorit/in favourite
Lieblings- favourite
Lied song
liegen; sich hinlegen lie
Lineal ruler
linke(r, s) left
links, auf der linken Seite on the left
links/rechts abbiegen turn left/right
Liste list
Loch hole
Löffel spoon
Löwe lion
Luft air
lustig, witzig, komisch funny

M

machen make
Mädchen girl
Magenschmerzen, Bauchschmerzen stomach ache
Mahlzeit, Essen meal
Mai May
… Mal … times
Mama, Mutti mum *(informal)*
man you
manchmal sometimes
Mann man (*pl* men)
männlich male
Mantel coat
Markt market
März March
Maschine, Motor engine
Mathe maths
Maus mouse (*pl* mice)
Medizin, Medikamente medicine
Meer, (die) See sea
mehr more
Meile *(= 1,609 km)* mile
mein(e) my
Mensch man (*pl* men)
Messer knife (*pl* knives)
Meter metre
Milch milk
mindestens, zumindest at least
Minute minute
mir, mich; *hier:* **ich** me
mit by *(+ Verkehrsmittel)*
mit with
mit dem Bus fahren take the bus
mit jdm gehen go out with sb *(informal)*
(mit)bringen bring
mitlesen read along
Mittagessen lunch
Mittwoch Wednesday
Mobbing bullying
Mobiltelefon, Handy mobile (phone)
Möchten Sie schon bestellen? Are you ready to order?
mögen like
Möhre, Karotte, Mohrrübe carrot
Moment mal! Wait a minute!
Monat month
Mond moon
Montag Monday
morgen tomorrow
Morgen, Vormittag morning
morgens, vormittags *(nur hinter Uhrzeit zwischen Mitternacht und 12 Uhr mittags)* am (= ante meridiem)
müde tired
Mülleimer, Mülltonne b n
müssen must

Dictionary German–English

Mund mouth
Museum museum
Musik music
Musiker/in musician
(Musik)gruppe group
Mustertext model (text)
Mutter mother

N

Na und?, Na wenn schon! So what? *(informal)*
nach after
nach dem Weg fragen ask for directions
nach oben, hinauf up
(nach) oben upstairs
Nachbar/in neighbour
hier: **nachdenken, sich überlegen** think
Nachmittag afternoon
nachmittags, abends *(nur hinter Uhrzeit zwischen 12 Uhr mittags und Mitternacht)* pm (= post meridiem)
nachschlagen look up
nachspielen act out
nächste(r, s) next
Nacht night
Nachtisch dessert
nachts at night
Nachtwanderung night hike
nahe (bei) near
Name name
Nase nose
natürlich of course
(Natur)wissenschaft science
neben next to
nein no
neu new
Neuigkeit; Nachrichten news *(no pl)*
Neujahr New Year
nicht not
nicht dürfen must not
nicht mehr not anymore
nicht stimmen, los sein be wrong with sb
nichts not anything, nothing
Nichts zu danken!, Gern geschehen! You're welcome.
nie(mals) never
niemand not anyone, nobody
nirgendwo(hin) not … anywhere
noch eine(r, s) another
noch mehr; weitere(r, s) more
Norden north
Norden; *hier:* **in nördliche Richtung** north
Nordirland Northern Ireland
normalerweise normally
November November
nun (ja), tja well
nur only
nur, bloß, einfach just
nützlich, praktisch useful

O

oberhalb; *hier:* **oben** above
oder or
offen, geöffnet open
oft, häufig often
ohne without
Ohr ear
Oktober October
Oma, Omi grandma *(informal)*
Onkel uncle
Opa, Opi grandpa *(informal)*
orange orange
Orange, Apfelsine orange
Ort; Platz place
Osten east

P

Paar pair
Papa, Vati dad *(informal)*
Papier paper
Pappe, Karton; Karte card
Parade, Umzug parade
Partner/in partner
passen zu go with
Patient/in patient
Patrone cartridge
Pause break
Penny p (= penny; *pl* -nies *or* pence)
Pferd horse
Pflanze plant
Pfund *(engl. Währung)* pound
Pinguin penguin
planen; vorbereiten plan
Platz, Raum; Zimmer room
plötzlich, auf einmal suddenly
Polizeibeamter/-beamtin police officer
Pommes frites chips *(only plural)*
präsentieren; *hier:* **aufführen** present
Preis price
Problem problem
Projekt project
Prüfung exam
Prüfung, Test; Klassenarbeit test
Punkt; *hier:* **Komma** point

R

Rad fahren cycle
Radiergummi eraser
Rat(schlag), Tipp tip
Raum; *hier:* **Weltraum** space
Recht haben be right
rechte(r, s) right
rechts (abbiegen) (turn) right
rechts, auf der rechten Seite on the right
Regal shelf (*pl* shelves)
Regel rule
Regen rain
Regenbogen rainbow
regnen rain
regnerisch rainy
reich rich
Reim rhyme *(no pl)*
Reise, Fahrt trip
Reise; Fahrt journey
Reisen travelling
reisen; fahren travel
Reisende/r traveller
Religionslehre religious education
Reporter/in reporter
(Republik) Irland (Republic of) Ireland
Restaurant, Gaststätte restaurant
richtig, in Ordnung right
richtig, korrekt correct
riechen; duften smell
riesig, riesengroß huge
Rock skirt
Rollstuhl wheelchair
Rose rose
rot red
Rücken; Rückseite back
ruhig bleiben stay cool

S

Saft juice
sagen say
sagen; erzählen tell
Salat salad
sammeln collect
Sammlung collection
Samstag Saturday
Sand sand
Sänger/in singer
Satz sentence
Satz; Ausdruck; (Rede)-wendung phrase
sauber clean
sauber machen clean
Schaf sheep (*pl* sheep)
Schal scarf (*pl* scarves)
hier: **scharf** hot
Schauspieler/in actor/actress
scheinen seem
schießen *(Tor)* score
Schiff ship
Schinken ham
schlafen sleep
Schlafzimmer bedroom
schlagen; *hier:* **besiegen** beat
schlagen; treffen; stoßen (gegen) hit
Schlange snake
schlecht; schlimm bad
schmecken taste
Schnee snow
schneiden cut
schnell fast, quick
Schokolade chocolate
schön beautiful
schon, bereits already
schön, hübsch; *hier:* **herrlich** lovely
schön; nett nice
Schottland Scotland
Schrank cupboard
schrecklich, furchtbar terrible
schreiben write
Schreibtisch desk
schreien; rufen shout
Schuh shoe
Schule school
Schüler/in pupil
hier: **Schuljahr, Klasse** year
(Schul)klasse class
Schultasche schoolbag
Schulter shoulder
Schwamm sponge
schwarz black

schwer; stark heavy
Schwester sister
hier: **schwierig** hard
schwierig, schwer difficult
Schwimmen swimming
schwimmen swim
schwimmen gehen go swimming
See lake
sehen see
sehen, schauen look
Sehenswürdigkeit(en) sight(s)
sehr very
Sehr geehrte(r) …, *hier:* **Liebe(r, s)** dear
Sei kein/e Spielverderber/in! Be a sport!
sein be
sein(e), ihr(e) its
sein(e, r) his
seit since
Seite page, side
Sekunde second
selbst; sogar even
September September
setzen, legen, stellen put
sich amüsieren have a good time
sich ansehen have a look (at)
sich anziehen dress
sich ärgern über be angry about
sich beeilen hurry up
(sich) bewegen move
(sich) brechen break
sich die Zähne putzen brush one's teeth
sich entscheiden; beschließen decide
sich erinnern (an) remember
(sich) fühlen feel
sich (hin)setzen sit down
sich informieren über find out about
sich interessieren für be interested in
sich kümmern um look after
sich kümmern um, versorgen take care of
(sich) Notizen machen (über) make/take notes (on)
sich öffnen, aufgehen open
sich schlecht fühlen feel bad
sich sicher fühlen feel safe
sich Sorgen machen worry
(sich) treffen meet
sich trennen, Schluss machen break up
sich verirren lose one's way
sich verkleiden dress up
sich verlieben (in) fall in love (with)
sich vorstellen imagine
(sich) waschen wash
sicher safe
sie she, they
sie, ihnen them
sie; ihr(e, n) her
singen sing
sitzen sit
SMS text message
so; auf diese Weise like this/that
Socke sock
Sohn son
sollen shall
sollte/müsste should
Sommer summer
sonderbar, merkwürdig strange
Sonne sun
Sonnenbrille sunglasses *(only plural)*
sonnig sunny
Sonntag Sunday
sonntags (on) Sundays
Soße, Sauce sauce
später later
später; danach, anschließend afterwards
(spätestens) bis by *(+ Zeitpunkt)*
Spaß fun
Speisekarte menu
Spiel game
Spiel match
spielen play
Spielzeug toy
Spinne spider
Sport treiben do sport
Sport(art) sport
Sport(unterricht) PE (= physical education)
Sprache language
sprechen, reden (mit) speak (to/with)
sprechen/reden (mit) talk (to)
springen jump
Stadt town
stark strong
starke Erkältung bad cold
stattfinden take place
stehen stand
stehen bleiben; (an)halten stop
stehlen steal
Stein; Fels rock
Stern star
Stiefel boot
Stift pen
Strand beach
Straße road, street
Strecke, Route route
streng strict
Stück piece
Stuhl chair
Stunde hour, lesson
Stundenplan timetable
Sturm storm
suchen nach look for
Süden south
Supermarkt supermarket
Suppe soup
süß sweet

T

Tafel blackboard
Tag day
Tante aunt
tanzen dance
Tasche bag
Taschendieb/in pickpocket
Taschengeld pocket money
Taschenlampe torch (*pl* torches)
Tasse cup
Tausend thousand
Technologie, Technik technology
Tee tea
Tee trinken have tea
Telefon telephone
(Telefon)anruf call
telefonieren make a call
Teller plate
teuer expensive
Theater(kurs); Schauspielerei drama
(Theater)stück play
Thema; *hier:* **Lektion, Kapitel** theme
Thema; (Schul)fach subject
tief deep
Tier animal
Tiger tiger
Tisch table
Titel title
Tochter daughter
toll, klasse brilliant
Tomate tomato (*pl* -es)
tragen; anziehen carry, wear
Training training
Traum dream
träumen dream
traurig sad
hier: **treffen** see
Treppe stairs *(only plural)*
treten, schießen kick
trinken drink
trotzdem still
Tschüss. Bye. *(informal)*
tun, machen do
Tür door
Turnen gym (= gymnastics)

U

üben practise
über about, above, across, over
über Nacht bleiben, übernachten sleep over
überfliegen skim through
überprüfen, kontrollieren check
etwa: **Übung macht den Meister.** Practice matters.
Uhr clock
(Uhr)zeit time
hier: **um** at
um (… herum) around
um Hilfe bitten ask for help
(um) wie viel Uhr (at) what time
hier: **umsteigen** change
und and
Unfall accident
ungefähr about
Uniform uniform
uns us
unser(e) our
unten, darunter below

unter below, under
unterrichten; beibringen teach
hier: **Unterricht(sstunde)** class
Unterschied difference
Urlaub, Ferien holiday
Urlaub/Ferien haben be on holiday
USA (= Vereinigte Staaten von Amerika) USA (= United States of America)

V

Vater father
Vegetarier/in vegetarian
(ver)ändern; austauschen change
verärgert; zornig; wütend angry
(ver)brennen burn
Verb verb
Verband bandage
verbringen *(Zeit)*; **ausgeben** *(Geld)* spend
verdienen earn
Vergangenheit past
vergessen forget
vergleichen compare
verheiratet married
verkaufen sell
Verkäufer/in (shop) assistant, seller
(Verkaufs)stand stall
verlassen leave
verlieren lose
vermissen; verpassen miss
verstecken hide
verstehen understand
versuchen try
vervollständigen complete
Verwandte(r) relative
Verzeihung., Entschuldigung. Sorry.
viel Glück good luck
viel, jede Menge lots *(informal)*, lots of
viel; sehr much
viele many
viel(e) a lot (of)
Vielen Dank! Thanks a lot!
Vielen Dank. Thank you very much.
vielleicht perhaps
vielleicht, möglicherweise maybe
Viertel (vor/nach) quarter (to/past)
Vogel bird
voll full
vollkommen, perfekt perfect
hier: **von** by
von of
von, aus from
vor before, in front of
vor (langer Zeit) (long) ago
vorbei an; hinter, nach past
vorne at the front (of)
vorsichtig careful
Vorspeise starter
Vorstellung idea

W

wählen; sich entscheiden choose
wahr true
während while
Wald forest
Wales Wales
wann; wenn when
warm warm
warten auf wait (for)
Wartezimmer waiting room
warum why
was what
Was ist im Angebot? What's on offer?
Was ist los? What's the matter?
Was ist mit …? What about …? *(informal)*,
Was kostet/kosten …? How much is/are …?
Was läuft? Was geht ab? What's on?
was man tun und was man nicht tun sollte dos and don'ts
Was nimmst du/nehmen Sie? What are you having?
Wasser water
Wechselgeld change
(weg)gehen; abfahren leave
wehtun, schmerzen hurt
weiblich female
Weihnachten Christmas
weil, da because
weinen; schreien cry
weit far
weiß white
hier: **welche(r, s)** what
welche(r, s) which
Welt world
Weltrekord world record
wem, wen who
weniger less
wenn, falls; ob if
wer; der/die/das who
werden become, get
werfen throw
wessen whose
Westen west
Wetter weather
wie how, like
Wie alt bist du/seid ihr? How old are you?
Wie geht es dir/Ihnen/euch? How are you?
wie man how to
Wie spät ist es? What time is it?
wie viele how many
Wie war es? What was it like?
wieder; noch (ein)mal again
wiederholen repeat
wild wild
Wind wind
Winter winter
wir we
Wir möchten bitte zahlen!, Die Rechnung, bitte! Could we have the bill, please?
wirklich really
wirklich, echt real
wissen; kennen know
Woche week
Wochenende weekend
wo(hin) where
Wohltätigkeitsorganisation charity
Wohnzimmer living room
wollen, dass jd etw tut want sb to do sth
Wort word
Wörterbuch dictionary
Wortfeld wordbank
Wortnetz word web
wunderbar, wundervoll wonderful
wünschen wish
wünschen; wollen want
würde(n/st/t) would
Wurst, Würstchen sausage

Z

Zahl; Ziffer, Nummer number
Zahn tooth (*pl* teeth)
Zebra zebra
Zeichen; (Straßen-/Verkehrs)schild sign
zeichnen draw
zeigen show
Zeitschrift, Magazin magazine
Zeitung newspaper
Zeltplatz campsite
Zentrum center *(AE* = centre *BE)*
Ziel; Tor goal
Zitrone lemon
Zoo zoo
zu essen geben, füttern feed
(zu Fuß) gehen walk
zu Hause at home
(Zu) Hilfe! Help!
(zu) spät (too) late
zu verkaufen for sale
Zucker sugar
zuerst at first
zuerst, als Erstes first
Zug train
Zuhause home
Zuhause; *hier:* **Heimat** home
zuhause; *hier:* **nach Hause** home
(zu)hören listen (to)
Zukunft future
zum Beispiel for example
zuordnen match (with/to)
zurück back
zurückkommen come back
zusammen, gemeinsam together
(zu)schicken send
zustimmen agree
zuvor, vorher before
zweimal twice
(zweimal) pro (Woche) (twice) a (week)
Zwiebel onion
zwischen between

Girls/Women
Alecia [ə'ləʃə]
Amar [ə'mɑ:]
Ann [æn]
Annette [ə'net]
Audrey ['ɔ:dri]
Barbara ['bɑ:brə]
Becky ['beki]
Berlie ['bɜ:li]
Beth [beθ]
Caitlin ['keɪtlɪn]
Cheryl ['tʃerəl]
Claire [kleə]
Dayna ['dænə]
Debbie ['debi]
Emily ['eməli]
Emma ['emə]
Emmeline ['eməli:n]
Gillian ['dʒɪliən]
Ha Tien [hɑ:tɪ'ən]
Hannah ['hænə]
Helen ['helən]
Janet ['dʒænɪt]
Jennifer ['dʒenɪfə]
Jenny ['dʒeni]
Josephine ['dʒəʊzɪfi:n]
Karen ['kɑ:rən]
Lennie ['leni]
Lindsay ['lɪndzi]
Lisa ['li:sə]
Mary ['meəri]
Monica ['mɒnɪkə]
Rosemary ['rəʊzməri]
Sabrina [sə'bri:nə]
Sally ['sæli]
Sarah ['seərə]
Sharon ['ʃærən]
Sheila ['ʃi:lə]
Sue [su:]
Susan ['su:zən]
Vanessa [və'nesə]

Boys/Men
Adam ['ædəm]
Amir [ə'mɪə]
André ['ɒndreɪ]
Benny ['beni]
Bill [bɪl]
Billy ['bɪli]
Björn [bi'ɔ:n]
Bob [bɒb]
Brian ['braɪən]
Calvin ['kælvɪn]
Charlie ['tʃɑ:li]
Chris [krɪs]
Christy ['krɪsti]
Chuck [tʃʌk]
Colin ['kɒlɪn]
Dan [dæn]
Daniel ['dænjəl]
Dave [deɪv]
David ['deɪvɪd]
Dennis ['denɪs]
Dick [dɪk]
Dirk [dɜ:k]
Dustin ['dʌstɪn]
Dylan ['dɪlən]
Elliot ['eliət]
George [dʒɔ:dʒ]
Greg [greg]
Hank [hæŋk]
Hans [hænts]
Harry ['hæri]
Herb [hɜ:b]
Jack [dʒæk]
Jacob ['dʒeɪkəb]
Jake [dʒeɪk]
James [dʒeɪmz]
Joe [dʒəʊ]
Joey ['dʒəʊi]
John [dʒɒn]
Jonathan ['dʒɒnəθən]
Kevin ['kevɪn]
Kieran ['kɪərən]
Lennie ['leni]
Levi ['li:vaɪ]
Lew [lu:]
Lionel ['laɪənəl]
Marc [mɑ:k]
Marcus ['mɑ:kəs]
Mark [mɑ:k]
Marlon ['mɑ:lən]
Martin ['mɑ:tɪn]
Oscar ['ɒskə]
Pablo ['pæbləʊ]
Paddy ['pædi]
Paul [pɔ:l]
Pete [pi:t]
Peter ['pi:tə]
Rajiv [rɑ:'dʒi:v]
Robert ['rɒbət]
Robin ['rɒbɪn]
Robinson ['rɒbɪnsən]
Rubayet ['ru:baɪæt]
Ryan ['raɪən]
Sam [sæm]
Steve [sti:v]
Tim [tɪm]
Tom [tɒm]
Tony ['təʊni]
Wallace ['wɒlɪs]

Families
Adler ['ædlər]
Alpert ['ælpət]
Andersson ['ændəsən]
Barclay ['bɑ:kli]
Batson ['bætsən]
Belafonte [ˌbelə'fɒnti]
Brando ['brændəʊ]
Brown [braʊn]
Collins ['kɒlɪnz]
Cooke [kʊk]
Crusoe ['kru:səʊ]
D'Angelo [d'ændʒələʊ]
Davis ['deɪvɪs]
de Mestral [ˌdə 'mestrəl]
de Vere Stacpool
[də ˌvɪə 'staekpu:l]
Defoe [di'fəʊ]
Denims ['denɪmz]
Denver ['denvə]
Ewalski [ju'vælski]
Garnerin ['gɑ:nəɪn]
Gordon ['gɔ:dən]
Gunning ['gʌnɪŋ]
Harmer ['hɑ:mə]
Harrison ['hærɪsən]
Hastings ['heɪstɪŋz]
Hood [hʊd]
Horn [hɔ:n]
Kessing ['kesɪŋ]
Klein [klaɪn]
Kosseris [kɒ'særiz]
Mann [mæn]
Miller ['mɪlə]
Monkhouse ['mʌŋkhaʊs]
Moore [mʊə]
Moskovitz ['mɒskəvɪts]
Murphy ['mɜ:fi]
Parlemois [pɑ:l'mwɑ:]
Picasso [pɪ'kæsəʊ]
Pistorius [ˌpɪ'stɔ:riəs]
Potter ['pɒtə]
Richie ['rɪtʃi]
Scott [skɒt]
Strauss [straʊs]
Taylor ['teɪlə]
Trippel ['trɪpəl]
Ulvaeus [ʌl'veɪəs]
Waterman ['wɔ:təmən]
Zuckerberg ['zʌkəbɜ:g]

Other Names
Acton Town [ˌæktən
'taʊn]
Air and Space Section
[ˌeər‿ənd 'speɪs‿ˌsekʃn]
Alexandra Palace
[ˌælɪgˌzɑ:ndrə 'pæləs]
Alexandra Road
[ˌælɪgˌzɑ:ndrə 'rəʊd]
Amphicar ['æmfiˌkɑ:]
Armani [ɑ:'mɑ:ni]
Arsenal ['ɑ:sənəl]
Avro Shackleton [ˌævrəʊ
'ʃækəltən]
Baby ['beɪbi]
Beatles ['bi:təlz]
Bermuda [bə'mju:də]
Bethnal Green [ˌbeθnəl
'gri:n]
Blackheath [ˌblæk'hi:θ]
BMX [ˌbi:em'eks]
Bollywood ['bɒliwʊd]
BP British Art Displays
[ˌbi:ˌpi: ˌbrɪtɪʃ 'ɑ:t
dɪˌspleɪz]
Brahmin ['brɑ:mɪn]
British Airways (BA)
[ˌbrɪtɪʃ‿'eəweɪz]
Buckingham Palace
[ˌbʌkɪŋəm 'pæləs]
Burger Queen
['bɜ:gə ˌkwi:n]
Butterfly ['bʌtəˌflaɪ]
calypso [kə'lɪpsəʊ]
Cambridge Heath Road
[ˌkeɪmbrɪdʒ ˌhi:θ 'rəʊd]
Capri [kə'pri:]
Centre for Alternative
Technology
[ˌsentə fər‿ɔ:lˌtɜ:nətɪv
tek'nɒlədʒi]
Children's bookshop
[ˌtʃɪldrənz 'bʊkʃɒp]
the Children's Trust
[ðə ˌtʃɪldrənz 'trʌst]
Ciao Bambino [ˌtʃaʊ
bæm'bi:nəʊ]
Comic Relief [ˌkɒmɪk rɪ'li:f]
Covent Garden
[ˌkɒvənt 'gɑ:dən]
Covent Garden Piazza
[ˌkɒvənt ˌgɑ:dən pi'ætsə]
Crowthorne Road
[ˌkrəʊθɔ:n 'rəʊd]
Dalit ['dælɪt]
dirtsurfing ['dɜ:tˌsɜ:fɪŋ]
Disneyland ['dɪzniˌlænd]
dungaree [ˌdʌŋgə'ri:]
the Eiffel Tower
[ði‿ˌaɪfəl 'taʊə]
Electric Theatre
[iˌlektrɪk 'θɪətə]
Emerson Park School
[ˌeməsən ˌpɑ:k 'sku:l]
Empire of Light
[ˌempaɪər‿əv 'laɪt]
Facebook ['feɪsbʊk]
Forest Hill [ˌfɒrɪst 'hɪl]

Fortis Green Road [ˌfɔ:tɪs ˌgri:n ˈrəʊd]
Game Land [ˈgeɪm ˌlænd]
the Gatecrashers [ðə ˈgeɪtkræʃəz]
Google [ˈgu:gl]
Grammy [ˈgræmi]
Greenwich Park [ˌgrenɪtʃˈpɑ:k]
Gromit [ˈgrɒmɪt]
Gunnersbury Lane [ˌgʌnəzbəri ˈleɪn]
Hammersmith & City Line [ˌhæməsmɪθ‿ən ˈsɪti ˌlaɪn]
Harvard University [ˌhɑ:vəd ˌju:nɪˈvɜ:səti]
Holiday Park [ˈhɒlɪdeɪ ˌpɑ:k]
Horniman Museum [ˈhɔ:nɪmən mjuˌzi:əm]
Jorvik [ˈjɔ:vɪk]
Junior Europe [ˌdʒu:niə ˈjʊərəp]
Kid's Cookery School [ˌkɪdz ˈkʊkəri sku:l]
Latimer Road [ˌlætɪmə ˈrəʊd]
Lee [li:]
Levi's [ˈli:vaɪz]
London Bridge [ˌlʌndən ˈbrɪdʒ]
the London Eye [ðə ˌlʌndən‿ˈaɪ]
London Marathon [ˌlʌndən ˈmærəθn]
London Road [ˌlʌndən ˈrəʊd]
London Transport Museum (LTM) [ˌlʌndən ˈtrænspɔ:t mjuˌzi:əm]
lowlining [ˈləʊˌlaɪnɪŋ]
M!ssundaztood [ˌmɪsˌʌndəˈstʊd]
the Mall [ðə ˈmɔ:l]
Man Friday [ˌmæn ˈfraɪdeɪ]
Man United (= Manchester United) [ˌmæn ju:ˈnaɪtɪd]
Manchester United [ˌmæntʃəstə juˈnaɪtɪd]
Manchester United Museum [ˌmæntʃəstə ju:ˌnaɪtɪd mju:ˈzi:əm]
Mexicana [mexiˈka:nə]
Microsoft [ˈmaɪkrəʊsɒft]
Millbank [ˈmɪlbæŋk]
Mini [ˈmɪni]
Museum of Childhood [mju:ˌzi:əm‿əv ˈtʃaɪldˌhʊd]
Museum of Science and Industry (MOSI) [mju:ˌzi:əm‿əv ˌsaɪəns‿ənd‿ˈɪndəstri]
Muswell Hill [ˌmʌzwel ˈhɪl]
Notting Hill [ˌnɒtɪŋ ˈhɪl]
Notting Hill Gate [ˌnɒtɪŋ hɪl ˈgeɪt]
Pimlico [ˈpɪmlɪkəʊ]
Pink [pɪŋk]
Pizza World [ˈpi:tsə ˌwɜ:ld]
Planet [ˈplænɪt]
Portobello Road [ˌpɔ:təˌbeləʊ ˈrəʊd]
Power Hall [ˈpaʊə ˌhɔ:l]
Queen [kwi:n]
rap [ræp]
Red Nose Day [ˌred ˈnəʊz deɪ]
reggae [ˈregeɪ]
rock [rɒk]
rock and roll [ˌrɒk‿ən ˈroll]
rollersoccer [ˈrəʊləˌsɒkə]
Sergeant Horn [ˌsɑ:dʒnt ˈhɔ:n]
slacklining [ˈslækˌlaɪnɪŋ]
St Mary's [ˌsənt ˈmeəriz]
Sussex Sharks [ˌsʌsɪks ˈʃɑ:ks]
Tate Britain [ˌteɪt ˈbrɪtn]
Tate Gallery [ˈteɪt ˌgæləri]
The Kid's Cookery School [ðə kɪdz ˈkʊkəri sku:l]
Ultimate Frisbee [ˌʌltɪmət ˈfrɪzbi]
Velcro® (fastener) [ˈvelkrəʊ]
Velodouche [veləˈdu:ʃ]
Verde [ˈvɜ:di]
Versace [vəˈsɑ:tʃi]
Via Veneto [ˌvi:ə vəˈni:təʊ]
Viking Centre [ˈvaɪkɪŋ sentə]
Westway [ˈwestweɪ]
Windsor Castle [ˌwɪnzə ˈkɑ:sl]
Wood Green [ˌwʊd ˈgri:n]
Wrangler [ˈræŋglə]
Xperiment [ɪkˈsperɪmənt]
Yahoo [jɑ:ˈhu:]
Young Pavement Artists Competition [ˌjʌŋ ˈpeɪvmənt‿ˌɑ:tɪsts ˌkɒmpəˌtɪʃn]

Geographical Names

Acton [ˈæktən]
Afghanistan [æfˈgænɪstɑ:n]
Australia [ɒˈstreɪliə]
Bala [ˈbælə]
Bangladesh [ˌbæŋgləˈdeʃ]
Barbados [bɑ:ˈbeɪdɒs]
Beijing [ˌbeɪˈdʒɪŋ]
Birmingham [ˈbɜ:mɪŋəm]
Brighton [ˈbraɪtən]
Cairo [ˈkaɪərəʊ]
California [ˌkæləˈfɔ:niə]
Canada [ˈkænədə]
Cardiff [ˈkɑ:dɪf]
the Caribbean [ðə ˌkærɪˈbiən]
Chartres [ˈʃɑ:trə]
China [ˈtʃaɪnə]
Croydon [ˈkrɔɪdən]
Dartford [ˈdɑ:tfəd]
Delhi [ˈdeli]
Doylestown [ˈdɔɪəlztaʊn]
Dublin [ˈdʌblɪn]
France [frɑ:ns]
Fulham [ˈfʊləm]
Genoa [ˈdʒenəʊə]
Greenwich [ˈgrenɪtʃ]
Hamburg [ˈhæmbɜ:g]
Hampstead [ˈhæmpsted]
Harvard [ˈhɑ:vəd]
Heathrow [ˈhi:θrəʊ]
Hendon [ˈhendən]
(the) Himalayas [ˌhɪməˈleɪəz]
Holland Park [ˌhɒlənd ˈpɑ:k]
Hornchurch [ˈhɔ:ntʃɜ:tʃ]
Houston [ˈhu:stən]
Hungary [ˈhʌŋgəri]
Hyde Park [ˌhaɪd ˈpɑ:k]
Iran [ɪˈrɑ:n]
(Republic of) Ireland [ˈaɪələnd]
Japan [dʒəˈpæn]
Kensington [ˈkenzɪŋtən]
Kerry [ˈkeri]
Las Vegas [læs ˈveɪgəs]
Liverpool [ˈlɪvəpu:l]
London [ˈlʌndən]
Madrid [məˈdrɪd]
Manchester [ˈmæntʃəstə]
Melbourne [ˌmelbən]
Monaco [ˈmɒnəkəʊ]
Moscow [ˈmɒskəʊ]
New York [nju: ˈjɔ:k]
the Niagara Falls [ðə naɪˌægərə ˈfɔ:lz]
Nîmes [ni:m]
North Wales [ˌnɔ:θ ˈweɪlz]
Notting Hill [ˌnɒtɪŋ ˈhɪl]
Nottingham [ˈnɒtɪŋəm]
Paddington [ˈpædɪŋtən]
Palo Alto [ˌpæləʊ‿ˈæltəʊ]
Pennsylvania [ˌpensəlˈveɪniə]
Perth [pɜ:θ]
Portobello Market [ˌpɔ:təˌbeləʊ ˈmɑ:kɪt]
Portobello Road [ˌpɔ:təˌbeləʊ ˈrəʊd]
Queen's Park [ˌkwi:nz ˈpɑ:k]
Reading [ˈredɪŋ]
Rome [rəʊm]
Russia [ˈrʌʃə]
San Francisco [ˌsæn frənˈsɪskəʊ]
Sherwood Forest [ˌʃɜ:wʊd ˈfɒrɪst]
South Pacific [ˌsaʊθ pəˈsɪfɪk]
Sri Lanka [srɪ ˈlæŋkə]
techno [ˈteknəʊ]
Texas [ˈteksəs]
Tunis [ˈtju:nɪs]
Wales [weɪlz]
Wembley [ˈwembli]
York [jɔ:k]

Numbers

0	oh, zero, nil [əʊ, 'zɪərəʊ, nɪl]
1	one [wʌn]
2	two [tu:]
3	three [θri:]
4	four [fɔ:]
5	five [faɪv]
6	six [sɪks]
7	seven ['sevn]
8	eight [eɪt]
9	nine [naɪn]
10	ten [ten]
11	eleven [ɪ'levn]
12	twelve [twelv]
13	thirteen [ˌθɜ:'ti:n]
14	fourteen [ˌfɔ:'ti:n]
15	fifteen [ˌfɪf'ti:n]
16	sixteen [ˌsɪks'ti:n]
17	seventeen [ˌsevn'ti:n]
18	eighteen [ˌeɪ'ti:n]
19	nineteen [ˌnaɪn'ti:n]
20	twenty ['twenti]
21	twenty-one [ˌtwenti'wʌn]
22	twenty-two [ˌtwenti'tu:]
30	thirty ['θɜ:ti]
40	forty ['fɔ:ti]
50	fifty ['fɪfti]
60	sixty ['sɪksti]
70	seventy ['sevnti]
80	eighty ['eɪti]
90	ninety ['naɪnti]

100	a/one hundred [ə/wʌn 'hʌndrəd]
101	one hundred and one [wʌn ˌhʌndrəd‿ən 'wʌn]
102	one hundred and two [wʌn ˌhʌndrəd‿ən 'tu:]
110	one hundred and ten [wʌn ˌhʌndrəd‿ən 'ten]
200	two hundred [tu: 'hʌndrəd]
1,000	a/one thousand [ə/wʌn 'θaʊznd]
1,001	one thousand and one [wʌn 'θaʊznd‿ən wʌn]
1,111	one thousand one hundred and eleven [wʌn 'θaʊznd wʌn 'hʌndrəd‿ən‿ɪ'levn]
2,000	two thousand [tu: 'θaʊznd]
10,000	ten thousand [ten 'θaʊznd]
100,000	a/one hundred thousand [ə/wʌn ˌhʌndrəd 'θaʊznd]
1,000,000	a/one million [ə/wʌn 'mɪljən]
1,000,000,000	a/one billion [ə/wʌn 'bɪljən]

1st	first [fɜ:st]
2nd	second ['sekənd]
3rd	third [θɜ:d]
4th	fourth [fɔ:θ]
5th	fifth [fɪfθ]
6th	sixth [sɪksθ]
7th	seventh ['sevnθ]
8th	eighth [eɪtθ]
9th	ninth [naɪnθ]
10th	tenth [tenθ]
11th	eleventh [ɪ'levnθ]
12th	twelfth [twelfθ]
13th	thirteenth [ˌθɜ:'ti:nθ]
14th	fourteenth [ˌfɔ:'ti:nθ]
15th	fifteenth [ˌfɪf'ti:nθ]
16th	sixteenth [ˌsɪks'ti:nθ]
17th	seventeenth [ˌsevn'ti:nθ]
18th	eighteenth [ˌeɪ'ti:nθ]
19th	nineteenth [ˌnaɪn'ti:nθ]
20th	twentieth ['twentiəθ]
21st	twenty-first [ˌtwenti'fɜ:st]
22nd	twenty-second [ˌtwenti'sekənd]
23rd	twenty-third [ˌtwenti'θɜ:d]
30th	thirtieth ['θɜ:tiəθ]
40th	fortieth ['fɔ:tiəθ]
50th	fiftieth ['fɪftiəθ]
60th	sixtieth ['sɪkstiəθ]
70th	seventieth ['sevntiəθ]
80th	eightieth ['eɪtiəθ]
90th	ninetieth ['naɪntiəθ]
100th	hundredth ['hʌndrədθ]

½	a/one half [ə/wʌn 'hɑ:f]
⅓	a/one third [ə/wʌn 'θɜ:d]
¼	a/one quarter [ə/wʌn 'kwɔ:tə]
⅛	a/one eighth [ə/wʌn‿'eɪtθ]
¾	three quarters [θri: 'kwɔ:təz]

Months

January ['dʒænjuəri]
February ['februəri]
March [mɑ:tʃ]
April ['eɪprəl]
May [meɪ]
June [dʒu:n]
July [dʒʊ'laɪ]
August [ɔ:'gəst]
September [sep'tembə]
October [ɒk'təʊbə]
November [nəʊ'vembə]
December [dɪ'sembə]

Irregular verbs

infinitive	simple past	past participle	
awake [əˈweɪk]	awoke [əˈwəʊk]	awoken [əˈwəʊkən]	aufwachen, erwachen
babysit [ˈbeɪbiˌsɪt]	babysat [ˈbeɪbiˌsæt]	babysat [ˈbeɪbiˌsæt]	babysitten
be [bi:]	was/were [wɒz/wɜ:]	been [bi:n]	sein
beat [bi:t]	beat [bi:t]	beaten [bi:tn]	schlagen; *hier:* besiegen
become [bɪˈkʌm]	became [biˈkeɪm]	become [bɪˈkʌm]	werden
begin [bɪˈgɪn]	began [biˈgæn]	begun [biˈgʌn]	anfangen, beginnen
bet [bet]	bet/betted [bet/ˈbetɪd]	bet/betted [bet/ˈbetɪd]	wetten
break [breɪk]	broke [brəʊk]	broken [ˈbrəʊkən]	zerbrechen
bring [brɪŋ]	brought [brɔ:t]	brought [brɔ:t]	(mit)bringen
build [bɪld]	built [bɪlt]	built [bɪlt]	bauen
burn [bɜ:n]	burnt/burned [bɜ:nt/bɜ:nd]	burnt/burned [bɜ:nt/bɜ:nd]	(ver)brennen
burst [bɜ:st]	burst [bɜ:st]	burst [bɜ:st]	platzen
buy [baɪ]	bought [bɔ:t]	bought [bɔ:t]	kaufen
catch [kætʃ]	caught [kɔ:t]	caught [kɔ:t]	fangen
choose [tʃu:z]	chose [tʃəʊz]	chosen [ˈtʃəʊzn]	wählen; sich entscheiden
come [kʌm]	came [keɪm]	come [kʌm]	kommen
cost [kɒst]	cost [kɒst]	cost [kɒst]	kosten
cut [kʌt]	cut [kʌt]	cut [kʌt]	schneiden
dig [dɪg]	dug [dʌg]	dug [dʌg]	graben
do [du:]	did [dɪd]	done [dʌn]	tun, machen
draw [drɔ:]	drew [dru:]	drawn [drɔ:n]	zeichnen
dream [dri:m]	dreamt/dreamed [dremt/dri:md]	dreamt/dreamed [dremt/dri:md]	träumen
drink [drɪŋk]	drank [dræŋk]	drunk [drʌŋk]	trinken
drive [draɪv]	drove [drəʊv]	driven [ˈdrɪvn]	fahren
eat [i:t]	ate [eɪt]	eaten [ˈi:tn]	essen
fall [fɔ:l]	fell [fel]	fallen [ˈfɔ:lən]	fallen
feed [fi:d]	fed [fed]	fed [fed]	zu essen geben, füttern
feel [fi:l]	felt [felt]	felt [felt]	(sich) fühlen
fight [faɪt]	fought [fɔ:t]	fought [fɔ:t]	kämpfen
find [faɪnd]	found [faʊnd]	found [faʊnd]	finden
fly [flaɪ]	flew [flu:]	flown [fləʊn]	fliegen
forget [fəˈget]	forgot [fəˈgɒt]	forgotten [fəˈgɒtn]	vergessen
get [get]	got [gɒt]	got [gɒt]	erhalten, bekommen; holen, kaufen; werden; kommen; nehmen
give [gɪv]	gave [geɪv]	given [ˈgɪvn]	geben; *hier:* nennen, angeben
go [gəʊ]	went [went]	gone [gɒn]	gehen; fahren
grow [grəʊ]	grew [gru:]	grown [grəʊn]	wachsen, größer werden
have [hæv]	had [hæd]	had [hæd]	haben; essen, trinken
hear [hɪə]	heard [hɜ:d]	heard [hɜ:d]	hören
hide [haɪd]	hid [hɪd]	hidden [ˈhɪdn]	verstecken
hit [hɪt]	hit [hɪt]	hit [hɪt]	schlagen; treffen; stoßen (gegen)
hold [həʊld]	held [held]	held [held]	halten
hurt [hɜ:t]	hurt [hɜ:t]	hurt [hɜ:t]	wehtun, schmerzen
keep [ki:p]	kept [kept]	kept [kept]	aufbewahren; behalten
know [nəʊ]	knew [nju:]	known [nəʊn]	wissen; kennen
lead [li:d]	led [led]	led [led]	führen
learn [lɜ:n]	learnt/learned [lɜ:nt/lɜ:nd]	learnt/learned [lɜ:nt/lɜ:nd]	lernen
leave [li:v]	left [left]	left [left]	(weg)gehen; abfahren; verlassen; zurücklassen
let [let]	let [let]	let [let]	lassen
lie [laɪ]	lay [leɪ]	lain [leɪn]	liegen; sich hinlegen
lose [lu:z]	lost [lɒst]	lost [lɒst]	verlieren
make [meɪk]	made [meɪd]	made [meɪd]	machen

infinitive	simple past	past participle	
mean [miːn]	meant [ment]	meant [ment]	bedeuten; meinen
meet [miːt]	met [met]	met [met]	(sich) treffen; abholen
pay [peɪ]	paid [peɪd]	paid [peɪd]	(be)zahlen
put [pʊt]	put [pʊt]	put [pʊt]	setzen, legen, stellen
read [riːd]	read [red]	read [red]	lesen
ride [raɪd]	rode [rəʊd]	ridden [ˈrɪdn]	fahren (mit); reiten
ring (up) [ˌrɪŋ‿ˈʌp]	rang (up) [ˌræŋ‿ˈʌp]	rung (up) [ˌrʌŋ‿ˈʌp]	anrufen; klingeln, läuten
run [rʌn]	ran [ræn]	run [rʌn]	laufen, rennen
say [seɪ]	said [sed]	said [sed]	sagen
see [siː]	saw [sɔː]	seen [siːn]	sehen; treffen; ansehen, anschauen
sell [sel]	sold [səʊld]	sold [səʊld]	verkaufen
send [send]	sent [sent]	sent [sent]	(zu)schicken
set [set]	set [set]	set [set]	stellen, legen
shine [ʃaɪn]	shone/shined [ʃɒn/ʃaɪnd]	shone/shined [ʃɒn/ʃaɪnd]	scheinen, glänzen
show [ʃəʊ]	showed [ʃəʊd]	shown [ʃəʊn]	zeigen
shrink [ʃrɪŋk]	shrank/shrunk [ʃræŋk/ʃrʌŋk]	shrunk [ʃrʌŋk]	schrumpfen
sing [sɪŋ]	sang [sæŋ]	sung [sʌŋ]	singen
sit [sɪt]	sat [sæt]	sat [sæt]	sitzen
sleep [sliːp]	slept [slept]	slept [slept]	schlafen
smell [smel]	smelt/smelled [smelt/smeld]	smelt/smelled [smelt/smeld]	riechen; duften
speak [spiːk]	spoke [spəʊk]	spoken [ˈspəʊkən]	sprechen, reden
spend [spend]	spent [spent]	spent [spent]	verbringen *(Zeit)*; ausgeben *(Geld)*
spin [spɪn]	spun [spʌn]	spun [spʌn]	rotieren; sausen
stand [stænd]	stood [stʊd]	stood [stʊd]	stehen
steal [stiːl]	stole [stəʊl]	stolen [ˈstəʊlən]	stehlen
stick [stɪk]	stuck [stʌk]	stuck [stʌk]	kleben, festhängen
swim [swɪm]	swam [swæm]	swum [swʌm]	schwimmen
swing [swɪŋ]	swung [swʌŋ]	swung [swʌŋ]	(hin- und her)schwingen; sich drehen
take [teɪk]	took [tʊk]	taken [ˈteɪkən]	bringen; nehmen; dauern
teach [tiːtʃ]	taught [tɔːt]	taught [tɔːt]	unterrichten; beibringen
tear [teə]	tore [tɔː]	torn [tɔːn]	(zer)reißen
tell [tel]	told [təʊld]	told [təʊld]	sagen; erzählen
think [θɪŋk]	thought [θɔːt]	thought [θɔːt]	denken, glauben, meinen; nachdenken, sich überlegen
throw [θrəʊ]	threw [θruː]	thrown [θrəʊn]	werfen
understand [ˌʌndəˈstænd]	understood [ˌʌndəˈstʊd]	understood [ˌʌndəˈstʊd]	verstehen
wake [weɪk]	woke [wəʊk]	woken [ˈwəʊkən]	aufwachen
wear [weə]	wore [wɔː]	worn [wɔːn]	tragen; anziehen
win [wɪn]	won [wʌn]	won [wʌn]	gewinnen
write [raɪt]	wrote [rəʊt]	written [ˈrɪtn]	schreiben

Bild- und Textquellen

Bildquellen
Umschlag außen: blum Design & Kommunikation, Hamburg;
Innenumschlag vorn: Ingenieurbüro für Karthografie Joachim Zwick, Gießen; Innenumschlag hinten: Dr. Peter Güttler, Berlin (Karte der Britischen Inseln);

11 Englischer Pub (Alamy/Pawel Libera);
12 Hamburger (Mauritius); Braten auf Teller (Alamy/Steve Cavalier); Burger Queen (Alamy/Dennis McDonald); Windsor Castle (Katja Nandorf, Frankfurt);
13 Pizza (Ullstein/Wodicka); Pizza World (Alamy/Francis Roberts); Geld (Nicole Bergemann);
18 indische Flagge (Stern, Jay Ullal); Indien: Straßenszene (Alamy/Peter Horree); Indien: Schule (Alamy/Norma Joseph); Indien: Junge (Alamy/Rachael Bowes);
19 Banana raita (Bärbel Drauschke, Egelsbach);
20/21 Camden Lock Market (Alamy/Pictures Colour Library);
23 Hähnchencurry (Stockfood, Frank Wieder), Tomatensuppe (Ullstein), Spaghetti und Ofenkartoffel (© Royalty-Free/Corbis);
24 Britain (Katja Nandorf, Frankfurt); Iran (Alamy/Ann Erikson); China (Fotoagentur Lade/BIM); India (Alarmy, Gerry Walden); Bratwurst (Alamy/Harald Theissen);
25 Radfahrerinnen (Alamy/Steve Skjold);
26 Mädchen mit Hund (Alamy/Michael Krabs), Kinder spielen Basketball (Alamy/Adrian Sherratt);
27 Fitness-Test (6) (Michael Tetzlaff, Mörfelden Walldorf);
28 Hockeyspieler (Photodisc/Twickham);
29 Rugby (Alamy/Janine Wiedel), englische Schüler beim Sport (Alamy/Mike Booth);
31 Aerobic (istockphoto), Rafael Nadal (Ullstein/Bergmann), Marta (flicker/Juan Rodriguez);
34 *My Left Foot* (pwe kinoarchiv, Hamburg);
35 Christy Brown (Mary Brown);
38 Oscar Pistorius (Pictures Press/Christiaan Kotze), Amerikanische Rollstuhl-Basketballerinnen (getty images/Feng Li);
39 verkleidete Mädchen (Ullstein/Meißner);
40 Funkenmariechen (Mauritius/Gilsdorf); Frau in Hexenkostüm (Mauritius/Pokorski); Kinderfasching (Alamy/Christoph Papsch);
41 Tänzer (© Halden Photography, London), Musiker (Gabi Uplawski, Hannover), Tänzer (Alamy/photolibrary, Janine Wiedel), Polizist (Alamy/Janine Wiedel);
42 Tänzerin (Zefa/Croxford), Mädchen mit Kopfbedeckung (IFA Bilderteam/TBC, Frankfurt);
44 Stadtfest (fotolia/Elena Elisseeva);
47 London Zoo und Sherlock Holmes Museum (Jutta Eckardt-Scheurig, Wiesbaden), Konzert (Verena-Susanna Nungesser, Frankfurt);
50 Mädchen mit Kopfbedeckung (IFA Bilderteam/TBC, Frankfurt)
51 Mann an Strand (Alamy/Emiliano Rodriguez);
55 Hütte am Strand (Alamy/Peter Adams); Palme am Strand (Alamy/Franz Marc Frei);
56 Erste Hilfe (Alamy, ST-images); Samen (Alamy/wsr); Spaten (Alamy/Mode/Wayne Forward); Streichhölzer (Alamy/David J. Green), Cover Robinson Crusoe (Penguin Books);
57 Jugendzimmer (Alamy/Angela Hampton);
58 Sarah (Manfred Jung, Frankfurt);
59 Junge (Alamy/Paul Brown);
63 Pyramiden (MEV);
64 Junge vor Graffitti (Alamy/Janine Wiedel);
65 Lokomotive in Museum (Alamy/Tony Morris);
67 MOSI, Kanalisationsrohr, der erste Computer-Nachbau, ein Auto hochheben, Lokomotive, Baumwollverarbeitung (Museum of Science and Industry);
68 Klettverschluss (Alamy/sciencephotos), Handy (Harald Thumser, Frankfurt), Fahrrad (Alamy/sciencefotots), Energiesparbirne (Zefa/Klaus Hackenberg); Flachbildfernseher (VISUM/A. Vosberg, Hamburg); Streichhölzer (Okapia, Frankfurt); Laptop (f1online); Penicillin (Mauritius/Miosga);
68 Laubbläser (istockphoto/Rob Belknap);
69 Stereo-Anlage (Hass-Karl/images.de), Toaster (fotolia/Wolfgang Kabisch), Geschirrspüler (Wolpert/f1 online);
70 Dampflok (Alamy/John Davidson);
71 Museumsgebäude (Alamy/Stu), Planet Lokomotive (Alamy/David Bagley);
72 *How nearly everything was invented*, Jilly MacLead, illustriert von Lisa Swerling und Ralph Lazar, Dorling Kindersley, London 2006;
76 Klette (istockphoto), Klettverschluss (Alamy/Natural History Museum;
77 Münzen in Hand (Alamy/DBurke);
78 Mädchen in Bekleidungsgeschäft (Corbis/Kevin Dodge), Eintrittskarte (Daniel Gonsior, Egelsbach);
79 Flohmarkt (Alamy/Tim Caddick);
82 Golden Couple (Picture Alliance/); Limousine (Alarmy/Alex Tino Friedel);
83 Marathonteilnehmer mit Turban (Picture Press/Alma Robinson),Marathonläufer als Smiley verkleidet (Alamy/Bob Deering), Rollstuhlfahrer beim Marathon (Alamy/Adrian Muttitt), Menge von Läufern beim London Marathon (Alamy/Dominic Burke);

84 Streckenverlauf (British Tourist Authority, London);
85 Red Nose Day Sugar Babes (Alamy/Mirrorpix);
88 Zuckerberg (Associated Press), Facebook (Alamy/Alex Segre), Harvard University Campus (Frithjof Nungesser, Erfurt);
89 Tate Gallery mit Spinnenskulptur (Alamy/David Pearson);
90 Pink (Picture Alliance/Isabell Schiffler);
91 Kanye West (Gettyimages/Kevin Winter), Portobello Road Market (Jutta Eckardt-Scheurig, Wiesbaden);
94 Kinder kochen (Alamy/jpb), Buchladen (Alamy/Paul Rapson);
96 L. S. Lowry, *Coming out of School* (Tate Gallery);
97 Marc Chagall, *The Blue Circus* (Tate Gallery);
98/99 Sean Henry, *Catafalque* (Alamy; Mike Booth);
100 Band bei Auftritt (fotofinder);
101 Pink (gettyimages/Frank Micelotta);
102 Pablo Picasso, Goat (Succession Picasso/VG Bild-Kunst, Bonn);
103 René Magritte, *Empire of Light* (Alamy/The Print Collector);
104 trauriges Mädchen (istockphoto);
105 Flugzeug (Alamy/Andrew Barker);
106 Ostseestrand (MEV/Tim Krieger), Moskau (istockphoto);
107 Pyramiden (MEV);
107 Schülerarbeit;
108 Do it 4Real Webseite (Do it for Real);
109 Kanu (Thorsten Eckerts, Braunsbach); Klettern (Alamy/Andrew McCandlish, Football/Rugby (dpa/Abaca Liewig), Musical Theatre (www.naf.edu);
110 Dylan (Alamy/Ian Murray), Brian (Alamy/FrankVetere), Barbara Harmer (fotofinder/Frank Boxler), Sue Monkhouse (Alamy/Vitaly Sokolovsky), Sheila Murphy (Alamy/Paul Kingsley);
111 Vereinte Nationen (dpa/A. Anderson);
113 Flughafen (Jutta Eckardt-Scheurig, Wiesbaden);
116 Flugzeug (Alamy/Andrew Barker);
118 Junge mit Krücken (istockphoto);
120 Dirtsurfing (NIXED Funsports/Nihat Uysal), Rollersoccer (www.citiskate.co.uk/Andreas Kollatek), Frisbee (PSU/Michael Merrick), Slacklining (wikimedia);
124 Levi Strauss Jeans-Etikett (Ullstein), James Dean in *Rebel without a cause* (USA 1955) (Alamy/Pictorial Press);
138 Tänzer beim Notting Hill Carnival (Alamy/Janine Wiedel/photolibrary);
140 Berg mit Seenlandschaft (Mauritius Images/Manfred Thonig), Stadt mit Landschaft (Pixelio/Andreas Stix);
141 Bildagentur online;
142 Sekretärin (Anika Mellinghoff, Frankfurt); Gartenarbeit (Mauritius);
144 Vincent van Goghs *Schlafzimmer* © 2001 The Yorck Project;
145 Weltkarte (istockphoto).

Textquellen

30 *Swimming*, Dayna; *The cricket ball's story*, Helen;
55 *Ocean Breezes*, aus: *Under the Breadfruit Tree*, First Boyd Mils Press paperback edition 2004:
64 *Tuff*, Annette Kosseris, Kindamindi Publishing, Sydney (1994);
72 *Fantastic inventions?* adaptiert von: *How nearly everything was invented*, Jilly MacLead, Dorling Kindersley, London 2006;
76 *A spiky story* adaptiert von: *Mistakes That Worked*, Charlotte Foltz Jones, Delacorte Press, New York; 94/95, 1991; adaptiert, aus: *Time Out, London for Children*, Time Out Group, London;
102 Texte von Rubayet und Ha Tien in: *Fantasien von Kindern aus aller Welt*, G. Rabkin (Hg.), © Ernst Klett Verlag Stuttgart;
118 *Kieran*, Berlie Doherty © Berlie Doherty, Edale/Derbyshire;
119 *Hearing the Ball*, adaptiert von Spot on!
121 *The Blue Lagoon*, Henry de Vere Stacpoole © Longman Group Ltd., Harlow/Essex.

Liedquellen

50 „All night long", Text und Musik: Lionel Richie;
55 „Island in the sun", Text und Musik: Harry Belafonte/Lord Burgess © Cherry Lane Music Publication Comp./Clara Music Publ. Corp.; für D/A/CH: 50 % EMI Music Publishing GmbH, Hamburg, 50 % Global Musikverlag, München;
61 „What a wonderful world" (Don't know much about), Text und Musik: Sam Cooke/Herb Alpert/Lew Adler, © Abcko Music Inc., für D/A/CH: Abcko Music Publishing GmbH Hamburg;
82 „Money, money, money", Text und Musik: Benny Andersson, Björn Ulvaeus;
104 „Conversations with my 13 year old self", Text und Musik: Pink, Billy Mann;
116 „Leaving on a jet plane", Text und Musik: John Denver

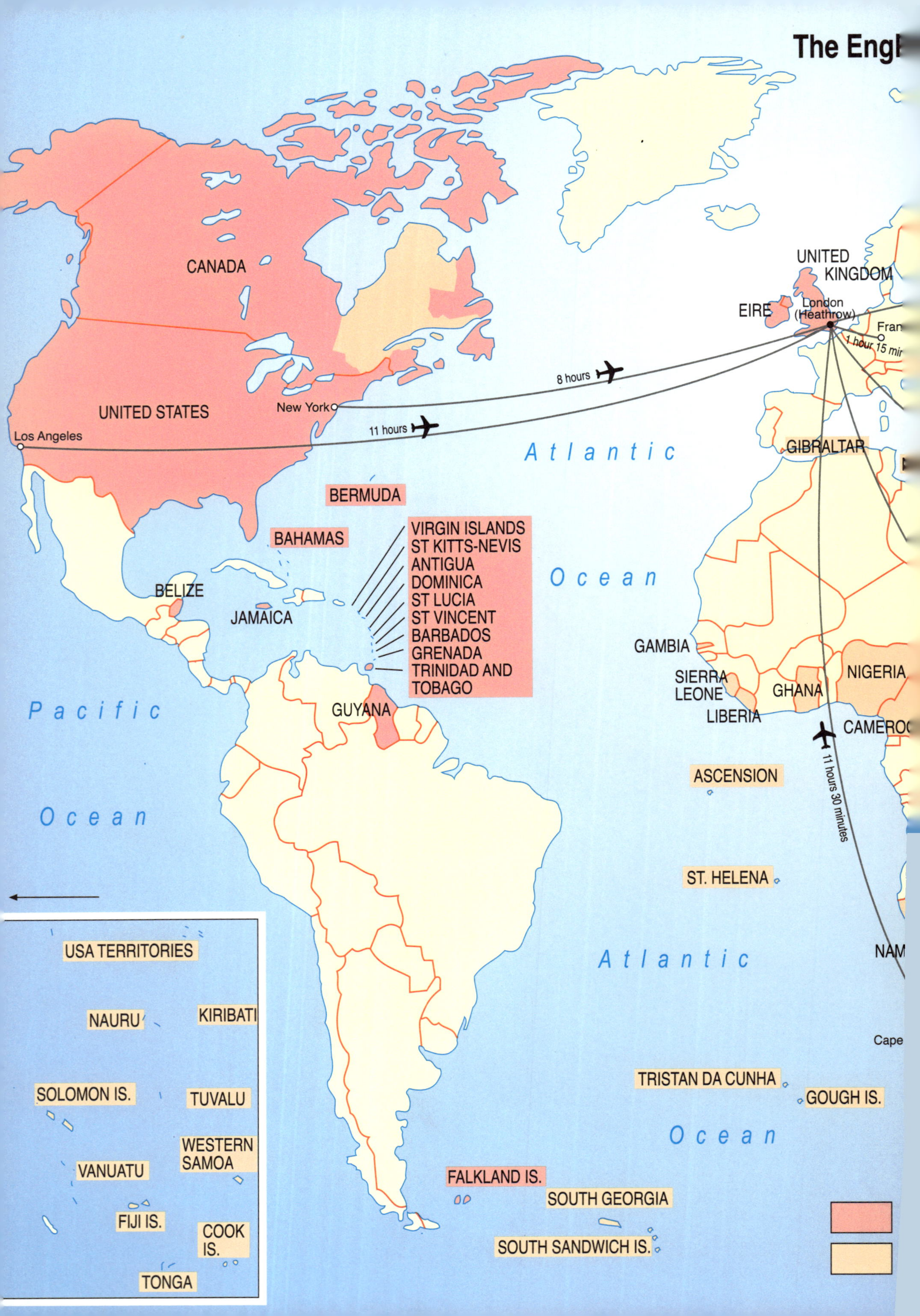

The Engl
CANADA
UNITED STATES
New York
Los Angeles
8 hours
11 hours
UNITED
KINGDOM
EIRE
London
(Heathrow)
Fran
1 hour 15 min
Atlantic
Ocean
GIBRALTAR
BERMUDA
BAHAMAS
VIRGIN ISLANDS
ST KITTS-NEVIS
ANTIGUA
DOMINICA
ST LUCIA
ST VINCENT
BARBADOS
GRENADA
TRINIDAD AND
TOBAGO
BELIZE
JAMAICA
GAMBIA
SIERRA
LEONE
LIBERIA
GHANA
NIGERIA
CAMERO
Pacific
Ocean
GUYANA
ASCENSION
11 hours 30 minutes
ST. HELENA
Atlantic
NAM
Cape
TRISTAN DA CUNHA
GOUGH IS.
Ocean
FALKLAND IS.
SOUTH GEORGIA
SOUTH SANDWICH IS.
USA TERRITORIES
NAURU
KIRIBATI
SOLOMON IS.
TUVALU
WESTERN
SAMOA
VANUATU
FIJI IS.
COOK
IS.
TONGA